UNDERMINING THE AMERICAN MIND

Reading Between the Lines of Public Deception

How Global Elites Are Using
the Art of Psychological Warfare Tactics
to Destabilize a Free-Thinking Society

DARLENE M. GROBEN

authorHOUSE®

AuthorHouse™
1663 Liberty Drive
Bloomington, IN 47403
www.authorhouse.com
Phone: 833-262-8899

Published by AuthorHouse 04/03/2025

ISBN: 979-8-8230-3471-5 (sc)
ISBN: 979-8-8230-3480-7 (hc)
ISBN: 979-8-8230-3470-8 (e)

Library of Congress Control Number: 2025900501

Print information available on the last page.

The *Art of War* states, "All warfare is based on deception. A skilled general must master the complementary arts of **simulation** and dissimulation (false realities) while creating shapes to confuse and delude the enemy. He **conceals his true disposition and ultimate intent**.

His **primary target** *is the mind* of the opposing commander, a victorious situation, a product of his creative imagination. Sun Tzu realized that an **indispensable preliminary to battle was to attack the mind of the enemy**. The expert approaches his objective "indirectly." By selecting a devious and distant route, he may march a thousand Li without opposition and *take his enemy* unaware.

> "CRITICAL thinking calls for a "persistent effort to examine any belief" or "supposed form of knowledge" in the light of the evidence that supports it and the further conclusions to which it tends."
>
> —*An Experiment in the Development of CRITICAL Thinking*. Teacher's College, Columbia University.

This book is not designed to determine whether you agree or disagree with its contents but to encourage you to evaluate your convictions based on logic and a healthy ability to reason.

> "Almost all devastating evil begins with good intentions."
>
> —D. M. Groben

CONTENTS

ACKNOWLEDGMENTS

I want to acknowledge my mother, who taught me the root meaning of endurance. To my children, Andreu, Alex, Deana, and Amanda, through all my mistakes, my love for you gave me the strength to persevere against incredible odds. Proud of each and everyone of you. To my friends: Elizabeth, throughout all our military escapades; Aileen, a blessed friendship; Alexa, my Mini me; and Matt, my confidant. Tony, for your spiritual insight; Jason, for your professional support; Jeremy and Jessica, for our insightful conversations; Webster for always keeping me in mind; Hanna, and Collete a blessing to know you; Mark and Cari, for the love and wisdom you have bestowed on my children; Julia an amazing doctor to whom I will be forever grateful and to all my friends who I have failed to mention who have played a pivotal part in the betterment of my life.

Thank you.

And in the loving memory of my father-in-law, who taught me the gift of hard work and due diligence in finishing what you start. To Aunt Zia for her wisdom, Aunt Rosemary for her kindness, and my maternal grandmother, until we meet again, my heart will forever grieve. You will be forever remembered.

I thank God most for placing *'His hand'* on all my travels.

"Live life with a sense of *purpose.*"

To Mrs. Giamarco, my Brentwood High School chemistry teacher. I hope I lived up to your standards.

ACKNOWLEDGMENTS

INTRODUCTION

> "The world has changed, and humanity has entered a dark period that few recognize for what it is. Troubles are sweeping the globe with noticeably with greater force; deceit, division, disorder, instability, lawlessness, corruption, and conflict of every kind are intensifying."
>
> —David C. Park

> "Many false prophets will rise and deceive many. Because lawlessness will multiply, the love of many will grow cold."
>
> —Matthew 24:11–12, HCSB

In the progressive worldview, most Americans fail to see this "greater force," which has gone unnoticed. My findings will reveal and emphasize how domestic and foreign globalists use the art of psychological warfare tactics to destabilize a free-thinking society by creating delusions and provocations of social conditioning by domestic and foreign entities without a verbal or written declaration of war. According to these tactics, the daily social construct in modern society has been studied extensively by social elites—politicians who then motivate societal emotions to distort reality and use predictable behavior in social constructs. They collaborate among multiple entities, intending to bend the will of the people like a well-orchestrated playbook.

I have spent many years and countless hours delving deeply into the multiple facets that govern society and how the psychological playbook and governmental deception have emotionally manipulated the social construct to the verge of exhaustion. I have found numerous authors steeped in professional and intellectual insights explaining the art of deception in simple terms. Globalists have configured this intricate playbook to manipulate words and bend truthful speech that goes against logic and human reason. The findings will allow the reader to see the hidden perspectives on how words, education, technology, and social media manipulate the emotions and normal functioning of the American mind.

Reading between the Lines of Public Deception will demonstrate how the modern-day nihilist uses militarized psycho-warfare tactics to coerce our mental ability to reason. They concentrate on conditioning the course of society, beginning with the most impressionable, **the youth**, creating the potential for divisive groups that lead to the breakdown of any society. Sun Tzu stated in *The Art of War* almost 2,400 years ago, "The supreme *Art of War* is to subdue the enemy without fighting." Many Americans have abandoned their logical use of deductive reasoning by surrendering their fundamental human rights and survival instincts to appease political subjectivism and relative truths.

I will attempt to reveal how the global politician is using psycho-warfare and neologisms while pushing the masses into mental, physical, and spiritual exhaustion, leading them into subjugation using tactful instruments of war to self-destruct. You may not agree with everything I say, and that's OK because the main objective here is to rethink your convictions and have open discussions, to conduct a healthy debate. Use deductive reasoning *and to not* immediately rebuke anyone who differs in thought or opinion. Time has made many into a collectively programmed society conditioned to believe or disbelieve and respond almost instinctively when triggered. The only thing we can all do now is pray and seek discernment for truth and reality are becoming blurred and undecipherable to human reasoning. While the globalists play on the premise of using delusional tactics as their form of attack, we must pray for truth as our first line of defense. If you can control the people's emotions, then the mind and the spirit will follow. This quote is attributed to Adolf Hitler: "I use emotion for the many and *reason* for the few."

CHAPTER 1

The Basis of Critical Thought and Human Reasoning

"An unexamined life is not worth living."

—Socrates

The first line of defense against tyranny and subjugation by any authoritative government is safeguarding our reasoning ability through logic and critical thinking.

Critical thinking is defined as the intellectual ability *to solve problems*. To help the individual arrive at a truthful conclusion based on *logic* and human reasoning. Critical thinking is a valuable tool to help you sort through controversy and conflicting thoughts and make sense of things.

According to Richard Paul and Linda Elder's *Guide to Critical Thinking*: "Critical thinking is the intellectually disciplined process of actively and skillfully conceptualizing, applying, analyzing, synthesizing, and evaluating information gathered from, or generated by, observation, experience, reflection, reasoning, or communication, as a guide to (a) belief and action. Its exemplary form is based on universal intellectual values that transcend subject matter divisions: clarity, accuracy, precision, consistency, relevance, sound evidence, good reasons, depth, breadth, and fairness."

A thought needs constructive steps similar to working through scientific calculations to reach a conclusion or to summarize a hypothesis not clouded or hindered by irrational egocentrism and sociocentrism. It needs to be a conclusion gathered with factual reasoning. The truth may not be popular or pleasing, but it is still fundamentally *actual*, given the evidence-based facts, contrary to relative speech and emotions that may blur or distort undeniable facts to fit a relative reality into one's back-pocket-size worldview. Decisions made through unfiltered emotions could be equally described as a physician's diagnosis based on their feelings instead of using the conclusions from the evidence-based data, like confirming cancer based on lab and MRI results but then out of subjective reasoning and the use of emotions deny reality.

Should a doctor make false claims or withhold medical findings and conclusions on evidence-based results because the client doesn't like the *prognosis*? Will their relative truth change the outcome? The preference for relativism over absolute truth for convenience can only create a subjective reality based on the individual, not a universal consensus based on unequivocal facts. Imagine 8.2 billion people having a subjective truth, all having a reality of their own, and then enforcing their subjective reasoning and moral standards onto the public as a universal truth. How is that even possible? How would the world function morally and empirically without absolute truth? A truth does not become *untrue* because it doesn't fit into a subjective reality.

Will the disease cease to exist because we deny the clinical findings, general reasoning, and basic logic? Will the academic understanding of the anatomy and physiology of the human body change a cancer diagnosis? Does the disease care about *how you feel*? Will the pathogen change its dynamics to fit a relative worldview to appease one's feelings? If so, then this illogical premise can be applied to multiple worldviews—medicine, law, physics, mathematics, accounting, and gravity. For the domestic and foreign globalists who feel they can fundamentally create any relative reality to fit their playbook by using relative speech and subjective reasoning through psychological warfare, as John Daniel Davidson wrote in *The Federalist* regarding the American voter, it is designed to **disorient and demoralize** the American. Deviating from the truth or denying its existence doesn't make the reality *untrue* but creates a *ruse*. This delusion will best suit the globally sympathizing politician and anti-American with much to gain in government. (John Daniel Davidson. September 11, 2024.

The Debate Was So Biased It Was Divorced From Reality. Trump Should Refuse To Do Another. The Federalist A Division of FDRLST Media.)

"Critical Thinking raises vital questions and problems, formulating them clearly and precisely by gathering and assessing relevant information and testing them against relevant criteria and standards."

According to the *Guide to Critical Thinking*, freedom of speech allows the mind to openly think within alternative systems of thought, recognize and assess assumptions, implications, and practical consequences, and communicate effectively *with others by figuring out possible solutions to complex problems.* Communication requires a speaker and a listener. To censor the freedom of speech silences one's ability to express and communicate, to form a thought, and smothers the speaker's ability to openly think objectively, instead of stifling any possible solution to resolve contentions and incivility. This thought could explain why dictators do all the thinking and the people do all the listening and then submit. No one would question the dictator's actions if the government had one idea and the people had been taught, convinced, or forced to renege in their innate ability to reason and morally question the status quo. Preventing critical thinking is like telling a scientist to stop experimenting or a mathematician to stop theorizing because they could be accused of being offensive or their reasoning be labeled as a crime against humanity, hence the word *hate crime.* Sounds absurd to some, and to others it is justified.

If people are silenced before they can reach a consensus, how can we achieve the answers we need as a people to solve the most complex problems permeating our society today? Can divisive ideological groups make *truth claims* that speech is oppressive while dominating the open forum? Will their relative ideology take precedence over other groups who disagree? Wouldn't that define fascism? Would the same narrative equal the oppressive nature they claim to defend? We create a new construct of reality under new conditions and new social constructs *that we accept without scrutiny*, no point of reference, and in reality, they defy the premise of tolerance.

This same ideology used in speech, and moral insight can be applied to multiple social facets where "those who call evil good and good evil, who turn light to darkness and darkness to light" (Isaiah 5:20, BSB) can be used as an effective tool to shape new social constructs and critical thinking patterns and change moral reasoning under the guise of being *good.*

> "Critical thinking, in essence, is self-directed, self-disciplined, self-monitored, and self-corrective thinking. It follows standards in ethics, morality, and truth. It entails effective communication and problem-solving abilities and a commitment to overcome our native egocentrism and sociocentrism."
>
> —Richard Paul and Linda Elder. *The Miniature Guide to Critical Thinking Concepts and Tools, Foundation for Critical Thinking Press*

Truthful Speech Gives Rise to Order

Jordan Peterson warned people when he said, "God used '*logos*' truthful speech to cast **a pre-cosmic and habitable order into existence** and then called it good." Hypothesizing in the Old Testament in *Logos,* Dr. Jordan Peterson surmised that "if *truthful* speech gives rise to order, then that order will be *good*."

> "To establish tangible merit regarding what is evidential and true. The principle is based on the logic that the simplest explanation is often correct."
>
> —J. K. Sheindlin, *The People vs Muhammad Psychological Analysis*

CHAPTER 2

WHAT IS A WILLING ACCOMPLICE?

What psychological tactics can be used to undermine the American Mind? According to Kent Clizbe, a former CIA operative who has summarized his intellect, that ***relative words*** are *being used to* 'depredate' **the mind by constructing a new reality**.

—Kent Clizbe, *Willing Accomplices, How KGB Covert Influence Agents Created Political Correctness, Obama's Hate—America—First Political Platform, and Destroyed America*

Using the pretense of social correctness, in social justice and diversity, while exploiting the very people the state claims to be defending. Creating an internal war against each other is a precursor to what lies ahead. If we destroy ourselves internally, having taken the bait, the outside forces have won the battle even before they declare war.

The art of constructing a new reality through relativism and distorting the "absolutes" will elevate subjective and emotional reasoning, leaving the ultimate discourse of bringing the citizen to an emotionally driven state of mind, unable to decipher what is true from what is false. Kent Clizbe states that the constant infiltration of false realities can alter our healthy ability to reason and the common sense to self-preserve, practice vigilance, and defend our inalienable rights given to us by God. "The step(s) needed to dismantle the very grounds of America is first **by polluting the thoughts instead of using arsenal.**"

The globalists have planted an internal war within our sovereign walls and caused internal strife within the people by patronizing division using relative words and race as arsenals to be used against one another. The social fabric that holds a nation together is being assaulted daily. Tactics in the *Art of War* by Sun Tzu states, "If your opponent is temperamental, **seek to irritate him;** if he is taking his ease, **give him no rest; if his forces are united, separate them. If sovereign and subject are in accord, divide them**. Attack him where he is unprepared; appear where you are not expected."

What does this all mean? Marxism is the theory of having two distinct classes: the proletariat (the lower class) and the bourgeoisie (business owners and merchants). In today's definition, the proletariat is the employee, the lower class of people, and the bourgeoisie, the upperclass, like a corporate CEO. According to Wikipedia, the bourgeoisie is defined as business owners and merchants who emerged in the late Middle Ages *as the middle class between peasantry and aristocracy.* I find that choice of words interesting. In the late Middle Ages, only the peasantry and the aristocracy existed. You were either in the confines of the rich or the poor. In Marxism, *there is no middle class.* As a capitalist country, we have a middle class. Karl Marx knew that the middle class was something to contend with and that it was more complicated to convince the public to embrace Socialism if the middle class existed. He thought if Marxism were to implore racial tactics and cause racial and class division, it could convince Americans to abandon the middle-class system. The globalists could then exploit the opportunity to institute internal civil warfare, create collectivism, and promote equal wealth distribution, with equal outcomes, essentially exploiting the masses into conformity—without resistance, which gives rise to **class warfare.** Even Adolf Hitler understood that. Why create an army and waste human and financial resources if one can invade a country using its own people as an arsenal against one another? Let them fight until they reach the point of exhaustion and social destruction by their own hands. Who will retaliate if we are mentally and physically fatigued? Who will retaliate when we have deconstructed our constitutional rights to speech, representation, property, and to defend ourselves from those who wish us ill? The opposite of freedom is prison (oppression). There is no glamor in Socialism.

"The merciful acts of the wicked are cruel."
—Proverbs 12:10, HCSB

Social constructs are convincing people that their God-given rights to freedom are oppressive. Chanting the past crimes of America, while denouncing the entire world's history of governmental tyranny in human suffering through forced servitude and slavery is left untouched and silent. Exonerating every tyrannical government that ever existed from their crimes and thefts in the spoils of war has all been forgotten, *except for America*. She must be punished. Foreign governments, comprised of every race and gender, have been subjected to human suffering, oppression, and slavery, unscrutinized by the anti-American mind. America needs to be portrayed as wicked and the most oppressive and should be convicted and punished, while the rest of the world is viewed as altruistic.

For over two hundred years, people have flocked to America to escape governmental tyranny under the aristocracy, Communism, and lawlessness. Yet we teach our children and citizens that American culture's underlying truth should be despised—a *playbook constructed by the globalist.* If you can manipulate the child's reality, you can control the future. Adolf Hitler understood this concept quite well when he said, "He alone, *who owns the youth*, gains the future."

By using logic alone, why would people leave a tyrannical Socialist country to come to America if America was also perceived as an oppressive country? It appears that the anti-Americans are convinced through propaganda that we too are an oppressed people. That would mean that no country is safe. Why not flee and migrate to China, Russia, Venezuela, or the Middle East? People do not generally leave a free country to migrate to one that is governed by an authoritarian dictator. Even though the anti-American seem to think otherwise, in constitutional reality, we are *free* to think so.

As with antisemitism and repeated rhetoric in systemic racism and phobias injected by mainstream media, academia, and politicians, the concept of "giving them no rest" until the last one conforms to the narrative is unrelenting. They are initiating a new social narrative that dominates the mainstream platform, where they circulate divisive information, and anything else is boxed into disinformation. They are portraying the conservative as a nonconformist, deplorable, intolerant, a dinosaur, and out of touch with reality. According to them, vice president Joe Biden when he called the middle Americans "the dregs to society" explains it all too well.

And those who are brave enough to think outside of their perceived identity groups have been ridiculed, shamed, and punished for daring to think and speak otherwise. Americans fought against slavery but were reminded to vote without fail, a party that has not changed their circumstance in decades. These voters do not even understand the history of their party. They protest oppression while staying loyal to a party that keeps them at bay. Where is the logic of thought placed on that? They continue to live under the same circumstances, poverty, cultural dissonance, communal ruins, and poor educational opportunities while maintaining a sense of loyalty to a party that only thinks about staying in power. The same thought process would define the mindset of insanity, doing the same thing repeatedly and expecting a different result. It is much easier to lay blame and abandon all sense in reasoning for leverage in exalting a political party that will give them more entitlements while usurping their independence.

Instead, blame the majority for your voting decisions. Blame the majority for your circumstances. If systemic racism were *real*, using critical thinking, then I suppose every minority, every film star, musician, talk-show host, politician, president, and athlete would be nonexistent. Can America do better for its people? Absolutely. There will always be room for improvement, as with any country. But when applying truth, *every man and woman is imperfect in the sight of God*. Improvement *for humanity* must begin with *the individual* first to form a better government that distributes tax-paying money to where it rightfully belongs. I will explain how government spending devastates our most vulnerable neighborhoods. How the government's playbook is designed to create societal dependency and social discord and bankrupt the country. *The Art of War* states, "First create **internal war** among the people by causing the mayhem in self-destruction, and **then the spoils of war will soon follow.**"

Should the American minorities dare stray from the Democratic party and face ridicule from their identity groups? Should their community ostracize them for noncompliance? Isn't that a form of discrimination, a dictatorship type of bullying within the ranks of the group? Has political correctness constricted the individual so *tight*, forcing classical conditioning into a predicted behavior with the unrelenting weaponized speech of oppression? Civilians use the same rhetoric that was used in antisemitism during WWII. They said Jews were less than human and using disparaging words of contempt to ostracize them from their community. They insulted them by creating a social construct that identified them as having beady little eyes and large noses or as selfish and greedy. Joking that the Jews mince children to make matzo balls was common practice. The Nazis were able to convince law-abiding citizens and subjects that stealing, beating, and berating the Jews was **collectively good** by using their **subjective standards**. But their oppression was irrelevant. Only my history and oppression has meaning, and no one else matters.

The anti-American will remember our country's crimes, while millions of Americans lay dead forgotten, and their historical sacrifices too trivial to mention.

Robbing people of the truth behind the Judeo-Christian religion that Catholicism rightfully began with them is historical thievery. Using replacement theology is a fallacy. Christ was a Jew, and the first disciples were also Jews. The Jewish people were severely persecuted for just existing. However, as with every **propaganda success**, *repetition is key*. According to Joseph Goebbels, Hitler's senior officer of propagandists, good propaganda is to provide the people with short verses so that most minors will understand your slogan. As for Hitler, he conceded that "The most brilliant propagandist technique will yield no success unless one fundamental principle is constantly borne in mind and with unflagging attention. It must confine itself to a few points and repeat them repeatedly. Here, as so often in this world, **persistence is the first and most important requirement for success**."

The same memorizing "images" are being used today. Words such as *white privilege*, *collective crimes*, *white supremacy*, *slavery*, *rape culture*, *oppression*, *racism*, radical, *Islamophobic*, *homophobic*, *-isms*, *Uncle Tom*, *pro-choice*, and *oppression* have become weaponized. Front lawn signs saying, "Hatred has no home here," and "Coexist," deliver the same message and associate the word *hate* with anyone who dares to question an ideology. You will be punished and ostracized by the **self-proclaimed righteous**. A government's tactical playbook is to deprogram the majority by strengthening the minority with unrelenting discontent and using *cultural differences and vulnerability* to exploit group dynamics. The playbook can **accurately predict a group's maladaptive behavior** in social conditioning.

Current events have revealed that today is no different than yesterday. People are paralyzed with derogatory words to subjugate and *dehumanize* them for the color of their skin, their religion, or their political affiliation. To drive guilt into the minds of a particular group and demonize their economic circumstance, even if the financial gains were obtained by personal sacrifice and hard work, has become irrelevant. You are a white American thus, you are *guilty by association*. To counterattack critical thinking before you have the chance to defend your right to exist does not imply *racism*. Racism is accurately defined as a prejudice that can be applied to everyone. The globalist has taken the predicted response and 'recoined' the word in a social construct to imply that only the white majority of people can be racial thus causing an intended social divide. Society had been well groomed by the universities, which have outwardly informed their students that only white men and women can be racist. You need only to repeat a slogan often enough to appease the emotional strife, and you can, in fact, convince a whole society that a square is indeed a circle—another thought-provoking slogan designed by the mastermind Joseph Goebbels.

These slogans have opened a new progressive era to the Jim Crow mentality, human value according to their skin color. How do you overcome a superior country? You first *attack the majority*; they represent *the biggest threat* to the global narrative. If defeated, you can weaken the country from the inside by using the tactics detailed in the *Art of War*. Blindside the people within mainstream and social media, blurring the lines of reality and distracting their minds. They will then fail to see the internal war being orchestrated before their eyes. The smartphone, along with technology, was ingenious. Most of our youth are becoming too preoccupied and paralyzed with social conditioning and have become less and less observant of their surroundings. Philosophers, anthropologists, archaeologists, psychologists (Pavlov dogs), sociologists, scientists, politicians, professors, academia, marketing, and social/mainstream media have studied the masses at *great lengths*.

If slavery was as detrimental as indicated by history, then why does one think that Socialism would be any better? Socialism is just another form of slavery, except this time, all Americans will feel the wrath at the same time, regardless of whether they fell under the majority, minority, tribal, or native group. The push for equality will cement global Socialism to where slavery will apply to all of us *equally*. How else can you have equal distribution with equal outcomes if it is not intended to apply to each and every one of us? Equal distribution is a concept that needs to be controlled and applied equally (equity) for all, regardless of education, position, experience, or occupation. Without constant vigilance in social conditioning, the past will inevitably return to the present.

> "The receptivity of the masses is '*very limited*,' and their 'intelligence is small,' but their 'power of forgetting is enormous.' In consequence of these facts, 'all effective propaganda' must be limited to a few points and harp on these in slogans until the last member of the public understands what you want him to understand by your slogan."
>
> —Adolf Hitler

Politicians and paid programming controlled by social/mainstream media giants use the same psychological tactics to engrain their ideology into social conditioning through repetition. They plant seeds of deceit and then convincingly present them as truth. It's the perfect platform to control what you see and hear, undoubtedly paid for by the 1 percent. The same 1 percent the minorities have been programmed to believe are their defenders. Everything is only valid if the thought police, the gatekeepers, and the fact-checkers state it to be true. Everything else is classified as disinformation. If you utter a single word contradicting the gatekeepers, you are "de-platformed, demonetized, publicly ostracized or arrested on prefabricate charges." This is how liars create the "illusion of truth."

The Nazis (gestapo) had perfected their militarized tactics in controlling social thinking. They had prepared extensively to manipulate the German masses, to rob them of speech and self-defense. They implemented their divisive ideology by way of fear and force. American politicians have become self-dictators, giving power to the universities to militarize our college students and permeate our elementary schools with adult issues. We were creating laws contradicting our Constitution enforced with federal and state mandates.

> "'Repeat a lie often enough, and it becomes the truth' is a law of propaganda often attributed to the Nazi Joseph Goebbels, the minister of propaganda for the German Third Reich under Adolf Hitler. A master orator and propagandist, he is generally accounted for and responsible for presenting a favorable image of the Nazi regime to the German people.
>
> And they bought into it."
>
> —Tom Stafford, *When and How Rational Argument Can Change Minds*

> "Think of the press as a great 'keyboard' on which the government can play."
>
> —Joseph Goebbels

CHAPTER 3

THE POWER OF WORDS

> "America is like a 'healthy body,' and its 'resistance' *is threefold*: its patriotism, morality, and spiritual life. If we can undermine these three areas, America will collapse *from within*."
>
> —attributed to Joseph Stalin*

*This quote cannot be authentically verified; nonetheless, there is truth to be found.

> "It would not be impossible to prove, with sufficient 'repetition' and a psychological understanding of the people concerned, that a *square is, in fact, a circle.* **They are mere words**, and words can be molded until they clothe ideas and disguise."
>
> —Joseph Goebbels

The tactic of using repetitive language is to have the power to deconstruct social norms. Social constructs are being accepted as truth and unconsciously conform the citizen to the will of the tyrant. American nationalism has been twisted to mean a Nazis form of social nationalism. Anyone flying the American flag or pledging American allegiance is attacked for being a racist or an oppressor and immediately attached to some collective crime. The Nazi regime and the American patriot idealism have become one similar thought. America has fought civil wars that protested for countless civil rights and accomplished much within its 247-plus years of existence. *Instead, we have chosen to cherry-pick which part of history will satisfy the global agenda and fulfill the international narrative.* The forgotten abolitionists, who fought against governmental tyranny and the social constructs of their day, have all been deleted from the American textbooks. Even the truth of human slavery has been blurred and twisted beyond recognition. It takes away the true suffering of the people from long ago to award those completely disassociated from the time period. The idea of retribution will continue until when? When will enough be enough?

These past heroes who went against the grain of society were victimized for having a different belief system. They fought against the social construct of the day with a conservative and moral objectivity aligned with the Judeo-Christian thought. They were persecuted as a radical ideological group from their day to defend the innocent, like the conservatives or nonconformists who refused to subjugate. The political party and social construct in the eighteenth and nineteenth centuries criticized and shamed all who fought against the system. Millions have shed their blood through war and made the ultimate sacrifice, which has gone unappreciated. It's like having the mindset that if you are praised 90 percent of the time and fail within the remaining 10 percent, then that 10 percent will represent your entire group's identity. A whole group of people are thus remembered for a systemic crime, for the actions of the few, and for the actions of the dead, punishing people for a collective crime without representation or Constitutional justice. But then again, how do you suppress the majority if not by using psychological warfare?

Can we hypnotize people with priming by interjecting collective thoughts disguised as free will?

Have you noticed that the newly revised Socialistic Democratic Party does not refer to itself as Socialist? The Nazi Nationalist Socialist regime used eugenics to purify their race. We have convinced Americans with prochoice (abortionist), euthanasia, and gender-reaffirming surgeries to sterilize our children. Hitler either praised the children or had them executed. The government is trying to outlaw guns, claiming it will decrease crimes while leaving Americans vulnerable to both inside and outside criminal forces. Indiscriminate immigration through our borders brings an unknown potential for war. The Nazis had the people register their guns; the government knew who had them. I can go on and on; I will go into more detail in later chapters, but you can see the pattern.

The nihilists are going after our children. If we do not dispose of them before they are born, then we will corrupt their minds and permantly damage their bodies beyond recovery. The country cannot be protected by its citizens if it creates a generation of disabled men and women by turning men into beta males. We inundate them with fentanyl, drugs, vaping, alcohol, and sexual/gender dysphoria. We attack the patriarch—the father figure—and the nuclear family. We have changed the pronouns of mother, father, son, and daughter. We shout toxic masculinity as evil while creating beta males and obsessive alpha females. We confuse evidence-based science, where men are women and women are men, starting at birth. Nazi social nationalism disrupted the social norms in Europe so quickly that the mass of people became profoundly disoriented, mimicking the same results in America.

Hitler's idea of nationalism was based on forming a "Socialistic, breed within a Communist regime." Unlike America, in the rule of law, the constitution, and the Bill of Rights, the laws were designed 'of the people, for *the people*, by the people." Hitler's nationalism was to form a *Socialist party and what we call today a democratic Socialist. A Democrat is one party and a Socialist party is another, but somehow, they have been combined and the two are represented as one.* America is not a *one-person ruled party.* America is not of one race but of multiple races, languages, and cultures **under the umbrella of Americanism**. Politics and colleges are notorious for defining the American culture as the most *abhorrent* while every other culture is to be embrace with open arms, regardless of their past and what they bring to society. Nationalism is accurately defined as having a common ground with citizenship. You will not defend what you don't love. That is the psychosocial warfare tactic used to undermine the citizens.

You will destroy what you think you hate and destroy yourselves while you're at it.

> "You just need to flood a county's public square with enough raw sewage ... you just need to raise enough questions ... spread enough dirt ... plant enough conspiracy theorizing ... let citizens no longer know what to believe. Once

> they lose trust in their leaders, mainstream media, and political institutions, in each other, **and in the possibility of truth**, *the game is won*."
>
> —Barrack Obama, addressing disinformation in his speech at Stanford University

Obama's arrogance and political intent were left wide open for all those wise enough to see. Truth be told, contradicting Obama's frame of thinking, the United States is not a democracy *but a republic*. Politicians often use the word *democracy* interchangeably with the word *republic*. Obama's speech was given under the pretense of "disinformation." The manipulation of words spoken by a charismatic speaker can deliver "disinformation and social classical conditioning" without being noticed or resisted. A persuasive public speaker can play their flute and hypnotize their audience as they watch the crowd willingly follow the flute player by weaponizing words to mean other than what they mean. Using the word *nationalism* is more evil than being a Communist. The Socialist who advocates for Socialism is actually grooming the citizen to become a subject under the rule of Communism.

Public speaking is an art of communication, a skill to persuade people. Professionals study the art of delivering the message, whether selling, marketing, educating, instructing, or convincing. The primary purpose is to persuade and even mesmerize the audience with their message. Public speakers can steer the masses in any direction they choose. If the lie is repeated often enough, will it become true? Then what is the truth? Is it relative or absolute? If the message is given by persuasive speakers who are gifted and talented, can they craft their speeches to seduce the unsuspecting without notice? Entertain their relative truth to satisfy the itching ear and suit their desires? People will follow the Pied Piper, and when they do, "will they not both fall into a pit?" (Luke 6:39, BSB).

> "For the time will come when men **will not tolerate sound doctrine**, but with itching ears, they will gather around themselves teachers to suit their own desires. So,

> they will turn their ears away from the truth and turn aside to myths."
>
> —2 Timothy 4:3–4, BSB

According to John Bouvier, "The guarantee of republican government was designed to provide a national remedy for domestic insurrection threatening the state governments and to prevent the rise of a monarchy." The Federalist Papers of 1787 and 1788 summarize that *the republic was designed to be **a contrast to democracy***, where the legislative would have no checks or balances; and the rights of the individual and the weaker party, personal security, and property would *always be in jeopardy*. This can be found in Republic, a law dictionary, adapted to the Constitution and laws of the United States.

This interpretation might explain the insights behind the need for the Electoral College.

> "There is no difference between Communism and Socialism, except in the means of achieving the same ultimate end: Communism proposes to enslave men by force, Socialism—*by vote*.
>
> It is merely the difference between murder and suicide."
>
> —Ayn Rand, philosopher

The Democrats do not use the term *Socialism*, because that would give the image of the German Third Reich. *American nationalism* on the other hand is one of those repeated words to associate the American nationalism as a form of oppression to despise, but yet it is not a term to define *pure breed*. The word *Americanism* is composed of multiple nationalities, unlike the pure Aryan race. Hitler was determined to create the Aryan race, which he considered superior beings similar to the belief system of a nihilist. That is not the premise of Americanism.

Hitler planned to murder *all the undesirable races discriminately*. A man who deliberately murdered millions of innocent lives to create a superior race, a country with systemic racism beyond reproach, does not in any way equate to American nationalism. Progressivism has allowed the crime of eugenics to permeate society as a subtle form of warfare. Abortion is a form of eugenics, ridding our society of the "undesirables," proposed by Margaret Sanger, the creator of Planned Parenthood. The global thought is that **fewer people represent less opposition** and allow more resources for the desirables and the politically powerful.

Any word-constructed repetition can make a good word appear revolting or a lousy word appear good. Any word can be twisted and taken out of context to represent anything the coiner wills it to be. Keep the word or verse relatively small and then incessantly repeat until "the mass accepts what you're trying to say." The global elitists have exploited the word *nationalism* to tear apart the fabric that holds us together as a people and as Americans.

Words are used in child's play, and globalists are using child tactics to lure in the unsuspecting.

Children are taught a language when introducing words. They associate the word with a given image, creating a social, classical conditioning. Children are given class assignments daily and homework to associate a word with the image. Then they associate the word with the image through repetition. Words create images, and images create language. To coerce a mass population into thinking a certain way, you repeat the message *until the masses not only believe you but will fight and protest to the death to defend the will of the tyrant.* Politicians are skillful actors, and social and mainstream media are paid to read word for word off the teleprompter to disseminate the narrative. MSNBC, ABC, CNN, and the BBC are paid by globalists and powerful corporations, like Disney, who use their platform to exploit their loyal followers. Academics and universities have the power to groom students as militants, while sports arenas exploit their fans. Elementary and high school students are required to take global studies, referencing our children as *global citizens.* Within time, the taxpayer will soon be the new subject under the global aristocracy—*the latest progressive monarch.*

Talk about controlling people's minds using simple childlike tactics in manipulating *words.*

> "Woe to those who call evil good and good evil, who turn darkness to light and light to darkness, who replace bitter

> with sweet and sweet with bitter. Woe to those who are wise in their own eyes and clever in their own sight."
>
> —Isaiah 5:20–21, BSB

Each original word has a root meaning. The writers who put together the dictionary have painstakingly collected the origin of words and definitions to preserve language to be domestically and universally understood. We have allowed the contradictions of truths to appease our pocket-size worldview, to dictate what we are to understand. Pronouns are no longer being used correctly in language and grammar. When using pronouns, you can't even construct a school paper without excessive grammatical correction. Pronouns are used to describe a noun. The word *they* is defined to represent more than one person and is now used to describe "a person" who identifies as a they. Why? The political playbook has created relative truths, blurring the lines in speech to cause disorder, confusion, and predictable set-up counter-attacks for not addressing *them* according to their assigned pronoun. We are changing the language used for hundreds and thousands of years. Words that were common knowledge are now used as a double-edged sword. Social conditioning has convinced the populace to accept a social construct by renouncing a truthful speech. If we can change words, we can change pronouns. If we can change the meaning of gender, regardless of evidence-based biology and science, then we can change the meaning of history. We can create a new reality without a point of reference or conjectures without empirical evidence. Without an approved word bank (a dictionary), any word can become subjective and used as a weapon to instill fear.

> "Be extremely subtle, even to the point of *formlessness*. Be extremely mysterious, even to the point of soundlessness. Thereby, you can be the *director of the opponent's fate*."
>
> —Sun Tzu, *The Art of War*

Changing the accuracy of American history by comparing American nationalism to Nazi nationalism is a travesty. The actions of the German SS who, in savagery, shot defenseless men, women, and children in the head in front of their graves that they dug for themselves have become irrelevant. During WWII the German Reich, invaded countries and killed Europeans like it was a sport. Now having said that, I do not imply that all German people or soldiers were Nazis. The Nazis were an elite group of people who held the power in government to exploit and murder the defenseless; the same can be said that not all Americans should be punished for a collective crime. They were people who joined the German Reich and committed horrific acts of human cruelty, while others fought to defend their motherland. Many Americans refused to subjugate to social constructs similar to the American abolitionists and the American soldiers. Both have been depreciated.

Webster's Dictionary defines a nationalist as a "member of a political party or group advocating national independence or strong national government." Nothing in the definition indicates oppression or racism. The word is defined as *national independence.* What would the global agenda benefit by robbing the *root meaning* of a word if not to manufacture a subjective view?

Would an opposing nation or billionaire *have anything to gain if America should turn against itself?*

To rob the word of its original root meaning can turn a patriot into a monster. The atrocities of the German Reich cannot in any way be compared to an American patriot. The gestapo should be held accountable for their atrocities and crimes against humanity and should not be redefined to equate to American nationalism.

Taking the innocence of a word to become a political vice removes the evils committed by the one and serves as an injustice to the other.

Being a patriot is not defined as "incomprehensible." *The action and brutality of the Nazis was incomprehensible and reprehensible.* Americans fought in the American Revolution and the Civil War. They marched in the suffrage movement and protested injustice in civil rights. Unjust idealisms are not caused by Americanism but by the European, century-old ideologies controlled by the aristocracy. America has only been around for 247-plus years. It was an experiment to create a *new world* different from Europe. And no, there is no "1619 project." *That is a global* propaganda designed to change the date to 157 years earlier, to a time controlled by the Europeans. North America was referred to as *the New World.* The United States did not exist 403 years earlier, even with college textbooks stating otherwise, which alters the truth. Logic tells you in the title alone: "The United States" did not exist until *after* the Revolutionary War.

The continent was called "The New World." Remember history: the English monarch controlled the first colonists to enter the New World, hence the need for the Revolutionary War to break free from the monarch and over taxation—the monarch's governmental tyranny. Our forefathers had committed treason in forming a new government where citizens created laws, a new government that would free the people from "subjecthood." They were free from governmental tyranny, over taxation, wars, religious persecutions, and misrepresentation, giving them the right to defend themselves against the monarch and creating citizens to break from subjecthood.

Repeating the past is not a progressive move *but a regressive one.*

As with all uncontrolled immigration, we run the risk of saving the many by inadvertently consenting to accept the few who bring with them the evils of sin. Evil men do not lag far behind. They follow to where they can do the most harm. There will always be psychopaths, sociopaths and tyrants who will carry with them their idealisms, greed, and lust for power. They follow where the people go, like bullies who pounce on the first opportunity to exploit. They find weakness in kindness until the people rebel. Many came to the New World with good intentions, to start a new life, while others came to bring misery, brutality, and death. That was over four hundred years ago, behaviors that are still reminiscent of today. Welcome to the modern-day nihilist progressivism for nothing has changed. There will always be those who thirst to rule by spilling blood and exploiting those who are willing to submit to the tyrant.

Saying that American nationalism is the foundation for oppression is unfounded. The lives of millions are controlled by powerful and influential people who have unlimited resources to coerce the masses. If the psychopath can find a *pin-size* chance to control the masses, the opportunist will act upon it. Respecting the historical significance that under the will of tyrants, Adolph Hitler, Joseph Stalin, and Mao Zedong, managed to murder an estimated 76 million people combined from 1939 to 1945. Today, the willing tyrant will wait to pounce on the next opportunity for mass murder following the Machievelli rule of government. WWII ended less than one generation ago. Will the crimes of a Romanian Socialist dictator, Nicolae Ceausescu, who was executed by a military tribunal for committing genocide of over sixty thousand Romanian people, be repeated? *And that was thirty-six years ago, from 2024.* How many more innocent lives need to perish before reason begins? What is the obsession with creating a utopian society under the rules and laws developed and governed by imperfect men? This utopic society can never be achieved, for only *God* can make a perfect government, but not within a sinful and imperfect world. The Declaration of Independence and the Constitution are as close as possible *to living in a just society.*

Henry Kissinger, the former US Secretary of State, said, "Today, Americans would be outraged if the UN troops entered Los Angeles *to restore order.* Tomorrow, they will be *grateful.*

This would be especially true if Americans were *told* there, was an outside threat." A biological disease, impending war, from beyond, whether 'real or manufactured', that would threaten *our very existence.*

"The one thing every man fears is the unknown."

> "When presented with this scenario, 'individual rights' will be 'willingly relinquished' for the guarantee of their 'well-being' granted to them by their world government."
>
> —Henry Kissinger (1923–), former US Secretary of State, speaking at Evian, France, May 21, 1992. Bilderberger's meeting. Unbeknownst to Kissinger, his speech was taped by a Swiss delegate.

An appalling statement, one might say, made by a former US Secretary of State responsible for mediating with foreign affairs. He insinuates that people would be "willing to relinquish their individual rights" to be governed by foreign entities without regard to their Constitution or Bill of Rights. Marxism is the beginning of grooming citizens into subjecthood. Repeat and deconstruct the social norms without the declaration of war. Katie Couric followed up with the same ideology when she said that 74 million Americans who voted for Trump needed to be "deprogrammed." She said, "How are we going to really almost deprogram these people who have signed up for the cult of Trump?" Can she be accused of treason by suggesting that these constitutionalists be *deprogrammed* and re-examined for obeying the laws of the country and having the Constitutional rights to vote? It makes no difference whether you agree with Trump or not, the people have a right to choose. The government does not have the right to choose for itself, which would define a totalitarianism.

A multimillion-dollar question: How do we deprogram a large amount of people without war? By altering the people's sense of reality, censoring their speech, public shaming, weakening the men, derailing women, and sabotaging the youth, while demonizing any form of patriotism. Attacking any form of opposition to globalism will be met with ridicule and punishment disguised as the failure *to conform.*

> "If you repeat a lie often enough, people will believe it, and 'you' will even come to 'believe' it yourself."
>
> —Joseph Goebbels

Let's summarize the impact of words (*logos*), repetition, and their ramifications. Learning words to form a language is the same process used to teach children to help them retain early developmental speech. As I said before, they learn their letters through repetition, jingles, music,_images, and word associations. These word associations can be implemented in psychological warfare and social conditioning. Suppose children learn that letters form words and words can create images and images can form ideas. In that case, these ideas, or reality, can affect behavior, executive function, cognition, and the ability to communicate with others—using childlike tactics but on a much broader scale. Implement these ideas in society through mainstream and social media, the music and film industry, journalism, and political diversions, and the citizens become trapped. Imprinting the social constructed ideas without knowledge.

Calculated words can cause a predictable response. In Pavlov's classical conditioning, he used images and sounds to get dogs to behave in a predictable manner. Pavlov learned through his experiment that dogs could be *conditioned* to associate certain sounds (the bell) to simulate food. The specific sounds would trigger a behavioral response, like salivating at the sound of a bell. As for human behavior within executive functions, we use them, as children, to learn, focus, and retain information, which can also be used to form new societal concepts. Classical conditioning is the process of learning by associating an image between two stimuli: the bell and the predicted response in salivating.

According to the results of this experiment, classical conditioning could stimulate a response in social construction. Classical conditioning, effective public speaking, professors use word associations and relative speech in classically conditioning their students. A politician using trigger words to form identity groups? Everywhere you go, you hear repetitive word associations. If not in social media, you'll listen to it in mainstream media, films, music, marketing, medicine, and all forms of social communication.

There are seven essential elements to public speaking. I will concentrate on three communication styles: informative, persuasive, and motivational. Pavlov's experiment in classical conditioning can be applied to all three elements, whether it is used to inform, persuade, or motivate a crowd of people or stimulate college students to act on a belief system other than their own by seducing them through incitement.

A narcissist or charismatic speaker *can motivate and persuade identity groups simply by provoking their Achilles's heel*, pretending to assimilate with their circumstance and then inciting them into a predictable behavioral response, like Pavlov's experiment.

Instead of salivating like Pavlov's dogs when smelling food, a man, woman, or child will react to their innermost desires, and temporarily permit themselves to behave undisciplined and for some lawlessly. Behaviors that are normally kept in check within the confines of societal laws, morals, and punishment are now being unleashed without recourse—for instance, looting and destroying property without accountability while protesting for retribution. Identity groups are protesting against a collective crime under the premise of self-proclaimed righteousness. I see no evil and do no evil, but you, *on the other hand*, must pay a price ...

If the mainstream media can market the skill of manipulating identity groups in classical conditioning, they can incite and produce a predictable response in any given gender or group. Politicians can do the same. Repeated verses like "my truth may not be your truth" or "my moral standards are not your moral standards" may trigger a *desired* result in changing social constructs where truth is arbitrary. An individual's perception of *truth* or moral standards can distort reality by creating a faulty script or schema in human behavior in social imprinting.

Nothing can be evidence based or received as an absolute truth if the **social imprinting** distorts one's ability to reason, commercial jingles that are so catchy they embed themselves deep inside the subconscious without the individual taking notice. These jingles and images can trigger and even emanate an emotional hypnotic reactive response. It's like breaking open an ice-cold can of soda. You hear the can crack open. You see the cold droplets drip alongside the can; you hear the fizzling of the carbonated water, and you immediately form an image in your mind strong enough to taste the drink without physically touching it. You can hear the sizzling sound of a steak on a grill. All are creating a physical response to salivate.

If multiple professions understand this behavioral response, then why wouldn't the globalist sociopathic politicians, both domestic and foreign, apply the same classical conditioning as Pavlov's experiment to society similar to marketing tactics?

Government and social elitists have adopted the same behavioral method to control the subconscious and allow unsuspecting citizens to believe almost anything. They use trigger words to create a new conformity, defying the old ways while succumbing to trickery. Marketing is a billion-dollar industry. Imagine how much time and money is spent in cornering the market by predicting a behavioral response, like turning a knob to raise the volume. Industrial psychologists, anthropologists, sociologists, professors, politicians, and the mainstream media have gathered enough clinical information and data to make calculated predictions.

If they can control the predictable response, **they can control the *outcome*.**

Now we understand how words can create images, images can create perception, and programmed perceptions can create predicted responses. Marketers can elicit an emotional response by using psychological tools and undermining tactics to exploit human reasoning. These are psychological tools that can be used to alter a person's reality, experiments that can cause one to salivate, crave, desire, or take a more deviant route by inciting aggression. Tucker Carlson interviewed Jacob Chansley when he said that "fiefdoms within the government are using psyops-neurolinguistics to program the way people ***perceive reality***. Neurolinguistics is the process of using words to create patterns in the subconscious to trigger responses. The *subconscious part of the brain* contains our Neurolinguistic activity.

"If you can **hijack** the pattern in someone's brain, you can **hijack** the conscious perception of reality." Joseph Goebbels and Adolf Hitler said the same thing when constructing propaganda. Isolate your words, keep them simple, and repeat them continuously until the last person understands your intended message.

Can the theory of classical conditioning be applied to social constructs like nationalism, toxic masculinity, patriarchs, collective crime, my body my choice, and American cultural oppression? People protest oppression based on their perception of reality, socio-economic circumstance, version of altruism, social justice, and self-righteousness, but by destroying their country, they inadvertently destroy themselves. Allowing the Pied Piper to play his flute, exhausting the people too weak to recover.

This allows the *coiner* **to control** what the word will mean, and the mass will follow.

Is this another tactic created by global verbal relativism?

We are punishing people who contribute to the federal government. Paying taxes to sustain a societal infrastructure, like Medicaid, Medicare, food, WIC, housing allowance, immigration, social security, disability, DACA, welfare, and military defense are just a few programs available in America. We are conditioning our citizens to hold this country in contempt while taking the taxpayers' money. Do we not work here? Do we not live here, raise our families, and attend school?

The US education system, controlled by multiple players, has a chapter of its own that addresses the complexities of how neurolinguistics is being used to create new conformities within the minds of our youths. The new conformist, having accepted classical conditioning, has consented to abandon the fundamentals of Americanism to chance their future for the unknown. It is deconstructing the American Constitution 'piece by piece' to create new laws to be enforced by nihilistic global politicians. What would a foreign government care about a former American citizen? Citizenship will become obsolete and make room for *serfdom*. Speech should be a universal form of communication. It's the logos that defend your inalienable rights as a human being. Without it, freedom cannot exist.

> "You are only a means to an end."
>
> —Machiavelli, *The Prince*

Imagine facing a crisis without a domestic or universal understanding of language, where society accepts relative speech coined by identity groups enforced by their subjective realities. This is deliberate by the power that be. Chaos within a society will someday require order, and this is when the nihilist will enter the stage to repair the disorder they first created. Society needs continuity and norms to function properly and thrive. We have abiding rules written in our Constitution, Bill of Rights, and the Declaration of Independence to help govern the 325-plus million people in the United States. If words and *logos* cannot be protected, then the most straightforward interaction between two entities within language could create chaos. The simplest act of getting from point *A* to point *B* would be a debacle. In a crime scene, words are imperative. Obtaining witness testimonies and evidence found must be communicated effectively to help investigators solve a case—*not subjectively but objectively.* Without a consensus on the use of language, understanding one another would be impossible. Logic and truth are cultivated in speech. They give directives. It allows for instruction to complete a task. It helps humanity to communicate effectively. Relevant truth, on the other hand, is the opposite.

Truth is absolute. Relative speech is *coined.* The logic behind nomenclatures, scientific and Latin terminology, is to explain the meaning behind the word. Prefixes and suffixes also work on the same premise. For example, the prefix *brady* means "slow" and the suffix *cardio* means "heart." *Bradycardia* means low blood pressure (BP). The prefix *arth* means "pertaining to a joint," and the suffix *itis* means "inflammation," making **arthritis** the inflammation of a joint or limb. The root of the word gives the word its meaning. It's not up for debate; it's Latin. Even science needs truthful speech to understand the laws of physics, gravity, and cosmology. *Neologism* is a word that defines the twisting of words to means other than what they were intended to mean.

According to Merriam-Webster dictionary, "Neologism: a new word that is coined, especially by a person affected with schizophrenia. **It is meaningless except to the coiner** and is typically a "combination" of two existing words or a shortening *or distortion of an existing word.*"

Triggers words are distorted versions of a neologism—words being circulated to cause a predictable response. Replace the words in American traditionalism with images of contempt and oppression, and **you have**

changed the image to suit the coiner's ideology, thus altering reality. *This is a tool used in neurolinguistics.*

> "And with every wicked deception directed against those who are perishing because they refused the love of the truth that would have saved them. *For this reason,* ***God will send them a powerful delusion so that they believe the lie***, in order that judgment may come on all who have disbelieved the truth and delighted in wickedness."
>
> —2 Thessalonians 2:10–11, BSB

God will give them over to their depravity. What does this quote in scripture mean? It means that most people will seek what they want to see and what they want to hear and thus reap what they follow. They would rather accept what is emotionally pleasing than accept what is true. So, **God will allow them to fall into their own desires** *because that is what they seek.* You think that everything you see and hear has good intentions? Stop. Stand outside the box. Examine the intent of the speaker and scrutinize the message. Be careful and methodical when using your sense of reasoning. Refrain from being too quick to agree *or disagree* **before examining the message.**

Scripture reminds us to keep a "clear mind" in all we do for many are plotting our ends. Should you be a progressive, a college student, a minority, or an identity group, you have been studied extensively, and the predicted pattern belonging to each identity group has already been predetermined and predicted. If we are led to despise our country, convinced to loathe the very word *nationalism*, and the representation of the American Flag is vile, then where will you go when your country falls? By consenting to divisive speech and social constructs, you have censored your own liberties. That is the same as putting shackles on your hands and feet and calling it good. *Censoring your neighbor's speech will one day* **censor you.**

Without speech, how can any civil movement go forward? How can logical discussions be made? How can others hear you think if you cannot speak?

Colin Kaepernick knelt in opposition to the National Anthem, claiming it represented fascism, oppression, and racism. Universities are producing college-groomed militants who are protesting our constitutional right to freedom of speech, the same speech they are using to protest. That's like bouncing two balls, but neither has a set direction. We are being indoctrinated and groomed to fit a global belief system. In George Orwell's novel *1984*, Winston is forced to believe in relative speech. Winston's job is to remove "information" *not approved* by Big Brother—*what we define today as disinformation.* Following neologisms and social conditioning, Winston is psychologically tortured until he reaches exhaustion. He submits and finally agrees that two plus two *does equal five.*

The population will soon grow exhausted too. Government and social media are relentless. Mainstream and social media conglomerates have thousands of paid employees whose primary mission is to censor our speech and act as gatekeepers to what they deem as disinformation. They aim to wear down the 325-plus million people through psychological and physical exhaustion. Psychological warfare is more effective than artillery.

Americans will be deceived into believing a preconditioned reality disguised as altruistic motives. Triggered words such as *oppression*, *social justice*, *toxic masculinity*, *the patriarch*, and *collective crimes* have been used to incite *public scoffing*, and shaming allowing the progressive fundamentalist to manipulate the subconscious by inciting primed triggered emotions disguised as free will.

Hitler once said, "I use emotion for the many and reasoning for the few." Global politicians will provoke relentlessly and with no rest until the entire country agrees that two plus two does truly *equal* 5. Where does the lie belong if we have relative speech? The lie and the absolute truth are polar opposites. If that were untrue, then where do we find relative speech? In geometry, when using the *X* and *Y* axis, where would we graph relative speech between true and false? Would the intercept point be anywhere within the middle of the graph? *X* and *Y* would be graphed opposite to one another. They will never intersect nor cross.

Question:

Shouldn't the very constitutional right for you to speak *against* me be used to censor you?

Identity groups have built a strong momentum, but it is all temporary.

You can only burn, loot, assault, and destroy property for so long and protest without respect for others until enough is enough. *There will come a time when group identity services will no longer be needed.* Exploiting gender/ sexual identities, derailing the minds of children, and making a mockery of mental health is, in itself, a social injustice. The treatment for mental health can now be questionable. Is the counselor providing a truthful diagnosis with an evidence-based treatment plan or providing subjective relativism based on ideology and social constructs.

There are social consequences in manipulating speech that can negatively affect the most vulnerable communities, and our government is more than aware of its resources. They have created social dependencies through specialized programs and will punish anyone not adhering to their rules. In welfare, if a woman marries, her federal support will stop. If she gets a job, her welfare will stop. If she tries to get educated, you guessed it, her welfare checks will stop. Where is the incentive to thrive? Where is the incentive to marry? Marxism does not support the individual or the nuclear family; it supports the idea of collectivism. Not unity. Not family cohesiveness. Not parenting and not individualism. The children will belong to the state.

So, what does incentive have to do with words that form images that incite an emotional response? It undermines the most vulnerable, weaponizing words and culture and marketing to change traditional thoughts and form divisive groups. **A country cannot stand if divided**. The family will fall *if divided*. The powerful World and Economic Forum (WEF) globalist elitists attend the G6 summit every year, where they discuss the finance, resources, immigration, education, and health care, *controlling the outcome of every man, woman, and child on the planet.* They see themselves as the world's gatekeepers. These unelected billionaires are making monumental decisions on our behalf. To them, we are just a means to an end. The WEF plans to incite internal warfare within America, Canada, and Europe by using undisciplined emotions, maladaptive behavior, politics, government elected policing and mass immigration *too diverse to assimilate* to form aggression within society to blur the lines in social reasoning.

Conditioning identity groups to shut down any possibility of thought and/or dialogue. Society is told through neurolinguistic language to censor the opposition even if the opposition is trying to reason with them. People are being programmed to fire at will at anything that remotely appears to defy their narrative and worldview. They shut down their intellect immediately and say to themselves, "I see and hear no evil." *The government will support the undisciplined and shut down those who resist before they have a chance to speak.* Wouldn't that define fascism? Defending the Constitution and the Bill of Rights is not a form of fascism. Not defending her, according to the law, is an act of treason. That would border the lines of espionage, jeopardizing the safety and security of the country. Society is declining in its ability to decipher the difference between what is true and false. The fallacies in social constructs that are politically driven are becoming increasingly difficult to differentiate. We have allowed distorted truth to become a reality of who we are, sending the message that a capitalistic country is riddled with racism and patriarchal oppression, but who would benefit the most from this relative reality?

Susan B. Anthony fought for the right of women to vote, attend universities, and have a voice in government alongside men. What we have today does not represent the women's movement first initiated by Susan B. Anthony and Elizabeth Cady Stanton. The feminist postmodern movement has become an organization to protest against men and their children, making women more aggressive and taking the role of toxic alpha male. To clarify proper speech and hierarchy, the patriarch is not a misogynist or a chauvinist. The patriarch is a father figure who is supposed to support and defend the family alongside the matriarch, *the mother figure.* A woman can be a form of misogynist. A woman can also be a female chauvinist (defined as a *misandrist*). These words are not specific to men only. The patriarch and the matriarch both hold vital positions within the family dynamics and in society, but social construct has disoriented the pivotal roles needed to sustain a nation's infrastructure and sustain a future for the children.

The speaker of the house, Nancy Pelosi, on the first day of the Biden Administration, officially changed the use of pronouns of mother, father, son, and daughter. The administration also changed the word *mother* to mean birthing persons. Changing the title of a mother is wrong on so many levels while deconstructing society's view on motherhood. The Marxist theory is set in motion to remove any resemblance to the nuclear family as

God had intended it. Women's position as the matriarch is being usurped and replaced with nihilism. Globalists are attempting to deconstruct social norms in family dynamics and language by changing the use of pronouns designed for proper identification (nouns) and roles along with dissecting the English grammar by redirecting speech to redefine a woman's self-identity. Why did the Biden Administration need to change the pronouns of father, mother, son, and daughter? Is this a ploy to separate the children from the parents? The administration is complying with Marxism, stating that children belong to the state and not to their parents. Would that change the woman of being the only gender capable of giving birth to become a progressive factory-style assembly line to make children for *der Führer* (the Socialist leader)?

It would help if you read Kitty Werthmann's testimony on how Hitler used unwed women to produce designer babies to serve the *der Führer.* He used women to produce future militants or have them fight as combative soldiers who then returned to their homeland emotionally damaged. Globalists are corrupting the minds of women to despise their matriarchal role and their motherhood, convincing them that they are oppressed and to emotionally despise the patriarch, the father figure. Yet, transgenderism is men taking the place of women or women becoming men and then calling it *good.* We can't even define what a woman is, yet men are becoming what cannot be defined.

> "Woe to those who are wise in their own eyes and clever in their own sight."
>
> —Isaiah 5:21, BSB

> "But the LORD your God will give them over to you
> and throw them into great confusion until they are destroyed."
>
> —Deuteronomy 7:23, BSB

Does God want people destroyed? *No, but confusion and instability within a society will.* American school districts are creating curriculums to indoctrinate our middle school and high school students by presenting the question of whether they should be allowed to decide on elective surgery without parental consent. Why even bring up such a topic unless it had a specific reason or purpose they hoped to achieve? Are they teaching our children to defy their parents? To teach our children that God created imperfect images of *Himself* and thus needs to be reassigned. These types of discussions have nothing to do with academics. Politically driven discussions undermine the parental role behind closed doors, introducing a new social conformity of defiance. The state is imploring to take the place of the parent. It's like playing the game of asking Mom first, and if that doesn't work, then resorting to Dad. It is easier to ask for forgiveness than permission. In this case, the parents go against the state or the state against the parents, who will control **the mind of the child**?

Unfortunately, it took a pandemic for most parents to realize what the districts were teaching their children, grooming them for Marxist thinking. Hitler used the same tactics when he removed all religious images from the schools and replaced them with his portrait as the centralized figure in the minds of children. How will parents safeguard their children's well-being if the school system is undermining them where they spend most of their days?

The board of trustees holds the power to convert the parental roles to the state. That's how Marxism is implemented. The children spend more time in school than at home since the system forces both parents to work. This was also strategically designed. I will discuss this in more detail in a later chapter. Using repetitive speech indoctrinates the minds of the youth into becoming a subject by robbing them of their citizenship. If the citizen reneges on their citizenship and becomes a subject, the country would then fall under international law. As a sovereign country, a republic, we have a border. If we remove the borders (mass immigration), then we would fall under international law. I will speak on this extensively later in the book. Still, for now, for this topic, the school district is gradually incorporating the term subject (*global citizen*) using neurolinguistic terms not associated with American citizenship. They are teaching our children subconsciously to renege on their American citizenship and attach themselves to global collectivism. Classical conditioning is Pavlov's behavioral conditioning at its finest. It is well played by the academic. Repetition is critical to creating a 'perceived' utopian society governed by a **small group of people** who will hold power while the rest become the regressive *1984* subjects. I thought

America fought a war to break away from subjecthood, but then again, I may be mistaken.

Jordan Peterson was quoted as saying, "Speech defends all your other rights, and without speech, you have consented to silence." If you oppose the new social post-modern constructs, then the globalists will weaponize their words to force you to conform. Hate speech, oppression, and intolerance are words that reflect more in the thought of fascism than Americanism. Oppressive speech will become hate speech, and hate speech will become a hate crime, and a hate crime will become *punishable.* In court, the legal terms for defamation or slander will not be required for criminal prosecution. The accuser would only need to accuse someone of hate speech, and that will be all the power required to imprison you.

> "All Scripture is God-breathed and is useful for instruction, for conviction, for correction, and for training in righteousness, so that the man (and woman) of God may be complete, (and) fully equipped for every good work."
>
> —2 Timothy 3:16–17, BSB

CHAPTER 4

What Is the True Meaning behind Social Injustice?

Only *my* woes are relevant.

I find it confusing when the leader of Hamas outright proclaims that he intends to annihilate an entire race of people, *the Jews*—a quantifiable hate speech to social injustice defenders that falls on deaf ears. To purposely announce the intent to drive an entire race of people into the sea, yet no respectable American journalist responded with horror to the injustice—no civil uprising. No protesting. No anarchy, no destruction, or burning down of businesses and personal property.

Jewish racism is not even defined as hate speech. It's not referred to as systemic racism; it's only understood as *antisemitism*. Identity groups have handpicked their trigger words and cause, but it is not designed or intended as social justice for all. Not all social identity groups fall under social justice. If it aids their cause and serves the narrative, all other injustices are permissible and even **desired**.

It amazes me how certain groups identified as some type of American, but the Jewish population is called a Jew, and the Puerto Ricans are called Hispanics. These two groups are not worthy of being represented as Israeli American or Spanish/Latin American but just a Jew and Hispanic. Puerto is a commonwealth of the United States, like Virginia, Boston, and Pennsylvania, but a Puerto Rican does not deserve to be called *American*.

Handpicked minority groups have been chosen for political gain. Globalists can start an internal war by using their handpicked subjects to wear down the enemy (the Americans), according to the *Art of War*. The officers (global elites) stay behind to plan the attacks. It is just a means to an end. Hamas advocating for the death of millions of people appears **irrelevant**—there is no global outcry against systemic racism. I suppose American oppression is far worse than calling for the death of over 6.5 million people. The American Institute for Economic Research wrote "that no one seems to be asking why Cuomo and selected governors made the fateful decisions that led to the excess deaths—and the coverup campaigns—of tens of thousands of senior citizens in New York and elsewhere across the United States." The Jewish population protested against the mayor, demanding access to see their loved ones and receiving very little mainstream media coverage. He was talking about the seventy thousand people who lost their lives without legal intervention by family members, representation, and advocates **who were left isolated**. Even military members were restricted from accessing their loved ones in rehab centers without family members **to advocate for them**.

This reminds me of the eugenics ideology proposed by Margaret Sanger, the founder of America's largest abortion chain, when she said, "I think the greatest sin in the world is bringing children into the world." Death to humanity, according to the powerful. According to Margaret Sanger. Older adults are not children, but they are our vulnerable population in need of protection. Let the subjects, the undesirables, die while the global elites wait and salivate for the prize of America will soon be in their hands. It sounds vicious, but it's all too true. Hitler did it. He murdered the elderly, children, infants, and the mentally and physically challenged. These people are expendable, according to the elitist.

Sanger had advocated "for a system requiring every American family to submit a request to the government to have a child." She told *America Weekly* in 1934 that it had become necessary to establish a system of birth permits. The Planned Parenthood founder noted that the chief aim of birth control is to produce a "cleaner race." Sanger's vision for birth control was to prevent the birth of individuals whom she believed were "**unfit for mankind**."

I thought Planned Parenthood was about pro-choice. Let us be reminded of the modern progressive woman. It is all about your rights to your body and the convenience that pro-choice brings. Planned Parenthood is a multibillion-dollar industry exploiting progressive postmodern woman aborting their unborn children like a manufactured assembly line. How's that for truth? Is it about *her* body, a ploy for politics to gain votes, a commercialized human tissue to make more money, or is it a form of eugenics to produce **a cleaner race**? They deliberately murdered the innocent and sacrificed to Baal, who the Canaanites burned their newborns for. The act of conception has not changed. This information is not new. Yet we continue to exploit the fetus. Millions of them. The unborn do not fall under a protected identity group. So they have no right to live and breathe. In the concept of slavery, the unjust thought the same thing. This concept is not to injure the woman, who felt cornered into making a distressful decision for multiple variables; it's for the woman to stop and think about what her actions dictate *before and after* and whose life she injures.

Hitler believed in eugenics. Eradicating all people deemed **unfit**. He murdered Germans and non-Germans. He murdered men, women, infants, and toddlers too young to defend themselves. Children were ripped from their mothers at birth and murdered or used for experimentation. Today, we have Planned Parenthood, who abort fetuses with a heartbeat, circulatory system, and a functioning neurological system to which *they feel pain*. The state has allowed reaffirming surgeries for children too young to understand, exposing them to possible and permanent health risks.

Where is their social justice? If you protest, you will be arrested and called a radical. Who will hear their cries and agony when they are ripped from the womb with forceps? Piece by piece, limb from limb. Who will march and defend them? Who will remember their intrinsic value and their demise? Can the history of the German Reich be rewritten and reborn into American history, where millions of lives perished for convenience and money? Will Josef Mengele's spirit return through our New York State Governor Andrew Cuomo? Will he be held accountable for the death of the elderly just so he could raise the number of deaths during the pandemic crisis and paralyze people with fear? No. He was forced to resign for sexual misconduct and not for murder. We as a nation have lost our way in moral integrity and true social justice as defined by God by ***His moral standards***. Legality doesn't make it *morally right* if the state and the government are *equally* immoral.

Margaret Sanger advocated for birth permits, where the government would decide who will be allowed to live and who would die. Sounds like the One Child Act by the Socialist Communist Party (CCP). Back in WWII, we had Josef Mengele, a Nazi physician who was branded the "Angel of Death," a doctor who performed medical experiments on children and the mentally disabled at the Auschwitz death camps.

Euthanizing all the undesirables, including newborns deemed unworthy to live, did Governor Cuomo deem the elderly unfit? By putting people who were sick back into nursing homes while the rest of us followed the mandate. Did he pose to inject fear into society to satisfy the status quo? Did he satisfy the narrative by allowing the unfit to die to elevate the number of deaths? Did he intend to raise the number of fatalities enough to call the president to implement Executive Order 13603, The National Defense Resource Preparedness and impose martial law?

Today, we have Bill Gates, the **largest financial donor** to the World Health Organization (WHO). His connection with the pharmaceutical companies, the introduction of microchips, and the global reset have an undermining narrative. He has bought thousands of acres of American farmland and is introducing synthetic beef. I suppose GMO, chemically engineered food wasn't enough, which may be causing undocumented illnesses, but that's for another topic. Eugenics is designed to eradicate the unfit to leave enough food and planetary resources for the fit, wealthy, and *cleaner race*. But first, the land needs to be taken from the undesirables; water needs to be owned and controlled, and people need to be discarded. America is on fertile land. Creating identity politics is just a ploy for the politicians to exploit the anti-American rhetoric, blinded by hate for one another.

The global and domestic Socialist sympathizers are stealing our resources while our minds are inundated with media minutia. The politicians are giving the herd all the room it needs to destroy itself through civil war. The globalists lie in wait like a predator salivating for a meal, ready to pounce on their prey. To one day usher in martial law, having defunded the police and disarming the populace with gun control.

To handpick a new police force **politically selected** to restore order. Australia is already feeling the brunt of the *hand-selected gestapo*.

The plan is to kill the unborn under the ruse of overpopulation, to incorporate mass immigration by forcing and condensing millions of people into cities unable to withstand the additional people and then inject the narrative of overpopulation, justifying the legality of murdering the unborn.

> "We want fewer and better children who can be reared up to their full possibilities in unencumbered homes, and we cannot make the social life and the world peace **we are determined to make** with the *ill-bred, ill-trained* **swarms of inferior citizens** that you inflict on us."
>
> —Margaret Sanger, *The Pivot of Civilization*

For the believer and the unbeliever, *pray for discernment.*

CHAPTER 5
COLLECTIVISM

America is torn with its political opposition. You against me and me against you. What good can come from an entire nation at war with itself? We have handed down a baton to the next generation of oppressors. We teach our children to hold contempt, despise one another, commit violence to feel power, and impose fear by seeking revenge. We fail to teach our children resiliency or perseverance. We teach our children tribal warfare and train them in guerrilla-style tactics. The Civil War and the civil rights movement should be used as a reference point. Instead, our point of reference is 1619. Monumental efforts were sacrificed by abolitionists, civil war soldiers, and civil rights advocates. We fail to acknowledge with experience the changes enacted throughout American history that have made great strides in correcting the failures and human errors that have gone unwritten and unappreciated. We have chosen to blame and make accusations. We make demands against those who are guilty by association—victims of circumstance or victims of government.

We have trained the mind with neurolinguistics to believe there is no room to agree *or disagree*, saith the collectivist.

Remember that preconditioned thoughts are also implanted by the collective group. You either agree with the group narrative and speak the same rhetoric or are excluded and ridiculed for having a different belief system.

Collective and identity groups will not take opposition from their group members.

They allow no one in, and they will allow no one out.

Collective groups have similar attributes of being part of a gang. In psychological maladaptive behaviors, people will join gangs for all sorts of reasons, with inside and outside variables. Some groups or communities may join a specific gang or identity group to feel a sense of belonging and safety in numbers. They form an attachment by creating a connective bond, self-identity, security, and acceptance not found in childhood. Primary caregivers may have exposed them to childhood traumas and/or abandonment. Failing to obtain Maslow's Hierarchy of Needs, people will resort to identifying with the closest group they feel represents them. The gang fills that ever-reminding void, the feeling of isolation and abandonment and powerless, under the pretense of having a sense of meaning and purpose within the identity group, regardless of cost and misguidance.

But the gang is a ruse. It's a mouse trap pretending to offer cheese. Within time, the gang or collective group will reveal its true colors. Hardcore gangs have codes and leaders, meaning someone is always in charge of making up the rules. You will adhere to the rules within the social construct defined in the identity group. If you disobey, you may experience ridicule, shame, abandonment (once *again*), aggression or punishment for not conforming. **Collective groups are not designed to create a healthy inclusion**. It's an illusion. It is a process that ropes you in and then pin you down. It creates fear and occlusion. You are not free to have thoughts of your own. If you dare to think outside the group dynamics, *you will become the enemy* you have been groomed to despise.

With a gang-like predisposition, how would diversity be accurately defined?

Does diversity mean allowing a set of people or a particular group to project an ideology and force their reality while suppressing the majority? *Isn't the very force defined as oppression*? It is another form of communication reflected through relativism. If so, then the act of oppression has not changed. It has only altered its internal color, appearance, direction, and disposition.

Another word that the coiner has changed in meaning from its original root, diversity is the difference we all have. Diversity does not have the right to force its idealisms on me, nor is it right for me to push my views on you. We are all held **accountable** for the choices we make, whether good or bad, moral, or immoral. But if an ideological group makes terrible choices, should society be punished or oppressed for their inequities? Will they commit collective crimes to be judged by? Where is the justice in that? If one person commits a crime, should society suffer the consequences for the other? If a doctor is negligent and causes his patient to die, should all doctors be punished for his negligence? Should all doctors suffer under a collective crime?

> "We must reject the idea that every time a law's broken, society is guilty rather than the lawbreaker. It is tme to restore the American precept that each individual is accountable for his (*her*) actions."
>
> —Ronald Reagan

We are following a devious precedence that the oppressed will now become the oppressor. Wouldn't the new oppressor become the new dominant figure in society, notwithstanding the fact that they are not the majority? The majority are now being oppressed and silenced by the minorities with words. Guilty by association. They are suppressing the majority with trigger words used as weapons without the declaration of war and fighting an internal battle without acknowledgment.

Punishing people for a collective crime is a narrative created by foreign and domestic politicians, social media, collective groups, and political correctness as an *Art of War* with an internal agenda to build power over the majority. Domestic and foreign politicians have created a powerful delusion to curtail the freedoms of the American taxpayer through the *Art of War*. These politicians advocate for social justice against the 1 percent to pay more taxes while they hold the very position, they claim they are defending us from.

A cloak and dagger disguised has an *altruistic* motive.

Let me ask a simple question: Who maintains the infrastructure of the United States? The 1 percent? The minorities? The influx of immigration? The progressives? The identity groups? The United Nations? The European Union? If not, then who? The main contributors to the American infrastructure are "the majority" of working-class American taxpayers. The majority are American citizens who work and pay taxes. That includes every American taxpayer, regardless of color, race, or gender. Punishing the *majority*, falsely claiming that they are only "white people" is improbable and faulty thinking. How is that even possible? The identity groups demand retribution when the majority pays into all social programs. Social programs are being diverted away from the innercity neighborhoods and redirected to support immigration.

Identity groups are 'literally' punishing themselves and the very people who sustain the country's infrastructure: its welfare system, education, food stamps (EBT and WIC), paid health care, and the cost of immigration. This so-called majority of taxpayers contribute billions of dollars to foreign aid, sustaining multiple countries without gratitude or compensation. The American taxpayer is accused of war crimes, racism, and collective crimes guilty by association and seen as the worst oppressors. It is seen as unrighteous and inhumane to want to build a wall that will protect the American people from any potential terrorists, drug infiltration, sex traffickers, and unvaccinated people, not just those with COVID-19. Undocumented people crossing the borders and coming from unknown places with an *unknown past* costs the American taxpayer millions of dollars each year jeopardizing the safety and security for the citizen. Open borders with mass immigration is not based solely on humanitarianism. We have trained customs officers at every border, at every airport, in every country to stop illegal human trafficking and drug cartels with weapons and protect our agriculture from potential disease. Does that not mean anything? I suppose that we should fire every customs officer at every border in every country since their jobs have become useless and discriminatory. I suppose we should stop airport TSA from screening flyers and luggage. We have completely abandoned our ability to reason and to self-preserve our way of life. Protecting our citizens has become an afterthought and irrelevant.

We are told that the increase in debt to our national deficit is based on the rising cost of health care, military defense, and baby boomers, bringing the national deficit to $26 trillion. Yet, the current Biden Administration has found money to pass a spending budget of trillions of dollars to support the Ukrainian war. There is no accountability for government spending and financial waste. The American people are given no gratitude for their financial support in foreign aid. The United Nations is budgeted to receive millions of American taxpaying dollars annually. The amount of money spent on foreign countries ***protecting their borders*** while we abandon ours could have paid off the American national deficit. We are told we are spending more than we are taking in; imagine that! The American taxpaying citizen, the modern progressive serf, is getting poorer while the politician is getting richer. *Public servants* making millions of dollars is not capitalism; that's called *theft*.

Go and look up the US Debt Clock. The constant spending is mentally disturbing, *and the clock keeps ticking*: https://usdebtclock.org/.

To add insult to injury, these identity groups have caused billions of dollars of destruction and property damage. Businesses have gone bankrupt, foreclosed, and with a pandemic catapulting in the United States caused more economic hardship, instability, and suspicion. The identity groups appear to have a sense of superiority. They have been given carte blanche: "Unrestricted power to act at one's discretion with unconditional authority" (*American Heritage Dictionary of the English Language*, 5th Edition). Acting out their self-righteousness with demands outweighing the needs of the public majority. The right to condemn those who sustain the infrastructure is like biting the hand that feeds you. The majority of taxpayers' contributions *directly affect* society.

Would people discriminate when it comes to free money? For some, it would be preposterous. Money given to support social programs is provided by the majority and those associated with collective guilt. The word *diversity* within a collective group will eventually mean collectivism. Collectivism is a Marxist tactic to separate the bourgeoisie from the proletariat—this is a real Russian collusion. True diversity is the acceptance of all people of every race and color. The question continues: Who is the majority? How is that classified? Does the majority consist of all taxpayers, race, gender, or religious affiliations? Do most politicians misuse their positions by pandering to minorities and unvetted migrants? Hoping to achieve what? Do they have something to gain by elevating themselves by exploiting groups of people with social handouts and uncontrolled immigration? Is that a conspiracy theory or a probability?

Some have spent decades in the same political party, and yet their financial, educational, and environmental circumstances have not changed.

Where do the politicians and the Hollywood elitists get their wealth and fame from? The minorities or the majority? It would depend on how you would classify the majority. For the Hollywood elites who defend the stance that the conservative Americans are the deplorables and/or the "dregs of society," they speak to middle Americans as if they walk about their lives aimlessly without rational thought or common sense and need help deciphering what is true or false, *unable to vote and tie their shoelaces at the same time.* Actors, musicians, and athletes use their fame as a political platform to project their propaganda as if **their message** has any significance or meaning. I pay you to entertain. I do not pay you to coerce me to think along your lines. I contributed to your capitalistic wealth while you promoted a Socialist government, which will only affect me *and not you.* A Socialist government will govern and control the *majority* and minority while you sit behind the enemy lines, safe and secure within your walls, wealth, connections, and armed with bodyguards.

They speak and 'act' as if they defend the underprivileged and deeply feel the hardships of the oppressed. They add to the divisiveness of society from the comforts of their million-dollar homes. However, the repetition of perceived oppression emulates images and association by attaching the image of 'white privilege' to anyone not connected to Hollywood's royalty. Athletes, musicians, and so-called artists have become millionaires, and some have become billionaires. That would make them a ***privileged* group**, the 1 percent of capital wealth. There is no racism among the elitists, only in social societies where oppression is *perceived* as prevalent.

So let me ask that question again: Who are the majority regarding position and wealth? They clamor against the capitalist, against the United States, by defending the identity groups that act with lawlessness and violence—destroying property and their neighborhoods. Even when the dust settles, they add fuel to the fire, inciting racism. They pick at the scab, reopen the wound, watch society bleed, get infected and feel a sense of satisfaction. They have controlled the public outcome.

Again, they do this from the comforts of their homes, behind cement walls, safe and secure and protected by their armed bodyguards. These progressive globalist sympathizers tell the working class how bad America is and that capitalism is the root of all evil while praising Socialism while they remain capitalist. But be reminded that Socialism is a form of government that caused hundreds of millions of people to suffer and die at the hands of the dictator. But history has been tampered with and exonerated. They speak to the public as if they are the underdogs, *seducing their emotions* while they support the globalists and the pedophiles. It's mind-boggling how they speak with such deceit and with empty minds. They sell their souls to the highest bidder and expect us to do the same. But then again, **they are paid actors**. Their job is to 'deceive' what truth is by distracting and entertaining.

If left unchecked, what will ultimately happen to a country if its people become too weak with its cities that have been destroyed and burned to the ground? An economic collapse? No more trust in one another? Anarchy? What will become of our nation? Divisive groups can be easily swayed using undisciplined emotions to dictate a predictable response. If I study an identity group, their language, and culture, I can insert **trigger points** and *wait* for a predictable response.

The function of a team is for the players to depend on one another. If a team member decides to undermine his team members, the team's objective will fail; it would be *inevitable*. You can't play against the opposing team *while simultaneously going against your team* and expect to win. Strength comes in numbers, not when grouped and broken into societal pieces. The American people are the whole piece of the pie—the body and everyone is integral to sustaining a nation. Slicing the pie takes away from the whole and weakens the body. It's a Marxist tactic to create group identies to weaken the whole. It's much easier to manipulate 'pieces' **isolated** from one another *than trying to control the whole*. How can a team win when players play against the objective and attack each other? How can a society survive if its 'pieces' have lost their ability to self-preserve and defend the basic principles of life, liberty, and the pursuit of happiness? Has the country become flawed beyond repair? Do we expect perfection in an imperfect world?

It only takes the global elitist to orchestrate the perfect crisis and then incite the masses to achieve their goals. These tactics are old, and the Machiavellian style of manipulation is nothing new. Our forefathers painstakingly wrote the Constitution, considering all the possible flaws in government. The right to a peaceful assembly did not mean rioting and acting lawlessly. Anarchy is borderline to criminality. It is a global opportunity to exploit the people's Achilles's heel, stirring the emotions by steering them into *predictable patterns of behavior.* Again, classical conditioning.

"All warfare is based on deception. A skilled general must master the complementary arts of simulation and dissimulation; while creating shapes to confuse and delude the enemy, he conceals his true disposition and ultimate intent. **His primary target is the mind** of the opposing commander, a victorious situation a product of his creative imagination. Sun Tzu realized that an indispensable preliminary to battle was to àttack the mind of the enemy."

> "The expert approaches his objective 'indirectly.' By selecting a devious and distant route, he may march a thousand Li '**without opposition**' and take his enemy '**unaware**.'"
>
> —Sun Tzu, *The Art of War*

They create an internal war by using the country's citizens as the combative enemy. You wouldn't need a foreign military to march in and take over; you would only need to plant a seed, **agitate**, and wait patiently for your reward. The enemy can continuously add more discontent, one after the other, unrelenting, keeping the mind engaged and without rest. Globalists will use the nation's own citizens to do their bidding, making people believe it's all for social injustice and acting on their own free will. The globalists have given the identity groups a false sense of power. When the groups have accomplished the global narrative, initial goal, and hidden intent, they will march in and take over. By this time, even the identity groups will have grown tired. No more money will be allocated to pay the protesters. No more forms of income or unlawful defense. No more bailing out of jail. The globalists, the wealthy, the United Nations, and the Counsel for Foreign Affairs (CFR) will march in and claim their winnings, and you will become the modern-day serf. When we become too damaged to help ourselves, our military defense has been dissected and destroyed from within, and we have no constitution or bill of rights to speak for us; the people will beg for the government to repair the damage they first created and orchestrated.

We fought the Civil War. We marched for civil rights. We defended the suffrage movement, fought WWI and WWII, and lost millions of American lives to protect the defenseless. People who fought believed in our freedoms and our way of life, but the anti-Americans shouted and demanded progressivism, Socialism through Marxism, while slowly regressing into a primitive mind. The progressive movement will enslave us all, regardless of color, race, *or gender.*

Is this a conspiracy theory? Do you think it won't happen to us? A scenario like this can only happen to *other* people from foreign lands or in the past, which we have so conveniently erased. People get exploited all the time, every day, not only the minorities but also the majority. **It's easy**. It's like studying a sample group population. Anthropologists, psychologists, economists, scientists, philosophers, professors, marketers, politicians, and journalists have studied human behavior extensively. They study their traumas, history, socioeconomics, political affiliations, spirituality, culture, and political loyalty.

They find the *weak points*, the Achilles's heel, and then exploit it. How difficult can that be? Bullies and premeditated murderers do it all the time. They watch their prey, like predators, waiting for the perfect crisis or *opportunity* when presented. That's a classical war tactic.

Sports coaches create playbooks based on the opposing team's *strengths and weaknesses.* They devise a strategic plan based on the opposing teams' *advantages and disadvantages.* Sociologists study societal behavior on the same premise. Psychologists study the human mind and cognitive behavior, while philosophers study the concept of humanity's ability to think and reason critically, like Machiavelli and Nietzsche studied politics and human nature. It's a childlike game. Siblings do it all the time. They provoke from a distance, wait patiently for the younger sibling to react, watch for the outburst, and then claim their innocence. The answer is always the same.

I didn't do it.

The oldest child will always have the advantage over the younger sibling, who is mentally and physically unable to challenge the elder. The younger and less experienced sibling will be unable to navigate around the tactical mind games the older one has perfected with age and will always be at a disadvantage.

The same ideology would apply to a group identity. They believe they hold the *conch*—the power to force their form of **justice and ideology** *while* *maintaining their innocence.* Manmade, imperfect self-righteousness. Have they accepted their right to "cast the first stone" regardless of their own inequities and sinful nature? Their intent is not for social justice. According to Saul Alinsky, a Socialist queue is designed to disrupt and "stir the ambers of discontent," a Marxist theology. Constructing a path where the *most* **will follow** is a politician's playbook, stirring up psychological warfare without the use of arsenal or the declaration of war. Plant a Communist in the White House and watch them breed more Communists. A country can be taken over without the expenditures and casualties brought in by war.

Nietzsche and Machiavelli wrote similar philosophies on governmental control. "In Germany, Nietzsche's ideas were adopted by Adolf Hitler and the *National Socialists,* who saw themselves as executing Nietzsche's concept of "will to power" in their political pursuit of domination under the rule of the "master race" (Larry Arnhart, *Political Questions,* 2003).

Note: Who is the master race? The global elitists? The *national* party promoting Democratic Socialism/Communism, orchestrated by the World Economic Forum, which is promoting eugenics. It's *not a national party* defending the Republic. The two are *not* the same.

Under Nietzsche's philosophy, the social justice warrior supports the nihilist approach. A form of philosophy that makes you a *godlike figure* by taking their cherry-picked social justice into their own hands. The new oppressed majority group will now be forced to conform or become labeled as a social outcast accused of being intolerant. There will be no justice for you, I say. We will repeat history by **oppressing the least favorable groups in society** (Conch from the novel, *The Lord of the Flies*).

Due process for me, but not for "*thee.*"

You did it to me; *now I do it to you.* This broken wheel will continue to turn. We have learned *nothing* for humanity is naturally corrupt and sinful—an imperfect opportunist. For revenge and power is mine and mine alone. All we have done is hand down the baton. The globalists have temporarily given identity groups carte blanched to freely suppress public speech and persecute all those who disagree with them. Their fearless leaders tell them, "Do not allow the oppressors to speak." Assault them should they dare to oppose you. Stir trouble on college campuses. Behave badly. *Be indignant,* and you'll dominate the platform. The lawlessness will be exonerated to return to the crime on release.

The objective is to topple a country by all means possible. The United States is blocking the great reset. The globalist elitist understands that you cannot have ***two opposing superpowers.*** One will stay and one needs to go. The nihilist believes that they were born to control the masses. Caesar, the Roman Empire, Catholicism, Napoleon, the Czar, Pol Pots, Mao Zedong, Kim Jong-Un, Adolph Hitler, and Joseph Stalin, to name a few, believed in the same psychopathology. History is replete with dictators and psychopaths wanting to rule over others with an iron fist. The horrific outcomes of genocides have shown the importance of keeping truth and accurate historical records; otherwise, people will repeat the same offenses without an end.

Let's think about this for one second: Why would the welfare of humanity be important to the powerful billionaires if there wasn't something in it for them? Do you think they care about your feelings? Your health? Do you think that foreign and domestic global bankers placate their entire investment in wealth to bid it farewell for the love of humanity?

Will the global motives be altruistic with the intent to bend to the will of the commoner for both sides of the socioeconomics spectrum to reach a shared equity and equal outcome? Will Jeff Bezos, the former CEO of Amazon, or Sundar Pichai, the CEO of Google, each reach a consensus to share their equity proposed in Socialism to achieve an equal outcome with the commoner? How is that even possible? Protest for social justice and inequality while oppressing the majority. What does Socialism propose? A systematic design for social order? No private property? No financial gain and no incentives. There are no rights to defend yourself, no rights to representation, no right to parenting, or the right to speak.

Equal wealth distribution in Socialism is to take from the haves and to give to the have nots. The question would be, from what pot are the Socialists taking? Will the elitists take what they want first and leave what's not wanted to the commoner? Aren't the Americans already paying into the social programs now, taking from the haves, who work, to give to the have-nots? The elitists are slowly taking our liberties, our freedoms, and our speech while convincing the anti-Americans to dissect the Constitution and present it as oppressive, *the only document that safeguards* our rights, liberties, and citizenship.

Take the time to ponder on that.

CHAPTER 6

THE DEMOCRATIC SOCIALIST

> "So long as the people do not care to exercise their freedom, those who wish to tyrannize will do so, for tyrants are active and ardent and will devote themselves in the name of any number of gods, religious or otherwise, *to put shackles on sleeping men.*"
>
> —Voltaire

Every historical document that has ever been written has shown that Socialism/Communism has cost the lives of millions. Where governments have confiscated all property and resources, depriving people of food and liberty; if it didn't contribute to genocide, then it contributed to higher taxes, social abuse, unmanned police forces, gestapo-style KGB tactics, starvation, extreme poverty, religious persecution, and slavery. A governing style similar to the "Communist Party, Prime Minister" Pol Pot caused the deaths of over 1.5 to 3 million Cambodians. Pol Pot was supported by the Chinese Communist Party (CCP) and its founder of the People's Republic of China, Mao Zedong, giving human cruelty and suffering a whole new meaning, where children were ripped from their parents and fed to crocodiles.

Where were the social justice warriors for these people?

Where is the written history for the Cambodians to educate Americans who received no justice? The Khmer Rouge regime, documented by *The*

New York Times back when journalism had a smidgen of credibility, took into account severe human atrocities.

The history of human slavery has apparently never occurred outside the United States, according to the anti-American narrative. College militants protest that this country is the most oppressive on the planet, undeniably the guiltiest of all in social injustice.

People never cease to boggle the mind.

For the other entire side of the world lies a dark history that fails to appear in American textbooks. For thousands of years, civilizations did not hold hands and sing "Kumbaya" without incident. Regardless of the truth, slavery was an unfortunate social norm that originated in Europe, Asia, South America, the Middle East, and Africa. All races and people have suffered the travesty of slavery. Every country is guilty of slavery, social crimes, inhumane torture, black marketing, human trafficking, and genocides.

Death came to millions of innocent people because their governments desired to rule, manipulate and **decimate any opposition**.

Our American politicians and judicial courts, designed to give a fair and just hearing, also use their resources to punish their opponents. They assimilate tribal warfare conducted in third-world countries.

People are free to disagree with other cultures or groups of people—whether by ignorance, trauma, or justification. No one is perfect. The preconditioned idea that everyone *must like and accept* one another regardless of behavior, conduct, character, morality, or offensive ideology is the will of a tyrant.

To use political correctness as a weapon to censor speech and thought is far more effective for tyrants than stationing a military to police citizens. That is the definition of dictatorship, totalitarianism, and fascism.

Intolerant of me for being intolerant of you and then demand respect.

Should we teach our children to despise one another to satisfy a political narrative, for pride and vanity, or for fleeting fame? Identity groups will become two bouncing balls with no direction.

CHAPTER 7

THE RIGHT TO SELF-DEFENSE

> "They have the guns; therefore, we are for peace and reformation through the ballot. When 'we' have the guns, then it will be through '*the bullet*.'"
>
> —Saul Alinsky, *Rules for Radicals* (1971)

All working toward a reformation through the ballots … working behind the scenes. What does David Rockefeller have to say about reformation?

> "We are on the verge of a global transformation. All we need now is the right major crisis, and the nations will 'accept' the new order."
>
> —David Rockefeller

> "If the Council on Foreign Relations (CFR) raises the **hackles** of the conspiracy theorists, the Bilderberg meetings must induce apocalyptic visions of omnipotent international bankers **plotting** with unscrupulous government officials to impose cunning schemes on an ignorant and unsuspecting world."
>
> —David Rockefeller

Let's define the word hackles. The word describes the hairs at the back of your neck that rise when confronted with immediate danger, producing fear.

Hackle is a normal reaction by an average person who feels the hairs behind their neck rise when suspecting danger. The normal biological response to self-preservation activates the sympathetic nervous system (SNS) in the fight, flight, or freeze response. In this quote, he is basically stating that we should abandon our natural and normal impulses in responding to danger and cough it up as a conspiracy theory.

Should we ignore the hackle as a normal response because social constructs expect us to? Political correctness and being labeled phobic are social constructs that allow us to accept what is questionable without scrutiny. Classical conditioning goes against our ability to reason, expecting the populace to receive the message and follow the direction of the herd. What other psychological ideology can be used today to alter reality and become a present-day Winston?

> "We are 'grateful' to the *Washington Post, The New York Times, Time* magazine, and other great publications whose directors have attended our meetings (the Bilderberg meetings) and respected their promises of '*discretion*' for almost 40 years."
>
> —David Rockefeller

> "Think of the press (*and social construct*) as a great keyboard on which the government can play."
>
> —Joseph Goebbels

A Nazi propagandist who poisoned his six children, committed suicide with his wife just before our American soldiers reached their doors—such courage and bravery.

Let me entertain your thoughts and pose a hypothetical scenario. If the Americans were to forfeit their constitutional right to bear arms, would the same forfeiture apply to every human being worldwide? What if the guns were to fall into the hands of a dictator, a criminal, or a politician? What would happen to those who obeyed the rules of law? Would we need to fight with rocks and pitchforks? Or are we to submit to Big Brother or the gestapo and be controlled by the overlords? Will they be the sole owner of the "conch" in *The Lord of the Flies,* and will we play the role of "Piggy"?

> "We are on the verge of a global transformation. All we need now is the right major crises, and the nations will "accept" the new order."
>
> —David Rockefeller

I found this piece interesting: According to Pennsylvania state laws, if you have a medical marijuana card an approving physician prescribed you, you cannot register a gun. In the state of New York, people who have marijuana cards fall under the status of being a criminal offender or mentally ill. So, if you smoke marijuana, and you try to purchase a gun, you will be denied the chance to buy a weapon, denying your constitutional right to own a firearm. Smoking marijuana, whether legal or not, if a police officer stops you, you can be arrested for driving under the influence—a DUI. People seem to think that if it's legal, it must be OK.

Interesting. Instead of transparency and openly stating the truth by mainstream media and public announcements, they hid the truth. If enough people become addicted to marijuana in New York and Pennsylvania, you would have denied them the right to defend themselves under the ruse that they are free to smoke. Clever politicians. Behind-the-scenes manipulation. You can take antidepressant and anxiety medications and purchase a firearm, but not if you smoke weed. Imagine if the state and the federal government legalize opioids.

> "To *conquer* a nation, first **disarm** its citizens."
>
> —Adolf Hitler

The preacher would say, "And the truth shall set you free!" Imagine the right crisis, the "right" political group divisions, the right propaganda of systemic racism, the right global pandemic for fear and isolation, and now the right new laws to deny the citizens the right to defense by passing a law to legalize a drug. What other false advertisements have the globalists conjured up?

We have the right to Pro-Choice, but under what pretense? The right to my body? The ingenious right to inadvertently apply eugenics "for the undesirables" and population control disguised as a personal right. All within good intentions with divisive outcomes. The industry meanwhile exploits the female body like a factory assembly line to which they make billions of dollars in federal funding and in selling fetal body parts for genetic testing and flavoring food. Psychological warfare has successfully convinced the woman that the fetus is a parasite, a separate entity with no God-given rights to exist. They are separating the identity of a mother and the child from her natural response to protect the unborn.

The government has managed to break the bond between the mother and the child to appease a political narrative. There is no discussion on the psychological torment, grief and depression that many women experience after such a procedure. There is no discussion on the repercussions and potential dangers that a surgical procedure like abortion could cause: a puncture of the uterine wall, excessive bleeding, possible sterilization, or infection. Some women must live with the consequences of their actions for the rest of their lives. Are these women provided with mental health? Some of these women may never recover. Having an abortion is not like running to the store to buy milk, even with the after pill. An event like this is traumatic by any means.

Political and social constructs dull the woman's mind, inundating her with repetitive jargon to follow the oppressive victim mentality without sensing the danger. They have been programmed to despise anyone pleading with them with facts. Let's not forget the theology of Marxism, with its agenda to dismantle the nuclear family and despise the patriarch. Obey the lawn signs that say: "Hate has no place here," except if you are a male and associated with a collective crime. The state is trying to usurp the roles of the matriarch so that the child will become the ward of the state or not exist at all.

Renounce the pronouns "he" and "she" and label that as intolerance. Those identity gatekeepers are erasing and eliminating the emotional connections with our significant others and our children, like China has implemented the One Child Act, permitting the murder of additional children who are not born male. The children will belong to a state like Venezuela. The House Speaker, Nancy Pelosi, is using Marxist tactics to disrupt language and family. Her actions border the line of treason, punishable with a prison sentence.

> "Never let a 'good crisis' go to waste."
>
> —Sun Tzu, *The Art of War*

CHAPTER 8

ALTERING AMERICAN HISTORY WITH THE "1619" PROJECT

In 1848, Karl Marx and Friedrich Engels, writing in *The Communist Manifesto,* declared: In bourgeois society ... the past dominates the present. In a Communist society, the "present" dominates the past.

Let's talk about the "1619 Project." What global tactic can be implemented by academia to rewrite history without resistance? Where textbooks are tampered with, and the truth disguised and hidden between the lines by their authors. Claiming that the Puritans entered the United States, not the New World, *is disinformation.* Truthful speech is paramount; without truthful speech, you cannot have truthful accuracy. One false move and everything written after that can be based on a false premise, where one lie is built on another. You cannot create a sturdy foundation in truth if the foundation is built on a lie. And if this falsehood is said often enough, a circle can thus become a square, and the lie will become a relative truth. Who would know the difference? Was the New World called America back in 1619? Was it called the United States, where no states existed? The British, the French, and the Spanish ruled and occupied the New World.

> "The man who has 'no sense of history' is like a man who has no eyes or ears."
>
> —Saul Alinsky, *Rules for Radicals*

Foreign entities had the authority in the New World. Since the purpose of propaganda is to twist and bend the truth using classical conditioning, like Pavlov's dogs, for example, deliberately deprogramming the college student, an unsuspecting citizen, into believing that any version of social justice is to attack all injustices committed in the distant past. If that were true, then all people should be punished for every crime, every doing, committed by everyone, every day! No race or gender could be excluded. For every day that passes becomes a yesterday.

Demanding reparation "will never be enough; it will never end." If you say America breeds racism, then that would mean all Americans yesterday *and* today breed racism, thus making all Americans guilty of a collective crime. Even minorities can be accused of a collective crime just by claiming that Americans are racist. The word American means citizenship. It's not a race. It's a commonality in citizenship of people from all over the world coming into one place, under one government. People who brought with them cultures, religions, languages, morals, and "state of affairs" concerning politics.

How can the average American contend with that? It would be like moving through a revolving door and not knowing when to get off.

The Aztecs, who have had a history highly exalted by anthropologists and archaeologists, were mesmerized by their well-constructed architectural aqueducts and progressive civilization, where a culture was exonerated for their brutality, and cruelty history of slavery. I will speak more on that later with more defined details regarding human abductions and savagery among their people to worship their sun god.

Americans persecuted with a pang of collective guilt pay the taxes that support those who condemn them. Where does that money come from to support all the underprivileged? Social programs, welfare, healthcare, WIC, immigration, and federal-funded college grants? Does it all come from the politician's pockets? Political parties? From the domestic and foreign globalists? From the underprivileged? From the unemployed minorities? Does the United Nations pay into America's social programs to fund the needs of the American communities? The United Nations first takes for itself and then pretends to give back, *but not for America.* The UN is like the middleman, getting his fair share—its "cut"—while the American taxpayer is villainized as the oppressor. Along with the government's excessive spending on foreign affairs while our communities are falling into disrepair.

> "The government has nothing that it first did not take from someone else."
>
> —Dr. Aiden Roger

The constant barrage of anti-American antics by social media with its relentless propaganda to "hate America" goes hand in hand with the Willing Accomplice outlined by the former CIA agent Clint Clizbe. For those who kneel in contempt for the National Anthem, burn the American flag, and propagate false journalism are controlled by the 1 percent. They incite divisive political parties, promote violence, and exploit identity groups in serving to align with their purpose of destroying personal and private property. Deface monuments (erase history) and use family-friendly sports arenas to advocate a Communist regime. For the amount of protesting we are experiencing in America, you would think we were in the middle of World War III.

Is America being equated to the atrocities of war, murdering millions of minorities, with this uncontrolled systemic genocide at every corner, causing unrest, and comparing the conservative majority to Nazis and fascists without even understanding what the words *actually* mean?

ANTIFA stands against injustice and oppression; meanwhile, they commit fascist crimes against anyone not agreeing with them. They call the "nationalist" fascists, while they force their idealism on society with brutal force, violence, fear, and intimidation. They are defining their actions as self-righteous. They can't even read well enough to understand the actual definition of fascism. You should read *Intellectuals* and *Race* by Dr. Thomas Sowell, who explains the truthful side of American history as an educated Black intellectual economist. Truthfulness is God's gift to man. Unfortunately, many have turned "a blind eye" and allowed their "itching ears" to govern their worldview, setting aside truth to serve a back-pocket version of revenge with carte blanche. Who supports these protesters if not for self-gain? Fascism is an attitude that is very intolerant according to *Oxford American Desk Dictionary & Thesaurus* (third edition, Oxford University Press, 2010).

> "Since this is an era when many people are concerned about 'fairness' and 'social justice,' what is your '**fair share**' of what someone else has '*worked*' for?"
>
> —Thomas Sowell

> "I have never understood why it is 'greed' to want to keep the money you have 'earned' but not greed to want 'to take' somebody else's money."
>
> —Thomas Sowell

> "The very first essential for 'success' is a perpetually constant and regular employment of "violence.'"
>
> —Adolf Hitler

> "He alone, who owns the youth, gains the future."
>
> —Adolf Hitler

Today, present-day Hitlerian militants are being created by university professors and administrators. We pay the school tuition, and the school receives additional wealth from unknown contributors and endowments while exhausting the federal financial aid provided by the majority. Grooming our students to become social militants devoid of knowledge.

> "I will make boys their leaders, and toddlers their rulers. People will oppress each other—man against man, neighbor against neighbor. Young people will insult their elders, and vulgar people will sneer at the honorable. In those days a man will say to his brother, 'Since you have a coat, you be our leader! Take charge of this heap of ruins!'"
>
> —Isaiah 3:4–6, NLT

If people were to look for one second and put aside their impulsive nature, they would see the damage they leave in their wake.

CHAPTER 9

RELATIVISM VS. ABSOLUTE TRUTH

> "When Christ is talking to Pontius Pilate and says that He has come to bear witness to the Truth, Pontius Pilate shrugs his shoulders and replies, 'What is truth?' and then walks away. A cynic who does not believe in the objective truth—the same cynicism that has affected much of society today."
>
> —Michael Knowles, *The Daily Wire*

What is an objective truth, and how does it compare to relative speech? Is it a social construct to condition and redefine language? And who is to decide what truth is? To say that truth is offensive, intolerant, and politically incorrect is determined by whom? Is relative speech another form of classical conditioning by forming new social constructs determined by whom?

Relative truth "may appear" aesthetically and emotionally pleasing and presumed humanely just, but what rules or moral standards are constructed to decipher what is just, wrong, or morally correct? What rules are being built to justify a relative reality, if not to serve a narrative?

I suppose one can make up a truth, even if the traditional and absolute truth is defended with evidence and scientific data, time as a reference, and supported by historical proof. Groups of people will still find it to be emotionally irrelevant. That science is a conjecture, and that religion is a farce. Confirming that a man can define himself as a woman without asking "why." Why does he feel he was born in the wrong body? Will changing his body parts change his mental health? What if these people are suffering from a childhood traumatic disorder or have been physically abused? I suppose we will never know because gender enlightenment has taken center stage without research or substantiated data.

We are allowing medical science to mutilate children's bodies before they are legally allowed to give their consent. Children do not pay medical insurance or make life-changing decisions. Children are not allowed to vote, buy cigarettes, buy alcohol, or join the Army. Science states that the human brain is not fully developed until the age of twenty-five years old—adulthood. A social construct is dictating that scientific data is irrelevant and that lifespan development across adults and children has also become irrelevant. The political narrative must be complied with.

Reality is just a blurred image of the unconscious, waved as insignificant. What we can *see and mentally process* **is no longer a reality**. So do as you please because nothing matters. Politicians hold no accountability to a society built on trial and error, eradicating any point of reference. Globalists construct new laws as they go, **almost to see the extent of chaos they produce**, regardless of whether it's true or false. May it be logical or illogical makes no difference and the thought becomes irrelevant. You cannot base logic without an empirical reference founded in truth. You cannot change science to please your feelings or worldview, and if you believe otherwise, then welcome to nihilism. Congratulations on thinking along the lines of Nietzsche; you have now become a *god*.

> "Nietzsche warned that Europe was approaching a nihilist catastrophe with the thought that since there are **no universal standards of truth** or value, and since all such standards are arbitrary creations of the human will, then life has **no transcendent meaning**, and human beings must choose **how to live without knowing that any choice is better than any other**."
>
> —Larry Arnhart, *Political Questions: Political Philosophy from Plato to Rawls*, Third Edition, 2003

"The Death of God and the Will to Power." Man is trying to become God by denying their conviction to sin. The nihilists will create new laws to serve themselves. The "me" movement has blurred the lines of true diversity. Diversity is the acceptance of all people, not just a selective few.

> "Everyone is *senseless* and **devoid** of knowledge."
>
> —Jeremiah 10:14, BSB

> "*They exchanged the truth of God for a lie* and worshiped and served the creature rather than the Creator."
>
> —Romans 1:25, BSB

> "To say that truth is not true (*in itself*) is a self-defeating statement. If absolute truth is not true and truth is relative, then the counter-argument would be that 'all truths are relative,' **thus making all truths not true**. If all relative truths are not true, then everything we say is untrue (*false*)."
>
> —Leslie Wickman, PhD

Leslie Wickman, a PhD, corporate astronaut, rocket scientist, and Hubble Telescope engineer, said in her book *God of the Big Bang: How Modern Science Affirms the Creator* **that reasonable faith is using logic and sound judgment**. She stated that the distinction between whether something is "true" or "false" only has meaning if sound reason applies.

Without logic, there could be no such thing as true or false.

According to Dr. Wickman, the notion of logic includes valid inferences that require systematic consistency. **The laws of logic** are understood by the fundamental laws of identity, such as non-contradiction, the excluded middle, and rational inference. The Law of Identity defines something as genuine if and only if it's true. In the Law of Non-contradiction, you cannot have a contradictory statement that is simultaneously true. Could this statement apply to relative speech?

The Law of the Excluded Middle states that one of the two mutually contradictory statements must be true. Dr. Wickman states there is no third or undecided option. In the Law of Rational Inference, the same theory that works with mathematical equations states that if A=B, and B=C, then A must = C. You cannot conclude evidence-based data or empirical findings based on **subjective reasoning**. You can hypothesize a theory. Before a scientist or scholar can write a scholarly paper and peer review, they must follow up with their empirical and evidence-based data to confirm their theory. With logic clearly defined, we can conclude that relative speech is not logical. Relative speech is designed to serve the coiner and, in this case, the globalists imposing their self-narrative to control social thinking.

Dr. Wickman states, "It would be nearly impossible to get along in the real world without logic. Even the thought process involved in preparing to cross a busy street would be a challenge. Is there a car coming or not? Maybe that object that looks like a car is simultaneously moving and not moving (you cannot have two opposing truths). Is it moving, or is it not, or maybe it's simultaneously something else altogether."

Maybe relative speech could trump an absolute truth regarding physics and the physical laws of nature. Highly improbable.

When using logic in a mathematical algebraic sequence, as when you apply PMDAS to a quadratic formula, it is imperative to follow the specific steps to solve the problem correctly. PMDAS stands for parentheses, multiplication, division, addition, and subtraction in that "specific" order. Could we arrive at the same conclusion if we were to apply relativism to change the sequential order of algebraic equations because it suits our emotional, subjective reasoning?

Completing the simplest basics of mathematical probabilities would be virtually impossible. Would subjective reasoning lead to progressive thought, or would it lead society into a regressive form of thinking like reinventing the wheel?

To *God*, truthful speech is good, and that truth (*logos*) brings order into existence. If that is logically true following the laws of logic, then relative truth would bring about what? You cannot have two truths simultaneously and not defy the Law of Non-Contradiction. If one is false, per the Laws of Non-Contradiction, the other statement must be true. It cannot be anything else; otherwise, it would defy the law. Can relative truth bring about order or disorder if truth brings order? Relative truth and absolute truth cannot both be true. That would create an illogical set of rules.

For the counterargument to be valid, relative truth must be false. Relative truth, solely dependent on the individual to whom it is coined, does not have a universal point of reference, is not supported by empirical data, nor is it evidence-based. You cannot conclude a true hypothesis, an experiment, or a theory if the testing experiment is relative. A scientist is trying to conclude a repetitive outcome to prove truthful validity in the experiment. If truth is relative, a relative truth could change at any moment and thus mean just about anything at any given time. The dictionary cannot affirm relative speech. Words were created and written by intellectuals who defined words and root meanings to prevent misuse in speech and written language. Words have meaning and set the premise to form language to communicate effectively.

Relative speech exists in a faulty state of reality, in which the individual cannot fully conclude that something is right or wrong, true or false, and has no conclusion to refer to. On the other hand, culture is neither definitive nor based on logic. Culture is created and can be subjective, making it neither true nor false. It does not fall under science but under sociology, anthropology, and the humanities, not within truthful speech. Let's take a hypothetical situation. If a state emergency were to occur, like a hurricane, tornado, or earthquake, the federal government and the state emergency mandates have preset protocols designed to aid the public during emergencies. These mandates were written with clear instructions on organizing and orchestrating an order for the good of the state and those affected by the national emergency. Using relative speech without specific protocols to follow distinctive directives could cause a language barrier that may lead to miscommunication and defy order. Relative speech cannot follow state procedures in the hierarchy of roles and positions needed to determine truthful guidelines to accomplish mission goals. Acting on a crisis without a clear understanding of the objectives could cause untold injuries and even deaths. If you inject relativism into speech, to be disseminated to a large number of people based on how one feels, without following a constructed order, then the normal reciprocating response would be to doubt those in charge and command. The simple act of moving from point A to point B could cost millions of dollars in wasted resources and workforce, not to mention cause unintentional harm and potential mayhem.

Let's take another probability. Imagine a motor vehicle accident involving multiple people. Triaging the injured could become a debacle if rules were not set in place. Triaging the injured without having specific training based on truth and order? Imagine medical personnel not following emergency protocols but instead triaging the wounded based on their *personal relative truth.* What would separate the message from being true or untrue? A correct procedure from a wrong procedure? Could the relative frame of thinking cause more significant harm or produce a greater good? Why bother training for such events if truthful speech and order have no significance?

Can we triage patients by changing the protocols to suit our feelings of the day, ignoring the main objective of saving the most lives? Maybe we can use relative speech by saying, "I think this injury should be coded yellow, no green, no black … and instead of red, I'll use pink. What subjective mood am I in today? For today, let's conclude that we are not to use the primary colors of yellow, red, or black because I personally find these colors offensive. Instead, I'll use relative speech and derail the universal colors by changing them to pink, purple, and blue. While we spend more time alternating new societal-constructed rules to accommodate feelings, we'll waste crucial time alternating the colors for every triage while the injured bleed.

Would you gamble and change your life on some random person's idea of truth? Would you chance some random person with a relative understanding of medical training to perform a complex surgery? Not even a culturally based practice can interfere with the evidence-based understanding of basic human anatomy. Bloodborne pathogens will continue to cause diseases, and handwashing before surgery is still a factual, evidence-based practice to kill pathogens, proven by science, not based on human emotions. Would you randomly accept a stranger's idea of truth without some logical frame of reference? Should a patient (*or client*) allow an untrained person to perform open-heart surgery while defying the medical standards of care? Untrained professionals performing a duty less than their medical competency and ethics is called medical negligence and malpractice and is punishable by law.

Norman L. Geisler and Frank Turek wrote *I Don't Have Enough Faith to Be an Atheist.* Both reached the same conclusion about truthful statements.

Would you trust relative speech with issues pertaining to life? Would you allow an untrained accountant to plan your retirement by investing your entire life's savings? Would you gamble your life savings according to their relative truth? Would you consider their job-related experiences, credibility, and education? Let's try another probability. Consider the purpose of a traffic light. We have traffic lights and stop signs for logical reasons. Let's examine a four-way intersection. We use three basic colors: green, yellow, and red. Imagine using relativism when trying to decipher the images that the colors represent. Instead of using green to go, you would stop. Instead of using red to stop, you would go. Forget using the yielding color of yellow. Not observing transportation laws alone would cause enough chaos to block traffic, cause undue accidents, and inflict unnecessary harm. Would pedestrians lose their right of way? Will laws become nonapplicable to citizens with physical challenges because relative speech has no universal standards, making society dangerous and least productive? In relative reality, universal laws do not follow logic. It would be like reinventing the wheel every day and never reaching a consensus—an exhausting feat in effort. The traffic flow would be virtually impossible and, at the very least, the most dangerous.

> "Without the moral principles in truthful speech, the laws of logic could not apply. Logic can be met with logic, while the illogical cannot. **It confuses those who think straight**. The Big Lie and monotonously repeated nonsense have more emotional appeal than logic and reason. While the people are still searching for a reasonable counterargument to the first lie, **the totalitarians can assault them with another**."
>
> —Joost Meerloo, *The Rape of the Mind: The Psychology of Thought Control, Menticide, and Brainwashing.*

Civic order that relies on cohesive truths to produce the greater good would then be malleable or divisive. You cannot bend the truth for convenience. To say I will use relative truth here or there would make reality incoherent. Having subjective truth would solely depend on the individual's relative thought at any given moment, mood, or time.

> "Jesus showed his frustration with stubborn hearts and heads in the face of reason and evidence."
>
> —Leslie Wickman, *God of the Big Bang: How Modern Science Affirms the Creator*

We have grown accustomed to accepting progressive conformity while abandoning traditional truths to suit a political worldview and forcing social contracts for a low percentage of people while disrupting the majority. No compromise has been introduced. We have abandoned our natural ability to reason. We follow society while we ignore our natural response to self-preserve rather than offend a stranger. We have allowed ourselves to venture into the unknown without question because society says we should. There is no thought process or version of reality without careful inquisition. We have allowed ourselves to accept without question the weaponry of words to control and paralyze our movements and speech for fear of an explosive emotional response.

We can't even hear ourselves think or have a dialogue with a human being without being attacked for having a contradictory or perceived hateful thought. Words that have been weaponized to steer us into social conformity while abandoning the traditional norms that took hundreds of years of trial and error to create and wars to defend the multiple civil rights movements we have today—all given to us by the untold number of sacrifices and bloodshed by others, only to dismiss it and speak of it as trivial.

Words that defy truth without a logical form of reference.

If speech is oppressive, then your right to say that speech is oppressive is oppressive and thus should be censored. Wouldn't that be a logical and truthful statement? What is truthful for you may not be truthful for me.

We are being conditioned through social constructs to think and feel according to social media, politics, school boards, and the Hollywood elitists' mandate. Each uses their platform of influence to convince and captivate the crowd with charismatic speeches. They are manipulating visual images and daily verbal indoctrinations through textbooks. They are changing the course of history, erasing the past while creating a new present with an unknown future, producing a society behaving like an assembly line of collectivists. The young behave as if they are acting of their own free will, unbeknownst to the fact that they are being played like a chess game. Each piece is moved across the board in a predictable manner, similar to a football playbook.

> "I use emotion for the many and *reasoning for the few.*"
> —Adolf Hitler

We have the well-paid academia with its monetary grants given with stipulations, like a lobbyist who is paid to advocate for a social agenda. Should the amount of money spent on an agenda be of concern? Is the agenda designed to coerce our free will by leading us into social conformity devised by the conformist? If an individual refuses to conform, they are met with direct opposition by those who feel that they can exercise their right to censor one's right to speech while, in the same breath, clamoring for social justice, inclusivity, and diversity according to their right to relative speech.

We have abandoned the years of evidence-based traditions, brought on through centuries of trial and error, to attempt to create a new, unknown progressive future that has no past or point of reference except for the historical facts of genocide. Unless you study and fully understand without bias how Socialism and Communism caused millions of deaths experienced by the Europeans, the Russians, and the Asians, you are ignoring history. Anti-Americans somehow feel that we are intellectually above every country that has experienced Socialism and Communism at its worst, insulting the people who have suffered under dictatorship. The anti-American nihilist feels that their insight, relative speech, and knowledge are beyond reproach.

The globalists are somehow privy to bringing this utopian society to fruition based on equal distribution, equality, with equal outcomes. This planned utopian society is not being designed for them. They are planning a delusion for us, the subjects, based on their version of disinformation. But let us first instill censorship, according to the globalists, using words like *disinformation*, *relative*, and *hate speech*; then everything will be good. Bringing about a progressive change, submitting to a new social conformity with all of us working for the same premise, in becoming one collective thought through Marxism.

> "Socialism is the doctrine that man has no right to exist for his own sake, that his life and his work do not belong to him, but belong to society; **that the only justification of his existence** is his service to society, and that society may dispose of him in any way it pleases for the sake of whatever it deems to be its own tribal, collective good."
>
> —Ayn Rand

CHAPTER 10

THE RUSE FOR POLITICAL CORRECTNESS

> "The Government Owns Nothing That It First Hasn't Taken from Someone Else."
>
> —Dr. Aiden Rogers

Put a financial burden on the American shoulders and, in the same breath, call them an oppressive capitalist.

Our Constitution states that people are presumed innocent until proven guilty. According to the law, a jury cannot convict an individual without reasonable doubt. Still, in today's social realm of political correctness, reasonable doubt is rendered null if you fall under the unprotected identity group. People are being groomed and preconditioned to believe that anyone not agreeing to progressive views is somehow guilty and oppressive and thus should be punished.

The progressive globalists equate reasonable doubt to having an "irrational fear." The reasonable doubt or irrational fear will then be attached to the stigma of being privileged, intolerant, racial, and accused of multiple "isms." It's like walking into a blaze of fire against your better judgment, against logic, against your natural ability to reason and self-preserve. Still, you do so to avoid being accused of any "isms." Let the citizen walk into the unknown against their better judgment, even to their death if needed. If you can get them to believe they are acting on their own free will, you can condition the mind without force.

Groomed to follow the intellectually blind, without question, agree without information, and expected to conform without resistance.

All to appear an unresisting conformist. Do we have people who are prejudiced? Of course. Do we have warped politicians, serial killers, sex traffickers, Big Brother, the black market, pornography, bullies, gangs, thieves, child abusers, and blasphemers? Of course. We can go on and on and on, paying attention to every human ill unfathomable. These unjust profiles fall into every category of people: every color, every race, every gender, and every identity group. No one is exempt, whether here or abroad. As long as there is sin in the world, injustice is inescapable.

In *The Art of War*, the enemy is well aware of your limitations, your Achilles's heel, and will use your obedience to comply with political correctness to their advantage.

Political correctness changes the normal programming in the human brain's synapses to deny your self-preservation and tread into the unknown without reservations. If the words are said often enough, a square will indeed become a circle. When our bodies react to a potential threat, instead of a normal biological mechanism to fight, flight, or freeze, you invite the danger and willingly accept it against your better judgment. Logic and the will to live find strategic ways to solve the unsolvable and persevere against the odds because they know it's right. That's like people who commit suicide against their natural impulse to self-preserve is illogical and goes against nature. There is an unnatural disconnect if you do not follow your gut feeling that something is wrong and instead follow societal conjectures rather than your internal message to survive—programmed into your DNA's genetic code. Your body's normal chemical mechanisms in response to danger confuse the biological impulse to react. The body and brain will unconsciously remain hyper-alert, keeping the sympathetic nervous system (SNS) in a state of hypervigilance.

Hypervigilance will cause physical exhaustion and mental distress. If left unaddressed, brain fog and illnesses can occur, lowering the immune system. For some, the high levels of dopamine and epinephrine will cause the effects of addiction. The body cannot withstand high levels of chemical reactions designed for fight, flight, or freeze mode. The parasympathetic nervous system (PNS) will keep trying to return the body to its homeostasis or normal balance. If not corrected, the sufferer will feel the need to sedate themselves to find relief.

A prolonged state of hypervigilance will exhaust the human body physically, mentally, and spiritually, causing depression and co-dependency. The body is trying to regain control of its environment and return to a healthy internal and external balance. Contrary to the SNS, your PNS is fighting to restore this normal balance. As with any post-traumatic stress disorder (PTSD), you will crave any stimulant to serve as a coping mechanism to counteract the effects of the SNS. This exhaustion is what the globalists are waiting for. You have been studied like a microorganism in a petri dish, and believe me, no stone has been left unturned.

It's like fighting yourself within yourself—the Law of Non-Contradiction.

For a normal chemical and biological response to self-preserve and escape danger, what would happen if you negate human reasoning and remain running on the central nervous system (CNS) for long periods? It would be like sprinting and never seeing the finish line. No rest to look forward to, no end in sight. Once sheer exhaustion is reached, will the residual endorphins, dopamine, and corticosteroids secreted by the body now imprint themselves as a routine exchange of chemicals? In other words, you have built a threshold tolerance level. People will experience symptoms of withdrawal associated with addictions. The sufferer will crave a higher chemical dose to find relief. Is it not so hard to believe why our country is in an opioid crisis? People needing antidepressants, energy drinks loaded with caffeine, cigarettes, vapes, alcohol, and every other substance abuse is becoming a norm and a daily consumption.

Our subconscious has taken over the mind's distress, attempting to stay alert and self-preserve against immense mental and physical expectations during distress. People will self-medicate and are vulnerable to depression, feeling trapped within themselves. Global elitists have disrupted society so profoundly within the content of human fibers that many have become disoriented. Society doesn't make sense anymore. What was once good is now wrong, and vice versa.

> "Woe to those who call evil good and good evil, who turn darkness to light and light to darkness, who replace bitter

> with sweet and sweet with bitter. Woe to those who are wise in their own eyes and clever in their own sight."
>
> —Isaiah 5:20–21, BSB

Nothing makes sense; there is no rhyme or reason. Members of society will connect to any identity group that remotely appears secure, safe, and familiar—groups that provide human connection and belonging, empowering them in places where they lack self-esteem or acceptance. Giving them that sense of purpose they longed for. A form of sedation to feel a moment of relief. Many have forgone their spiritual side and instead see a quick fix in the new social constructs and new age enlightenment as the antidote, as if we can only possess true peace *within ourselves* or by what body or group we connect ourselves with. Without God, there is no peace, truth, or logic. God said to rest the mind and the body on the Sabbath, once a week from sundown on Friday to sundown on Saturday. Just as God had rested on the seventh day, that is the time to find peace and to be still. Taking the time to unite with your creator through prayer and being still will replenish your soul. New Age spirituality commits to yoga for thirty minutes or an hour, but God said it takes twenty-four hours to rest the mind and the body; yoga states otherwise.

You cannot give what you do not have. Faulty reasoning is expected and even demanded by the world.

Tucker Carlson wrote in his book *Ship of Fools*:

Let's say you were an authoritarian who sought to weaken American democracy. How would you go about doing that? You'd probably start by trying to control what people say and think. If citizens dissented from the mandated orthodoxy *or dared to consider unauthorized ideas*, you'd hurt them. You'd shame them on social media. You'd shout them down in public. You'd get them fired from their jobs. You'd make sure everyone was afraid to disagree with you. After that, you'd work to disarm the population: you'd take their guns away. That way, they would be **entirely dependent on you for safety**, *not to mention unable to resist your plans for them.*

> "Then, just to make sure you'd quelled all oppositions, you'd systematically target any institution that might oppose or break on your power."
>
> —Carlson, 2018

> "All warfare is based on deception. A skilled general must be master of the complementary arts of simulation and dissimulation; while creating shapes to confuse and delude the enemy, *he conceals his true dispositions and ultimate intent.* The expert approaches his object **indirectly**. By selecting a devious and distant route, he may march a thousand li **without opposition** and take his enemy unaware."
>
> —Sun Tzu, *The Art of War*

Can the opposition take the enemy unaware? Can they inundate the minds with relentless trouble until they exhaust the public into submission? Can the enemy overtake the Americans without resistance? Can the anti-American globalists overcome the masses, disguising their true intent? All on the pretext of an altruistic motive. Using pretentious word associations, they aim to unite people to consent to a One World Government (OWG) through climate change and social constructs. Maybe the quote by David C. Park is not so far-fetched when he said:

The world has changed, and mankind has entered a dark period that few recognize for what it is. Troubles are sweeping the globe with noticeably greater force; **deceit, division, disorder**, instability, lawlessness, corruption, and conflict of every kind are intensifying.

(Social) justice is a social construct using associative words to bypass human reasoning in self-preservation. Is it reasonable to question the absurd and caution oneself in following a crowd without scrutiny? This is the panning of the Orwellian thought circulating in the American mind today.

> "To argue with a man who has renounced the use and authority of reason, and whose philosophy consists in holding humanity in contempt, is like administering

> medicine to the dead or endeavoring to convert an atheist by scripture."
>
> —Thomas Paine, *The American Crisis*

> "Enter through the narrow gate. For wide is the gate and broad is the way that leads to destruction, **and many enter through it**. But small is the gate and narrow the way that leads to life, and only a few find it. Beware of false prophets. They come to you in sheep's clothing. You'll recognize them by their fruit."
>
> —Matthew 7:13–15, BSB

Prophets are not just religious leaders. False prophets represent every platform and domain, including politics, journalism, education, films, the music industry, social and mainstream media, and academia. They lurk everywhere in search of a victim.

CHAPTER 11

WHY ARE THEY TRYING TO UNDERMINE THE AMERICAN MIND?

> "Doubt is our product since it is the **best means of competing with the body of fact** that exists in the minds of the general public."
>
> —Tobacco Executive at Brown & Williamson (1969)

Tristan Harris is convinced that all human minds can be hijacked, and their choices are not as free as they think. The Atlantic stated in its November 2016 issue that Harris is "the closest thing to Silicon Valley has to a conscience." He coined the phrase "human downgrading" to describe the idea that computers are changing people's lives and minds for the worse.

Tristan Harris is an ethicist who studied under psychologist B. J. Fogg. He taught *persuasive technological principles in behavioral design* at Stanford University. He introduced persuasion tactics that conditioned people to respond to sounds like a clicker, a bell, or whistles. These sounds work to trigger a euphoric response, a psychological experiment similar to Pavlov's dogs, which salivated at the sound of a bell even in the absence of food. Las Vegas uses slot machines on the same premise, employing bells and lights to trigger a dopamine-driven reward response. Harris describes these triggers as persuasive tactics used to hijack the brain "with likes," comparable to slot-machine rewards (Bosko, 2016).

Formerly employed as a design ethicist at Google, Harris studied the ethics of human persuasion. He concluded that the art of persuasion relies on the individual's capacity to reason **against** social media's definition of reality. Whether this reality is healthy or unhealthy, people tend to follow the same mental pathways outlined in Maslow's hierarchy of needs—a foundational model of human development.

According to Maslow's hierarchy of needs, people require basic human interactions to achieve self-actualization, which includes understanding truth, morality, problem-solving, and accepting facts. Maslow also detailed the need for self-esteem, confidence, respect for others, and an understanding of the self. The final stage of human development, per Maslow, is achieving self-actualization and ultimate reality.

Harris explains that technology and social media **monopolize reality by controlling** the social environment. These **platforms** use marketing strategies to steer our thoughts and actions by controlling our 'attention span' and **manipulating our emotional states**. Social media communication alters reasoning by creating social constructs **where rules are undefined**. For example, selfies foster a craving for unlimited attention and affirmation, creating addictive behavior. If affirmations are positive, individuals receive reinforcement and continue the behavior, but is the affirmation itself good? Negative affirmations can lead individuals to alter their moral and intellectual standards to satisfy the status quo.

The issue lies in the social contract: Is the status quo in the receiver's best interest? Has it altered their intellectual reality to meet an unknown agenda? We are glued to our phones, receiving messages 24/7. How can this not adversely affect how we think, process information, and contemplate foresight?

Social structures also influence our ability to make appropriate decisions, including decision-making and sense-making. Executive function, a cognitive skill set, plays a vital role in planning, focusing attention, remembering instruction (retention), and managing multiple tasks successfully.

According to the Center on the Developing Child at Harvard University, executive function and self-regulation enable us to filter distractions, prioritize tasks, set and achieve goals, and control impulses. These skills are crucial for learning and development. They also foster positive behavior and allow us to make healthy choices for ourselves and others. **Self-regulation**, specifically, helps resist impulsive behavior.

If the mind is inundated with a constant flow of messages, leaving little time to decipher them, attention spans diminish. This conditions the mind to accept social conditioning due to the rapid pace of information. Repetition becomes a form of communication, similar to Pavlov's experiment. Applied on a global scale, the results could be catastrophic.

An experiment orchestrated by Silicon Valley—the minds behind **algorithms** that know our likes and dislikes—manipulates attention spans and **fosters dependence on external stimuli**, whether technology, caffeine, alcohol, or other substances. Combined with media propaganda, these tactics distract us from real issues, **isolating** us from truth and facts.

These manipulations tug at society's fabric, especially among vulnerable populations and youth. If they can alter the mind's ability to think, reason, and react to distress, they can shift society's moral compass subtly.

> "Modern technology teaches man to take for granted the world he is looking at; **he takes no time to retreat and reflect**. Technology lures him on, dropping him into its wheels and movements. No rest, no meditation, no reflection, no conversation—**the senses are continually overloaded with stimuli**. Man doesn't learn **to question his world** anymore; the screen offers him answers—ready-made."
>
> —Joost Meerloo, *The Rape of the Mind*

In medical terminology, a pathogen is any disease-producing agent, especially a virus, bacterium, or other microorganism. Now consider technology, charismatic politicians, and university professors. If their objective is to steer students into a new social conformity designed to cause divisiveness, the stage is set for internal war—not against an enemy but ourselves.

If *The Art of War* is intended to destroy freedoms, speech, liberty, and the right of the citizen to defend oneself, then who is the enemy? Those positioned to attack from within.

Collective groups are casting the first stone, proclaiming themselves as self-righteous and blameless of any wrongdoing. They have insinuated that they have "eyes only for you." All human beings have fallen short. Not one of us is good or righteous—not one.

From the social justice perspective, to avoid being branded as a **socially unjust adversary**, you would have to think about every word you say, every action you make, every step you take, and every thought you dare to think. This would cause a paranoid state of mind and spirit. Instilling into the citizen an intense feeling of being interrogated 24/7 would eventually become exhausting. This social construct will eventually force you to believe in anything and still feel guilty for it.

What does this imaginary interrogation do to the human psyche? Will it not raise our sympathetic nervous system (SNS) and elevate our vigilance? And if it does, how long can the body sustain itself at this high level of hypervigilance before experiencing a mental and physical breakdown? But I suppose the globalists have prepared for this. Americans have access to a score of self-medicated drugs—prescribed, over-the-counter (OTC), legal, *and illegal*—all for the taking. Sedate, sedate, and sedate some more.

If society is making you sick, then maybe something is wrong, and you'd be right to think so. You don't need to be hammered by anyone for thinking that something is terribly wrong. Social political correctness is a social construct—planting the seeds of corruption into the mind, then attacking first and asking questions later. A dialogue in communication is prohibited—no room for error and no room for discussion. Perfecting the use of Hitlerian thought and function.

Some accusers may like to present the mistake as someone else's good fortune. To regurgitate the one dark moment in your life, crush every good intention you ever made, and minimize your accomplishment to triviality. Exploit your victimhood, your self-righteousness, your shady intentions. They choose to shine a light on your brother's error; shout it out for all to hear while they lay covered in their pool of sinful inequities. The social elites use the claims for social justice as a tool to exploit the group's dynamics and punish anyone with ridicule who disagrees. They use their relative words as weapons and batons, calling the masses, according to scripture "to see the splinter in your eye while they cover the log in their own."

—Matthew 7:5, NLT

These people are what you may call opportunists—those who lie in waiting for their next victim while holding themselves to zero accountability. Bullies are everywhere, and we have given them carte blanche to decide what is moral and immoral. The progressive nihilist has taken the baton to control society's moral compass, creating rules in morality as they move from one state of mind into the next. You either agree or suffer the consequences—and the atheist calls the Judeo-Christian God *harsh.*

If your ideas differ from the group's, you are deemed mentally corrupt, and they make sure you know it. You are then considered the enemy of the state, an outcast—with repercussions. You can lose your job, your livelihood, and your integrity and be imprisoned for having a thought outside the gestapo. There is no room for individuality or personal thought, yet they consider themselves diversified **and tolerant** while refusing to let you get a word in. How repressive and regressive at the same time.

The social collective mind is not designed for the free-thinking individual. It is intended for those who want to be taken care of regardless of the consequences of social programs. An individual who clamors about diversity while thinking and behaving **collectively** is like a trained poodle. These political identity groups are not for diversity as much as they claim they are. They are advocating for the Marxist theology of collectivism, following the route of Karl Marx's theory of governmental tyranny—a gamebook ploy to create division among the people.

> "To separate the people into believing that the American has no common ground, no common interest, and no shared history. If that were the case, then the progressive nihilist is open to create a whole new common ground to serve our best interest—or not."
>
> —Tucker Carlson

It is so much easier to manipulate potential thought when the masses are against one another in emotional heat. When a person is angered, they become centered and focus on retaliation. No emphasis is placed on communication or compromise; the focus is solely on brute force and immediate action to control the situation. Why? Because you are aiming to get immediate results.

Some people are naturally violent and will act on their nature with no remorse when instigated. In contrast, others lay dormant, waiting for the opportunity to behave badly and then justify it as a common good. This innate behavior defines the lawless and undisciplined.

For mainstream media and vile politicians, their keyboards are running rampant. Relentless in circulating **out-of-control** systemic racism and societal uprising while limiting our ability to reason with half-baked truths. There is no end in sight to this pandemic or the economic crisis. It is like the country has gone haywire, and the American people are driven into turmoil with no rest in sight. Major distractions keep the mind inundated while treasonous politicians work behind the scenes to undermine the American citizen.

Let's consider isolation, for example. How does isolation affect the human mind? How would Pavlov's dog conditioning experiment affect people?

> "Pavlov made a significant discovery (in addition to Pavlov conditioning dogs): the conditioned reflex could be developed most easily in a **quiet laboratory with a minimum of disturbing stimuli**. Every trainer of animals knows this from his own experience; isolation and patient repetition of a stimulus are required to tame wild animals. The totalitarians have followed the same rule. They know that they can condition their political victims most quickly **if they are kept in isolation**."
>
> —Joost Meerloo, *The Rape of the Mind*

An interesting thought. Did the pandemic isolate people and control them with fear? Was this a Pavlov experiment to see how far the government could go in mandating people into submission? There was no discussion on preventive medicine or the use of Ivermectin (the so-called "horse pill").

What was there to lose if the person was dying and wanted to try every avenue to preserve life, but the CDC and the FDA disapproved? The only remedies for the pandemic were wearing masks, getting vaccinated, and being isolated. The government kept people isolated for almost two years, delivering constant propaganda without rest.

Was COVID-19 serious? To a certain point, yes. But isolation is the perfect crisis and opportunity to revamp the mind into submission—not to mention change how society and the world function going forward. This isolation also affected other vulnerable patients with diseases such as cancer, and diabetes. This pandemic will forever alter society's patterns economically and socially, opening doors we never thought we would open. The theory of Marxism is being introduced, disguised as a crisis.

We institute the concessions of lawlessness, but it doesn't correct the problem; it entices more. We have the constitutional right to protest peacefully, but these chaotic demonstrations are supposed to resolve what and intimidate whom? What is the present day white man expected to do with determining the past? Does culture play into individual circumstances? Parenting styles? Truth? Social media? Films and the music industry have coerced the minds of people to remain in their socioeconomic circumstance, and intellectual level. Silicon Valley has shortened attention spans, promoted bad behavior, and lowered the ability to reason. Welfare produces dependency supported by most taxpaying citizens and enforced by politicians.

Is it possible that politicians are playing to keep minority groups oppressed to get votes and remain in power? No! That can't be it! That would be speculative—a conspiracy theory. That would insinuate that the most vulnerable populations and identity groups were being exploited for a political agenda. If you vote for the same party and expect a **different** result, isn't that the definition of insanity?

Some people want freedom and accountability, while others hunger for handouts—a precursor to Socialism and submission. These identity groups get angry for not achieving success while ignoring the fact that hard work and perseverance are required to achieve what you hope for. If something is handed to you, then somehow, somewhere, something must first be taken from someone else to give it to you. The politician didn't give you the handouts; the majority did. The political party first took from your perceived oppressor—the American taxpayer.

How long will the white man or woman pay for a crime they didn't commit? How much does the white man need to bend for the sins of the dead? What type of reparation will suffice for the identity groups? To reap what you haven't sown? Would that be a fair assessment of social justice—to take from one and give to another without any accountability for where the money came from?

Perhaps all the welfare money, all the social programs, housing subsidies, healthcare for the underprivileged, education, WIC, and food assistance—all the money, past and present—can be returned to the American taxpayer. Then, we can start from the bottom, ground zero, and discuss reparations. That would only be fair. Fair across the board and not just for a select few, for the premise of social justice in socialism is equal distribution.

A Brief Account of American History Not Taught in Schools

The United States was established in 1776, 248 years ago (as of 2024), and has since been revised, altered, and tampered with. History books of propaganda have stated that we are 528 years old (as concluded in the 1619 Project).

The New World welcomed the Europeans, the English, the French, the Spaniards, and the Africans—immigrants from every continent on the planet, each carrying their wounds of human suffering and despair. The Europeans, including the English, French, and Scottish, had to contend with oligarchs and the aristocracy, who forced their subjects into barbaric wars against one another. These wars filled the oligarchs' pockets with stolen goods, land, and power for themselves while their *subjects* lay rotting in some remote ravine on foreign land. Wars left their countrymen dead, their women ravaged, and their children orphaned.

The aristocracy abused their subjects most brutally, and if the subjects did not conform, they were tortured, burned, or beheaded. That's what I call the "white man's paradise"—the English aristocracy's barbarity. And they claim to be more refined than the Americans. Europe had thousands of years to refine the society they have today, whereas America has had less than 250 years—founded on different principles and government.

Subjects are not citizens. Subjects are people who are "owned" by the Crown.

The Europeans learned from the Roman Empire, who had perfected the art of slavery, war, and torture to create what Machiavelli considered "good government." They destroyed and pillaged every city they conquered. The Romans crucified the Jews and nailed their bodies to city walls to intimidate anyone who dared to rebel. The Europeans praised the Machiavellian style of government—a style of corruption that also permeated the Roman Catholic Church, an institution that mimicked the aristocracy.

The Romans used enslaved people, Christians, and Jews at the Roman Colosseum, where men, women, and children were eaten alive by wild animals for entertainment. The Roman emperor used such spectacles to *preoccupy and distract* his citizens. Today, we have the music and film industries to keep us distracted and preoccupied with scripted narratives that serve the global agenda.

During Roman times, was there human cruelty? Was there racism? There will be no social justice for those people and no reparations—just "white man's privilege in the white man's paradise."

The Romans trained wild animals to defy their natural instincts, exposing themselves in open arenas against loud bursts of cheers—enjoying a day of spilled blood.

The spectators were the real culprits who sat behind the stone walls. No genocide or inhumanity was experienced here—just "white people problems." And don't get me started on China, Germany, or Russia. The CCP runs a black market in the selling of human organs, monitors society like an Orwellian government, and recruits children into guerrilla warfare in Africa. They rob the child's innocence and punish their spirit until death becomes their constant companion.

America started with an idea. It was an experiment where the people made the laws, and the government answered to the people. Our forefathers took the European experience, with its long history of persecution, subjecthood, and taxation, and implemented new laws to restrain the government.

The founding fathers were not perfect, nor good, *nor are we.* They were imperfect men, just like the rest of us, but they felt a firm conviction to come together and sacrifice everything they had to write a new set of standards, morals, laws, and ideals for a new nation.

Since its founding, the United States has had high and low moments on its road to ensuring freedom and liberty for its citizens. Let's look back to summarize the eight monumental moments in American history. How quickly people forget the heavy sacrifices steeped in blood. Forgetting their names is an abomination and a crime against humanity.

Remember—what the government does is one thing, and what the people represent is another.

What has the American ideology done for its citizens? What was devised to repair the damages and consequences of human bondage under dictatorships? Below are eight pivotal moments in American history, contributed by people of all classes, positions, races, and genders—all of whom have advanced the nation's betterment.

The Declaration of Independence was written to break away from England's tyrannical oppression, taxation without representation, religious persecution, and punishment without judges and juries (1775–1776). The Bill of Rights was first enacted in 1791. At the time, England was colonizing much of the world, including India and Africa. The abolition of slavery through the 13th Amendment occurred in 1865. Similarly, the Emancipation Proclamation of 1863 and the Gettysburg Address delivered by Abraham Lincoln declared liberty and equality as central tenets of the nation's values. Lincoln's words remain powerful reminders:

And by virtue of the power, and for the purpose aforesaid, I do order and declare that all persons held as slaves within said designated States, and parts of States, are, *and henceforward shall be free;* and that the Executive government of the United States, including the military and naval authorities thereof, will recognize and maintain the freedom of said persons. And I hereby enjoin on the people so declared to be free to abstain from all violence, unless in necessary self-defense; and I recommend to them that, in all cases when allowed, they labor faithfully for reasonable wages. And I further declare and make known that such persons of suitable condition will be received into the armed service of the United States to garrison forts, positions, stations, and other places and man vessels of all sorts in said service. And on this act, sincerely believed to be an act of justice, warranted by the Constitution, on military necessity, I invoke the considerate judgment of mankind and the gracious favor of Almighty God. In witness whereof, I have hereunto set my hand and caused the seal of the United States to be affixed. Done at the City of Washington, this first day of January, in the year of our Lord one thousand eight hundred

and sixty-three, and of the Independence of the United States of America the eighty-seventh.
By the President: Abraham Lincoln
William H. Seward, Secretary of State (Public Domain)

And in his Gettysburg Address, Lincoln profoundly stated,

Four score and seven years ago, our fathers brought forth on this continent a new nation, conceived in Liberty and dedicated to the proposition *that all men are created equal.* Now we are engaged in a great civil war, testing whether that nation or any nation so conceived and so dedicated can long endure. We are met on a great battlefield of that war. We have come to dedicate a portion of that field **as a resting place for those who gave their lives that the nation might live.** It is altogether fitting and proper that we should do this. But, in a larger sense, we cannot dedicate—we cannot consecrate—we cannot hallow—this ground. The brave men, living and dead, who struggled here have consecrated it far above our poor power to add or detract. The world will little note nor long remember what we say here, but it can never forget what they did here. It is for us the living, rather, to be dedicated here to the unfinished work which they who fought here have thus far so nobly advanced. It is rather for us to be here dedicated to the great task remaining before us—that from these honored dead we take increased devotion to that cause for which they gave the last full measure of devotion—that we here highly resolve that these dead shall not have died in vain—that this nation, under God, shall have a new birth of freedom—and that government of the people, by the people, for the people, shall not perish from the earth.

Abraham Lincoln, November 19, 1863

Between 1880 and 1920, immigrants came from all over the world. They endured poor living conditions and starvation, often without social programs, but persevered. The Irish and Italians were met with signs reading, *"Need not apply,"* but they pressed on. In 1920, the 19th Amendment was enacted, supporting the women's suffrage movement during the Great Depression. Women persevered and triumphed.

American soldiers and civilians made countless sacrifices during

WW I and WW II, including the D-Day invasion of 1944, marking the beginning of the end of Hitler's Nazi regime. This monumental effort spared Holocaust victims from certain death, combating the human suffering imposed by Socialist and Communist dictatorships. However, it's worth noting that the American government has not been without faults, including moments of betrayal, such as cooperating with Communists—an issue explored in James Perloff's *The Shadows of Power.* The American government has grown excessively large and unaccountable, no longer representing the people but rather its own interests.

In 1963 and 1964, the civil rights movement achieved landmark victories, outlawing discrimination based on race, color, religion, sex, or national origin. The progress achieved within 187 years of the nation's founding far outpaces the centuries of systemic oppression experienced by Europe, Asia, and Russia.

To those advocating for the "1619 Project," it is essential to remember that in 1619, the continent was not America but the New World. No states, Declaration of Independence, Constitution, or Bill of Rights existed. Colonists brought European ideologies, both good and bad, much like the dynamics of uncontrolled immigration today. Americans only came into existence after the Revolutionary War and the signing of the Declaration of Independence, which solidified the nation's break from British rule.

The New World belonged to Europe, and any critique of slavery's origins must address the Monarch's collective crimes. America was built as a Republic, not a democracy, ensuring each state a voice within a central government controlled by its citizens. To claim otherwise is historically inaccurate.

Now, the question today would be: Were the new white European migrants cruel to the Native Americans? For some, the new migrants brought their cultural norms, political rules, and caste systems, as British royalty had done for thousands of years. They arrived with the same brutal mentality of conquering lands through war, as they had on their European shores. This was not solely race-based; *it was cultural dominance.* The aristocracy viewed anyone outside their class system as *inferior.* They had the aristocracy (the barons) and the subjects. Embracing Socialism will only invite the same class system that has historically murdered millions of people. That will never change, regardless of the perceived altruistic motives they claim to have for their fellow subjects.

These psychopathic behaviors and entitlements were carried to the New World to conquer and replicate the same governmental tyranny imposed on their white subjects. This was the same brutal government the new immigrants had escaped from in the first place. These people came intending to start a new life free from persecution by those we define today as the 1 percent. This kingship would be classified as the ruling 90 percent of the government. Remember, England was notorious for controlling other countries, such as Africa and India, and we were conditioned to be enamored with the royal family, which, for centuries, brutalized its subjects.

That ingrained mentality of controlling the masses still exists today. The United Nations, the Council on Foreign Relations (CFR), the World Economic Forum (WEF), and the world bankers want to control America. They will say whatever needs to be said and do whatever needs to be done until they get what they want, with *or without your consent.*

The world will always have psychopaths and dictators, whether we accept it or not. Sin exists in the world. We may not always have the brave to stand against adversities and governmental tyranny because we are tearing down the walls, dismantling our national defense, and attacking the majority who can still fight against the enemies wishing us ill. We are at war with ourselves—the perfect crisis for the future oligarchs. Why expend resources, money, and manpower when citizens can be persuaded to attack their neighbors? When the people become too weak and disillusioned, and their children too mentally and physically damaged, the enemy can invade without resistance. They live and breathe among the commoners until they find the right opportunity, the Achilles' heel, and the perfect crisis to reveal their true colors. It's only a matter of time. The majority and the minority do not need to be punished for the acts of the few.

When I say "the few," I compare that to today's population of 323 million versus census data from the 1700s and 1800s. The identity groups forget that the world, including Americans, experienced two World Wars in which millions of people perished. World War I, from 1914 to 1918, resulted in some 8,500,000 people listed as killed, wounded, or missing. In World War II, over 60 million were killed, with Stalin responsible for an additional 62 million deaths. That doesn't even include Cambodia, China, and Japan. Enough blood has been shed, and enough minds have been broken.

Our children do not understand the full ramifications of war. Hate solves nothing and only instigates more wars. Don't blame God for mankind's initiation of wars. Dictators, totalitarians, and Socialist/Communist governments have repeatedly devised plans to control the masses and extend their power across the world. Some say World War II was just a dry run—a way to work out the kinks in perfecting the ultimate goal.

Today, we have the globalists, the progressive fundamentalists, the Hollywood elitists, and the film and music industries pushing the Hitlerian dream forward. We have the United Nations with its international laws, the European Union, the Council on Foreign Relations, the Federal Reserve (which is not governed by the US government but by wealthy world bankers), the politicians, corporations, and mainstream media controlled by domestic and foreign interests—all advancing agendas of their own. This 1 percent, following a well-defined and orchestrated playbook, sees us, the citizens, as "a means to an end." Watch and listen carefully to their messages—they're all the same. They twist and repeat a single message to suit their audience, but the core remains unchanged: Submit.

> "The most brilliant propagandist technique will yield no success unless one fundamental principle is borne in mind constantly—it must confine itself to a few points and repeat them over and over."
>
> —Joseph Goebbels

Do we need reform? Every society does from time to time, because we evolve as a people. But certain inalienable rights and principles that maintain a moral compass are in danger of falling into complacency. We are losing sight of how precious freedom is, forgetting the sacrifices made by so many to ensure it. These lives should never be forgotten or buried in bureaucracy.

However, for reform to succeed, both parties must reach a civil consensus to find a suitable resolution. Reckless decisions made to satisfy political correctness or to bully one side over another by infringing on constitutional rights achieve nothing. Political identity groups operate within a complex landscape of cultural variables: language, family dynamics, socioeconomics, environmental factors, morality, and spirituality. All of these influence individuals and groups in their processing of language and reality. Whether one chooses a moral or immoral path, some will take the path of least resistance and obey anarchy's incentives and cash. Sabotaging neighborhoods, burning buildings, and attacking innocent bystanders to have their voices heard plays directly into the hands of the global elitists, who orchestrate these crises by inciting emotions like whispers from evil intrusive souls.

Think about it: Who is controlling what? These Marxist sympathizers are organized, convinced to act out for their continuants. Like puppets manipulated by a master puppeteer, they act while those in control remain hidden. Belief in anarchy is a betrayal of your country and any chance at a just society. A countryless society leaves you without a home, property, or future. Anarchy has no rules, forcing the government to invent new ones. Martial law becomes inevitable when chaos reaches its peak, impacting even law-abiding citizens.

Remember, evil for evil produces only evil. Changing the pattern of vulnerability is the only way to alter the path forward. Good for good produces good.

Marxism employs tactics reminiscent of Russia's, overpowering minds and reducing citizens to serfs. Citizens can vote, possess rights, property, Liberty, and freedom. Serfs are subjects, enslaved without inherent rights. They cannot vote, own property, or enjoy personal freedoms. This distinction underscores why the American anthem is sung at sports arenas—to remind us of what it means to be American. Destroying that cohesion destroys a unified people willing to defend their country. You will only fight for what you love. Condition the people to despise their country, and the country will fall without the cost of war.

Sports complexes bring together people of all ages, races, and socioeconomic backgrounds to celebrate a shared identity and interest and to be reminded, however briefly, of what unites us.

Strength comes in numbers, and **division creates broken pieces**. A broken leg will never be as strong as the original bone unless supported with metal rods. Broken glass glued together will never be as strong as the original piece.

It amazes me how other social events are free to express their pride, like high school and college athletic events—supporting their team members, motivating the players supported by their fans, beaming with pride, and cheering for their accomplishments as an institution. We have frat houses and alumni who share their pride in their schools and universities, cherishing their long-lasting memories. For Penn State, if an alumnus is seen with a Penn State emblem, they shout out, "Who are we? We are Penn State!" College pride unites the students regardless of race, color, or gender. They share a commonality that fosters a sense of pride and the feeling of being part of something bigger.

People will only defend what they love. They will oppose and abandon whatever they are taught to hate. If you hate your country, you won't fight for her. If that is the case, then the globalists have succeeded, and you have lost a country.

The global goal is to undermine your feelings toward the idea of America and erase your sense of being part of something greater. If the US falls under the United Nations as the One World Government through the Great Reset, every person in the United States will fall under international law, making you a subject. (I write more intensively on this topic in later chapters.)

Let me put it in other words: violent identity groups believe they are acting on their own free will, but in reality, they are paving their way into modern-day serfdom, an alias for enslavement. A position in serfdom is handed to the elites with your consent, and it will be your undoing. Unfortunately, you have aided the rest of the country in plummeting into the worst governmental tyranny ever devised by man. History has shown that governmental tyranny was once contained within a country, but with the Great Reset, the entire world would be controlled by the unknown.

Klaus Schwab, the founder and chairman of the World Economic Forum, asked Google co-founder Sergey Brin at the WEF's annual gathering in Davos, Switzerland, in 2017 if he could imagine a world in which elections are deemed **unnecessary** *because the outcome can be predicted.*

> "The World Economic Forum's chairman didn't call for A.I. to replace elections."
>
> —Associated Press, August 11, 2023

As expected, fact-checkers twisted the conversation to make it appear like a conspiracy theory. Occam's razor? Is it improbable that the WEF and the UN have considered **using AI and algorithms to predict future elections**, excluding the citizen's right to vote? Then why have the conversation at all? Schwab even suggested using implants in the brain, where subjects could simply think about who they will vote for, making it "**unnecessary**" *to vote in person*. Nothing could possibly go wrong with that, since technology always follows ethics and moral standards—let alone the idea of people lining up to have chips planted in their brains. How will American citizens feel about that?

At COP26: The UN Climate Change Conference (UK 2021), King Charles gave a speech.

"Here we need a **vast military-style campaign** *to marshal in* the strength global private sector with trillions *at his disposal* far beyond global GDP (Gross Domestic Product) and with the greatest respect beyond even the government of the world's leaders it offers the only real prospect of achieving fundamental economic transition."

> For the theist, this only means the Antichrist: one man having trillions at *his* disposal 'beyond the government of the world's leaders.' Could this **bypass and interfere** with global elections if A.I. can '**predict**' *the outcome*? Was this just a simple conversation between Klaus Schwab and Sergey Brin?
>
> —Prince Charles calls for a vast military-style campaign to fight climate change. ABC *News Politics*

What does Paul Harvey have to say about warning America?

Paul Harvey's "Warning to America" in 1965 predicted America's downfall in specific detail. He said if he were the devil, he would engulf the planet in darkness. He would own a third of its real estate and four-fifths of its population and then "seize the ripest apple on the tree" and take whatever measures were needed to take her over. He would whisper the wisdom of the devil, as he once whispered *to Eve*, and say to the young, "Do as you please." He would tell them that the Bible is a myth and convince them that man created God instead of God creating man (the nihilist approach to the progressive superman). He would change the moral compass by saying that what is bad is good and that good is "square" (meaning dull and out of touch).

> "Woe to those who call evil good *and good evil*, who turn darkness to light and light to darkness, who replace bitter with sweet and sweet with bitter. Woe to those who are wise in their own eyes and clever in their own sight."
> —Isaiah 5:20–21, BSB

If Harvey were the devil, he would whisper into the ears of married couples that work is beneath them and that drinking parties are good. He would caution them *to refrain from extreme religious idealisms, patriotism, and moral conduct.* He would teach them to pray after him, "Our Father who art in Washington…"

He would educate authors "to make lurid literature exciting so that anything else would appear dull and uninteresting. I'd threaten T.V. with dirtier movies and vice versa." He would **desensitize the viewer** *to death, sex, and horror.* He would **preoccupy the young** with video games and technology, keeping them in a constant state of suspension, far from a truthful reality. He would get organized and infiltrate unions to incite more loafing to produce less work because idle hands work best for him. "I'd peddle narcotics to whom I could, and I'd sell alcohol to ladies and gentlemen of distinction, and I'd **tranquilize the rest** with pills."

In today's society, we are in an opioid crisis. We sell energy drinks loaded with caffeine, cigarettes, coffee, and drugs, and we legalize marijuana (except medicinally) for dependency and abuse. Politicians want to legalize drugs for votes, while billionaires invest in pharmaceutical companies, benefiting from addiction and dependency. Vaccines are mandated, threatening citizens with the loss of jobs, livelihoods, or even medical care if they do not comply—all for the betterment of society, of course. Addiction and mandates can always *be controlled by the supplier.*

I would encourage schools and universities to refine young intellects but "**neglect to discipline the emotions**," imposing a false sense of reality and proposing safe spaces *not found in society*, thereby weakening the future generation's ability for resilience. I would allow them to run wild. I would designate an atheist to speak for me before the highest courts in the land and get preachers to say, "She's right."

Biased courts and prosperity preachers corrupt justice and scripture for wealth, using *God's name in vain* and breaking the Second Commandment: "You shall not take the name of the Lord your God in vain" (Exodus 20:7, BSB). They claim that God *ordained their actions*, but *He* **did not.**

> "Woe to those who are heroes in drinking wine and champions in strong drink, who acquit the guilty for a bribe and deprive the innocent of justice."
>
> —Isaiah 5:22–23, BSB

"I would evict God from the courthouse, school districts, Congress, and churches. I would solicit in favor of pornography in court to go against God. **I would no longer require people** *to swear on the Bible and state the truth*, so help me, God. I would substitute psychology for religion and defy science by making mankind believe they are smarter and more clever in creating weapons of mass destruction—but not wise enough to control them."

The Iranian nuclear deal brokered by the Obama administration could have been disastrous, and the sale of 17 percent of American uranium to the Russians under former Secretary of State Hillary Clinton was treasonous. Yet these actions were apparently not considered a danger to national security, nor were they labeled as Russian collusion. Homeland Security conveniently turned a blind eye to them.

Former President Bill Clinton sold the capabilities to produce nuclear weapons to North Korea—a move also not considered collusion. Instead, it was seen as the decision of supposedly smart people who swore an oath to protect the country and its citizens, but who instead treated nuclear weapons like toys. **The public is told just enough to distract** from what is truly detrimental and then further distracted by issues like climate change. Here's a thought: you won't need to worry about climate change if the entire planet is annihilated by radiation.

> "If I were Satan, *I would take from those who have and give to those who wanted*, **until I had killed the incentive of the ambitious**. I would then police the state and force people to work, institutionalizing Socialism for the supposed betterment of society. I would separate families and parents from their children. I would put children in uniforms and women in coal mines. I would imprison the objectors and eject them into slave camps. In other words, if I were Satan, I'd just keep on doing what he's doing."
>
> —Paul Harvey, "Good Day"

Fifty-eight years later, Harvey's words continue to resonate. His mention of camps aligns disturbingly with Federal Emergency Management Agency (FEMA) camps and facilities already established for illegal immigrants. A tactic of Karl Marx? Those who refuse to use pronouns are punished—it's no longer a choice to speak proper English. Even computers struggle to keep up when writing. Hate speech morphs into hate crimes, punished by unwritten laws. Children rebel against their parents; parents turn against their children. Bureaucrats change laws affecting children without parental consent.

The censorship of free speech serves the global elite, dictating what we can and cannot say. Piece by piece, our constitutional rights are dissected and stripped away, while Congress becomes increasingly criminalized. The FBI and Homeland Security break the law internally, serving elitist agendas without accountability. Immigration policies serve what purpose? Compassion and humanity? If so, then child trafficking, which crosses American borders unchecked, should be a top priority for Homeland Security and the CIA, along with terrorism and drug infiltration—like the fentanyl crisis killing Americans.

Passports, visas, and proof of vaccinations are required for lawful entry into the country, yet none of these are enforced at the border. Vulnerable children enter the United States unaccounted for, with no trace of their safety. America, as we once knew it, has been infiltrated—not for the good of its citizens, but for an agenda we are only beginning to comprehend. For God-fearing people, these are undeniably interesting times.

CHAPTER 12

Fanning the Embers of Discontent within "Feminism"

> "The organizer's first job is to create the issues or problems, and organizations must be based on many issues. (In other words, presenting too many issues for the common thinker to gather their thoughts to notice that something is wrong.) The organizer must first rub raw the resentments of the people of the community; fan the latent hostilities of many of the people to the point of overt expression. *He must search out controversy and issues*, rather than avoid them, for unless there is controversy, people are not concerned enough to act ... **An organizer must stir up** dissatisfaction and discontent."
>
> —Saul Alinsky, *The 12 Rules of Radicals*

This chapter is for the progressive feminist incapable of moving beyond the 1920s. What prohibitions does a woman face today? Our textbooks keep going back to the 1960s. The media and film industry relentlessly push the narrative that women are victims, falling prey to men, and that we are a nation built on sexual predators. Yet, the music videos created by most female artists resemble pornography.

Women sell sexuality in films and music, then complain when men look at them with lust—sending degrading messages to today's young people that it's OK to undress through perversion with zero accountability. So, what is it that a progressive feminist wants to project? You say you want respect while sending messages that you can undress and behave as you choose, without moral consequence. These women complain that the patriarch controls positions held by men in the workplace, yet we are constantly told that women are stronger, smarter, and more clever than men. So, which one is it? Victimhood or superhero?

It appears the progressive feminist movement focuses more on stripping men of their manhood and asserting the superiority of women instead. This makes the progressive female intend to replace the alpha male. I find it confusing when men are allowed to play in women's sports and dominate the field without contention. Feminists argue that men are oppressive and misogynistic, yet the global system allows men claiming to be women to play gender politics and dominate women's sports. Feminists cannot abide men dominating business as corporate CEOs, but they allow men to enter locker rooms and wrestle women in sports and find it fair. It feels like living in the *Twilight Zone*, waiting for Rod Serling to explain how bizarre things have become.

No one criticizes the music industry, film, or pornography, which make millions—if not billions—of dollars exploiting women. They call it "art" and claim freedom of expression, but money is the root of all evil. Even progressive women won't complain. You cannot say you are not luring men into sin. Women sell their bodies for money, then complain they don't make as much as men. Meanwhile, society is constantly reminded of its accusations against the American male—a construct of the so-called American "rape culture." Yet progressive women contribute to this ideology by posting their bodies on social media, such as OnlyFans.

There is no intellectual or moral accountability for what women bring to social constructs. Masculinity is labeled as toxic, and the patriarch is vilified as a chauvinist. Progressive women sell their bodies, yet men are lured to pay the price for their oppression.

What about this new social construct of pronouns and sexual identities where biological men identify as women? If they identify as women, how do we now identify a biological woman? And can women protest against men invading their biological space while society allows men to control the narrative? Men who identify as women dominate the women's sports arena, yet no progressive feminist objects. They talk about a rape culture while biological men are allowed in women's locker rooms and bathrooms—all by saying two words: "I identify." If a biological conservative woman feels uncomfortable with men in these spaces, society deems *her irrelevant*. She has no rights.

Can "I identify" as the President of the United States and sit in the Oval Office? Can I use *logos* to speak things into existence, or is that reserved for God?

It's bizarre. We have allowed irrational thinking to permeate society while sitting silently. Social justice should be equal for all, *not just for the few*.

If identity politics precede medical science, and "feelings" supersede biological facts, is all science now relative, regardless of empirical formulas or evidence-based findings? Does this include evolution and the age of the earth, theories versus facts? Under the standards of relative speech, all scientific reasoning can be questioned and scrutinized, further undermining logic and human reasoning.

Where do we draw the line between what is logical and *illogical* or true and false?

> "The problem in disbelieving in God is not that a man ends up believing nothing. Alas, it is much worse; he ends up believing *anything*."
>
> —Gilbert K. Chesterton

Science is defined as the "systematic knowledge of the physical or material world gained through observation and experimentation."

Let's take stability and the notion that men and women play pivotal roles in society. Equality does not mean what many think it does. If the roles in society were usurped, a tyrant would undermine your freedom to choose. A tyrant would gravitate at playing both roles by owning the children because adults have become too disoriented by identity politics. The proletariat would be reclassified as servants, and the state would become the parent.

Animals understand this hierarchy through the laws of nature.

Progressive men and women are the only species failing to grasp the social order within human hierarchy. Pride and self-interest cloud their understanding—the same knowledge promised by the serpent in the Garden of Eden. Identity politics is rooted in the "me" movement: *me, myself, and I.*

> "A society that puts equality before freedom *will get neither*. A society that puts freedom before equality will get a high degree of both."
>
> —Milton Friedman

A society can only function with an understanding of civic order.

I came across a phenomenal description for understanding the hierarchical order and group dynamics—a social order not constructed by the progressive social order but by the order in the animal kingdom. Interestingly enough, where a mare is a mare, and a stallion is a stallion, using the herd dynamics described by Naomi Sharpe in addressing the social order in horses.

She begins her article with the masculine role of the lead stallion; his role within the herd is to keep the herd moving while ensuring their safety. The female lead mare is positioned **at the front of the herd** while the stallion *pushes from the back*, leading the "community" to food and water. Within the herd dynamics, the male holds the position of alpha male, and the female has the position of alpha female. The additional responsibility of the male stallion is to resolve conflicts among the community horses. The author states that, through her observation, the lead stallion sometimes *chooses not to intervene in conflicts*, depending on the situation. Could this be a genetic or learned behavior in patriarchal wisdom? She explains that for minor disputes, the stallion chooses not to interfere, thinking it would be best for the horses *to work it out and learn a lesson*, while he maintains a watchful eye to intervene **if necessary**. However, if the dispute escalates and threatens the herd or the stallion's position, he will step in with aggression to demonstrate his dominance. Once the message is understood, the stallion becomes passive and resumes his activities.

For men, the patriarch is the father figure—a position that should be respected and earned. For women, she is the matriarch of the home and the community—a role that is honored and loved. If either role is depleted, neglected, or belittled, it affects both the home and the community. When homes fail in their roles within the community, society itself is adversely affected.

Dominance is not toxic masculinity. Dominance is the role of the male who exhibits it to keep or restore order. The patriarch is not a "chauvinist." A chauvinist degrades women, himself, and those around him. A chauvinist is a man who doesn't respect others or himself. By that definition, both men and women can behave like chauvinists—not just men. Like a narcissist who feels the need to be the center of attention, a chauvinist behaves as though others owe him or her something.

It is interesting to me how a chauvinist needs a woman to feel better about his manhood, contrary to the patriarch, whose leading role is to protect and maintain order. If a chauvinist (misandry) woman raises herself above a man to elevate her own status, what makes her different from a chauvinistic man? What would be the difference between the two? Would they not both be at fault? Women can also be insecure and feel the need to degrade men to feel better about themselves—and then teach their daughters to think likewise. Neither sex deserves to be trampled on to serve the other's vanity.

No one is stopping a woman from becoming an engineer, a firefighter, or a golf pro. In reality, certain jobs are better suited to a particular sex, and you know what? That's OK. No one will suffer or perish from it—except the prideful.

As a woman, I have gifts given to me by God, which a man cannot possess. That is my gift and mine alone. Men have their gifts as well, given to them by God. Yet, within the confines of our present reality, we have failed to raise our daughters and sons with a foundational understanding that they are gifted with unlimited possibilities. However, we must remind them that we are also expected to uphold our roles for society to function and for families to prosper.

Progressive feminism seems to suggest that men are depriving women of something. Again, it draws on how women were treated back in the 1920s through the 1950s, as though we still live in that era. That was seventy to one hundred years ago in a country that has only been around for roughly 247 years. If fathers were more involved in their daughters' lives, their daughters would learn what to seek in potential relationships. If mothers were more engaged with their daughters, those daughters wouldn't feel the need to compete with men. Demonizing men for their genetics and accusing them of scheming to conquer women is a form of discrimination and self-hatred.

No one stops me from succeeding except for myself. Often, we are our own worst enemies. Women clamor for equal pay without considering that pay depends on skill, depth of education, years of experience, perseverance and how many hours one is willing to work. Yes, in the 1950s and 1960s, there was a significant gap in pay due to men being viewed as the primary financial providers. But that was decades ago. We no longer live in the 1920s, 1930s, 1940s, or 1950s. Stirring up anger for something that doesn't exist in modern-day America is counterproductive. Do we have remnants of discrimination, of course, but that is not, the 'be-all and end-all' to those who aspire.

Certain jobs are better suited for men, such as working on an oil rig or in heavy construction. You don't see many women in those fields, as they are physically demanding and virtually impossible for most women.

People keep talking about the past as though nothing has changed. Progressive academics and professors rarely highlight the Women's Suffrage movement, the contributions of Susan B. Anthony, or the work of Elizabeth Cady Stanton. There's little mention of these great strides toward women's equality—the right to vote and attend college. Instead, the focus remains on relentless narratives that men are keeping women down through unequal pay, toxic masculinity, and misogyny.

Unfortunately, in the corporate world, all sexes face ruthlessness. Men are often just as ruthless toward each other. Yet women who enter this "competitive environment" often expect to play by different rules. When they encounter opposition or competition, they call it sexism, racism, or discrimination—**not competition**.

Progressive women demand inclusion in the so-called man's world but then insist the climate change to suit their preferences. Men continue to compete with each other, while some women demand positions based on gender rather than merit. This isn't equality; it's a demand for privilege. It's similar to letting someone win at chess simply because she is female. Where is the *incentive* to improve or achieve?

Demanding equal pay or opportunities while ignoring qualifications, education, or experience creates a dangerous precedent. Affirmative action policies that prioritize identity over merit are both negligent and irresponsible. Imagine hiring an unqualified female surgeon over a man with years of experience simply to meet a gender quota. The consequences would be catastrophic.

This mindset is rooted in the "participation trophy" culture, where everyone is rewarded equally, regardless of contribution or skill. This approach has already crept into the elementary and middle school grading systems. Replacing the traditional A–F system with vague evaluations like "below level," "at level," and "above level" confuses children and undermines accountability. Even educators struggle to explain these systems, which only serve to coddle feelings at the expense of fostering resilience.

Women today are not only achieving equality but, in some cases, are becoming oppressors themselves. They weaponize terms like sexism, rape culture, and toxic masculinity to suppress and control men in the workplace and beyond. Men are increasingly forced to walk on "eggshells" to avoid lawsuits or accusations, further destabilizing gender dynamics. Male employers are understandably hesitant to hire women, given the risks associated with a single unsubstantiated claim.

None of this benefits society. To rob a woman of her womanhood is morally wrong, but to rob a man of his manhood is equally damaging.

Consider the military. Its hierarchical structure, known as the "chain of command," is essential for maintaining order and functionality. Each rank comes with specific responsibilities, career specialties, education, and experience. If a commander were to abandon this structure and act like a dictator, it would undermine the entire unit. Enlisted personnel and officers would no longer respect rank or authority, and the chain of command would break down.

The same principle applies to other hierarchies. If students are equal to teachers, why bother teaching? If children are equal to parents, why have parents? A functional society requires roles and responsibilities. When these roles are neglected or abandoned, chaos ensues.

When parents fail to fulfill their roles, political entities or ideological groups step in to fill the void. This is not a hypothetical scenario; we've seen it before, such as with Hitler's Youth. Progressive social constructs now convince children they were "born broken." Boys are told their masculinity is inherently oppressive, while girls are told their existence is inherently unjust.

To make matters worse, children's impressionable minds are further confused by narratives that defy science and logic. Teachers increasingly introduce adult topics—often without parental consent—forcing children to grapple with issues far beyond their comprehension. This is blatant child abuse.

According to Jeremy P. Shapiro, "Children, *usually do not choose the situation in which they find themselves*. They do not choose the family environment, neighborhoods, **and schools that influence their development**. People also do not choose the genetic endowment, physical constitutions, and neurophysiologically based temperaments that, operating from within, strongly influence their experience and behavior. Within these constraints, people try to do the best they can for themselves, seeking happiness where opportunities present themselves and avoiding pain when danger occurs. People become therapy clients when their efforts to adapt are disrupted by neurophysiological dysregulation, *environments* (and *social*) *that are harmful* or poorly matched to their needs, **unrealistic thinking, and painful emotions.** Shapiro, Jeremy. 2015. *Child and Adolescent Therapy. Science and Art.* 2nd Edition. Published by John Wiley & Sons, Inc., Hoboken, New Jersey.

Adulthood and childhood occupy different stages of life, with distinct developmental needs. Forcing adult sexual identities or ideologies onto children undermines *their natural development*. The human brain isn't fully developed until age 25, yet we expect young children to process complex topics **that even adults struggle with**.

Occam's razor suggests the simplest explanation is often the correct one. Ignoring the obvious—that children need time, guidance, and protection to develop—only leads to unnecessary confusion and harm.

Eradicating the hierarchy of needs in human development disrupts the level at which we should feel safe and secure. We think we are evolving and progressing, but in reality, we are regressing to a factory-style, cookie-cutter mindset. Imagine how confusing it must be for a young male to navigate today's society. Every day, new social constructs **redefine what it means to**

be a man. He must tread carefully, watching every step and word, knowing that *one accusation* could ruin his life. Yet in the realm of transgenderism, a biological male is allowed to enter a girls' locker room without recourse. In this scenario, the biological heterosexual male is punished, while the biological male claiming to be a woman is free. Meanwhile, the biological conservative female is not permitted to express discomfort without risking accusations of intolerance or bigotry.

This rejection of natural reasoning throws caution to the wind. Scripture declares, "I will put My teachings within them and write it on their hearts" (Jeremiah 31:33, HCSB). God has instilled in us an innate understanding of right and wrong. "No longer will one teach his neighbor or his brother, saying, 'Know the Lord,' **for they will all know Me**, from the least to the greatest of them" (Jeremiah 31:34, HCSB). This inherent moral compass is often overridden by operant conditioning.

Operant conditioning is "the learning of a specific behavior or response because that behavior has certain rewarding or reinforcing effects." It operates outside of morality, rewarding or **punishing based on frequency** rather than what is right or wrong. Social constructs rooted in operant conditioning guide the masses to perceived altruistic motives that serve global narratives, not the majority's interests. The question remains: Who is making these decisions? Operant conditioning defined: Graham Davy. 2021. *Psychopathology*, 3rd Edition. Wiley Blackwell.

Words alone cannot change someone's biological sex or *override scientific laws*. It is illogical to assume all speech is truthful. Neither sex is fully protected in this construct.

Returning to herd dynamics: aside from the lead mare and stallion, each member of the herd finds its place in a hierarchy, climbing the "pecking order" based on dominance and opportunity. If a position becomes vacant, it may be filled without resistance, similar to climbing the corporate ladder. In parenting, if roles are left vacant, the state assumes them, usurping parental authority. The welfare system exploits this principle, promoting dependency by discouraging strong family structures. For example, an unmarried woman receiving financial help from a man forfeits welfare benefits, and married couples in financial need receive no assistance. This diminishes the strength of families, forcing both parents to work or remain unmarried, leaving children unattended.

Social constructs have misled women into believing post-modern feminist is synonymous with inner strength, independence, and invincibility. Progressive narratives encourage women to despise their natural roles, even to the extent of rejecting motherhood and terminating pregnancies. The feminist mantra of "I need no one but myself" undermines the value of men, leaving them as *beta males* deemed useless, while women pursue traditionally male roles. This dynamic harms children, who are neglected in daycare centers or treated as afterthoughts. Men are robbed of their masculinity while women deny their unique gifts.

If the roles of parents are left vacant, the totalitarian state will gladly fill them. **A society that fails to raise its children responsibly** creates a void, leading to dependency on the state. Feminists often resent men's hierarchical roles without acknowledging their own unique strengths. Such resentment may stem from societal conditioning that portrays motherhood as a limitation rather than a gift. Rejecting the opportunity to nurture future innovators like Leonardo da Vinci or Madame Curie deprives society of untold potential.

Historically, the social construct of male dominance in the nineteenth and early twentieth centuries exploited women's roles, but blaming all men for the actions of a few is unjust. Similarly, blaming all women for the failures of some is equally destructive. Men and women both play essential roles in maintaining social order. Undermining these roles leads to societal disarray, paving the way for Marxist ideologies to take root.

Marxists and Socialists exploit familial dysfunction to reshape society. By undermining family structures, they condition children to pledge allegiance to the state rather than their parents. The ruling elite—the 1 percent—remain untouched by these upheavals, manipulating the class system to maintain their power. The family unit, once the bedrock of society, becomes subservient to political agendas.

The advocacy for abortion is another means of societal control. The government frames the issue as a woman's right, emphasizing convenience over accountability. But is this narrative genuine? Margaret Sanger, a prominent figure in the abortion movement, revealed the darker motives behind this facade:

> "We want fewer and better children who can be reared up to their full possibilities in unencumbered homes, and 'we cannot make the social life and the world-peace we are determined to make, with the "**ill-bred, ill-trained swarms of inferior citizens**" that you inflict on us.'"
>
> —Margaret Sanger, *The Pivot of Civilization*

An astonishing statement—you would think humanity was a swarm of fleas needing to be disposed of and disinfected. But let's remember what our top priority is: my rights, my body, and all its conveniences. Of course, it has nothing to do with eugenics or serving a billion-dollar industry. There is no better way to exploit the rights of a woman than to appease her need to abort solely based on the claim of bodily autonomy. Convincing her to view her pregnancy as a burden or parasite while simultaneously despising her counterpart ensures the narrative persists. With the amount of money spent on abortions, one might think the government would advocate against such excessive spending. Yet that would defy the globalist narrative, which subtly pursues population control and the cleansing of so-called "undesirables."

Question: If a tree falls in the forest, does it make a sound? When a life is terminated after twenty-one days, does he or she make a sound?

- The heartbeat and circulatory system in a fetus begins at five to six weeks.
- The neurological system and **the ability to feel pain** develop after twenty-one days.

> "The most merciful thing that a large family does to one of its infant members *is to kill it*."
>
> —Margaret Sanger, *Woman and the New Race*

> "They have filled this place with the blood of the innocent. They have built high places to Baal on which to *burn their children in the fire as offerings*."
>
> —Jeremiah 19:4–5, BSB

For this, God killed the Canaanites. Did they not deserve death for murdering the innocent, for burning newborns alive? Did God not answer the cries of the innocent?

> "Jesus once said to His disciples, 'It is inevitable that stumbling blocks will come, but woe to the one through whom they come! **It would be better for him to have a millstone** (which weighs hundreds of pounds) **hung around his neck and to be thrown into the sea** than to cause one of these little ones to stumble. Watch yourselves. If your brother sins, rebuke him; and if he repents, forgive him.'"
>
> —Luke 17:1–3, BSB

> "The word of the LORD came to me, saying: 'Before I formed you in the womb, I knew you, and before you were born, I set you apart and appointed you as a prophet to the nations.'"
>
> —Jeremiah 1:4–5, BSB

We are not created equal in outcome; we are created equal *in birth and by humanity.* Some will contribute to the well-being of society, and some will bring turmoil and death. Some will persevere, and some will quit. Some will heal, and some will cause pain. Some will lead, and others will follow. Some will condemn, and others will save. Some will live idle lives, while others bring prosperity.

No animal or person, fingerprint, or snowflake is the same. We cannot freely assume that each individual will contribute equally or believe that any one group is more deserving than another. Men and women each have their God-given roles that make society function, homes stronger, and lives safer. Either we embrace the absolute truths given to us by God or leave those roles to tyrants to assume on our behalf.

You decide …

CHAPTER 13

LIVING IN "ALLURING" TIMES

> "The 'organizer's' first job is to create the issues or problems, and (*the*) organization must be based on many issues (simultaneously, stirring the pot without giving public rest). The organizer must first 'rub raw the resentments' of the people of the community; 'fan the latent hostilities' of many of the people to the point of overt expression (excessive protesting). He must '**search out controversy and issues**' rather than avoid them, for unless there is controversy, people are not concerned enough to act."
>
> —Saul Alinsky

The breeding grounds for the modern-day gestapo. According to Saul Alinsky, "Where despair can be found, we must go in and '**rub raw the sores of discontent with the unrelenting sentiment**,' galvanize them 'for radical change.'" He states we must "stir the amber of discontent."

Can the calling to dismantle the police force create a form of anarchy and disorder, and then claim it to be for the betterment of society? But does anarchy create order, or does it create disorder, (the law of contradiction)? The government and the state will have no choice but to usher in martial law. Your community will have a curfew, and anyone found outside their homes will be disciplined.

The politicians have called in the Pied Piper to play its song so that they can watch the identity groups dance to their tune. They are playing right into the hands of the globalists: *stir the ambers of discontent.*

Is this the making of "our own free will?" Once the police have been dismantled, the government will have no choice but to "handpick" their newly assigned police force. The new Americanized "black and brown shirts," equating them to the modern-day gestapo, will march down our streets enforcing martial law to restore order.

A random reader might say, "Groben, you are overreacting." Am I? We are *defunding* our police force; how long will it take before vulnerable and protected neighborhoods fall into anarchy? Oh, wait—California has beaten us to it with billions of dollars in revenue lost to looting businesses **while making no arrests**. *"Fan the ambers of discontent and* search out controversy and issues."

WWII was only a trial run, and the globalists have been preparing for these moments. This time, more people will be adversely affected, and there will be no America to seek refuge from.

It makes identity groups powerful when gathered in large numbers to intimate, dominate, and suppress a neighborhood by looting, destruction of property, and violence. They deprive law-abiding citizens of their right to live peacefully. The politicians have hired the Pied Piper to play an alluring tune to get the people to desecrate their own country, demanding retribution belonging to someone else. No conception or knowledge of truthful history. It's like the blind leading the blind.

> "Can a blind man lead a blind man? Will they not both fall into a pit?"
>
> —Luke 6:39, BSB

Foreign bodies have noticed how aggressive we behave in adversities, and they say, "What a mess." I'm not implying that these foreign countries behave any better; I am convinced they are going through the same attack we are. This is a world government trying to set the stage for the great reset, but we, as a people, should set the example.

> "If you are born at the right time, with some access to the family fortune, and you have a 'special talent for whipping

> up other people's hatred and sense of depravation,' you can arrange to kill large numbers of unsuspecting people. With enough money, you can accomplish this from far away, and you sit back safely and watch with satisfaction."
> —Laura Knight-Jadczyk, *Political Ponerology: Science on the Nature of Evil Adjusted for Political Purposes*

What other types of radical intervention could be used to maintain the division they are trying so hard to instill? Perhaps introduce mandates through political interventions, interject mind games into our children's education, or promote gender dysphoria? Maybe creating safe spaces within college campuses will somehow build resilience in our youth **to resolve future problems**—and I write this with extreme sarcasm. On what premise does Critical Race Theory (CRT) placate its theory on social justice, introduced by the will of the tyrants? Do people genuinely believe CRT is meant to bring closure to society's disconnects and injustices, or was it designed to create more divisiveness, implementing an endless barrage of hate and regression back to segregation?

"There are a series of euphemisms deployed by its supporters to describe [ideologies and identity politics] of critical race theory, including 'equity,' 'social justice,' 'diversity and inclusion,' and 'culturally responsive teaching.' Critical race theorists, masters of language construction, realize that 'neo-Marxism' would be hard to sell. **Equity**, on the other hand, sounds non-threatening and *is easily confused with the American principle of equality.*" Christopher Rufo goes further to say that since we fought the Civil War, instituted the 14th Amendment, enacted the Civil Rights Act of 1964, and the Voting Rights Act of 1965, CRT was rejected. If you don't know history, you can be led to believe anything."

"Critical Race Theory: What It Is and How to Fight It." March 2021 • Volume 50, Number 3 • Christopher F. Rufo, Founder and Director, Battlefront. Hillsdale College *Imprimis*. Adapted from a lecture delivered at Hillsdale College on March 30, 2021.

Eric Metaxas interviewed Os Guinness on his platform *Socrates in the City*. Guinness spoke about his new book, *The Magna Carta of Humanity*. Guinness stated, "The deepest division in America is between those who understand the Republic and freedom from the perspective of the American Revolution and those who understand it from the ideas that came down from the French Revolution. Radical multiculturalism, post-modernism, the sexual revolution, identity politics going down the line, cancel culture—*every single one of those is a child of ideas that have come down from the French Revolution,* **now called Revolutionary Liberationism**. Revolutionary Liberationism or *cultural Marxism or Neo-Marxism,* user-friendly Marxism."

He explained that Antonio Gramsci, the founder of Italian Communism "shifted the ideas of revolution" from economics and politics **to culture**. Gramsci believed that when *the cultural gatekeepers of a society* are won over, the radicals would win "the long haul." Colleges, the press, media, Hollywood, and the entertainment industry became the new tools for shaping culture and controlling the masses. In other words, these tactics being used today are not new. Every great society and civilization has been taken down or dismantled because its people forgot what made them great **to begin with**. According to Guinness, they lose the main objective and forget the meaning of why virtue and freedom are essential.

This mirrors words spoken by the World Economic Forum (WEF) when Yuval Noah Harari, lead advisor to Klaus Schwab and author of *COVID-19: The Great Reset,* said, "The big political and economic question of the twenty-first century will be, 'What do we need humans for, or at least what do we need *so many humans for*?'" Asked if he had an answer in his book, he responded, "At the present, the best guess we have is to **keep them happy with drugs and computer games**."

In *COVID-19: The Great Reset,* Harari attempts to address the main objectives of understanding the multitude of domains affected by the pandemic. "Published in July 2020, in the midst of the crisis and when further waves of infection may still arise, it is a hybrid between a contemporary essay and an academic snapshot of a crucial moment in history. First, *assess what the impact of the pandemic will be* **on the five key macro categories**: the economic, societal, geopolitical, environmental, and technological factors. The second considers the effects, in micro terms, on specific industries and companies. The third hypothesizes **the consequences at the individual level.**"

Does this statement contradict the social justice theory, or does it confirm what has been suggested? Social justice ideology is predicated on collectivism, **not individualism**. You either belong to specific groups, submit to the rules and behavior of an identity group, or become excluded. There is no room for individualism *or independent thought*; group identity demands groupthink.

The Declaration of Independence states, "We hold these truths to be self-evident, that all men are created equal, that they are endowed by their Creator with certain unalienable Rights, that among these are Life, Liberty, and the pursuit of Happiness."

True Americanism is rooted in individual rights. Yet consider Vice President Kamala Harris's speech addressing the fiftieth Anniversary of Roe v. Wade, where she omitted the right to life from her remarks. Bit by bit, the rights of the individual are being eroded and replaced by progressive thought through collectivism. Subtle concessions, some not-so-subtle, are changing historical documents to appease emotional doctrine rather than defend the moral ground of objectivity, logic, and ethics.

During the 2024 DNC, Planned Parenthood provided an abortion mobile clinic outside the complex.

> "From vasectomies to abortion pills, Planned Parenthood sets up a mobile clinic near DNC."
>
> —Sarah McCammon, August 20, 2024. Planned Parenthood Mobile Clinic Near DNC. Margaret Sanger would be proud.

In today's Marxism, the progressive system cannot rely on the old bourgeoisie–proletariat class system. Instead, the globalists are dissecting the middle class, the "deplorables," and the conservative nationalists. Neo-Marxists must contend with the conservative, God-fearing middle class and patriots. Their plan is to eradicate the middle class and remove all forms of God from public spaces, academia, courthouses, and forums.

Unlike the progressive American, the middle class is not as easily swayed by charismatic speeches riddled with repetitive language. The neo-Marxist strategy aims to rid society of these so-called deplorables, who pose a monumental problem for the globalists' objectives. These conservatives uphold foundational truths enshrined in the Constitution, and any governing body that threatens our Republic must be scrutinized with discernment. Some might call that nationalistic, but would you prefer surrendering your country to foreign entities intent on eradicating your constitutional rights *and reducing you* to a progressive subject?

The middle class aspires to improve their current circumstances and provide hope to the vulnerable by contributing to infrastructure and funding millions in social programs. Political parties do not create money; they take money from the working class and spend it like a credit card without a limit. Socialism has crept into American society through welfare, social programs, the public school system, and Obamacare's socialized healthcare. The drive to implement Socialism has been brewing since the 1800s with the Rothschilds, Warburgs, and Rockefellers. While we are obligated, as a people, to help those less fortunate, we are not obligated to pay public servants to become modern-day oligarchs, turning citizens into taxpaying subjects. Taxpayers have little say in how the government spends their money. Thousands are dying on the streets from fentanyl, yet we provide little aid for their needs, while offering endless financial support for wars not our own.

The social class system in the United States would take too long for the Marxist system to take root. As a result, the globalists devised another plan, using propaganda to divide Americans into identity groups, erasing any commonality they once had as citizens.

With the pandemic and accusations of systemic racism, these goals have gained traction. Middle-class businesses were forced into bankruptcy during lockdowns. Law-abiding citizens were arrested for wanting to work. Stimulus packages acted as a precursor to governmental Socialist handouts, redistributing from the haves to the have-nots.

Newly instituted federal mandates have forced people to become more subservient to the government. Vaccine mandates pressured compliance through fear, portraying the 'unvaccinated as criminals' and carriers of disease. Citizens were shamed by mainstream media and labeled noncompliant if they did not adhere. To work, eat, shop, travel, or even access medical care, individuals were required to show vaccine cards, or face potential arrest. This echoed Nazism's "Show me your papers!" rhetoric.

Vaccines, designed to build immunity, were depicted as ineffective if others remained unvaccinated—a paradoxical narrative. The government seemed unconcerned about allowing millions of undocumented immigrants into the country, *regardless of their vaccination status*, creating further confusion.

This appears to mirror a progressive version of Hitler's playbook. The globalists and anti-American sympathizers are manipulating the masses through fear and shame. Even more absurdly, the American taxpayer has funded this enslavement through mandates and massive payments to pharmaceutical companies without empirical data.

With a $1.5 trillion spending bill, the United States faces bankruptcy, and China may call in its debt, which we cannot pay. What then? Open borders, the eradication of the Constitution, and submission to international law may turn US citizens into subjects under a new aristocracy.

The globalists have groomed obedient teachers, law enforcement, journalists, corporate leaders, politicians, and professors since the 1960s, creating a new generation of academic militants. Parasitic ideologies infiltrate the country with little resistance. Even pastors have lowered their standards, engaging in prosperity preaching and replacing scripture with man-made doctrines for financial gain.

God said, "Judgment will come to the house of the Lord **first**" (1 Peter 4:17, NKJV). Exploiting diversity for political gain is dangerous and divisive, threatening the very fabric that unites Americans. What we need is education and mutual respect—not internal war.

> "Keep oneself from being 'polluted' by the world."
>
> —James 1:27, BSB

> "A society that puts equality before freedom will get neither. A society that puts freedom before equality will get a high degree of both."
>
> —Milton Friedman

CHAPTER 14

THE PATHOLOGICAL DOMINATOR

Alan Harrington described a "psychopath as the new man produced by modern life's evolutionary pressures. Uninvolved with others, he coolly saw into their fears and desires and maneuvered them as he wished." Can a mass population sense that something is terribly wrong, and do they need to be reeducated, deprogrammed, and socially conditioned to see a reality not their own? Globalists are hard at work orchestrating a deceptive reality with the intent to blindside the public by any means possible.

Andrew Lobaczewski, in his book *Political Ponerology*, describes the psychopath as a "virulent pathogen in a body" that strikes at the "weaknesses where the entire society is plunged into a condition that always and inevitably leads to horror and tragedy *on a large scale*." He saw the psychopath as a **predator** that will "adopt all kinds of stealthy functions in order to stalk their prey, **cut them out of the herd**, get close to them, *and reduce their resistance*." Similarly, psychopaths can "construct all kinds of elaborate camouflages composed of **words and appearances**—lies and manipulations—*to assimilate their prey*." Would predatory tactics include inciting identity groups and grooming emotionally motivated future academic militants to protest their cause?

Remember that strength comes in numbers. **Divide the herd**, *reduce their resistance*, and you weaken their defenses.

Can the political psychopath use the same philosophy of predatory stalking on a larger scale than just the United States? Consider the

United Nations and the European Union, which plan to initiate the 17 Goal Sustainable Development Agenda by 2030. This initiative aims to address poverty, hunger, health, education, gender equality, clean water, sanitation, affordable energy, economic growth, innovation, reduced inequality, sustainable communities, responsible consumption, climate action, conservation of life in water and on land, justice, and partnerships. If that summary isn't a mouthful, there's also the Annual Global Summit and the Economic Forum—all controlled by wealthy bankers. They aim to dominate future transactions without the people's consent. Their reach even extends to controlling religion, which comprises billions of people worldwide.

What good can come from **one entity having total control** of the world's population, economics, natural resources, and religions? Wouldn't that amount to the power of an autocracy, an emperor, *or a Caesar*—a single entity with unlimited power? If the world falls into the wrong hands or under a political party **you disagree with**, what will become of those not in power?

At the COP26 United Nations Climate Change Summit, then Prince Charles delivered these words:

"I know you all carry a heavy burden on your shoulders, and you do not need me to tell you that the eyes and hopes of the world are on you to act with all dispatch and decisively because time has quite literally run out. The scale and scope of the threat we face call for a **global system-level solution** based on radically transforming our current fossil fuel-based economy to one that is genuinely renewable and sustainable. So, ladies and gentlemen, my plea today is for countries to come together to create an environment that enables every sector of industry to take the action required. We know this will take *trillions, not billions, of dollars.* We also know that countries, many of whom are burdened by growing levels of debt, simply cannot afford to go green. Here, (*again*) we need a **vast military-style campaign to marshal** the strength of the **global private sector with *trillions at its disposal***, far beyond global GDP and, with the greatest respect, beyond even the governments of the world's leaders, it offers the only real prospect of achieving fundamental economic transition."

Does that statement bring reassurance *or alarm*? Should Americans be concerned about footing the bill for a "vast military-style campaign"? Who benefits from these trillions?

Let us add the United Nations' 17 Goal Sustainable Development Agenda, which aims to control every resource and challenge the inalienable rights given to us by God. The UN also constructed the Paris Climate Accord, a measure that could cost American taxpayers trillions of dollars with **minimal effects on the environment**. Why? Because **we cannot control** how other countries use their resources *or pollute their environments*. Why should American citizens pay for crimes committed by other countries?

Can the United Nations control climate change? If so, why wait until now, after decades of receiving billions from over 195 countries? Are they waiting for a total collapse of the world's infrastructure, forcing mass immigration into concentrated areas, then blaming "overpopulation" and "rescuing" us *from ourselves*?

We have the Annual G20 Summit 2023, where the heads of state and governments worldwide come together to discuss the existence of life, from microorganisms, plants, and animals to human beings.

These organizations mentioned above attract the interest of those who possess psychopathic tendencies. A psychopath is incapable of having remorse, enjoys inflicting pain on others, and lacks the moral consciousness of their actions. They are progressive nihilists who feel superior to the commoners. Imagine these people discussing and dictating your future outcome without your vote or consent.

The World Health Organization (WHO) also works on the same premises, and its biggest investor is Bill Gates. Gates is the most significant financial contributor compared to the 195 countries. What does he hope to gain in his investment? The same man who owns stocks in pharmaceutical companies and bought up thousands of acres of American farmland—what a coincidence. He has no medical degree. He is not a scientist, yet he contributes monumental decisions to the World Health Organization that affect the entire world.

He introduced the microchip tattoo, a precursor to a mandate to medical laws, by attempting to make the vaccine passport mandatory for every human being. This is not just any passport for the common citizen to use when traveling outside the United States but a precursor passport that will mimic the Real ID Act, permitting American citizens to travel within the United States. The Real ID Act, introduced by former President George W. Bush through the Patriot Act, was a subtle mandate to be implemented on our driver's licenses. The states will require you to have the Real ID Act to enter federal buildings and/or military bases. Concurrently, you will need a vaccine passport to travel to your neighboring states, board a plane, or travel by train or bus.

The pandemic was the right opportunity for the right crisis, allowing the state the opportunity under the guise of a pandemic to implement mandated laws. This was an experiment to see who would comply *and who would not.* Government mandates could seize control of employment, medical care, and food accessibility. The CDC is even creating mandates on personal property.

> "In the beginning, the organizer's first job is to create the issues or problems."
>
> —Saul Alinsky, *Rules for Radicals: A Pragmatic Primer for Realistic Radicals*

> "We are on the verge of a global transformation. All we need is '**the right major crisis**', and the nations will accept the New World Order."
>
> —David Rockefeller

The American soldier swore an oath to defend the country against foreign **and domestic threats**. What does that ultimately mean? Who will the soldier need to bypass to honor their oath? The United Nations Peacekeepers and the French European Army are being groomed as the new progressive World Army. Imagine the gestapo in charge of the world. They would only need to build bigger concentration camps for those gun-loving, freedom-loving, God-and-country traditionalists. That, my friend, is not going to end well.

> "Do not let wisdom and understanding out of your sight, preserve sound judgment and discretion."
>
> —Proverbs 3:21, NIV

CHAPTER 15

The Grooming of a Socialist

> "With the diverse levels of morality, intelligence, and skills. Equal distribution only means that a low percentage of people will work while the mass majority will reap what they have not sown."
>
> —Dr. Adrian Rogers, 1931

Dr. Adrian Rogers's statement reflects that we are **not all the same** *in producing equal outcomes.* For equality and equal outcomes to transpire, "the government" will need to interfere with our personal gains and disrupt individual "incentives" to give to those who have not sown. This is not to say that there are people within the population who are vulnerable and require help. I am addressing the people who have adapted to a social dependency without incentives to change the course of their circumstances.

Imagine having no aspirations, no need to explore, no desire for higher wisdom, or need to create. If the government interferes with how you work, what you aspire to, what you sow, and what you contribute, supporting an entire society without your needs being met is defined as what? A government that does not define the standards and has no moral absolute would then preach to you what is good. Is it good to control the population's money, their private property, their goods, and their savings? Under Socialism, what political entity *will decide who will get what and why*? Who will get the spoils? Who will plunder and navigate through violence, looting, and mandates?

Garret Geer summarized *Rules for Radicals,* which interpreted the intent of the democratic Socialist Saul Alinsky by highlighting the steps needed to subjugate a country and its people. He outlined step by step how Saul Alinsky's propaganda was designed to indoctrinate the social justice warrior, grooming the academic militants to give up their rights and force others to do the same. Geer recalls, "Hillary [Clinton] did her college thesis on Saul Alinsky's [work], and Barrack Obama wrote about him in his books. Saul Alinsky died forty-three years ago, but his writings still influenced those in political positions of power in our nation's capital, following the steps outlined in Saul Alinsky's book Rules for Radicals. If anyone doubts this global governance is an improbability and that it couldn't possibly happen to the US, they need to remember how Hitler was able to control multiple countries under his regime using the same tactics outlined in the *Rules for Radicals.* Europe didn't think it could happen to them either, but it did."

According to Geer, "All eight rules are currently in play."

There are **eight steps** needed *to create a social state.* The government first needs to establish social healthcare, then poverty, consume the country with debt, initiate gun control, create dependency through welfare, control education, suppress religion, and create class warfare. According to Saul Alinsky, "Control healthcare, and you control the people."

Under the Obama Administration, we no longer had a choice in healthcare. The administration, along with the IRS, mandated that all American citizens maintain healthcare *or pay a penalty tax.* If you remain uninsured and do not pay into the social healthcare system, the average American will be penalized by the Internal Revenue Service. A 1098 is required to show proof that you are insured. Without the form, the Internal Revenue Service can attach a tax fee. This is the same logic used by credit card companies, which charge a high delinquency fee for not paying on time. Apparently, if you didn't have the money to pay the credit card bill to begin with, you could afford the fee through some miraculous intervention.

This law **does not apply** to illegal immigrants; by the way, the law only applies to taxpaying American citizens. This healthcare system is creating forced labor. In a social healthcare system, the doctor's income will be controlled by the government. Despite their professional training, student loans, and personal sacrifices, all will become irrelevant. Forced labor is illegal and unconstitutional.

Many defend social welfare and social healthcare systems because they believe being cared for is better than being free to choose. Why have these insurance companies in the United States become so challenging to work with, forcing many healthcare providers *not to accept insurance*? Is this a symbiotic relationship only about money, or is there something more sinister brewing behind the scenes? Everything comes at a price. What will happen if the government is the only insurance company and mandates that all physicians accept what is given at a set price to see a set number of patients a day and get paid minimally? No freedom of choice. Socialist sympathizers see Canada as a winning deal in healthcare, but how much does it cost for the average Canadian to pay for the rest of the country? It's not free healthcare; **someone is paying for it**.

"Increase the poverty level as high as possible; poor people are easier to control and will not fight back if you provide everything for them to live."

Create the welfare state while providing pseudo-free healthcare, all paid by the American taxpayer. This will be a financial pot of money controlled by the politicians, while our public servants and their families get free healthcare for life. No 1098 is needed.

Poverty aids in accepting the Marxist theology by creating the class system: the bourgeoisie and the proletariat. The proletariat will depend more on social programs, housing allowance, welfare, food, healthcare, subsidies, and education. Obama gave away free phones at one point to create more dependencies. Even though he was seen as being gracious, he was actually exploiting the people. These cell phones were all paid for by the hard-working American taxpayer—*the majority*—not the federal government or any administration. The majority of working-class citizens *will support the other half through taxes* before providing for themselves, **taking from the haves** to give to the have-nots. A Socialist idealism.

Increase the debt to an "unsustainable level." That way, you can **justify increasing the taxes and produce more poverty**.

Let's begin with the current $1.4 trillion spending bill as of 2023, adding to the already $22 trillion national deficit with an annual interest rate costing the American taxpayer $371 billion in **interest each year**. "The *interest alone* will soon outcost the national defense budget and quite possibly Social Security." This could be another national crisis. The federal government could exercise power to initiate Obama's Executive Order 13603. If we increase the debt, the excuse made by the federal government will be to **increase the taxes**. We are regressing back to the subjecthood under the Crown, which forced taxation without representation. If both parties are working together, who can deny them? I thought we fought a Revolutionary War to escape tyranny from England, but apparently not.

This executive order allows the government to mandate total control of the entire country's assets, property, and money should a national crisis occur. It gives the government carte blanche to take from the American people, like freezing the banks and taking over your property and food distributions. It was signed into law by Barack Obama on March 16, 2012.

The entire Executive Order 13603 and the role of FEMA propose that all secretaries of state have the power to seize assets, beginning with the Secretary of Defense, who will have power over all water resources. The Secretary of Commerce will have power over all material services and facilities, including construction materials. The Secretary of Transportation has power over all forms of civilian transportation. The Secretary of Agriculture has power over food resources and facilities, livestock, plant health resources, and the domestic distribution of farm equipment.

Remember, *Bill Gates is buying up thousands of acres of farmland* and is introducing synthetic meat under the guise of combating climate change. We have the Secretary of Health and Human Services, who has power over all health resources—hospitals, medical care, and pharmaceutical companies—and finally, the Secretary of Energy, who has power over all forms of energy.

Is the government eliminating oil production to convert all cars to battery-operated, electric-driven vehicles, claiming it's for climate change, while engaging in insider trading without recourse? Should every American buy a new car? How does the government plan to recycle gas-operated vehicles without adversely affecting the planet? Will we still need fossil fuels to power battery-driven cars? The states and countries are investing in installing wind turbines for energy to support climate change, yet no one seems to suggest planting more trees to combat air pollution. Only a few companies propose planting more trees. Unlike trees, wind turbines cannot clean the atmosphere from carbon dioxide.

The United Nations' 17 Goal Sustainment of Development works on the same premise as Executive Order 13603 but on a much larger global scale. This initiative promotes taking over all planetary resources and the sustainment of people by the year 2030.

Barack Obama spoke on how to win the game using misinformation and propaganda:

> "You only have to flood a county's public square with enough raw sewage. You just have to raise enough questions, spread enough dirt, and plant enough conspiracy theorizing that citizens no longer know *what to believe*. Once they lose trust in their leaders, the mainstream media, political institutions, and each other **in the possibility of truth** … the game is won."
>
> —Barack Obama's speech at Stanford University on April 21, 2022

Obama used an interesting choice of words, possibly a Freudian slip. Will the mainstream media treat this speech as **disinformation** *or as a distorted truth* that needs to be repaired by his public relations (PR) team?

The social state would then need to enforce gun control, claiming it's for the betterment of society, safety and the government's effort to reduce gun violence and crime. However, this removes **law-abiding citizens**' right to defend themselves and portrays them as criminals without committing a crime. Gun control gives the government the ability to create a "police state."

Social constructs are activating willing protesters to advocate defunding the police, leaving the government with the power to hire *new law enforcement*. The government can use this opportunity to handpick their new police force—progressive versions of Hitlerian brown and black shirts, *or redcoats*, as our forefathers warned us about.

That's why we have written constitutional rights to defend ourselves against governmental tyranny. These "outdated laws" written by "dead white men" were written with heavy heart and deep foresight, brought to us through their experience.

According to the *Epoch Times*, Roman Balmakov explains the recent legislative effort to ban citizen militias. A bill, introduced by Democrat lawmaker Mr. Markey, was presented to the Senate and House of Representatives in Congress in 2024. This legislation, *H.R. 6981 — Preventing Private Paramilitary Activities Act of 2024,* would explicitly **outlaw** the formation of citizen militia groups.

Balmakov comments, "If they are trying to outlaw it, **then it must be legal**." He adds that the federal government distinguishes the term "militia" in the Constitution as representing the state's National Guard. **However**, *this conflicts with the understanding* that in 1776, the states did not have a National Guard. The people were allowed to assemble as a militia to defend themselves and property against a government that could become tyrannical.

Outlawing a constitutional right leads to what? The word *outlaw* itself recalls the aristocracy and oligarchs of medieval times.

Disarm the citizens. Call in martial law.

The Constitution was made and created *for Americans*. The next course of Socialistic action is to create a welfare social state designed to take control of every aspect of people's lives. By creating dependency, you can control the crowd (groups). Take away the incentive to work and eliminate self-reliance, and people will abandon any desire to improve their circumstances, falling prey to **socially conditioned inertia** to work less with the mindset *of receiving more.*

Money does not grow on trees, nor do we receive wealth from the lining of politicians' pockets—who first take for themselves. This is especially true when a social program provides for able-bodied men and women who feel entitled to someone else's money they didn't work for or earn. This is a moral dilemma, exonerating oneself from moral responsibility and accountability for one's choices. Those who take advantage of the system deprive those genuinely in need. One can only imagine if this is a deliberate act of breaking a functioning society from the inside and from the bottom up.

Next on the social agenda would be to take over American institutions in education. Control and manipulate **what is read, seen, and heard**, *and precondition the minds of the young.* The classroom can alter students' minds and change their perspectives on truth, history, and civics. Program the minds of the young like Hitler's youth, and you have imbued the social collective narrative. Teach the children to disobey their parents, and have the government usurp parental roles. PTA meetings have become a battleground, with parents attempting to voice their outcries against schools and districts' boards with no resolutions. School curriculums force political ideologies and *adult issues* into the minds of our children, who are too young to understand the differences.

This mass psychological warfare is being thrust on our children as a social construct *intentionally* applying *The* Art of War tactics. If it's not sexual dysphoria, addict them to substance abuse. Desensitize them with video games and smartphones occupying their minds 24/7, and then create drone-like behavior following the music and film industry without reservation. If all of this does not prevail, then abort them before they take their first breath.

Applying eugenics using psychological warfare to first damage the mind and the spirit will follow. The Obama Administration threatened state school districts with the deprivation of federal funding if they didn't comply with new federal laws to integrate girls' bathrooms with transgender children. The rights of the presumed dysphoric child have superseded the rights of the heterosexual child, assuming that all people claiming to be transgender *are truthful.* A **situational awareness** that could have been *resolved* by simply installing a new bathroom would not have satisfied the Marxist theory of disrupting society.

Again, this is another tactic where the state exploits the child to serve a Socialistic political ideology.

The Obama Administration's executive decision goes against our constitutional right for states to govern themselves. The United States is a republic governed by individual states with the right to manage their own school districts. It is federally and state funded by the American taxpayers, not by self-proclaimed oligarchs. That is how the federal government controls the curriculum at state universities—through federal funding. The budget belongs to the taxpayers and to the district of that state.

Regardless of where your political beliefs lie, *all children should feel safe,* not just a few identity driven groups. Schools should be a place where a child feels secure, yet they have become breeding grounds to appease political objectives. What is a truthful reality, and who is to say what the truth is? What is in the best interest of our children? Safety and securing Maslow's hierarchy of needs.

We have added mental instability to children unable to decipher what is true and what is false. These children follow the *guidance of adults* who use them as pawns to appease their political ideologies.

Current school districts are mandating children to take global studies, referring to them as global citizens. This is social conditioning. School districts use their power to demonize capitalism and vilify anyone promoting nationalism. Forbid a student from going to school wearing a symbol of the American flag or standing for the national anthem, and they are somehow considered the enemy of the state. Ironically, the youth in China proudly wave the American flag while our youth burn it.

College students are conditioned to despise their country, indoctrinated by social sympathizers. College militants, knowingly or unknowingly, serve the global agenda—politicians who have sacrificed nothing in exchange for your total submission.

Religion is a major factor affecting billions of people today—"Remove the belief of God from the government and schools." Change morality by allowing the *atheist to speak* while **suppressing the theist**. Identity politics are free to protest, but the conservative Judeo-Christian is silenced and criminalized as a radical conservative or Christian nationalist. It boggles the mind that the mainstream journalist refers to the Christian as a nationalist and portrays them as worse than a criminal. Should anyone speak against Islam and Sharia law, they could be arrested for 'hate speech'. Christianity is the only faith deemed unacceptable and intolerable.

Freedom of religion is a constitutional right, but that constitutional right appears to be disintegrating. The oligarchs have regressed the American citizen to medieval times of religious persecution. We have not progressed as a society; we have regressed to the oligarchs' oppressive example of tyranny. We have learned very little—if anything at all.

If the word *phobia* means an "irrational" fear, then what do you call a rational fear, and who will coin and define what is "rational"?

Words are lost in translation, and their root meanings are redefined through relative speech. Millions of Christians are being slaughtered across the globe **just for having faith**. Why isn't the word "irrational fear" applied here *or social justice implemented and defended*? The Marxist believes that Jews and Christians are expendable, while identity groups are protected. They cherry-pick to serve the narrative, ensuring no opposition to their agenda. You are to serve the state and not *God*.

Is the term *social justice* a matter of public opinion or a subjective reality designed to serve the political agenda? Is social justice truly for humanity's well-being, or is it a ruse—a form of psychological warfare *exploiting the emotions* of the desired group? The masses are steered toward their demise and marched to their progressive 'final solution'. The finale sounds very much like Hitler's plan when he gave the command to annihilate the Jews **in his** *Final Solution*.

Life is trivial for some, but power is the endgame for others.

The final act in creating a social state through class warfare is to "divide the people into the wealthy and the poor." By decimating the middle class, you create class warfare between the rich and *the poor*. The excessive propaganda of the "1 percent" in politics is designed to divide the rich from the poor. Sound familiar? It's the Karl Marx bourgeoisie and proletariat class restructuring. The middle class must be abolished for Marxists to gain traction in American politics.

According to Kent Clizbe's *Obliterating Exceptionalism*, Stalin described his sympathizers as "useful coverts." Groomed college militants declare war on anyone who dares to battle their indoctrinated ideology through conservative thinking—disrupting society with mass immigration, open borders, and intensifying crises with pandemics. The socioeconomic situation for all Americans worsens. The poor remain poor, and public servants grow richer.

The existence of the middle class defeats the global agenda—the Marxist theory of government, whose ultimate plan is to usher in a new democratic-Socialist form of government. But what does that mean? Will there be opposing systems of government that are supposedly contradictory to one another?

Perhaps someone should inform Bernie Sanders to surrender his multimillion-dollar empire and live among the poor since he happens to be part of the very "1 percent" he campaigns against.

The "useful coverts" have destroyed every nation in which they have seized power and control, and it's happening right now before our eyes.

> "A people without understanding will come to ruin."
> —Hosea 4:14, BSB

Pray for discernment—for what will it cost you but a few moments of your time?

CHAPTER 16

The Ills in Chemically Engineered Foods

Let us revisit the United Nations and its 17 Goals Sustainment Development plan, which convinces the masses of its altruistic motives to produce zero hunger while promoting sustainable agriculture. Could these motives be introduced through the Executive Order of 13603, where the United States Secretary of Agriculture has unlimited power over food, facilities, livestock, plants, health resources, and the domestic distribution of farm equipment? Will this permit wealthy corporations to produce genetically engineered foods (GMOs) for the entire planet? Does the billionaire entrepreneur Bill Gates, who recently bought thousands of acres of American farmland and is personally investing in synthetic meat, have anything to do with the UN and the 17 Goals in Sustainment Development?

Producing GMOs with genetically engineered seeds designed to reproduce once *or twice*—is this contributing to world starvation? Laws protecting patented GMO seeds prohibit farmers from saving them for future harvests. These laws force American farmers to buy more seeds annually from a **controlled, monopolized entity**. Should these seeds fall or grow onto adjacent farmland due to wind or inclement weather, farmers are being sued as if they were thieves and criminals. These same measures are being imposed on poorer countries, leading to starvation. Dairy farmers in Ireland are being forced to kill 200,000 cows to promote efforts against climate change, while Bill Gates produces synthetic meat for human consumption. Will the Government's Sustainment and

Development plan allow people to grow their food and access water and resources to provide for themselves and their families—*or will* that become unlawful and punishable? This mirrors the medieval period when peasants, caught stealing potatoes to survive, were sentenced to death.

Will American citizens be allowed to plant their food, build their homes, and own property? Under Socialism, likely not. Citizens will depend on what is given to them, and rebellion will bring harsh punishment as an example to others. Social dependency is not progression but regression—returning to serfdom and subjecthood as the oligarchy regains its throne. Astonishingly, the simple act of planting more trees could clean the air and save the lives of 200,000 animals. Yet the Government has opted to cut down trees to make room for windmills, which they claim will produce clean energy, creating the very climate issues they seek to resolve (*The Guardian*, October 27, 2021).

Where has all the money from capitalist taxpayers and charitable non-profits gone? Billions of dollars have been spent subsidizing global needs and financially supporting the impoverished, yet starvation, disease, and human trafficking persist—with no accountability except to criminalize the West and its taxpayers and American soldiers as warmongers and oppressors.

Society and academia are being reconstructed to believe that Socialism will eradicate capitalism's evils. The message is clear: we need a "World Government" to feed and aid the impoverished. Yet, people continue to starve, even after decades of funding. Must we wait until 2030 for the UN to act, or are they waiting for the right crisis to impose subjugation under the One World Government?

The United States contributes billions in foreign aid, while its citizens shoulder a $23 trillion debt. This spending leaves Americans grappling with overpriced healthcare, homelessness, mass immigration, human trafficking, and an opioid crisis. To "take from the haves and give to the have-nots" turns the former into the latter—a Marxist style of governance.

American civil servants have failed to hold other nations accountable for their financial mismanagement. Instead, US taxpayers fund these countries' needs, further deepening the debt. Should the UN or EU succeed in enforcing wealth redistribution, would the elites—such as monarchies and religious institutions—share their wealth equally? History suggests otherwise. Redistribution will affect only the commoners, leaving the elites untouched.

Adding to this, the Biden Administration has increased the national deficit by $1.4 trillion to support the Ukrainian war, further antagonizing Russia and risking a third world war. Will the military once again send its youth to fight wars not their own, while progressive ideologies weaken America's defense? Protesters advocating for social justice and diversity *drain national morale*, paving the way for **external threats** to take advantage.

January 6th event saw barbed wire fences, FBI involvement, and the National Guard deployed to protect the Capitol. Why, then, does the government fail to protect schools from harm? Instead, they post "Gun-Free Zone" signs, which criminals ignore, and use these incidents to further restrict the constitutional right to bear arms—leaving *law-abiding citizens* to suffer for the guilty's crimes.

I wonder if this is another deliberate attempt to wear down the masses.

> "The State must declare the child to be the most precious treasure of the people. As long as the Government *is perceived* as working for the benefit of the children, the people will happily **endure almost any curtailment** of liberty and almost any deprivation."
>
> —Adolf Hitler

> "The end will justify the means."
>
> —Niccolò Machiavelli, *The Prince*

Let us get back to the seeds. I will go on a tangent from time to time to show how many political variables are connected, working against Americans. So, please bear with me as I return to the bioengineered GMO seeds. The term GMO stands for genetically modified organisms. This is when food or seeds *naturally produced by nature* **are chemically altered**. The next time you shop, be vigilant and notice all the fruits and vegetables advertised *without* seeds. Let's use seedless grapes and seedless bananas as examples. You will see that GMO foods *are placed next* to organically grown foods. The GMO produce will always appear "brightly colored" and much healthier than the organic foods, which will appear less desirable, with organic bananas looking more tinged with brown decay than the brightly colored yellow GMO bananas. It is an amazing display. Every arrangement in a food market is strategically designed *with purpose*. Nothing is by chance. People are paid millions of dollars for marketing. The same principles apply to marketing public perceptions, social constructs, and social conditioning.

According to Dr. Mercola in *Genetic Engineering: Seeds of Profit and Dominance*, "Monsanto has become the world leader in genetic engineering of seeds, winning 674 biotechnology patents, which is more than any other company. If you are a farmer who buys its Roundup Ready seeds, you must sign an agreement promising not to save the seed produced after each harvest for re-planting. You are also 'prohibited' from selling the seeds to other farmers *and breaking the law*."

This allows the company to "monopolize" access to seeds.

In short, you must buy "new seeds" every year. This reminds me of the medieval European courts, when a subject was sentenced to hard labor or death for stealing a chicken or a royal deer from the king to feed himself and his family. Imagine that a human life was valued less than poultry or venison. Today, saving seeds is considered a *patent infringement*; anyone who saves genetically engineered seeds (GMO seeds) must "pay a license fee" to re-sow them. This results in higher prices and reduces product options. (Mercola.com, *GMO Foods*, February 10, 2014).

Why is Big Tech allowed to monopolize seeds? Is monopolizing seeds part of a larger scheme? Playing god with humanity, controlling food like a chess game—where we are the expendable pawns. When a government controls *food distribution*, what will happen to those who refuse to obey the laws imposed by the oligarchs? Will people be handpicked to live or die based on obedience? Already, the Government is picking sides. According to mainstream media, any voter choosing Trump is anti-democratic and a radical nationalist. The press even pits Christians against "Christian radical nationalists." Resources like food will be allocated to those deemed worthy by the oligarchs.

Could these GMO bioengineered seeds adversely affect and contaminate the environment, water, and animals that consume them? Could biohazards, unnatural environmental interventions, and slight mutations contribute to climate change? Globalists have interfered with food, water, education, healthcare, socioeconomics, the roles of men and women, and family dynamics—creating ripple effects in how the world *and biological nature operate.* Yet, to politicians, the greatest threat to democracy is nationalism. So, which is the greatest threat to American politics today: democracy or climate change?

According to the *Genetic Literacy Project*, "Hybrid seeds, including those widely used by organic farmers, **are not found in nature** and have been patent-protected for more than 90 years by a *variety of laws*, nationally *and internationally*, that protect the intellectual property of breeders who develop unique seeds."

These laws echo those of fiefdoms and faceless monarchs.

The same predicament applies to impoverished countries forced to buy patented seeds, cornering the market on **food production**.

> "Then God said, 'Let the earth *bring forth vegetation*: seed-bearing plants and fruit trees, **each bearing fruit with seed according *to its kind*.**' And it was so. The earth produced vegetation: seed-bearing plants according to their kinds and trees bearing fruit with seed according to their kinds. **And God saw that it was good**."
>
> —Genesis 1:11–12, BSB

Producing seedless grapes, seedless cucumbers, seedless bananas—seedless, seedless, and seedless. No more naturally, organically made fruits and vegetables. Even labeled organic foods are questionable. This paves the way for bioengineering and controlled food distribution.

The United Nations Plan for 2030: 'The Sustainable Development Goals are a universal call to action to end poverty, protect the planet, and improve the lives and prospects of everyone, everywhere.' The 17 Goals were adopted by all UN Member States in 2015 as part of the 2030 Agenda for Sustainable Development, which set out a '15-year plan' to achieve the Goals."

It's *their* goal to control every resource and person, whether we consent to it *or not.* Even with the billions of dollars in foreign aid given by the American taxpayer to support the UN, the money is still *insufficient*. The capitalists must surrender to this ideology, submit to this equal wealth distribution, and accept equal outcomes, thus becoming global serfs. If billions of dollars haven't ended world hunger, disease, or war, will equal wealth distribution achieve the elusive utopian society promised by globalists? All of this would be accomplished on the shoulders and backs of the American and European taxpayers. Remember, this cannot happen until America falls. You cannot have two conflicting *world powers.* If Americans want sovereignty and globalists want a world government, **can both exist without conflict**? Sovereignty and globalism are as irreconcilable as freedom and Socialism/Communism (prison) conflict.

What will become of Putin, Kim Jong-un, or Xi Jinping, President of China? Are they likely to relinquish their wealth and positions of power to cooperate with the idea of equal wealth distribution and outcomes? Will they not choose for themselves before others? They already operate as Socialist and Communist dictators. How will globalism alter their treatment of people or the distribution of resources? Will they not implement the same oppressive ideology that mirrors their political systems? Has any Socialist or Communist country ever genuinely achieved equal wealth distribution or outcomes for its citizens while the United States continues to pay to support Venezuela and Mexico? What does the United Nations propose to eradicate poverty, disease, human trafficking, civil war, or China's genocide? They pocket the money and demand more under the guise of altruism. The United States of America stands as a barrier to their global agenda, which is total control.

According to Wilfred J. Hahn, author of *Global Financial Apocalypse Prophesied*: "You cannot have two superpowers, *for they will oppose one another.*" Even *Yehoshua* (Christ) said—"No one can serve two masters: Either he will hate the one and love the other, or he will be devoted to the one and despise the other" (Matthew 6:24, BSB).

Whenever I've touched on every subject and am ready to close my book, I find more disturbing plans. Consider this from the United Nations Sustainability Act in Decolonization and Self-Governing Territories:

"Since the birth of the United Nations, more than 80 former colonies comprising some 750 million people have gained independence. At present, 17 Non-Self-Governing Territories (NSGTs) across the globe remain on the list of Non-Self-Governing Territories, home to nearly 2 million people. Thus, *the process of decolonization is not complete.* **Completing this**

mandate will require a continuing dialogue among the administering Powers, the Special Committee on the Situation, with regard to the Implementation of the Declaration on the Granting of Independence of Colonial Countries and Peoples (also known as the 'Special Committee on Decolonization' or the 'C-24') and the peoples of the Non-Self-Governing Territories, in accordance with the relevant United Nations resolutions on decolonization."

Decolonization—eradicating self-governing territories or states—must occur before the One World Government, the "Great Reset," can take place. The United Nations' 17 Goal Sustainment Development Plan will be enforced without opposition. Implementing the 17 Goals initiative plan must become a reality, with or without your consent.

Now, does our Constitutional right and the Declaration of Independence, written over 247 years ago (depending on when you read this book), with the breaking away from the British monarch, appear old to you? Does the United Nations intend to act as a ruling government for the entire world? These unelected officials make decisions without your consent or vote. And if you object, you are a rebel, an outcast, deplorable—needing to be deprogrammed, shamed or punished. Remember the words of former Speaker of the House Nancy Pelosi: "The **biggest threat to democracy** are the nationalists" who are American voters. I suppose I can congratulate those who play identity politics while they keep the country divided with no resolution in sight.

> "Don't interfere with anything in the Constitution. That must be maintained, for it is the only safeguard of our liberties.' And not to Democrats alone do I make this appeal, but to all who love these great and true principles."
>
> —Abraham Lincoln, August 27, 1856, speech at Kalamazoo, Michigan

Why did Abraham Lincoln say, "And not to Democrats alone do I make this appeal"? Shouldn't *all people* want to safeguard their liberties regardless of their political affiliations? Unless you want to return to subjecthood under the oligarchs, then moving to England or Canada might be of interest to you.

> "America will 'never be destroyed from the outside.' If we lose our freedoms, it will be because we have destroyed ourselves *from within*."
>
> —Abraham Lincoln (paraphrase), resonating well with the tactics of *The Art of War*

As we continue with the Global Sustainment Intent Goal: "Today, progress is being made in many places, but overall, action to meet the Goals is not yet advancing at the speed or scale required. 2020 needs to usher in a decade of ambitious action to deliver the Goals by 2030."

Could a global pandemic usher in the ambitious goals needed for a worldview to progress? How many people need to die before the action takes place in 2030? Maybe add another war like Ukraine and Israel and disperse more American soldiers to die in its wake. I wonder what those ambitious actions entail behind the farce of goodwill.

"A Decade of Action: We only have six years left as of 2024 to achieve these Sustainable Development Goals (SDG). The world leaders corralled at the SDG Summit in September 2019 and called for a decade of action and delivery for sustainable development, and pledged to mobilize financing, enhance national implementation, and strengthen institutions to achieve the Goals by the target date of 2030, leaving no one behind."

That, my friend, is *equality*—where we all suffer the same fate *with equal outcomes*.

They use an altruistic platform of good intentions with no definitive action plan other than their proposed agenda, which is only expressed in words. Dramatic changes in effort to aid the less fortunate. Regardless of the damage first created by foreign and domestic governments with breaking Federal laws and ushering in open borders, mass immigration without Homeland Security interventions, identity politics, gender-affirming surgeries, abortions, human trafficking, climate change, feminism, and systemic racism. The Government is leaving *breadcrumbs*, and the people follow the crumbs piece by piece, walking forward to their demise, as in the story of *Hansel and Gretel* (Disney). The United Nations has done nothing for the United States, yet they dare to make demands on the American citizens. The UN expresses concern about defending other countries; while

Americans are facing terrorist attacks or an environmental crisis, no one seems to come to our aid.

And to some extent, *not even our own*. The US government has dispersed our military men and women to foreign countries, neglecting their domestic duties to answer against those who wish us harm. The enemy walks around, parading itself in broad daylight on American soil. The Government has prevented our men and women from serving their sworn calling:

I _______ do solemnly swear that I will support and defend the Constitution of the United States against all enemies, foreign and domestic, that I will bear true faith and allegiance to the same.

> "The military men mentioned in the New Testament are all men and women of character."
>
> —*The Soldier's Bible*, Holman Bible Publishers

> "Our Constitution was made **only** *for a moral and religious people*. It is wholly inadequate to the Government of any other."
>
> —John Adams

The United Nations feels this overwhelming desire to proclaim "altruism" by making a UN proclamation of equal wealth distribution beginning from *where* and taken from *whom*? They are planning to control all the powers on the planet to where the poor will become poorer, and the middle class will become non-existent, defining the theory of Marxism. The rich and powerful, on the other hand, will remain just where they are—standing above the rest of us.

In a Socialistic government, *no one owns property*—only the government. All the people will need to depend on government handouts, like welfare and social programs, to which they will "own you" like property, what an oligarch calls a *subject*. The government will take first according to his or her needs, they say, and the government will then **decide** *what your needs are*, according to them—thus applying Communism.

"You will each get a carton of milk, and a loaf of bread, and nothing more and nothing less, regardless of how much you work."

A Socialist government "does not live among the people." They live "above" the people. According to the UN incentive, this altruistic intent has nothing to do with money. They claim that there is no power to be gained, no selfish agendas to be glorified or exalted. All these ambitious actions are solely for the betterment of the world—or so they say. For the good of mankind. Something we cannot possibly achieve as we currently stand. We need to usher in global governance for any good to happen, and remember, **only after** you submit and forfeit your rights to own property, to vote, defend yourself, *and to speak.*

You must understand that America must fall first *to usher in this utopian society.* Still, when people finally wake up from this illusory nightmare, they will have no place or Country to run to, no more refuge, and no more hope for asylum seekers; in essence, freedom seekers will be a thing of the past, and "we the people" will be trapped, spiraling back into a regressive medieval aristocracy without representation.

"The UN Secretary-General called on all sectors of society to mobilize for a decade of action on multiple levels. They call for global action in securing greater leadership. They call to secure more resources and using smarter solutions to sustain the 17 goals, 'local action embedding the needed transitions in the policies, budgets, institutions, and regulatory frameworks of governments, cities, and local authorities and calling the people to action, including the youth, civil society, the media, the private sector, unions, academia, and other stakeholders.'"

Could the additional stakeholders include pharmaceutical companies, medical institutions, academia, the film and music industry, food marketing in synthetic meat, and new bioengineered drugs and vaccines? They plan to generate an "unstoppable movement pushing for the required transformations."

> "We are '**five days away**' from fundamentally transforming the United States of America."
>
> —Barrack Obama, speech in Columbia, Missouri, October 30, 2008

Obama was completely transparent in his intent to transform the United States. He opened Pandora's box: the one world government regime planning to initiate its narrative by bringing in that "*ever-lasting peace*" so desperately needed in the world's present-day "perfect crisis."

The United Nations 17 Sustainable Development Plan Resolutions are

1. No Poverty
2. No Hunger
3. Good Health and Well-Being
4. Quality Education
5. Gender Equality
6. Clean Water and Sanitation
7. Affordable and Clean Energy
8. Industry, Innovation, and Infrastructure
9. Reduced Inequalities Responsible Production and Reduction
10. Climate Action (*I thought climate change was a top priority. It's number 10 on the list.*)
11. Life Below Water
12. Life Online (*Life above water is a broad statement.*)
13. Peace, Justice, and Strong Institutions
14. Partnership for the Goals

—Mark Horoszowski, August 18, 2015, *The Full List of the 17 United Nations Sustainable Goals*

That surmises total governmental control with the One World Government (OWG), the One World Economic System (also known as the World Economic Forum), and the One World Religion, which covers every resource a human being needs to survive. What's next after economic control through the One World Government?

Hitler's vision and idealism didn't die. They just lay dormant, like a viral pathogen, waiting for the right opportunity to strike its host when they least expect it.

The UN Sustainable Development Goals set by the United Nations have been brilliantly orchestrated and supported by all the Hollywood self-righteous elitists. They have the money and the means to secure their position as the world falls prey to the world bankers and the politicians disrupting society's infrastructure and group dynamics. These are the very same people who advocate for eugenics to preserve the world's resources to sustain their existence while claiming these goals are in the best interest of all people.

How will the UN propose to execute this perfectly orchestrated plan? Maybe they will burn houses down to make room for an oceanside view. Hawaii sounds like the perfect place to begin a climate-preserved utopian society for elitists.

What will be expected from the people to execute this utopic society? They have listed all great ideologies but no clear-cut plan on how to implement them except by introducing the Green Peace Deal and climate change, which will forfeit the voice of the people and give the power of all the earthly resources to foreign entities, costing the American taxpayer everything they own. Talk about robbing the American people—and for the most part, and with all good intentions, they will forfeit their rights.

This agenda mentions nothing about child welfare and human trafficking, a billion-dollar industry.

There is no mention of the black market, Big Brother, organ harvesting, or the ever-present Chinese genocide by the CCP Communistic dictatorship. San Francisco is riddled with homelessness, the opioid crisis, and human waste. Yet, Governor Gavin Newsom cleaned the streets and relocated all the homeless people to present a clean environment to welcome a dictating Communist. Instead of posting American flags, Newsom posted the Communist flag. Where are all the social justice warriors and environmental protestors? I suppose no one was available or paid to orchestrate a protest.

According to the Constitution and Federal Laws, Newsom poses a threat to the Republic, putting the foreign Government's interests above his sworn allegiance to the American people. The US Government, Homeland Security, the FBI, NSA, and the CIA remain absent and silent—like Canada treats Trudeau.

Do people genuinely believe that all the dictating Communist leaders are going to relinquish their dictatorship, their money, their reign, and their perceived "godlike" power over the citizens because it might "hurt your feelings?" There is no safe place in a truthful reality. Indoctrinating the global ideology to our college students and ingraining the future followers in elementary school. Forbid the child to have the time to rationalize their circumstance, use critical thinking, and see reality for where it lies—to recognize tyranny as it unfolds.

The universities have constructed our safe spaces just for that. Very clever! Ignore the existence of truth and hide behind safe spaces. Colleges have created a ruse to weaken the resiliency of the young. No civility allowed, and no dialogue condoned. Oppose anyone having a contradictory thought. Open conversation is immediately attacked and shut down.

The government has federally funded the beast, with its desire to rule and control unsuspecting citizens—all paid for by American and European taxpayers. It's brilliant!

The Pope should be the first to give up his wealth and position since he advocates for social justice. Christ owned nothing, and even His last piece of property was taken and gambled for. He was buried in a borrowed grave, while the Catholic Pontiff lives in opulence.

> "Again, I tell you, it is easier for a camel to pass through the eye of a needle than for a rich man to enter the kingdom of God."
>
> —Matthew 19:24, BSB

Imagine a dictating psychopath presiding at the UN—one dangerous platform for a single psychopath or sociopath to dictate from. Deciding how every human being will be governed. Proposing the Sustainability Development Act, blindly accepting the "all-feel-good ideas" of humanism, proclaiming that it's all based on "good intentions"—a proposed new government controlled by the unknown globalist elitists. Abandoning the ideals of the dead white men, our Founding Fathers created, to follow new laws erected by whom? Releasing the safety of my family to unknown global political leaders with no history or ties with you. It is the greatest gamble you will ever make, outside of giving up on your own life.

What is in it for them, and where will global politicians and journalists live? Where will the music and film industry reside after betraying their country and countrymen for "thirty pieces of silver?" Will they partake in Socialism and share their wealth with their subjects? The global government will control all the money, all the properties, all the resources, healthcare, jobs, academics, water, shelter, food, and all your children, including you.

To think that putting your trust in something that will have total control over your life could somehow be good? What driving force do they possibly have? Could it be out of love? Does Amazon love us, or do they see us as a dollar sign cornering the market until we grow entirely dependent on them? Can this become a future monopoly? Is it illegal to monopolize a market in the United States? Will they, too, become the "haves" to give to the "have-nots"? Or will they remain wealthy and not partake in the equal wealth distribution they have planned for the commoners? Will the globalists change their upper-class lifestyle to live in a suburban neighborhood without walls separating them from the commoners?

Did they fail to mention how they would need to topple every other government in the world to rule without opposition? Did they also fail to say that the only opposition they foresee is the United States and Israel? It's not the Middle East. The United States, Hungary, and Israel are the remaining free worlds. The UN and the EU are neither attacking China nor the Middle East. These countries have paid their way to control the UN. They only go against the United States and a country the size of a postage stamp—Israel. Better yet, introduce the "Small Arms Treaty vs. The Constitution." A law where the United Nations subverts the Constitution and invokes a new international law to limit and abolish the rights of Americans to bear arms. Our constitutional right to defend ourselves against this governmental tyranny. These opposing forces are working diligently to convince the masses to give up their rights to defend themselves, all for the better good of society. The United Nations will keep their "peacekeeping troops armed" while Americans give up their self-defense. Can we rely on American military forces that are being indoctrinated by leftist Socialist ideology?

What will happen with the likes of Kim Jong-un surrendering his totalitarian form of government and dictatorship to appease the UN to bless the commoner? The same dictator who wanted to send missiles to annihilate 323 million people. The same man who punishes his people for generation on generation—talk about social injustice. Will he surrender peacefully? Will each government relinquish its power to become like the rest of us? Equal wealth distribution with equal power and equal outcomes. Will the Communist regime give up its power to control the masses, control their wealth, and control their freedoms? A country where the young people hold up our American flag instead of their own, while our youth desecrate the flag, kneel in defiance at the American anthem, and protest to censor their own freedom of speech.

Maybe we can make an exchange.

We will take their Chinese youth and give them ours. Where are their social injustice defenders when it comes to Chinese genocides? I suppose they are sitting in their safe rooms with their pacifiers, rocking back and forth, throwing tantrums, screaming bloody murder because Steven Crowder put up a fascist sign, "Change My Mind!" I'm sure—without a doubt—every corporate CEO will leap for the chance to hire a college militant, who won't hesitate to call him or her a racist and then sue them for social injustice. That way, they can jeopardize everything s/he worked for, down to the shirt on their back, in defending political correctness. We have Harvard and Yale University students defending Hamas after the brutal attack on the Israelis. Where do we draw the line in defining social justice for one and not the other? Is it humane to murder innocent children, burn them alive, or decapitate them in their cribs? We have American academic militants fighting a cause with very little to no knowledge. They speak without thinking; they follow without scrutiny, and these are the future intellectuals who know less than a third-grade child. They have no emotional discipline, and they express violence because they can, instead of asking if they should. They fail to see that their actions have consequences. They are driven blindly by those who exploit incisively for their global political agenda.

Childish and undisciplined minds are devoid of knowledge and unable to cope with the realities of life. Protected in their college safe spaces, they take it on themselves to defend the deaths of others not outlined in their protective groups, and they call the conservative American a fascist. We have allowed these empty minds the permission to cripple the country. But let us congratulate the professors for doing a job well done. You have transformed our youth into a future of pure nonsense, with zero resiliency and empty logic. A wasted generation unable to decipher what is true and what is false. They base their logic on appeasing their emotional state of mind rather than truthful facts. Even worse, they wasted American taxpaying money to grant the semi-educated militant. They feed the global beast with tuition money, to where a university will turn around and exploit the youth and the American taxpayer to their advantage. They get paid to destroy the country from within, paid for by the American taxpayer—those evil, privileged people.

> "These men are discontented grumblers, following after their own lusts; their mouths spew arrogance; they flatter others for their own advantage."
>
> —Jude 1:16, BSB

Where else did I see this, in the taking advantage of people? Oh yes, in the Declaration of Independence, as our forefathers have written. I will highlight a few of our current and present-day conditions similar to days past. The political atmosphere of today remarkably resembles the atmosphere of the 1700s. The antics politically used today were also used back then as well. Our forefathers outlined what the oligarchs were guilty of.

- He has called together legislative bodies at places unusual, uncomfortable, and distant from the depository of their public Records, for the sole purpose of "**fatiguing them into compliance**" with his measures.
- He has dissolved Representative Houses **repeatedly for opposing with manly firmness his invasions on the rights of the people**.
- He has refused for a long time, after such dissolutions, to cause others to be elected, whereby the Legislative powers, incapable of Annihilation, have returned to the People at large for their exercise; the State remaining in the meantime exposed to all the dangers of invasion from without, and convulsions within.
- **He has obstructed the Administration of Justice**, by refusing his Assent to Laws for establishing Judiciary powers.
- **He has made Judges dependent on his Will alone for the tenure of their offices and the amount and payment of their salaries. (Politicians and civil servants.)**
- He has erected a multitude of New Offices and **sent hither swarms of Officers to harass our people** and eat out their substance. **(The FDA, the IRS, the CDC, credit bureaus, and multiple agencies**

in bureaucracy set in place without our consent—laws created by the unknown and who are unaccountable.)

- He has affected to render the Military independent of and superior to the Civil power. **(Dispersing our military men and women to foreign countries to fight wars, not our own, leaving the country defenseless against tyranny.)**
- He has combined with others to subject us to a jurisdiction foreign to our Constitution and unacknowledged by our laws, giving his Assent to their Acts of pretended Legislation. **(Global international laws; mandated global studies for American academia, and referring to our children as global citizens.)**
- For imposing Taxes on us without our Consent. **(Four trillion dollars in the national debt, UN budgets, and the cost of foreign wars. Providing an exorbitant amount of money in support of Ukraine while leaving our state of Hawaii to burn.)**
- For taking away our Charters, abolishing our most valuable Laws, and fundamentally altering the Forms of our Governments. **(E.g., fundamental progressivism.)**
- For suspending our own Legislatures and declaring themselves invested with power to legislate for us in all cases whatsoever.
- He has abdicated Government here by declaring us out of his Protection and waging War against us.
- He has plundered our seas, **ravaged our Coasts, burnt our towns, and destroyed the lives of our people**. (Out-of-control lawlessness, identity politics, protesting, burning down cities, pillaging businesses, and attacking anyone opposing their idealisms is not a constitutional right. This is anarchy, inciting crimes by identity groups that have been given carte blanche by both domestic and foreign sympathizers. Each party has a global agenda with the intent to infiltrate the American social construct by bidding against her, just like the British aristocracy did in their attempt to destroy and dismantle the New World from within. History has a fierce way of repeating itself. It's human nature.)
- He is at this time transporting large Armies of foreign Mercenaries to compleat the works of death, desolation, and tyranny, already begun with circumstances of cruelty & perfidy scarcely paralleled

in the most barbarous ages and totally unworthy of the Head of a civilized nation. **(Paying into social disorder, planting seeds of discontent to have fellow citizens attack one another unprovoked.)**

- He has constrained our fellow Citizens taken Captive on the high Seas **to bear Arms against their Country, to become the executioners of their friends and Brethren, or to fall themselves by their Hands.**
- **He has excited domestic insurrections** among **us and has endeavoured to bring on the inhabitants** of our frontiers, the merciless Indian Savages, **whose known rule of warfare is an undistinguished destruction of all ages, sexes, and conditions.**

The tactics of the British Aristocracy in the 1700s to provoke fear, discord, and chaos are eerily mirrored in today's social and political climate. Psychological warfare, identity group manipulation, and exploiting internal divisions are not new strategies—they are recycled tools of oppression used to dismantle unity and sovereignty. The parallels between then and now underscore how history repeats itself, especially when people fail to learn from it. Did the British exploit the natives to serve their narrative and pillage what didn't belong to them?

> "What is the source of wars and fights among you? Don't they come from **the cravings that are at war within you?**"
>
> —James 4:1, HCSB

In every stage of oppression, as noted in the Declaration of Independence, petitions for redress were met with repeated injury. The colonists and natives faced tyranny from a ruler **unfit to govern** a free people, and today, a similar battle unfolds, this time against ideological subjugation disguised as altruistic progress.

The modern war against the mind, especially targeting the young, is strategic. The grooming of youth through identity politics and social justice platforms aims to dismantle the foundations of the very country that provides the freedoms to protest. The narrative is clear: America must be vilified, while the atrocities of other nations are conveniently ignored.

Global leaders, like the Apostolic Pope, have taken it on themselves to redefine education and morality. Initiatives such as "Reinventing the Global Educational Alliance" aim to recondition children toward a new global theology. But the Pope is not just a religious figure—he is a head of state with vast political and economic influence. Despite his calls for equal wealth distribution, the wealth of the Catholic Church remains untouched, and his opulent lifestyle contrasts sharply with his purported concern for the poor.

> "For there is one God, and there is one mediator between God and humanity, Jesus Christ (Y'hoshua), who gave Himself as a ransom for all ..."
>
> —1 Timothy 2:5–6, HCSB

> "For false Christs and false prophets will appear and perform signs and wonders that would deceive even the elect if that were possible. So be on your guard; I have told you everything in advance."
>
> —Mark 13:22–23, BSB

The Pope's rhetoric, while compelling, raises questions. Who truly benefits from his initiatives? Are his actions guided by faith or political ambition? He calls for wealth redistribution while living in splendor, leaving one to wonder if his concern for the poor is genuine or another tool for influence. Furthermore, his church, exempt from taxes and funded by parishioners, stands as a monopolized corporation.

Christ, on the other hand, owned nothing but the garment gambled away at His crucifixion. His teachings and life stand in stark contrast to the wealth and power wielded by religious institutions today. Would it be wrong to question whether a Jesuit or Socialist would employ any means necessary to achieve their goals? After all, it is not the church or the wealthy global elite funding the world's foreign aid—it is the American and Euopean taxpayer. They are the unsung heroes, vilified by the global elites.

Can we advocate financial and social injustice for the American taxpayer? No, because they are not listed as a protected group. They have been labeled as the "privileged group," ignoring the fact that this majority is composed of every race and gender. Facts need not apply. Bankrupt the country, and then clamor for Socialism. Demand global governance to help repair the damage first incited by the globalists. The law-abiding citizen keeps the law, while politicians break the rules for indiscriminate amounts of money—and then demand more. Could bankruptcy be the crisis the government is waiting for? Or perhaps we should brace ourselves for another pandemic, systemic racism provocation, or open-border terrorist attack. May it be whichever comes first.

> "When the US government declares a state of emergency, will it have the right to confiscate everything the public owns for the sake of the country? Take control of all the resources, food, water, property, your checking account, pension, 401K, and savings—unless the United Nations doesn't get to it first."
>
> —International Council of Christian Churches, January 29, 2020, *Reinventing the Global Educational Alliance*

A law signed in by Barack Obama, Executive Order 13603, states, "This means (that) all of our water resources, construction services and materials (steel, concrete, etc.), our civil transportation system, food and health resources, our energy supplies including oil and natural gas—even farm equipment—can be taken over by the President and his cabinet secretaries. The government can also draft US citizens into the military and force them to fulfill labor requirements for the purposes of national defense."

No congressional oversight is required, only briefings. It remains unclear why the order was signed and what its consequences are for our nation—especially during times of peace. This type of martial law imposes a government takeover on US citizens that is *typically reserved for national emergencies*, not during periods of relative peace.

Perhaps Congress will amend Title 18, prohibiting unauthorized private paramilitary activity. Introduce the Bill to Ban Citizen Militia and deny law-abiding citizens the right to own a firearm. Under the Obama administration's philosophy, may the citizens fall where they may.

"Sen. Markey, Edward J. [D-MA] (Introduced 01/16/2024) S.3589 - Preventing Private Paramilitary Activity Act of 2024. 18th Congress (2023-2024). This bill establishes a federal statutory framework *to prohibit* certain conduct involving actions as a part of (or on behalf of) a *private paramilitary organization while armed.* An individual who violates the prohibition **is subject to criminal penalties**." https://www.congress.gov/bill/118th-congress/senate-bill/3589

Will this Bill interfere with the Constitutional Right to bear arms?

CHAPTER 17

May the Dominoes Fall Where They May

Did the National Defense play a part in the pandemic? Can a pandemic create a national crisis, or was this just a trial run to estimate how many people would comply and how many would rebel? Interestingly, while most were inundated with fear, overwhelmed with advocating social injustice, and protesting to keep tensions high on systemic racism, Kensington and San Francisco were overdosing on fentanyl. Our youth were imbued with sexual dysphoria, mass immigration persisted, school districts were controlled by socialist sympathizers, and inflation, food shortages, and unemployment escalated. Meanwhile, Bill Gates—a billionaire—invested millions of his own money into pharmaceutical companies supplying vaccines and mandates. Gates also became the most significant financial supporter of the World Health Organization (WHO) after the United States withdrew under the Trump administration.

Gates has been a busy bee, buying thousands of acres of farmland and introducing "animal stem cells" through what he calls "tissue engineering" to create genetically synthetic meat via 3D printing. The Biden administration is paying American farmers not to grow food for the next 75 years. In Ireland, 200,000 cows were killed, and multiple reports surfaced of fires at egg-laying farms, killing millions of chickens. Some claimed the birds were sick, yet everyone cleaning up the dead birds was fired, and no one was accused of tampering with evidence. No foul play was called, and no inquiries were made.

"The New York meeting with Bill Gates, Warren Buffet, David Rockefeller, Eli Broad, George Soros, Ted Turner, Oprah, Michael Bloomberg"—and Schwab—"are all conspiring together to control the marketing in food production." Along with idealisms rooted in eugenics, Margaret Sanger convinced a large number of progressive women to murder their unborn children, enabling a progressive legal genocide. This is progress to the final solution—without FEMA camps or gas chambers.

> "We have fallen into the pit of human despair, **where truth and moral judgment** are subject to relativism."
>
> —Maddi Ruhl, *Bill Gates Invests in Genetically Engineered Food Products: Billionaires Try to Shrink World's Population, Report Says*, August 7, 2013; Robert Frank, *Wall Street Journal*, May 26, 2009.

Bill Gates, in his entrepreneurship of "tissue engineering" to make synthetic poultry, has also invested heavily in pharmaceutical companies by buying large amounts of shares. This man started in software, *not chemical or medical engineering.*

We have the CDC, the FDA, and pharmaceutical companies—all supported and controlled by stockholders, not by the Centers for Disease Control (CDC) or the National Institutes of Health (NIH). Add to this the fact that interest rates in the United States are regulated by the Federal Reserve, a small group of members similar to the Council on Foreign Relations (CFR), who are not bound by the statutes of civil servants.

Gates promoted the introduction of the microchip to store information within the human body, stating it was a convenient way to detect if someone was fully vaccinated—not for immigrants *but for citizens.* Imagine the amount of money generated by every human being on the planet after these stockholders monopolized the world pandemic.

COVID-19 vaccinations cost between $10–20 or $35, and rapid testing costs between $95–$135—a brilliant idea proposed by the global elitists to kill two birds with one stone. The WHO also suggested creating a vaccine passport. Meanwhile, the states have been pushing for the Real ID Act. The government can impose mandates proposing, "No vaccine, no job. No vaccine, no food. No Real ID Act, you cannot enter a federal building, cross state lines, or board a plane."

Where have we heard this before? Checkpoints? "Show me your papers! Show me your rations!" Is this a reintroduction of the Third Reich?

> "Why is the FDA funded in part by the companies **it regulates**?"
>
> —C. Michael White, *UConn School of Pharmacy*, May 21, 2021

The Real ID Act of 2005 required every American to have a stamp on their driver's license, pushing the Patriot Act Homeland Security *mandate* imposed by former President George W. Bush after 9/11. First introduced because of **terrorism**, *today we have open borders*, where millions of undocumented people cross like a Trojan horse, with no knowledge of their backgrounds or intentions. We are taught to assume that all people crossing the border have good intentions toward Americans. Meanwhile, Customs and Border Protection (CBP) and the Transportation Security Administration (TSA) work at airport terminals scrutinizing travelers. Appears to be counterproductive.

> "Customs at the airport is a security process led by Customs and Border Protection (CBP) to check passengers and their belongings before allowing entry into a country. **It ensures safety, controls the flow of goods, and prevents security threats**."
>
> —Debra Carpenter, *Travellers Worldwide*, January 2, 2024

> "The United States Department of Homeland Security (DHS) is the US federal executive department responsible for public security" and safety for the American citizens. "Its mission involves anti-terrorism, *border security*, immigration and customs, cybersecurity, and disaster prevention and management."
>
> —United States Department of Homeland Security, *Wikipedia*

> "On May 7, 2025, US travelers **must be** REAL ID **compliant** to board domestic flights and access certain federal facilities."
>
> —*Are You REAL ID Ready?*, Department of Homeland Security, https://www.dhs.gov/real-id/are-you-real-id-ready

The new mandate by the Department of Homeland Security implies that American citizens **will need a permit** *to travel from state to state.* The Real ID Act must be stamped on your driver's license to board a plane or enter a federal building, like a courthouse, post office, or military installation—except for those who cross the borders *illegally.* The ever-growing mandates are superseding our constitutional freedoms. They may seem trivial at the moment for some, but these "mandates" only open the door to additional mandates not enforced by the US Constitution.

The Real ID Act remains an alternative under the ruse that we have a choice. A day will come when the government 'will force' a federal mandate for all citizens who travel from state to state—such as from New York to New Jersey—and for all those who enter a federal building to be monitored. How will the tolls be charged if an ID is required to validate travel? I suppose *more* Big Brother surveillance will need to be imposed.

We need an ID to buy cigarettes—an ID to purchase alcohol. The government will mandate the Real ID Act to enter a federal building, travel from state to state, or board a plane, but you don't need an ID to vote because requesting proof of your citizenship is somehow discriminatory. This statement of discrimination for asking for evidence that you are a citizen borders on delusion. Mass undocumented immigration does not require an ID. This implies that citizens have fewer rights than those who illegally enter the country.

Undocumented and unsupervised entries into the country raise questions about open borders and mass immigration. Is it really for the sake of humanity? Bringing in millions of people irresponsibly allows women and children to be murdered or sold into human trafficking, while the American citizen remains unaware. We cannot answer their cries for social justice because they are brought into the country unaccounted for. How can you 'protect' what you don't know?

That's why we pay Homeland Security *with tax dollars*—to uphold the laws. But what happens when they don't? Can a government agency be fired or dismissed?

H.R.418 - REAL ID Act of 2005

REAL ID Act of 2005 - Title I: Amendments to Federal Laws to Protect Against Terrorist Entry

—*Congress.gov*, https://www.congress.gov/bill/109th-congress/house-bill/418

Another question is whether these people are immunized before entering the country. We know that the laws are being manipulated to give undocumented immigrants the right to vote and to reap where they didn't sow, subjecting American citizens to rethink the purpose of the law. Bill Gates wanted every citizen to be microchipped as proof of vaccination. What will happen to those who refuse? The American citizen is expected to comply, while the undocumented immigrant faces no consequences.

To add insult to injury, social media enforces laws like bureaucratic fiefdoms, solidifying their position in global governance, which they helped create. They manipulate people's minds with social construction and deprogramming until they surrender their rights and freedom without resistance, subjugating their loyalty to the new rulers.

Remember, you cannot have **two opposing powers**. You cannot have two superpowers, like the United States and the United Nations. Otherwise, there will be *a conflict of interest*. Serving an allegiance to one and rejecting the other diverts the masses from their global governance and total rule. No stone has been left unturned. Freedom needs to be abolished, beginning with open borders and federal mandates that oppose the Constitution.

Programming a future in which people are unwilling to think critically or scrutinize reality is a dangerous position to be in.

I have come across people who will bend the truth to fit their narrative and worldview instead of following the truth to where it leads. If you respond immediately by calling me a conspiracy theorist, you have already been conditioned. What will it cost you to search for the truth, except your time and pride?

We are bombarded daily with messages that shift our minds to accept whatever new political propaganda is presented at any given moment. We are relentlessly exposed to public ridicule, fear, hate, division, and social injustice without giving the mind a moment's rest.

> "In the beginning, **the organizer's first job** is to *create the issues* or problems."
>
> —Saul Alinsky, *Rules for Radicals: A Pragmatic Primer for Realistic Radicals*

We have been socially conditioned to invest yearly in new technology, with smartphones every two years, keeping us in perpetual debt. You'll never truly own a phone; once you pay off the balance, they entice you with a new upgrade—just as you'll never truly own your home. You will always pay school taxes and property taxes. The bridges will never be paid off, and every year, the cost of travel will increase. Taxes will continue to rise while politicians line their pockets with arbitrary spending of taxpayer dollars on any "fluke" they desire without recourse.

> Meanwhile, we fall deeper into debt, and the globalists tell the world how American capitalists exploit minorities, arguing that Americans should be punished for their collective crimes. According to former Attorney General Eric Holder, "Michelle always says, 'When they go low, we go high.' No. No. When they go low, *we kick them*"—speaking at an event for Georgia gubernatorial candidate Stacey Abrams. I suppose no violence was incited, no Twitter suspension, no hate speech accusations—just the freedom for him to speak his mind.
>
> —Analysis by Aaron Blake, October 10, 2018, *The Washington Post*, https://www.washingtonpost.com/politics/2018/10/10/eric-holder-when-they-go-low-we-kick-them-thats-what-this-new-democratic-party-is-about/

Bombard them with relentless noise, incite hatred, have them oppose each other and hate their country for the perceived "social good" until they have nothing left to connect them as a people.

Creating opposition within political parties is like creating militants for a cause. What is so divisive about being a nationalist versus a Socialist? How do we break the resistance of those unwilling to bend to the new rulers? There are innumerable, subtle variables willing to infiltrate in ways so minute that the intent eludes even the most vigilant.

Imagine gathering a large group of people, like a sports event. Pay the players to present themselves as "militants." Use marketing skills to persuade fans to share a "truthful" narrative, much like Joseph Goebbels did. Repeat the narrative's key words until everyone understands, accepts, and is willing to fight for your cause.

Let's begin with the National Anthem, attaching historical symbolism and poetic lyrics as representations of oppression and social injustice. Frame it as a "white-privileged collective crime" committed against formerly enslaved people and Native Americans, all while conveniently exonerating Europe's thousands of years of human oppression and bloodshed. The fans are now fueled to protest, burn, pillage, and destroy private and federal property.

Yes, we have a constitutional right to protest. What we do not have is the right to cause civil unrest that leads to lawlessness.

Let's also debate with the same fervor whether American law-abiding citizens should retain the right to bear arms. Protesters already oppose speech, nationalism, and capitalism. Should we also disarm law-abiding American citizens for fear of crime? Would that mean disarming every citizen or military defense from *every country* to follow a totalitarian style of government where the government will be solely responsible in controlling the access of guns?

What guarantees would safeguard the American people's safety as the Constitution is dissected and seemingly rendered null? The Constitution was written to safeguard liberties, yet it's now being rewritten to serve whom?

Athletes soon plant the seeds for their next attack, serving their global leaders while grooming their fan base. The globalist institution holds no allegiance to the country, its citizens, or even to God. Their allegiance is to themselves, luring the commoner into seductive illusion. Global reasoning spins these efforts as "for the good of the people" or "for climate change."

> "He will use every kind of evil **deception** to fool those on their way to *destruction* because they refused to love and accept the truth that would save them. So, God will cause them to be greatly deceived, and they will believe these lies. Then they will be condemned for enjoying evil rather than believing the truth."
>
> —2 Thessalonians 2:10–12 NLT

As an American, you must decide where you stand or, sooner rather than later, pay the price for your consent or negligence.

> "So, God abandoned them to do whatever shameful things their hearts desired. As a result, they did vile and degrading things with each other's bodies. They traded the truth about God for a lie. So, they worshiped and served the things God created instead of the Creator Himself."
>
> —Romans 1:24–25, NLT

Brigitte Gabriel provided an insightful rebuttal to a question about the evils of humanity throughout history. When a Muslim student stated that it was unfair to criticize an ideology based on less than 25 percent of its adherents (e.g., Taliban, ISIS), Gabriel's response highlighted a compelling historical truth:

> "When you look throughout history, when you look at all the lessons of history, most 'Germans' were peaceful, yet the Nazis drove the agenda, and as a result, 60 million people died, **almost 14 million in concentration camps**—6 million were Jews. The peaceful majority were *irrelevant.*"
>
> —Brigitte Gabriel, *YouTube: Brigitte Gabriel gives a FANTASTIC answer to a Muslim woman claiming that all Muslims are portrayed badly,* https://brigittegabriel.com/

Her argument extended beyond Nazi Germany. Gabriel explained that in Russia, the peaceful majority could not stop a small minority from murdering 20 million people. "The peaceful majority were irrelevant." Similarly, in China, a peaceful populace could not prevent the slaughter of 70 million under Communist rule. "The peaceful majority were irrelevant."

> "What is the **source of wars** and fights among you? Don't they come from the **cravings** that are at war within you?"
>
> —James 4:1, HCSB

Genocide and forced organ harvesting continue today in China, yet no social outcry emerges. Selective outrage cherry-picks oppressions like college students choose term paper topics. Anti-American rhetoric incites fear and weaponizes political correctness. Meanwhile, Socialist and democratic leaders deflect accountability, enabling the dysfunction of group dynamics. Social justice is reserved for select groups, regardless of broader suffering.

Even Japan, prior to World War II, demonstrated how a peaceful majority could become irrelevant. Japan's forces **butchered** their way across Southeast Asia, killing 12 million—many with **bayonets and shovels**. Yet these atrocities are rarely included in conversations about historical reparations or systemic oppression.

> "On September 11 in the United States, we had 2.3 million Arab Muslims living in the United States. It took 19 hijackers and 19 radicals to bring America down to its knees, destroy the World Trade Center, attack the Pentagon, and kill almost 3,000 Americans that day."
>
> —Brigitte Gabriel

"The peaceful majority were irrelevant."

Americans seem to forget the staggering death toll caused by dictatorial regimes—92 million murdered under Socialist and Communist leaders. Human cruelty *transcends* race, religion, and geography. It is a universal affliction seen throughout history, from European monarchies to the Roman Catholic Church's crusades and inquisitions.

Despite its faults, America became a haven for the peaceful—though a minority of evildoers inevitably followed. Evil thrives by feeding on good, seeking domination wherever it can. History repeatedly demonstrates that when left unchecked, tyranny escalates to unimaginable atrocities.

When no one else came to liberate the Holocaust victims, Americans and Allied forces answered the call. Yet today, anti-American narratives persist, portraying Socialism and collectivism as inherently virtuous.

> "Give me your tired, your poor, your huddled masses yearning to breathe free. Send these, the homeless, tempest-tost to me, I lift my lamp beside the golden door!"
>
> —Emma Lazarus, *The New Colossus*

This poem did not say, "Bring me your immigrants so I can enslave, exploit, or oppress." That's not what America was founded on. Little did they know that oligarch thinkers were already waiting like vultures gathering for a meal. The undermining of society plants seeds of civil unrest until the people bend to the will of the tyrant. *The New Colossus,* written by Emma Lazarus—a woman who didn't feel oppressed—was far from an endorsement of such exploitation.

A brief synopsis of the *Declaration of Independence*, written for the state follows:

"We hold these truths to be self-evident, *that all men are created equal*, that they are endowed by their Creator with certain **unalienable Rights**, that among these are Life, Liberty, and the pursuit of Happiness.—That to secure these rights, Governments are instituted among Men, **deriving their just powers from the consent of the governed**.—That whenever *any Form of Government becomes destructive of these ends, it is the Right of the People to alter or to abolish it*, and to institute new Government, laying its foundation on such principles and organizing its powers in such form, as to them shall seem most likely to affect their Safety and Happiness."

When can the people hold the government accountable for excess spending, mandates, and wars while actively working to dismantle the Constitution? Can Americans abolish progressive, unjust laws that are unconstitutional and destructive without being accused of being insurrectionists? This is clever maneuvering by the globalist Socialists.

They **invoke** the events of January 6 until it becomes seared into citizens' minds as a warning: to think or conspire against the government risks being labeled a traitor.

"Prudence, indeed, will dictate that Governments long established should not be changed for light and transient causes; and accordingly, all experience hath shewn that mankind are more disposed to suffer, while evils are sufferable, than to right themselves by abolishing the forms to which they are accustomed. But when a long train of abuses and usurpations, pursuing invariably the same object, evinces a design to reduce them under absolute Despotism, it is their right, it is their duty, to throw off such Government and to provide new Guards for their future security. Such has been the patient sufferance of these Colonies; and such is now the necessity which constrains them to alter their former Systems of Government. *The history of the present King of Great Britain* **is a history of repeated injuries and usurpations**, all having in direct object the establishment of an absolute Tyranny over these States."

Let's review the branches of the United States government, as established by the *Declaration of Independence* and the *Constitution*, which states:

"We have three legislative branches that our forefathers **designed to prevent** *the British-style oligarchs from resurrecting.* These branches create a '**check and balance**' over each branch. We have the Legislative Branch, which proposes and drafts new laws, confirms or rejects presidential nominations for heads of federal agencies, federal judges, and the Supreme Court, such as the Federal Bureau of Investigation (FBI), the Central Intelligence Agency (CIA), Homeland Security, the Internal Revenue Service (IRS), and the National Security Agency (NSA). This branch includes Congress, the Senate, the House of Representatives, and special agencies. The Legislative Branch can also declare war.

The Executive Branch represents the president, vice president, and cabinet members who serve as the president's advisors, while the vice president presides over the Senate.

The last branch is the Judicial Branch, encompassing the Supreme Court, which **interprets** the meaning of the laws and decides whether they are unconstitutional."

This configuration was carefully written from experience and designed to oppose potential future tyranny because, where there is power and wealth, the ruthless will always be drawn to it, leaving the commoner **defenseless**. Within 247-plus years, people have forgotten that America is a piece of land controlled by civil servants sworn to represent the whole. Each civil servant must pledge an oath before taking office, and if they betray that trust, they border on the lines of treason.

"I do solemnly swear (*or affirm*) that I will support and defend the Constitution of the United States **against *all enemies*, foreign and domestic**; that I will bear true faith and allegiance to the same; that I take this obligation freely, without any mental reservation or purpose of evasion; and that I will well and faithfully discharge the duties of the office on which I am about to enter: *So help me God*."

The government's sole purpose is to 'represent and protect' *the citizens* to whom they swore a civil duty, but unfortunately, this has not always been the case. The government and its legislative branches have conspired to commit human atrocities through wars for profit, excessive spending, and poor decisions. The American people stand guilty *only* by **association**.

Our forefathers strategically placed the name of 'God' into this oath to establish **moral ground**. In the Judeo-Christian tradition, God sees what lies in the heart and mind of the deceiver. Those who fear God are kept in check by *His* reprisal and punishment for sin. But those who lack fear of God will follow their own subjective rules to serve themselves. What rules will they follow? Can an atheist know the true intent within the heart of a man or woman? If a psychopath assumes power, will they possess the moral integrity and just character to do what is right? If so, what moral framework will guide them **if they neither fear God** *nor respect man*?

History offers examples of human atrocities and genocide committed across continents, from Africa to China, North and South America, and Europe. Mexico is no exception. The history of the Aztecs reveals their barbaric practices, including the brutal treatment of enslaved indigenous people. Anthropologists and archeologists often admire the Mayans' architectural advancements and societal structures while ignoring their violent acts, such as pillaging and blood sacrifices. Even the French were astounded by their cruelty. Should the people of Mexico today be held collectively guilty for the atrocities of the Aztecs or Mayans in the 1300s? Could we call this "*The 1300 Project*"? Of course not, as it doesn't serve the global narrative, even if historical evidence of slavery and brutality exists. Instead, the globalist focus remains on America.

In this case, the Mexican government exploits its people for political gain. What benefit does it bring to a country to lose its population to mass migration across the American border if not for an **ulterior motive**? Is this just a strategy to create open borders, fulfilling the vision of George and Alex Soros's Open Border Foundation?

> "Mexican President Andres Manuel Lopez Obrador on Wednesday **condemned** a Texas law that would give state authorities broad powers to arrest foreigners suspected of illegally crossing from Mexico into Texas. After a day of back-and-forth court decisions that had left the law in effect for just hours, the Mexican president labeled the Texas statute 'dehumanizing' and 'anti-Christian.'"
>
> —Patrick J. McDonnell, *Los Angeles Times*, March 20, 2024

Doesn't the state of Texas have a right to protect itself from undocumented individuals crossing its borders and adding financial strain? At airports, Americans face stringent checks by Customs and TSA. Meanwhile, millions cross borders without accountability, and President Obrador feels **entitled** to condemn Texas's state law as inhumane. Are American citizens obligated to support an entire country's population while they face inflation, taxation, exorbitant healthcare costs, homelessness, the opioid crisis, and unemployment, all while staying true to a progressive interpretation of Christianity? Calling something "anti-Christian" has become a convenient buzzword to serve political narratives. You are either anti-Christian or a Christian radical nationalist. Using relative speech to define what *true* Christianity entails.

America is, after all, a piece of land. The government is supposed to represent the people, protect them, and maintain order under the Constitution. If the government acts corruptly, makes human errors, and enforces poor decisions, should Americans bear collective guilt? Should identity groups pay for collective crimes they didn't commit and also **fund social programs** for people who despise them?

The abolitionists who fought against slavery have faded from public memory. Their contributions are overshadowed by narratives that encourage resentment as a trophy. Some perpetuate animosity and unrest, while others stand back, observing. Throughout history, the psychopathic, the manipulative, and the ruthless have always sought power and exploited any opportunity to behave unethically. These individuals—politicians, journalists, thieves, murderers, and Hollywood elites—will always watch for their next chance to deceive and manipulate.

America fought for freedom in the Revolutionary War timeline from 1763-1783 and again during the Civil War, which ended in 1865—just eighty-two years later. The first broke away from British tyranny, while the latter ended slavery. Unlike Europe, Asia, and South America, which took thousands of years, Americans fought to end oppression in a relatively short time. They marched for women's suffrage and civil rights. Yet people today are easily swayed. Idle minds are captivated by charismatic speakers and repetitive journalism. If something is repeated often enough, it becomes "truth," even when reason tells us *otherwise.*

We are not all designed the same.

The Socialist sympathizers are teaching the young to burn the American flag, kneel at the American national anthem, and rebuke the American people in front of the entire world during the Olympics. Athletes who were given the opportunity of a lifetime to excel—supported by the American people—*chose instead to lobby against their country* for the world to see. They stood proud, having gone to the Olympics under the premise of being proud Americans. These athletes should have been stripped of their silver and gold medals and required to return all the money given to them to represent the United States. You did not see athletes from other countries conspiring to behave as vilely as the anti-American athletes. Try such antics in China, Russia, or the Middle East, and you would find yourself in an unfortunate situation—stripped of any future aspirations, with your athletic career terminated. If you hated America that much, you should have forfeited your invitation; instead, you elevated your narcissism at the expense of the country you claimed to represent.

In North Korea, their Communist leader incarcerates and punishes generations of families for a crime committed by one. That defines a 'collective crime'. I suppose anti-Americans wish to outdo this, imprisoning a newborn for deeds committed by their great-great-great-grandparent. It is intellectually *illogical*, yet this concept is well received by some with open arms. Guilty before being proven innocent. Talk about being born with a "fettered start." That is social injustice in its purest form.

The very same ideology is indoctrinated in the rhetoric of "white privilege" as a collective crime—punishing an unborn child before they take their first breath. Meanwhile, the UN Humanitarian Defense and the World Health Organization (WHO) have ignored ongoing human sacrifices. Where is the Human Relations Department that we, as Americans alongside 193+/- other countries, have paid billions of dollars to support? The UN holds senseless conferences and purposeless meetings where they shake hands and play politics while unprecedented human suffering continues. I suppose the UN has a plan to have in effect by 2030; until then, it seems these people can wait.

So, we will wait patiently for the UN to reveal its utopian plan, until these euphoric ideas come to fruition.

> "In the last days, there will be very difficult times. For people will love only themselves and their money. They will be boastful and proud, *scoffing at God*, disobedient to their parents, and ungrateful. **They will consider nothing sacred**. They will be unloving *and unforgiving*; **they will slander others and have no self-control**. They will be cruel and hate what is good. They will betray their friends, be reckless, be puffed up with pride, and love pleasure rather than God."
>
> —2 Timothy 2:1–4, NLT

CHAPTER 18

THE AGE OF REASONING

George Orwell's *1984* predicted a future society of mindless subjects controlled by Big Brother.

America was an idea called the 'Great Experiment'. Its purpose was to try a new form of government that would serve the people instead of the unchecked power of the oligarchs. The new Americans won the Revolutionary War, but the aristocracy, elitists, and the world bankers have not receded in their quest to control the most powerful country in the world. They wait patiently, orchestrating a progressive plan to win back the country they lost. These people are called opportunists. These are people in power, and immense wealth lies waiting to pounce on their prey when they least expect it.

If you take the time to stand outside the box, allow yourself to find silence, free from socially conditioned biases, remove your deep-seated worldviews *just for a moment*, and then pray for discernment, God will reveal a truth that is becoming harder and harder to decipher. Be still and watch. Listen to those who speak the loudest. Politicians, journalists, the Hollywood elitists, the film and music industries, and the protesters seem to have an endless amount of time and money to protest and cause civil unrest. All these entities appear to be speaking the same language: disrupt and cause civil disorder. Meanwhile, these elitists have no idea of the plights of the commoners. They live in ivory towers, claiming to be **all-knowing**, while "*we*," the commoners, have grown clueless and unenlightened as time progresses.

They expect—almost demand—our **undivided** attention. They want us to idolize their fame and wealth without questions or resistance. They inundate the young with reality shows, embedding them to wish they were them. These stars have become godlike figures, idols by image and perceived glory. They state claim to some invisible power to encapsulate the mind and the spirit. They hold the influence to steer the masses in any direction they see fit, and all of it goes unnoticed. All that is needed is for the **jester** to act, sing, dance, and seduce the captivated and visually hypnotized audience. They are praised and awarded an Academy Award and the Golden Globe, supplemented with a hefty paycheck. Narcissism is at its full potential in the worldview.

It's not enough to have their faces plastered on television and movie theaters up to ninety feet wide and thirty feet tall. It's not enough to make millions of dollars and live in a mansion surrounded by thick walls, panic rooms and armed bodyguards. They travel the world in luxury personal jets while simultaneously advocating for climate change.

These people have sold out their country for *thirty pieces of silver.* Their relative reality is disassociated and detached from the common man. George Orwell had this to say about the progressive Socialist Democrat in his highly acclaimed novel *1984*:

"Winston Smith is a member of the Outer Party; he works in the Records Department in the **Ministry of Truth**, *rewriting and distorting history.* To escape Big Brother's tyranny, at least inside his own mind, Winston begins a diary—an act punishable by death. Winston is determined to remain human under inhuman circumstances. Yet telescreens are placed everywhere (New York Times Square, airports, bus stops, schools, smart phone, social media and all public spaces)—in his home, in his cubicle at work, in the cafeteria where he eats, even in the bathroom stalls. His every move is *watched.* No place is safe."

All of this sounds eerily familiar, like living currently in the United States, resembling a Socialist/Democratic state.

We have Alexa listening to our every word and recording our daily conversation, which we consider 'convenient'. AI **records** our speeches, taking notes of our political and religious affiliations. We have home monitoring for home security. We have our cell phones tracking our daily activities. We are managed and tracked through algorithms that predict our next moves, monitor our interests, and accurately predict what we'll buy. We have GPS installed on our smartphones and televisions. The National Security Agency (NSA) monitors our home computers. We have public monitoring with Big Brother cameras at traffic sites, intersections, and inside and outside businesses watching. We have the internet and social media tracking our social connections. We have television at gas stations, airports (predominately CNN), bus stations, malls, and city streets. Some will say this is done for our safety, to guard against criminals. However, a time will come when the state will 'redefine' what a criminal is, according to the Ministry of Truth.

We have the World Health Organization (WHO) in bathroom stalls and textbooks. We have global professors pushing the academic curriculum towards Socialism, emphasizing the "hate America" rhetoric and conditioning our children to refer to themselves as *global citizens.* We have the Hollywood elitists who are glamorizing Marxism, attracting the young into idol worship while invoking anti-social constructs aganist American traditions and cultural norms at an alarming rate. We have the music and film industry pushing a demonic narrative, enticing the young while simultaneously interjecting contempt for their country and the Christian faith in movies, commercials, and identity politics. These people are **paid** actors, **skilled** in *deceiving.* If that doesn't construct the plan to deprogram society and distort our reality and American history, they'll resort to infiltrating American academia. Granted, they have our children three-quarters of the day. It's ironic how the American education system *appears* to be the worst on the planet; even with the amount of money we have budgeted for the Ukrainian war, the government does not seem to have a **financial interest** in the American school systems. Still, they have time and money to support identity politics. I wonder why? Could there be an unbeknownst global political agenda?

Conditioning the mind like a programmed recording makes us believe we are *acting* on our free will. We have become a product of society—classic and operant conditioning through social constructs—tiny whispers deprogramming our ability to think critically. Socially constructing the masses like Pavlov's dogs to accept their subjective truth without inquiry. We have high school global studies training our children to identify themselves as global citizens. Academia is convincing our children to abandon their Americanized citizenry while mass immigration is pouring into the country, bearing children in the US and creating citizens by birthright. In other words, the undocumented immigrant will become the new American citizen while the citizen becomes a globalist governed under international law.

We, as law-abiding citizens, pay taxes to allow the districts to indoctrinate our children, subconsciously teaching them not to honor their country and to think globally. If one forfeits and denies their country, they abandon their freedom and liberties to become a future **subject**.

The *Art of War* states, "All warfare is based on **deception**. If united, *divide* him." Divide their allegiance. Divide them as a people by splitting them into smaller groups, such as African *American*, Asian *American*, and Latin (Spaniards). There's no such thing as Caucasian American or Puerto Rican American. Instead, we have "white privilege" and "the *Hispanics*."

The same concept is being advocated within American identity politics and universities, where college militants are groomed, and students are exploited toward social warfare. Academia is intentionally inciting civil unrest on campuses, targeting conservative speakers and forcing social group identity divisions. College liberals are pitted against conservatism, with students blocking others from hearing conservative speakers—a practice permitted within public institutions funded by American taxpayers. Academic institutions condone militant-style Fascism—violence and oppression—protesting their **intolerance** against anyone *opposing* their agenda and self-righteousness. Public land is free for anyone to speak without restrictions, yet universities allow disruptions to silence opposing views.

These institutions have become the new "brown shirts," pulling the Jews into the streets, beating them, and sentencing them to death. We are one hair's breadth away from emulating the same antics of Nazism. Adversarial students have become defenders of the Progressive Fourth Reich—Hitler's "progressive" youth. Is it harsh to say this? Consider: how is it allowed for university students to lack jurisprudence on the Palestinians and Jewish conflict? College students tear down posters of Jewish **hostages** *still missing*, treating them as less important than a lost pet. The atrocities committed by Hamas on October 7, celebrated by some in the United States and Europe, are abominable. The Jewish blood of infants and children was shed, yet no social justice warrior protested the cruelty. Cherry-picking which humans will live and which will die mirrors the same historical injustices that **Americans fought** *to overcome.* It is mind-boggling.

Social justice is an institutionalized buzzword, a sanctioned tool for legalizing social bullying toward globally preferred identity groups. Academia has redefined the root meaning of "fascism" to include legalized bullying and, in some cases, advocating for murder. College militants physically obstruct students from attending conservative speech rallies at taxpayer-funded public universities, ensuring that only their Fascist voice is heard. Who funds this behavior in colleges and universities? What global entity has the most to gain? A walk through a college library reveals much without words—what you see on the shelves speaks volumes, particularly regarding politics and religion.

> "In the beginning, *the organizer's first job* is to **create the issues** or problems."
>
> "True revolutionaries do not flaunt their radicalism; they cut their hair, put on suits, and infiltrate the system from within."
>
> —Saul Alinsky, *Rules for Radicals: A Pragmatic Primer for Realistic Radicals*

"The Supreme art of war is to subdue the enemy *without* fighting."

Plant the seeds of discontent (*Rules for Radicals*), invoke disinformation, and allow the people to fight among themselves until they are exhausted and confused in emotional chaos. Discipline and order cannot be achieved through the undisciplined acts of those who sow disorder.

> "The Lord of Hosts says this: Think carefully about your ways."
>
> —Haggai 1:7, HCSB

> "A worthless person, a wicked man, walks with a perverse mouth, winking his eyes, speaking with his feet, and pointing with his fingers. With deceit in his heart, he

> devises evil; **he continually sows discord**. Therefore, calamity will come on him suddenly; in an instant, he will be shattered *beyond recovery*."
>
> —Proverbs 6:12–15, BSB

There are consequences for bad and undisciplined behavior. If you are **not** part of the solution, you are part of the problem. Where do you stand?

> "There are six things that the Lord hates, seven that are detestable to Him: a haughty eye, a lying tongue, hands that *shed* **innocent blood**, a heart that devises wicked schemes, feet that run swiftly to evil, a false witness who gives false testimony, and **one who stirs up discord** among brothers."
>
> —Proverbs 6:16–19, BSB

Do you think the enemy does not see your limitations and your flaws? Do they not exploit your anger and vulnerabilities? You defend Hamas, but does Hamas hold any loyalty to you? If they come for you as they came for the Jews, will your life be spared? Will they spare the life of an infidel? Will they spare your children? And if not, who will come to defend you?

> "Hence, that general is skillful in attack whose opponent *does not know what* **to defend**, and he is skillful in defense whose opponent does not know what to attack."
>
> —Sun Tzu, *The Art of War*

No one has the right to intrude on and bully a student who has **paid tuition** to attend an institution. Nor do they have the right to subject students to political grooming. However, college campuses are the perfect breeding ground where students pay *their captors*—professors, lobbyists, and foreign financial contributors—to mold them into future global supporters. They are trained to become **obedient** poodles for professors who wield the power to indoctrinate the minds and spirits of Americans, programming students to act and behave according to the grand puppet master's design.

If these seeds of discontent had not first been planted in the college-groomed militant, would they have sought out the issues on their own? Bullies use the same tactics when recruiting others—attacking those who disagree and defy them, redefining and legalizing Fascism under the guise of social justice.

Colleges and universities receive undisclosed amounts of money from unknown sources that lobby the institutions for self-interest in exchange for financial gain. Who are these special interest groups, and what are their intentions with our American youth? Globalists keep their distance while Academia plants the seeds of Fascism, grooming the minds of our youth to facilitate foreign global narratives and attack from within—without the proclamation of war. Supporters of Hamas, for example, infiltrate these institutions through money laundering and whisper to those who are easily swayed, particularly the weak, the disenfranchised, and the outcast **seeking purpose and inclusion**. Opportunists eagerly sow discord and run toward chaos with profound excitement.

The agitators remain at a distance, watching as we devour ourselves without direct involvement, ensuring they stay free from harm. Globalists incite and fund riots and protests, leaving no trace of their names behind. Tribal identity groups serve as an organized distraction from the true collaborators.

In *1984*, Winston was tortured and ordered to change his way of thinking—forced "to employ the concept of 'doublethink,' or the ability to simultaneously hold two opposing ideas in one's mind and believe in them both. Winston 'believes' that the human mind must be free, and to remain free, 'one must be allowed to believe in an objective truth, such as 2 + 2 = 4.' Winston is forced to believe that 2 + 2 = 5, but Winston resists."

The truth will always have a point of reference. Relative truth, by contrast, is subjective reasoning expressed by each person separately and dependent on who "coins" the phrase or idea.

How can one compare relative truths if there is **no objective standard for comparison**? A subjective truth is malleable, shifting as quickly as the wind according to an individual's thoughts *or feelings*.

Katie Couric, for example, undeniably insulted the populace by suggesting the need to "almost deprogram" anyone opposing her idealism. She stated, "How are we going to really almost 'deprogram' these people who have signed up for the cult of Trump?" Does her political affiliation lack cult-like tendencies? Have foreign entities not infiltrated American politics to serve their interests? Is she blind to this, or is she complicit?

Instead, the question should be how to "deprogram" her collective Socialist sympathies. Were Obama's supporters ever called a cult? Couric insults law-abiding citizens exercising their Constitutional right to choose. Is it wrong for Americans to defend their Constitutional rights and sovereignty by standing against foreign global governance? Is such a stance truly absurd? Our Forefathers—those "dead white men"—warned us to be **vigilant** *against* foreign influence. Perhaps Couric should be 'deprogrammed' and *reeducated* on the basics of human rights. A journalist who betrays her country for global foreign interests and personal gain is no patriot. Don Lemon, similarly, does not stray far behind. Perhaps Couric deserves the title of the modern progressive "Benedict Arnold."

Orwell's other dystopian novel, *Animal Farm*, suggests the possibility of a utopian society—then makes very clear, with each horror that takes place, the price humankind pays for "perfect" societies.

Who pays for these "perfect" societies? For any utopian society to function, there must always be a leader to implement equal wealth distribution and ensure equal outcomes.

Both ideas are improbable. The variables associated with equal distribution and outcomes are endless, similar to throwing dice and expecting the same result every time. Human beings are as unique as fingerprints. It is impossible for all to achieve the same outcomes. We are born with distinct attributes, genetic endowments, and unique abilities—some intellectual, others physical. Some are driven to succeed; others are complacent. Some thrive on adrenaline; others fear their shadows. Some are heroes; others are *cowards*. Some save lives; others take them. How can any self-serving politician ensure equal outcomes when honesty, morality and the basic of economics eludes them? The national deficit for 2024 exceeds 36 trillion dollars.

Editor Laura Knight-Jadczyk wrote in the preface to Andrew M. Lobaczewski's *Political Ponerology: A Science on the Nature of Evil Adjusted for Political Purposes*, "People are not all the same. Even the profoundly unscrupulous are not all the same. Some people—whether they have a conscience or not—favor the ease of inertia, while others are filled with dreams and wild ambitions. Some people are brilliant and talented, some are dull-witted, and most, conscience or not, are somewhere in between. There are violent people and non-violent ones, individuals who are motivated by blood lust and those who have no such appetite ... [If] you have the special talent for whipping up other people's **hatred and sense of deprivation**, you can arrange to kill large numbers of *unsuspecting people.* With enough money, you can accomplish this from far away, and you can sit back safely and watch with satisfaction."

Global political figures, *not elected* by the American voters, are controlled by fiefdoms appointed by both foreign and domestic entities, bankers, politicians, and billionaires, with no ties to the *Bill of Rights* or the Constitution and no allegiance to the American citizen. They operate only in their self-interest, following international laws set by the United Nations, with little to no opposition from the US, Canada, or Europe.

George Orwell wrote *1984* shortly after World War II, warning readers about the possibility of totalitarianism, a reality in Spain, Germany, the Soviet Union, and other nations. These governments maintained iron control over their citizens, where freedom was almost nonexistent and hunger, forced labor, and mass executions were common.

Are we teaching the harsh realities of Socialism and Communism to our university students, who are defending these ideologies while labeling capitalism as fascism? Orwell described a state where government control **suffocates** the citizens, where hunger and forced labor are routine, and non-conformists are "vaporized." Is that not what we see today in the increasing push to censor dissenting views and silence and shame those who oppose progressive thought?

Katie Couric suggested, "How are we going to almost 'deprogram' these people?" Should we condition people to self-censor, like Pavlov's dogs, and punish those who refuse to conform? All of this is in service of an illusory utopia, one that serves only a select few.

The collectivism promoted by tribal identity groups is not the diversity they claim to fight for—it mirrors fascism, enforcing **a singular worldview** at the cost of *true diversity.* These identity groups are 'unwittingly' undoing the very progress fought for by civil rights leaders like Rosa Parks.

Students today are calling for segregated dorms, professors, and spaces, claiming these actions make them feel **safe**. But are they asking for segregation *or inclusion*? This contradicts the integration that was fought for in the civil rights movement. **Safe spaces** are not preparing students for the real world, where there are no such comforts. They foster intolerance and weaken resilience, creating students who cannot face adversity once they graduate.

Instead of unity, campuses today promote division. Students who demand tolerance are intolerant of differing opinions, turning from the oppressed into the *oppressors*. This division is not measured in strength. Strength comes from unity.

America is different than any other country in the world. We are a melting pot of diverse backgrounds—Germans, English, Scandinavians, Russians, Spaniards, Indians, Asians, Africans, Jamaicans, and more. We are not all Christians. We are Jews, Muslims, Buddhists, atheists, and secularists. Nationalism is simply pride in one's country.

It is disgraceful that highly paid American athletes, given the opportunity to represent their country on the world stage, instead choose to berate America. Their actions reflect poorly on themselves, not on the nation that gave them the chance. If America were as racist as they claim, why do millions of people risk everything to cross our borders for a better life?

I suppose the subjective reality of a college student would say that these unfortunate people have unconsciously left their utopian society to migrate to a country that is much worse—a country drenched in racism, capitalism, and oppression. What do these migrants seem to know that the college students fail to see? Nowhere is it written in the United States documents that Nationalism implies discrimination or oppression. Nationalist/Socialist are combined words used as a 'social construct' of neologism first constructed by Nazi Germany to serve an agenda. Changing nationalism to mean KKK or Nazism conferred as relative speech, also known as doublespeak.

Neologism is defined as a coinage, a buzzword associated with relative speech. A progressive example is "racist, white privileged, toxic masculinity and safe space" are just a few examples. Doublespeak is "any language deliberately constructed to disguise or **distort** its actual meaning, often by employing euphemism or *ambiguity*. Typically used by governments or large institutions: any language that **pretends to communicate** but actually does not (The American Heritage Dictionary of the English

Language, 5th Edition). It wouldn't make the least bit of sense if the word America meant the New World. These two words express two different time periods. Both represent two different beginnings and outcomes.

The Art of War states that "All warfare is based on deception. A skilled general must master the complementary arts of simulation and dissimulation; while creating shapes to confuse and delude the enemy, he conceals his true disposition and ultimate intent. (What better way than to conceal truthful speech?). His primary target is the mind of the 'opposing commander' (or people), victorious situation, a product of his creative imagination."

Sun Tzu realized that an indispensable preliminary to battle was to attack the mind of the enemy. (for the globalist, freedom and the right to speech is the enemy.) The expert approaches his objective **indirectly**. By selecting a devious and distant route, he may march a thousand Li (an Army) **without opposition** and take his enemy ***unaware.***

"Orwell despised the politics of the leaders he saw rise to power in the countries around him. He **despised** what the politicians did to make their countries totalitarian states."

Using doublespeak and ambiguous speech causes people to lose sight of where the rights of the citizen begin and where the law *ends*. New laws that are serving the politicians and the social democratic elitists deleting the rights of the citizen. They *say* we are doing what's best for you while disrupting the traditional social norms and injecting new conformities under the pretense of social justice. Disorder brings about chaos. In medical terms, a disease is caused by an internal "disorder" within the body disrupting the normal and natural order of how the body functions to maintain homeostasis, a holistic balance for a healthy body.

A disease is defined as an **abnormal condition** of an organism's part, organ, *or system* resulting from various causes, such as infection, inflammation, environmental factors, or genetic defect, and characterized by an identifiable group of signs, symptoms, or both. A disease defined for a society is the condition or tendency, as (a) society, regarded as **abnormal and harmful**. Andrew Lobaczewski describes psychopathic thinking as similar to a disease that injects its harmful doctrines into the core of society, appeasing the politically correct, even if your **mind** tells you otherwise.

> "The psychopath (is) like a 'virulent pathogen in a (societal) body,' (who) strike(s) at the weakness, and the entire society is plunged into conditions that always and inevitably lead to 'horror and tragedy' on a very large scale."
>
> —Andrew M. Lobaczewski *Political Ponerology*

Giant tech companies are as guilty of implementing the same modus operandi. They have become monopolized, maintaining an unlimited amount of power to inject their idealisms, gatekeeping in censorship, and buying power onto the unsuspecting "subject." Call it a conspiracy theory, if you will, but it will make no difference. The progressive future is coming to us at an alarming speed. Whether you believe it or not is irrelevant.

It is important to remember that Orwell based *1984* on the facts **as he knew them**; hunger, shortages, and repression did actually happen due to these countries' extreme governmental policies. Creating social conformities under the guise of social justice is just Big Brother steadily at work, redefining how society should function under collectivism. Collectivism is just another word to **assimilate** "togetherness." All working *together* for the greater good while simultaneously creating division. That's like walking in two different directions and expecting to reach what? Where are we going with this? What is the result?

Collective thinking is being ingrained into society, attempting to change American history, repeatedly implying that the 1619 Project is factual. The House of Representatives passed a vote to no longer use the pronouns of mother, father, brother, and sister in the English language. Forcing the doctrines of Marxism into a free society is treason. The government is changing the grammar of speech. The LGBQ+ and transgender community has free will in creating pronouns, even if it goes against the English language, like the pronoun "they." Still, the House of Representatives feels compelled to eradicate the specific pronouns attached to a nuclear family. It is a divisive ploy to separate the child from their parents. The brown shirts are storming the White House with their leather boots. We deny that we are at war with an enemy we cannot specifically **identify** or touch. They have guarded themselves with fences and military support at their disposal, all paid for by the American taxpayer. Claiming the use of protection is to prevent another staged insurrection. The Constitution states that the people have the right to dismantle a tyrannical government. The government is designed to serve the people, **not the people** in service to the government. This perceived insurrection appeared staged and seen as a third-world political response.

"[Machiavelli] introduced no moral standards. Instead, he merely judges whether political leaders have selected **the most efficient means** for their chosen end, and he assumes that the final end of political activity is requiring and holding power. He [taught] that in the pursuit of political power, the end justifies the means [and] that *cruelty* can be justified as a tool of political rule" (Larry Arnhart, 2003; pg. 110).

> "(The) revolutionaries do not flaunt their radicalism. They cut their hair, put on suits, and infiltrate the system **from within**."
>
> —Saul Alinsky

No one in history has had the luxury of escaping human oppression—no group of people, not even children. Children at the hands of psychopathic adults have suffered as enslaved and indentured servants until the Child Labor Laws were enacted. Historically, children have been exploited for a variety of reasons. Indentured servants, child laborers, and child soldiers. Children of every race, gender, and color have been used as pawns to serve the tyrants and those who exploit them. The modern-day tyranny is still active today, with child trafficking, Hollywood pedophilia, the black market in the selling of orphaned children's organs, forced labor for money, and child soldiers groomed to kill. They will always be those willing to take advantage of the innocent and the non-combative. Why? Because they can. If the right crisis presents itself, the tyrant and the opportunist will soon follow the predictable pattern of the 'will of the tyrant.'

History repeats itself without restraint until the agenda is fulfilled. Narcissists are incapable of accepting failure or feeling moral obligations. They will achieve their goals by any means possible, even if it takes theft, deception, oppression, cruelty, and death. Political gain for those who are willing to take that upper hand in government to usurp positions of power within a government, business, *or Church*. Let's take Cardinal Cesare

Borgia, the illegitimate son of Cardinal Rodrigo Borgia, Pope Alexander VI, who used the Machiavellian style of government as a political tool. In his book *Political Questions*, Larry Arnhart wrote that Machiavelli believed that "the end justifies the means."

"Even if the political action in question states' human cruelty' is justified, he is convinced that he is enforcing **good government** by maintaining a political order." You would first need to instill *disorder* to create the envisioned political order to maintain (power) and present it as good government.

I wonder if school shootings and the acts of police brutality caught on video, viewed by those with tightly wound pocket-sized worldviews, as a form of human cruelty, justified to steer the masses into a political order. As brutal as that may sound, could maintaining good government be found in such a scenario? The opportunist can capitalize by using social media, one-sided bias journalism, sports affiliation, and the film and music industry to fuel and perpetuate the fire. Politicizing that America's sins have been attributed to systemic racism and the need for gun control. What would be the results of the Machiavellian form of government where "the end will justify the means," forcing the citizens to consent to dismantling our Second Amendment under the pretext of protecting our children? But if we were invaded, would we protect our children with rocks and pitchforks? Should law-abiding citizens be punished alongside criminals for the crimes they commit? What would differentiate a law-abiding citizen from a lawbreaker?

> "We must reject the idea that every time a law's broken, society is guilty rather than the lawbreaker. It is time to restore the American precept that **each individual is accountable** for his/her actions."
>
> —Former American President Ronald Reagan

> "The state must declare the child to be the most precious treasure of the people. As long as the government is perceived as working for the benefit of the children, the

> people will 'happily' endure almost any curtailment of liberty and almost any **deprivation**."
>
> —Adolf Hitler

Interesting choice of words. Even if the government or school districts believed that putting up signs would deter violent acts, what would be the logic in putting up signs, to begin with, in proclaiming a 'Gun Free Zone' announcing that our children are 'sitting ducks' without protection? Wouldn't this **provoke** the criminals and *terrorists* to commit heinous crimes and allure the undesirables to commit the unspeakable?

> "Cesare Borgia (Cardinal) appointed an unusually cruel man to **restore** peace where the previous rulers had created **disorder** (imagine that; a ruler creating disorder?). Once the agent had done his job, Borgia judged that he should avoid the hatred stirred up by his minister by publicly punishing him. So, Borgia had the man cut in two and the pieces of his body placed in the public square. The ferocity of the spectacle left the people at the same time satisfied and stupefied. Machiavelli insisted that this was **virtue** in action and the actions of *good government.*
>
> —Political Questions, Larry Arnhart, 2003; *The Prince and Discourse Machiavelli*

Would gun violence curtail parents from their liberties and endure any **deprivation** to secure the safety of their children? Hitler thought so. No counter law was enacted to hire trained security guards for the school districts and college universities, implementing stiffer penalties for gun violence and maybe using the CIA and Homeland Security all paid for by the American taxpayers to protect our children. Could the death of many children in the end *justify the means*? Will this finally convince the stubborn patriot to give up their Constitutional right to bear arms? The foreign globalist and anti-Americans are staking their claims on it.

Again, according to Cesare Borgia, where there is **disorder**, a time will come when the people will beg the government to **restore order**. But what would happen, by today's standards, if the psychopaths in politics, journalism, and those in the position to steer the populace were the ones who created the disorder to begin with? Would this disorder create the stage of opportunity to change the social construct to serve the Machiavellian? Who or what identity group would need to be 'cut in half' and *displayed* in the public square? Could it be the majority? The privileged since they are the ones who outnumber the underrepresented. Using hate speech as a political weapon to subdue any potential retaliation is better orchestrated than open and direct warfare.

The disorder can begin with unpeaceful civil protesting, disrupting colleges and recruiting student militants, assimilating systemic racism, food shortages, wars, climate disasters, uncontrolled mass immigration, and inflation. These social disorders have **always** seemed to happen to the *common people* and never to the civil servants. Civil discourse never endangers bankers, politicians, CEOs, journalists, the Hollywood elitist, or the music and film industry. Why? They always seem to be the most insightful spectators, watching society fall, waiting to advise us on **how to fix** the chaos, repair the disorder, and *how to vote*. They seem **privy** to knowledge that always appears to evade the commoner.

The young have abandoned traditional norms learned through years of trial and error to unquestioningly accept the 'unwritten rules' the global Machiavellians have laid out for the masses to follow. The platform and **social gatekeepers will decide** what is virtuous and self-righteous, providing *no reference point*. What constitutes 'hate speech'? The platform will decide. What constitutes 'violence,' the gatekeepers will decide. Will the social media conglomerates controlling social and mainstream media determine and enforce these 'unwritten' rules? Will the Patreon suffer the consequence of not knowing one way or another? Conservative voices are shut down without rhyme or reason, except that it doesn't align with the Machiavellians.

> "Think of the press as a **great keyboard** on which the government can play."
>
> —Joseph Goebbels

> "It would not be impossible to prove with sufficient repetition and **psychological** understanding 'of the

people' concern that a square is, in fact, a circle. They are mere words, and words can be molded until they clothe ideas and disguise."

—Joseph Goebbels

Another 'Machiavelli form of government' would be the positional control of the churches. Christianity has over ten thousand denominations, some of which are steeped in the Roman system of idolatry. The aristocracy and their belief system claim the possession of royal blood ordained by God. The Pope believes he alone holds the key to all the souls on earth. Only *Yehoshua* (Christ) is the mediator. The only Kingship ordained by God was King David, King Saul's earthly Kings, whose lineage and descendants would bring the coming of the Jewish Messiah. How and when did the idea of Kingship begin? "The first King of Wessex proclaimed himself King of Wessex in 802–839, and Athelstan was the First King of all England." God did not ordain these men, and Peter was not the first Pope, nor was he a Christian. He was Jewish through and through. Reality and history are distorted, like the phone tag game.

—Encyclopedia Britannica, T. Editors of Encyclopedia (2023, September 20). *Kings and Queens of Britain.* Encyclopedia Britannica

"He traps the wise in the snare of their own cleverness. And again, the Lord knows the thoughts of the wise; he knows they are *worthless.*"

—1 Corinthians 3:19–20, NLT

"For the time has come for judgment, and it must begin with God's household. And if judgment begins with us, what terrible fate awaits those who have never obeyed God's Good News?"

—1 Peter 4:17, NLT

> "If anyone adds anything to what is written here, God will add to that person the plagues described in this book. And if anyone removes any of the words from this book of prophecy, God will remove that person's share in the tree of life..."
>
> —Revelation 22:18–19, NLT

In other words, adding to the word to empower your position in the Church and or in government, you will be **judged first**. For all the atheists who believe what the Church represents, rethink your position. If an enemy cannot beat you at your will, it will join you and corrupt you from within.

To elaborate on the King's 'subjects' intellectual psyche during the Medieval times under the aristocracy rule, the subjects could not read or write. What advantage did they have in going against the Church, much less the government? The ruling class used **psychological warfare** to manipulate the subjects and convinced them that the reason they suffered and were poor and sick was because they **deserved punishment** from God, making God *a tyrant*. God was used as a deterrent to prevent retaliation from the people to oppose the ruling class. The country was in constant 'disorder' with wars, rewriting the laws to preserve the noble empowerment with unspeakable cruelty and without representation. The subjects were convinced that their circumstance in life was brought on them because they sinned against God, and poverty and pain were the result.

Without biblical knowledge, the subjects depended **solely** *on the ruling class* and the clergy for education. If the subjects refused to obey the Church and the ruling clergy, they were essentially disobeying God and accused of heresy, punishable with torture and/or death. Do any of these actions parallel the accusations made today of hate speech and censorship? People were kept in line using God's wrath and fear of physical and spiritual death.

The only feasible outcome in this scenario is either you submit to the will of the tyrant to preserve your life or be tortured to death for being a heretic. What theist wouldn't become an atheist, given the choices? The subject would be conditioned to believe that God is cruel and unjust. To live in fear where your choices in life are limited, and your circumstances are bleak. Medieval traditions override scripture, translating doctrines unbiblically to serve the unethical and brutal ruling class.

> "These people honor me with their lips, but their hearts are far from me. Their worship is a farce, for *they teach man-made ideas* **as commands from God.** For you ignore God's law and **substitute** your own tradition. He said, 'You **skillfully sidestep** God's law in order to hold on to your *own traditions.*'"
>
> —Mark 7:6–9, NLT

> "Therefore, confess your sins to each other and pray for each other so that you may be healed. The prayer of a righteous man has great power to prevail."
>
> —James 5:16, BSB

Was the King's/Queen's subject taught about righteousness?

God has appointed the faithful into the priesthood. The aristocrats, the Church, or the government will **intercede** if you do not hold fast *to reason.* If it's not the government, then the Church will intervene; if not the Church, then it will be the economist, the system of class, the rich man vs the poor man. We will have to contend against science, which has chosen to experiment with the human body and create AIs designed intellectually to surpass man. Existing within a society **without a discerning eye**, people will become trapped in this progressive worldview that will lead many into a pit to where there is no escape. There, the ruthless will devour the mind and spirit by any selfish means possible. The end goal is to have total control over the lives of their subjects: no more citizenship but peasantry. The middle class will exist no more.

> "But you are a chosen race, a royal priesthood, a holy nation, a people for *His* possession, so that you may proclaim the praises of the One who called you out of darkness into His marvelous light. Once you were not a people (Gentiles), but now you are God's people (grafted)."
>
> —1 Peter 2:9–10, HCSB

The Catholic Church does not represent or mediate for Christ here on earth. For *Yehoshua* (Christ) said, "I am the way, the truth, and the life. *No one comes* to the Father except through **Me**" (John 14:6, NLT).

That means *no one*. That would delineate the Pontiff's position as a mediator. Is the Catholic Church trying to resurrect its former glory through replacement theology, to rule again and resurrect the Roman Empire? What is the obsession with trying to rule over the masses? The Pontiff owns his own country and police force and is viewed as the supreme leader in discerning God's word. The Pontiff is a leader in multiple-cultural-driven institutions with daughter cells worldwide that receive money from their parishioners *without* taxation. That's a win-win situation. This institution is similar to the United Nations, where both receive billions of dollars annually, paid by the taxpayer or the parishioner. It is resurrecting a new institution of multiculturalism under the Roman Empire with the intention of creating a One World Religion under the pretext of altruism. Catholicism has the attention of over a billion people. If united with other religious entities, their authority will surpass any historical power ever documented in history. The Pontiff is aware of this potential power that he may one day exalt.

Some may find my speech offensive and even revolting, but remember, truth is truth. My writing is not based on opinion but is supported by evidence. You may read and decide whether to accept the truth or defend manufactured traditions and social engineering.

> "I will put My law in their **minds** and *inscribe* it on their hearts. And I will be their God, and they will be My people. No longer will each man teach his neighbor or his brother, saying, 'Know the LORD,' because they will all know Me, from the least of them to the greatest, declares the LORD. For I will forgive their iniquities and will remember their sins no more."
>
> —Jeremiah 31:33–34, BSB

This biblical verse means that all people have the law written upon their hearts and have the same chance, according to God.

What about the convenience of the New Age religion that absolves itself from the meaning of sin while laying claim to being the most tolerant of all people yet is the most intolerant to anyone with contradictory thoughts? Some people will become hostile and ready to defend what they believe as just while simultaneously being unjust to the freedom of speech and thought, cherry-picking their definition of self-righteousness to self-serving their itching worldview.

The New Age is a political religion just as Atheism has a religion of its own; they choose not to believe, and that is a belief system, nonetheless.

Even evil has convinced most that it doesn't exist. He is just a little red man running around in red tights with a pitchfork and horns. Take the time to watch today's music videos, lyrics, and the film industry. Even commercialism is steeped in highlighting evil, making it unremarkable. I am not telling you what to believe. I am telling you to scrutinize what you believe and why. Suppose you are against God because of social injustice. In that case, you may need to reevaluate social conditioning, like Pavlov's dogs' experiment, and then compare it to God's words that advocate for wisdom and keeping a clear mind. Are the wicked misleading those who wish to do good through altruism and social awareness but instead harm themselves and others without knowledge?

> "Sin whispers to the wicked deep within their hearts. They have no fear of God at all. In their blind conceit, they cannot see how wicked they really are. Everything they say is crooked and deceitful. They refuse to act wisely or do good. They lie awake at night, **hatching sinful plots**. Their actions are never good. They make no attempt to turn from evil."
>
> —Psalm 36:1–4, NLV

What can this verse mean? Can the politicians, the wealthy, and those who can influence have the powerful to stir the outcome of the many into a given direction "by hatching sinful plots?" This creates a social crisis to the point of unsustainability, where the citizen drowns in self-doubt and produce a social instability elicited by what seems to be unknown. These unknowns become richer while the poor become poorer. The middle class is disappearing into a wasteland of despair, funneling the remaining two classes and turning them into the new progressive proletariat and the bourgeoisie within the Marxist theory of government. Imagine controlling billions of people through religion and by enforcing identity politics. If one doesn't submit, the other one will. Have the two conflicting sides turn on one another, divide them with identity politics, take God out of the equation and you have won a war. This will serve the agenda better and be more cost-effective than deploying military actions against the American citizen. Infiltrate from within.

The ruling class and the Church used their manufactured crisis against God's name as a ploy to allure the remaining subjects to submit. If you control the people, you can control the world. This is not a Hollywood scene, but a Roman Empire being resurrected by the modern-day Caesars and their minions. *The Art of War* tactic is at play. It is not buried and forgotten by the psychopaths, but alive and well and living among us, taking any opportunity afforded to disrupt with disinformation. The Catholic Church used the Crusades and the Spanish Inquisition as a means to control the 'mass' and conquer the world. They did it then, and they will do it again if left **unchecked**. It's inevitable.

Where there is greed, there you will find deceit and chaos.

The Church used fear with spiritual damnation, physical torture for those accused of heresy, and death to force non-Christians to convert. The English crown perfected the art of torture so violent and gruesome; I'm dumbfounded that the English aristocracy is still thriving today. I question whether the Roman Apostolic Church doctrines were meant to convert the subjects for salvation or just a means to force the unwilling into a regime. This concept is similar to the ploys used today to implement fear, outcasting, deprogramming, mandates, and causing political division. They are changing the social norms, moving towards collectivism, and using anti-American tactics to subliminally force people into accepting Socialism, abandoning their freedoms and their inalienable rights *given to us by God*.

Religious and political leaders are paving a path for the herd to follow, all in the name of God, good government, and social justice. This deception is an abomination to God, for we are free to choose *Him* without oppression or constraints. People may debate that civilizations were forced into Christianity through the Crusades and the Spanish

Inquisition. However, remember that those wars were initiated by the ruling class and by the authority of the Church, which worked alongside the aristocracy. These wars were not initiated by God; these wars were created by the ruling class to obtain wealth and dominance, breaking God's Third commandment, "You shall not take the name of the Lord your God **in vain**, for the Lord will not hold him guiltless who takes *His* name in vain" (Exodus 20:2–17, NKJV). That would be equivalent to slander and disinformation by the gatekeepers.

Anything contradictory to the Church or *Kingship* was deemed heretical or, as we would say today, social justice intolerants. No written verse in scripture validates wars against the unbeliever, only against idolatry. Now having said that, there is nothing in scripture that defends the Apostolic catechism of 'purgatory' or the 'praying' to dead people canonized as Saints. This is called idol worshipping. The Church claims that loved ones who have passed are somehow watching over them, which is a tumultuous idea. Should I want to see the daily sufferings of my children while having no control in consoling them? What kind of peace is that for me? I can see them but not touch them. I can hear them, but not speak to them. I can watch them cry and suffer while I remain distant. I would have to stay silent and grieve without comfort. I would feel trapped in a world with no escape. What kind of eternal existence would find that to be just?

These inaccuracies in Catholicism give validation to the atheist, the Jew, and the secularist because they would be right. You may now be asking what the government and God have in common. Nietzsche predicted this. This new nihilist, the progressive "superman," will now create their own laws regarding morality and human nature to become God-like. They read one sentence in the Bible and condemn the entire book but then read Marxism and think it's divine. You cannot have two controlling opposing forces. You will either love the one or despise the other (Matthew 6:24, BSB).

You cannot serve two masters. The Bible's credibility has been tampered with, and its words have been twisted to change its meaning and purpose. Injecting, adding, and subtracting the original text, all to serve the narrative imposed by the nihilist. Repeating the lie until the masses believe it as truth. The progressives are becoming the center political stage and manipulating worldview, and nihilism is becoming the new moralist and the all-knowing god. False prophets, disguised as false teachers and leaders, have become opportunists claiming to be speaking on *God's* behalf while devouring the innocent out of their money and spirituality and corrupting their natural ability to reason. Using nihilistic tactics in relativism as bait. Progressivism is actually a *regressive* thought. Progressives and secularists have elevated Science as truth disproving the existence of *God*, yet science and basic biology cannot define what a woman is. I am not a geologist; therefore, I cannot tell you that this ***is a rock*** or an automotive mechanic to tell you that this is an engine or a car. I am not a mathematician therefore I cannot tell you whether these are numbers or mathematical equations. It's incredible that I know everything at all.

We are now being socially conditioned to accept the term birthing persons. Demeaning the biology of a woman and robbing her true anatomical function to conceive a child. Women advocate for feminism while allowing a biological male to take the place of women in sports. Social conditioning biological men to compete in women's sports while having an anatomical advantage to win at every event. If feminism is stating that men are oppressing them in the corporate world, then why allow biological men to interfere in the healthy development of women by posing as women? Confusing language is the beginning of a social **deconstruction** of the delicate balance to function adequately in society. No consistencies, no absolutes, no norms, bringing people to walk around aimlessly, in a perpetual fog, unable to speak or think without a negative political recourse.

Subverting speech and language by assuming the word *women* can be applied without discernment.

I suppose the same relative ideological conditioning in social justice can be applied in forensics. Can a decomposed body be identified as an x, y, and z gender? Can we alter the DNA that differentiates body composition in men and women to serve a social construct? Then science, as well as the existence of God, can be circumvented by the nihilist. Within relative truth, I can determine that the findings of an archaeologist can be predetermined and changed to suit the narrative and thus alter history. Maybe Henry VIII was actually a woman. Facts will eventually mean nothing, and identity politics will become the subjective reality. What is science? I unfortunately cannot answer that question because I am not a scientist.

"Science is a rigorous, systematic endeavor that builds and organizes knowledge in the form of **testable explanations** and predictions about everything." Science defined by *Wikipedia*, https://en.wikipedia.org/wiki/Science.

CHAPTER 19

SOCIALISM VS. SOCIAL LIBERTIES

How does one describe Socialism? It's like putting an entire country under welfare. Imagine this concept on a much larger scale where 323 million US citizens are economically controlled by an unknown globalist who has zero ties in the making of one's country. Foreign elitists who have not been voted into civil service by taxpaying citizens have elected themselves to key positions to make life-changing decisions that will affect the entire world. These decisions will affect economics, government, and religion. Each entity is capable of adversely affecting billions of people. Are we to safely assume that these unknown delegates will act in our best interest?

Did they have the European citizen's best interest in mind when they committed themselves to receive mass immigration far beyond the country's infrastructure capacity to financially sustain itself?

Imagine a political ruse where society is given the appearance of being **overpopulated** to validate its citizens to condone abortions. Imagine risking *all* of the earth's power into the hands of *one collective* identity group like the United Nations or the European Union, where political leaders are not voted into critical positions but are 'handpicked' to suit their self-serving narrative. The United Nations is paid billions of dollars by over 193+ (as of 2023) countries in order to have a voice at the UN. Truth be known, no payment to the United Nations, and that country has **no voice**. The United Nations is preparing itself to control every resource on the planet, all governments, economic systems, World Health (WHO), and the One World Religion with the 17 Goal in Sustainability Program, as mentioned in the last chapter. That would be like resurrecting Hitler but at a much larger scale.

But what would happen to people if they lost their voice in defending their freedoms, liberties, and the power to exercise their right to vote? What would happen to these people if they were robbed of their thoughts and their 'natural' ability to reason? Would this allow these unknown entities to trespass and alter the outcome of your future? Can they gain momentum in changing their perception of reality by creating **new thoughts** without a valid point of reference? To create a new generation that will submit their freedoms and ability to think critically under the guise of a ruling oligarch who promises a utopian society?

> "Paradoxically, as the utopian (idea) metastasizes, and the society ossifies (solidifies), **elections become less relevant**. More and more decisions are made by the masterminds and the experts, who substitute their self-serving and dogmatic judgments—which are proclaimed righteous and compassionate—for the individual's self-interests and best interest."
>
> —Mark R. Levin, *Liberty and Tyranny*

Kent Clizbe, the author of *Willing Accomplices* and a former Central Intelligence Agency (CIA) agent, wrote, "The first steps needed to manipulate the minds of the American people would be to dismantle the very grounds of America, **pollute their** 'thoughts' instead of using subversive propaganda (or arsenal). To implant political correctness into the American ethos with the intent to destroy the moral fabric within America." Implanting Pavlov's experiment is socially constructing triggering words to motivate undisciplined emotions at the sound of a bell, in this case, with the use of emotionally offensive words.

Clizbe believed that covert operatives working within society can help deliver anti-American sentiments by instilling racism, sexism, and intolerance, instilling the Art of Warfare without suspicion.

The Marxist sympathizer can undermine American thoughts, cause emotional instability, and think they are working toward a utopian society that will be governed *by whom*? We have social media and academia glamorizing Marxism, a government that works on a two-class system: the proletariat and the bourgeoisie. In Capitalism, the two-class system is equivalent to the upper class and the lower class, the rich and the poor. But first, the country must do away with the middle class and the farmers. The middle class defies this type of system and will inherently pose resistance. But who are these proletariats?

According to Britannica, the proletariat was (or still is) **the lowest** or one of the lowest economic and social classes in a society. In ancient Rome, it was a class with little opportunity for productive work, but which, at times, **played a political role**. In Marxism, it refers to wage workers whose chief source of income came from the sale of their labor power. Britannica

Or defined as "the class of industrial wage earners who, possessing neither capital nor production means, must earn their living by selling their labor. The poorest class of working people. The **propertyless class** of ancient Rome constituted as the lowest class of citizens. Property gives people leverage and independence." (The American Heritage Dictionary of the English Language, 5th Edition.)

Contrary to what Socialism confers, "no subject will own property." Let's dissect these two definitions: "In Marxism, the proletariat is referred to as a **wage worker** whose chief source of income came from the sale of their labor power." The 'sale of their labor.' Interesting choice of words. Is this the byproduct of the exchange between the seller and the buyer? As in a free enterprise, free market defined as entrepreneurship or as in Capitalism, the citizen can either be an entrepreneur or apply for employment to work under an employer. In either case, the citizen will earn an income, a free choice.

Under the Constitution, **the laborer** can have the opportunity **to purchase** "property," unlike the proletariat. Too often, the word *capitalism* has been used as a form of exploitation by the 1 percent elitist. Still, in Marxism, the proletariat will not have employment choices nor the security of owning property and must depend on daily support from the working class enslaved by the haves and have-nots. This is not Capitalism but another form of imprisonment, a welfare state under the authority of the government.

The welfare system, using the concept of Socialism, appeared to serve under altruistic motives but was **essentially designed** to get people *to* *acclimate* to dependency on the welfare state. It's like a child becoming the ward to the state. Americans with skills and education who are self-employed or employed by others are not dependent on the state for income, and having the freedom to own property will pose a problem for the oligarchs. The welfare state will dictate what the subject will give (Proletariat) and receive. In a Socialist country with her 'subjects' becoming the wards of the state, dependent on 'equal distribution' like a proletariat.

> Repeating the Russian history of the Gulag Archipelago, where the Russian government orchestrated forced labor camps exploiting nearly three million *proletariats* under Soviet rule.
>
> "The Nazis in the early 1920's **closely observed** Soviet concentration camp practices with the intention of emulating them once they came to power."
>
> —Richard Pipes, *Lenin's Gulag*, September 23, 2018.
> Harvard University, Academic Research Journals.

Under Socialism, the "subject" will own no property or capital; you are forced to work under the pretext of the betterment of society. A form of collectivism. A class system with no intrinsic value. We will all collectively work for the betterment of society while owning no property, working, and surviving for the day. There will be *no diversity.* We will all have the same equal outcomes regardless of education, incentives, drive, aptitudes, race, or gender. Your efforts to rise above your station will be **futile.** Reeducate yourself with the class system of India. You are *born into a class* denoted by a dot on your forehead, and there you shall remain, affecting all your future generations. We will become a regressive society destined to repeat the medieval era. In addition to reliving the past in forced labor, we will also be "conditioned" and socially constructed to enter into a collective state of conformity, with or without our consent.

Taking from the haves to give to the have-nots will comply with equal distribution and equal income, **but it will not** begin with the 1 percent; it will start with the taxpayers and the middle class until they are forced out and eliminated. Take from the middle class to give to the have-nots, the poor, then the poor and the middle become one. The bourgeoisie will be the rich landlords. The untouchables. The politicians, the journalists, old money, the film and music industry, and all who partake in the evil scheme to rob us of our inalienable rights given to us by God to live freely. The nihilists will become the new lawmakers and the new superhuman race of gods.

Equality of opportunity is not equivalent to receiving an equal outcome. For someone else to reap what you have not sown is not a fair measure. Don't confuse the poor, the widow, and the severity in disability with those who can physically contribute to their own circumstance.

Furthermore, our American President Abraham Lincoln (also) interpreted this equality of rights as equality of opportunity, *but not* equality of results. He thought the aim was "**to lift artificial weights** from all shoulders—to clear the path of laudable pursuits for all to afford, all an *unfettered* start, and a fair chance, in the race of life."

Equality of opportunity with equal outcome is the thinking of a Marxist.

President Abraham Lincoln did not advocate for entitlements. For another to prosper on the backs of the citizen, is to reap without sowing, a Marxist idealism. We, as Americans, fought against slavery, hence the Civil War. The Truth of equality is for the man to excel on his own **merits** and to reap from the **sweat** of his brow. It is not freely given to any man or woman just because. The same would be true for respect. For respect is 'earned' not demanded or given on a whim. You cannot make a human being respect you if you are undeserving, and poor in character, nor can you expect others to follow you if you are unworthy and unjust. People with depth will see through you, leaving your lie exposed for ridicule. You either lead by example or lead with deceit. The undisciplined and emotionally driven will follow the latter.

Now, the problem lies with human nature.

"People have competing desires, which cause a struggle between classes. Different groups select different leaders as their champions to satisfy their group desires, but people change their minds so quickly about what they want that their leaders soon realize that the only way to remain in power is to crush all opposition. This, becoming Tyrants, and those who aren't tyrants become slaves to the will of the Tyrant."

(The two-party system in politics and within society. As other philosophers have pointed out.)

> "Once the division in society destroys stability, people will submit to the tyrant if only to add some stability. When Freedom destroys order, the yearning for order will destroy Freedom."
>
> —Eric Hoffer

> The idea of a utopian society under the guise of altruism will only achieve enslavement. Capitalism vs Socialism in a nutshell. "There is no difference between Communism and Socialism, except in the means of achieving the same ultimate end: Communism proposes to enslave men by force, Socialism—**by vote**. It is merely the difference between murder and suicide."
>
> —Ayn Rand

"You cannot legislate the poor into freedom 'by legislating the wealthy out of freedom.' What one person receives without working for, 'another person must work without receiving.' The government cannot give anybody anything it does not first take from somebody else. When half the people get the idea that they do not have to work because it does no good to work because somebody else is going to get what they worked for, that, my friend, is about the end of any nation." The welfare state, the proletariat who will work to survive daily with no aspiration toward a future he or she will have no control over.

> "You cannot multiply wealth 'by dividing it.'"
>
> —Dr. Adrian Rogers, 1931

Equal wealth distribution will kill the incentive. The logic is: Why would anyone work hard if they knew they would only get what Socialism would dictate? The new modern-day serf will not be able to manage or change their circumstance should they decide to change their mind. Equal wealth distribution only means precisely what it states: some unknown politicians will decide *your equal distribution* and thus determine **your outcome**. There is no citizenry, but subjecthood, without the freedom to change your circumstance by vote…

CHAPTER 20

"BEHIND THE SCENES" POLITICAL INFLUENCE

Both foreign and domestic political strings have pulled the American government since the United States became a superpower. We had the wealthy barons, the Rockefellers, Carnegie, and the Rothschilds, to name only a few, who schemed against the best interest of the United States and its citizens. Rockefeller wrote in his memoirs, "The few who can understand the system will be either so interested in its profits, or so dependent on its favors, that there will be no opposition from that class, while, on the other hand, the great body of people, **mentally incapable of comprehending** the tremendous advantage that capital derives from the system, will bear its burden without complaint and, perhaps, without even suspecting that the system is **inimical** to their interests."

Inimical: 1. Injurious or harmful in effect; adverse: 2. Unfriendly; hostile. *Inimical.* (n.d.)

American Heritage® Dictionary of the English Language, Fifth Edition. (2011). Retrieved December 28, 2021, from https://www.thefreedictionary.com/inimical

> "The Rothschild brothers, in a letter written from London in 1838 to the Rothschild's New York agents on introducing their banking system to America. For more than a century, ideological extremists at either end of the political spectrum have seized on well-publicized incidents

> such as my encounter with Castro to attack the Rockefeller family for the inordinate influence they claim to wield over America's **political and economic institutions**. Some even believe we are part of a secret cabal working *against* the best interest of the United States, characterizing my family and me as 'Internationalist' and of conspiring with others around the world to build a more integrated *global political and economic structure* – **one world**, if you will. If that's the charge, I stand *guilty*, and I'm proud of it."
>
> —David Rockefeller, from his "Memoirs"

Under this statement with the International (Globalist) versus Nationalist (autonomist, self-directing), which one do you deem as being the worst?

The enemy resides within us using psychological warfare through the *Art of War* tactics. Infiltrate and go unnoticed. We pay taxes and vote for people into office and civil service, but do we? The American public has recently been notified that other countries play a part in our civil service. We have unknown bureaucrats in positions employing subjectivism with no intent to act on our behalf or in the best interest of the people to which they serve. Instead, they create bureaucracy, 'RED TAPE,' inundating us with laws that are too complicated or convoluted for the average American to decipher. So, we concave to their web and accept their laws without opposition—FDA, CDC, the IRS, etc. All of these have been deliberately designed with the intent of exhausting people's time by drowning them in words that only a lawyer can *decipher*. How convenient.

They inject unreasonable laws and then hold us to them. If we were to oppose these unreasonable and *subjective laws*, we would be fined or criminalized. The Credit Bureau has a tremendous amount of power. One late payment and you can be denied credit. The country went through COVID-19, and people lost their jobs, yet the Credit Bureau continued as if nothing happened. Who are these Rothschilds and Rockefellers? Who are these bureaucrats? These billionaires are using their money to manipulate the **outcome** of this country or any other. The Rothschilds profited in the Napoleonic wars. People die, and bankers get rich. "The secret cabal is working against the United States," and those are the words of a World (Global) Banker.

If you are working *against* the United States, then who are you working for? If you are working against the United States, you are working 'against' the American citizen and taxpayer. It can't be just the United States Government since the bureaucrats work within the system. This statement alone makes them guilty of treason! But what is treason to the untouchables and the global elites?

> "We are grateful to the Washington Post, the New York Times, Time magazine, and other great publications whose directors have attended our meetings and respected their promise of **discretion** for almost 40 years ... but the world is more sophisticated and prepared to march towards a world government. The supernatural sovereignty of an intellectual elite and world banker is surely preferable to the national auto-determination practiced in past centuries."
>
> —David Rockefeller

Collaborators? Do you see the parallel effect of what's happening to the country today? Collaborators secretly orchestrate how the American stage will exchange one reality for another. A new reality through social construct designed to serve the globalist. Using rhetoric in systemic racism orchestrated by wealthy world bankers and politicians. They both play the people into the hands of the tyrant. Using the *Art of War* tactics while implementing Cesare Borgia Machiavelli's style of good government.

> "Think of the press as a great keyboard on which the government can play."
>
> —Joseph Goebbels

> "We are on the verge of a global transformation. All we need is the **right major crisis**, and the nation will accept the New World Order."
>
> —David Rockefeller speaking at the UN Business Conference, September 14, 1994

World pandemic, financial collapse, vaccine mandates, no vaccine, no jobs, foreclosures, political party dissonance? Systemic racism? Endless protesting? College indoctrinations with the theory of Marxism? What other crises do these bankers and politicians have in store for us commoners?

Executive Order 13603—National Defense Resources Preparedness

This order will allow the government to control our lives entirely through the "industrial and technological bases" should the President declare a national emergency. This Executive Order (EO) 13603 will give (the resigning President) the power over all commodities and products that are capable of being ingested by human beings and animals; *all forms* of energy; *all forms* of civil transportation; all usable water from all sources; health resources; forces labor such as military conscription; and federal officials can issue regulations to prioritize and allocate resources.

Obama signed this into law on March 16, 2012.

> "We are on the verge of a global transformation. All we need is the **right major crisis**."
>
> —David Rockefeller

To summarize, this executive order states that if the proper crisis occurred, the government would control every human necessity for life and resources, and the human being would be under a draconian subjugation. Will this also apply to our retirement plans, savings, bank accounts, and property? What does it mean to print an excessive amount of money to support Ukraine? Will the dollar lose its value, *and if so*, what will happen to our retirement plans, savings, bank accounts, and property? Will it become worthless and depreciate the value of the dollar? Is this another avenue to force citizens to comply with the welfare state? We would have no choice; how would we self-sustain? The British Red Coats have arrived, and the Constitution is ready to be burned and discarded.

Draconian is defined as a seventh-century Athenian statesman and lawmaker, or his code of laws, which prescribed death for almost every offense. 2. harsh: draconian legislation. *Draconian.* (n.d.) Collins English Dictionary – Complete and Unabridged, 12th Edition 2014. Retrieved December 29, 2021, from https://www.thefreedictionary.com/Draconian

> "We shall have world government whether or not we like it. The only question is whether world government will be achieved by *conquest* **or consent.**"
>
> —Warburg, son of Paul Moritz Warburg

They have won half the battle with our consenting college militants and divisive movements protesting on behalf of identity politics.

"Warburg was an architect and first chairman of the Federal Reserve System and Chairman of the Council on Foreign Relations (CFR), 1921-1932. The Federal Reserves and the CFR are controlled **by members**, not by the United States Government or act on behalf of the taxpayer.

George Clooney and Katie Couric, to name but a few, are part of the controlled members of the cabal. Remember, she made the statement that the MAGA supporters should be "almost deprogrammed." It doesn't matter what side you defend; she advocates for the deprogramming of people, insinuating that *we are the problem.* We are progressing toward an Orwellian nightmare reserved for the many *and not for the few.* https://en.wikipedia.org/wiki/Members_of_the_Council_on_Foreign_Relations

> "If the Council on Foreign Relations (CFR) raises the hackles of the Conspiracy theorist, the Bilderberg meetings must induce apocalyptic visions of omnipotent international bankers plotting with unscrupulous

> government officials to **impose cunning schemes** on an ignorant and unsuspecting world."
>
> —David Rockefeller https://www.cfr.org/membership/corporate-members https://www.cfr.org/backgrounder/american-presidents-council-foreign-relations

Hackles are defined as the long hairs that, when erected, form a crest along the neck and back of a dog.

> "[The New World Order] cannot happen without US participation, as we are the most significant single component. Yes, there will be a New World Order, and it will **force** the United States to change its perception."
>
> —Henry Kissinger, World Affairs Council Press Conference, Regent Beverly Wilshire Hotel, April 19, 1994

Henry Kissinger, former United States Secretary of State, a position once held by Hillary Clinton responsible for the 2012 Benghazi incident where four Americans died, told the White House Committee, "What difference does it make?" Their qualifications and moral obligations as Secretary of State are indeed questionable.

We should take a moment to understand some of the duties required by a Secretary of State. The United States Secretary of State's job is described as follows:

"Under the Constitution, the President of the United States determines US foreign policy. The Secretary of State, appointed by the President with the advice and consent of the Senate, is the President's chief foreign affairs adviser. The Secretary carries out the President's foreign policies through the State Department and the United States Foreign Service. This position was first created in 1789 by Congress as the successor to the Department of Foreign Affairs; the Department of State is the senior executive Department of the US Government.

The Secretary of State is also responsible for ensuring the protection of the US Government, the American citizens, property, and interests in foreign countries; supervises the administration of US immigration laws abroad; provides information to American citizens regarding the political, economic, social, cultural, and humanitarian conditions in foreign countries; informs the Congress and American citizens on the conduct of US foreign relations; promotes beneficial economic intercourse between the United States and other countries; administers the Department of State; supervises the Foreign Service of the United States.

In addition, the Secretary of State also serves as the channel of communication between the Federal Government and the States on the extradition of fugitives to or from foreign countries." https://www.state.gov/secretary/115194.htm

Henry Kissinger was the United States' former Secretary of State. Was he not quoted saying, "[The New World Order] cannot happen without US participation, as we are the most significant single component? Yes, there will be a New World Order, and it will force the United States to change its perception."

Is this treason? An appointed civil servant is also a member of the CFR working against the best interest of the United States. Conspiring with foreign interests and global dignitaries, paid for by the American taxpayer. This is not a theory to conspire; this is an act of treason.

> "The 'New World Order' will have to be built from the bottom up rather than from the top down ... but an *end run* on **national sovereignty**, *eroding* it piece by piece, will accomplish much more than the **old-fashioned frontal assault**."
>
> —Richard Garner-Council on Foreign Relations Journal, April 1974, page 558

The "end run on national sovereignty" anti-American sentiments parallel with the demonization of American Nationalism, which makes perfect sense. We should personally thank each and every American athlete playing in the NFL and the NBA, as well as the American players who represented the US in the World Olympics, for treason—refusing to stand up and respect the Flag. The owners and the players who actively participated in their 'full frontal attack' against the playing of the "National Anthem" exposed their lack of respect for the country and its citizens, who contributed to their fame and fortune. Richard Garner's speech, 'Eroding our National Sovereignty piece by piece, can be accomplished more effectively than the full-frontal assault,' set the stage for what would occur. I wonder where Kaepernick and Mark Cuban got this idea from. An institution using the 'American sports arena' as a political leverage to "Erode the country piece by piece." Are these taxpaying fans expected to support players who are paid millions of dollars, making them part of the 1 percent, while **enforcing their views** on social morality and planting divisiveness among its citizens?

The process of creating more incivility will not cultivate a productive change. The full-frontal assault will create MORE animosity, more divisiveness, and more social deconstruction. To give the National Anthem its defense, it is a moment in time when people can stop and remember to be **grateful** for all the *sacrifices made by the many* so that we can reap the benefits as a whole. It is a brief moment in time where socioeconomics, education, race, and gender do not separate us as a free people. Freedom is a gift, bought at a price and yet lightly discarded. Thousands have lost their lives so that we can be free, and the National Anthem has been robbed and disgraced.

"The Star-Spangled Banner" became our National Anthem on March 3, 1931. When our nation recognized it as our official Anthem, the future generations of America were called with heart and lips to affirm that government and faith were allies in regard to the praise that is due to the providential "Pow'r that hath made and preserved us a nation!"

We have allowed the acting gatekeepers to skulk about and use tactics to hypnotize the masses at every waking moment. Whose whole intent is to convince us to accept the lie. I lament how many young Americans fail to see the ever-growing deceit. A veil has been purposely draped over their eyes. We have our soldiers fighting wars abroad, fighting for democracy for others. Yet, it is **us who are in dire need** of our American military. To protect the Republic from global entities with invested interest by both *domestic and foreign* bodies who wish us harm. We live among the traitors, the wolves, and ever present-day Benedict Arnold's pretending to love us but, in reality, loathe us. We keep our patriot protectors abroad. We have the global elitists and terrorists right here on American ground, in our front yards, whose greed and psychopathic tendencies have nothing to do with unity, diversity, or social justice. These Bankers and billionaires have one thing in mind and one thing in common: our demise.

The fact is the world cannot have two superpowers.

One must go for the other to reign.

Progressive thought in eroding national sovereignty, calling the national anthem racial, outdated, divisive, and having **outlived** its purpose. Most free-loving people in multiple countries play their national anthem with pride and sing as a reminder of their love for their country, except for the anti-American.

The flag and the anthem help connect them as a people, and for a brief moment, they have no differences.

It reminds us of our humanity, regardless of race or gender. Remember our fallen soldiers and their sacrifices to keep our country the land of the free and home of the brave. Maybe Mark Cuban, a billionaire, can interfere with the nationalism of other countries and share his **contempt** with them. Perhaps they, too, can rethink whether their national anthem is dead, outdated, and divisive. The global conglomerates have found multiple ploys and distractions to disrupt the American ethos by forming new words through neologism and doublespeak. To change the root meaning and redefine words in their attempt to alter reality and American history to serve a progressive end. They are playing identity politics with their fan base, eroding the country piece by piece by exploiting those most vulnerable and easily persuaded. The global elites use the community's predictable patterns to trigger an emotional response. Pick an identity group, speak a few "trigger" words, and then predict an emotional response. Easily said and quickly done.

> "In the beginning, the organizer's **first job is to create** the issue or problems."
>
> —Saul Alinsky, *Rules for Radicals: A Pragmatic Primer for Realistic Radicals*

> "If people don't think they have the power to solve their problems, they won't even think about how to solve them."
>
> —Saul Alinsky, *Rules for Radicals: A Pragmatic Primer for Realistic Radicals*

To be in the position to manipulate reality is a human travesty. More and more American traditions are being presented as **toxic pollutants**, while the Marxist theory of government is enticing and appeases the social justice narrative without contemplating the end result. The theory of Marxism sets the stage for the *final solution* to end all societal problems initially set by those who wish us ill. Sports organizations receive their wealth from their American fans while exploiting the very people who provided their wealth and fame through capitalism—complying with the term 'Full-Frontal Attack.' They are using Americans as militants against one another like a playbook while hiding their true intentions. Remember, highly paid coaches are experts in building defenses and offenses between two groups or teams.

> "For those who care to see and for those who *dare to see*."
>
> —Kent Clizbe, *Willing Accomplices*

> "The NFL should eliminate playing the national anthem before games. A major theme in the movement for change in the United States for unity. In order for the NFL to remain in step, it is time to end what has become a 'divisive tradition.'"
>
> —https://touchdownwire.usatoday.com/2020/06/08/nfl-national-anthem-colin-kaepernick-george-floyd-peaceful-protest/

Use a few trigger words, and the statement becomes a relative truth. "To end this divisive tradition" and then fill in the gaps with collective speech to help promote **a new collective conformity**, but based on what? These players and the NFL billionaires will not share in the 'haves and have-nots' in equal distribution. They are just a vessel, a tactic, a route in promoting Socialism by vote and then Communism **by force**. On the other hand, they will not participate in this social government conformity. If the NFL coach changed his playbook tactics and had his team players oppose each other, would he achieve in building a winning team? If so, would there be a need to play against the opposing team? The whole narrative would be self-defeating. Americans against Americans, and in the end, who will be left standing?

With this new suggested step towards progressive playbook tactics, turning on each other instead of playing cohesively as a team, the same outcome can be achieved, or they will likely fail and lose every game.

> "We must reject the idea that every time a law is broken, **society is guilty** rather than the *lawbreaker*. It is time to restore the American precept that each individual is accountable for his [or her] actions."
>
> —President Ronald Reagan

What other systemic frontal assaults are being injected? Unrelenting rhetoric on all social platforms without rest. We are perpetually reminded of systemic racism, toxic masculinity, feminine oppression, anti-*God* rhetoric, anti-sovereignty, speech censorship, hate speech, and hate crime. Yet, we expect to somehow find **divine unity**. It will somehow repair itself once every identity group reaches equality, equal distribution, and equal outcomes, whether you are the one to sow (*work*) or reap what you didn't sow (Welfare state).

In other words, it's the anti-Americans who are seeking to destroy the country to rebuild by protesting for tolerance while being violently *intolerant*, orchestrating a civil war that will ultimately lead to America's demise. If we were to fall into a civil revolution, the government would gladly take over and usher in martial law and arrest anyone non-compliant. The perfect crisis. According to Saul Alinsky repeated again and again:

> "The organizer's first job is to create the issues or problems and the organization must be based **on many (unrelenting) issues**."
>
> —Saul Alinsky, *Rules for Radicals: A Pragmatic Primer for Realistic Radicals*

Multi-tasking the social narrative and exhausting the mind. Attacking every facet of traditional respects in conservatism ultimately creates a nihilistic form of postmodern progressivism—an ideological belief system.

The Marxist replacement theology goes against capitalism and the nuclear family and, in a nihilistic society, replaces God. A man or woman without a country will have no place to lay their head. If you have no country, you will have no ownership and no guarantee of your survival. The theory of Socialism is to become dependent on the unknown.

> "The organizer **must first rub raw the resentments** of the people of the community **and fan the latent hostilities of many of the people to the point of overt expression.**"
>
> —Saul Alinsky, *Rules for Radicals: A Pragmatic Primer for Realistic Radicals*

Identity politics are turning into tribal groups whose sole purpose is to cause civil unrest, destroy private property, and attack the unprovoked with actions that define fascism. We have a constitutional right to protest; what we don't have is the right to destroy and intimidate with violence to force others to accept the nihilistic idealisms.

> "He must **search out controversy** and issues, rather than avoid them, for unless there (is) controversy, people are not concerned enough to act … **An organizer must stir up dissatisfaction and discontent.**"
>
> —Saul Alinsky, *Rules for Radicals: A Pragmatic Primer for Realistic Radicals*

What other undermining schemes are being orchestrated behind the Iron Curtain and on college campuses?

> "Clearly, I consider the Trump Administration a danger to the world, but I regard it as a 'purely temporary phenomenon' **that will disappear** in 2020 or even sooner. I give President Trump credit for motivating his core supporters brilliantly, but for every core supporter he has created, a greater number of core opponents **are equally strongly motivated.** That's why I expect a *Democratic landslide* in 2018."
>
> —George Soros, *Bloomberg*

There is no "suggestive" allegation of election tampering; he is just expecting a *Democratic landslide.* This idea is left only for the conspiracy theorist, spoken by a man who sent an untold amount of people to their deaths as a Nazi sympathizer and collaborator at the age of 14. George Soros spoke with such conviction and certainty you would have thought he was controlling the ballots. Having been given the same conclusion, the Supreme Court refused to hear any litigations brought to them by the individual states, the Republic, who found voter discrepancies. It doesn't matter what political side you defend; voter fraud is manipulation; either way, he is stating that your voice wouldn't have mattered.

> "It's not the people who vote that count. It's the people who **count** the votes."
>
> —Joseph Stalin

Will we ever have a fair election? Will money, power, AI, and technology have an unfair advantage accompanying those who design and program the voting machine? Of course not. That could never happen, and if it did, how would we know?

CHAPTER 21

THE MAKING OF INTERNATIONAL LAW

Romania has a very interesting history. I read a book by Nadia Comaneci called *Letters to a Young Gymnast.* In it, she tells us about her experience representing her country during the Olympics, including her trials and difficulties and her defection from Romania. She was the most beloved child star in the entire world, especially in her country. When she defected, the country was outraged. Nicolae Ceausescu was later assassinated, along with his wife for crimes against humanity.

Nicolae Ceausescu was the country's general secretary of the Romanian Communist Party. His regime lasted from 1965 to 1989, and he *suspiciously* won every election for 24 years, even as the Romanians suffered under the brutal hands of a dictator. His form of the Hitlerian gestapo and KGB secret police kept strict control over free speech and the media and tolerated no **internal opposition**. "Ceausescu and his wife Elena were executed after a revolt where Ceausescu ordered his security forces to open fire on the demonstrators in the city of Timișoara on December 17, 1989. Under the military tribunal, both were found guilty of crimes against the State. They were charged and convicted of genocide and undermining the national economy."

He was the last Communist leader to rule Romania 35 years ago. Nevertheless, this dictatorship ended not long ago. (BBC News. *1989: Romania's 'First Couple' Executed.* Britannica, T. Editors of Encyclopaedia (2023, August 16). *Nicolae Ceaușescu.* Encyclopedia Britannica. https://

www.britannica.com/biography/Nicolae-Ceausescu http://news.bbc.co.uk/onthisday/hi/dates/stories/december/25/newsid_2542000/2542623.stm).

Nicolae Ceausescu deprived the country of electricity for over two years, and food was scarce. He exported much of the agricultural and industrial production, leaving the country starving. He bulldozed thousands of Romanian villages to create an agrotechnical center for the government to control food production through Genetically Modified Organisms (GMOs). Today, we have Bill Gates tampering with food production by introducing synthetic meat and the Biden Administration paying the farmers not to farm in support of climate change. We suffer through a pandemic, high inflation, mandates, speech censorship, and demands for more gun control. Try processing these recent events for the long term. What seems convoluted and incomprehensible right out of a Communist playbook.

Britannica, T. Editors of Encyclopaedia (2023, August 16). *Nicolae Ceaușescu.* Encyclopedia Britannica. https://www.britannica.com/biography/Nicolae-Ceausescu

Grain. *La Via Campesina.* 8 Apr 2015. *Seed Laws That Criminalize Farmers: Resistance and Fightback.* https://grain.org/article/entries/5142-seed-laws-that-criminalise-farmers-resistance-and-fightback

Where there is power and greed, the psychopaths will soon follow, gathering around like a swarm of vultures at a roadkill. They did it at the beginning of the New World, and they will repeat it with their ill intent for the New World Order. At least for now, you can choose whether to work for any capitalist *or not* or become self-employed as an entrepreneur. No one is forcing you to comply. But in Socialism, you either work or you perish. You will have no property to sell or savings to reap. Failure to comply with this quasi-utopian society will undoubtedly lead to certain death for those who refuse to comply. Re-read history, refresh your memory, and pray for discernment.

Could this be the future for America? Some might argue that voter fraud is a statistical improbability equal to the improbability that people are generally attracted to oppression.

Discernment is "the act or process of exhibiting keen insight and good judgment," which implies discipline in following the truth. (The American Heritage Dictionary of the English Language, 5th Edition).

In my travels through life, I was fortunate to meet a well-educated and refined medical doctor who migrated from Romania, where both her parents were college professors. They tutored for income and exchanged education for meat, eggs, and bread. Her story was captivating yet alarming at the same time, knowing that my country was eerily following in the same footsteps. Returning back to the topic of American traditionalism and the American sports arena, I will warn you, though, that I frequently divert into tangents simply for the reason that my mind wonders how interconnected the functionality of social construct is, slipping the nation into new conformity unrecognizable with subtle realization. If I am bombarding you with multiple variables in discerning the deconstructing of the American ethos, now you can understand what Saul Alinsky tried to state when he said that an organizer "must stir up dissatisfaction and discontent through controversy while *continuously stirring* the ambers of discontent," meaning one must stir up **multiple variables** all at once, to the point of confusion. The National Anthem and the American Flag represent something whole, not something designed to fragment America or its people.

- I pledge (my) Allegiance to the Flag of the United States of America
- To the Republic for which it stands
- One Nation under God
- Indivisible (*not divided*!)
- With liberty
- Justice
- For all = (not for some, *but for all*)

Nowhere in the Pledge of the American Allegiance does it state, I pledge my Allegiance to multiple nations, within divided groups, with no liberty and justice **for none**. If you do not pledge Allegiance to your country, then where and to whom will you pledge your Allegiance to?

Ponder on the thought of forfeiting your citizenship and electing instead to be a subject under an unknown Socialist government. Let's look at this former president whose statement goes against our consent. We had a president who swore under oath to serve and protect the Constitution and to serve the American citizens *in their* best interest.

> "It is the sacred principles enshrined in the United Nations charter to which the American people will henceforth **pledge** their *Allegiance*."
>
> President George H. W. Bush addressing the General Assembly of the UN, February 1, 1992

George W. Bush pledged his and the entire country's Allegiance to the United Nations without the people's consent. The UN Charter under international laws will make the American citizens the subjects under the UN oligarch. The UN recently erected a statue in their honor, which was forcefully taken down after much dispute for it resembled *the beast* yet to come prophesied in Daniel 7:1–8, BSB, and the Apostle John who also gave his account of the same **beast** in Revelation 13:2, "And the beast which I saw was like unto a leopard, and his feet were as the feet of a bear, and his mouth as the mouth of a lion."

> "These prophetic visions closely mirror the UN's new statue. The patterning on the new monument could undoubtedly be what Apostle John meant when describing the beast as similar to a leopard. Further, the right front paw of the beast looks immensely large, befitting that of a bear claw."
>
> —John Di Lemme, CBJ REAL NEWS, December 30, 2021 https://www.conservativebusinessjournal.com/2021/12/un-erects-statue-of-end-times-beast/

We have Americans protesting against kneeling at the National Anthem, but will they turn their attention to kneeling for the UN? Will Americans forfeit their sovereignty and freedom to pledge Allegiance to a foreign entity and thus become global subjects? What has a foreign entity contributed to American idealism? To submit freely to 'unknown' politicians, who are self-appointed into positions rather than by vote. Will Americans chance their future and forfeit their freedom and faith in submitting to a foreign self-interest group? The UN Charter makes the American citizen a "subject under international law once the States become borderless."

Do you see the parallels?

> "[In] 1945, Truman signs the United Nations Charter; President Harry S. Truman signs the United Nations Charter, and the United States becomes *the first nation* to complete the ratification process and joins the new international organization."
>
> —https://www.history.com/this-day-in-history/truman-signs-united-nations-charter

How does International Law under the UN Charter affect the United States?

> "The body of law that governs the legal relations between *or among states* or nations. **To qualify** as a 'subject' under the traditional definition of international law, a state had to be sovereign: It needed a territory, a population, a government, and the ability to engage in diplomatic or foreign relations." **Individual states do not qualify**, but if the States become *open borders*, the State will no longer exist and thus become sovereign, falling under international law. Open borders now raise the question of whether mass immigration into the United States was based on altruistic motives *or if having open borders* **qualifies** the states to fall under international law.
>
> —https://legal-dictionary.thefreedictionary.com/international+law

According to Cornell Law School, the Subjects of International Law are defined as follows: "Traditionally, individual countries were the main subjects of international law. Increasingly, individuals and non-state international organizations have also become 'subject' to international regulation."

> Notice that the American Constitution, Bill of Rights, and the Declaration of Independence *are not mentioned.* Becoming a 'subject' to international regulations is not citizenship. Defining subjecthood entails its ramifications in being governed by foreign bodies. The United States and International Law Dictates: "The United States typically respects the laws of other nations unless there is some statute or treaty to the contrary. International law is typically a part of US law only for the application of its principles on questions of international rights and duties. International law, however, does not restrict the United States or any other nation from making laws governing its own territory. A State of the United States is not a 'state' under international law since the Constitution does not vest the 50 states with the capacity to conduct their own foreign relations." Unless the states become ... **borderless.**
>
> —Cornell Law School, Legal Information Institute: https://www.law.cornell.edu/wex/international_law

This brings the question of George Soros's true intent with his Open Borders Foundation newly renamed Open Society Foundation.

Let's read that again!

> "States within the United States, provinces, and cantons "**were not considered subjects**" by international law, because they lacked the *legal authority* to engage in foreign relations. In addition, individuals did not fall within the definition of subjects that enjoyed rights and obligations under international law. Enjoy what rights and obligations? What does the American citizen have to gain in becoming a 'subject' under international law."

Give the United Nations more money, assets, and property, forfeit our citizenship, and submit to subjecthood. Attempting to make our country borderless is deliberate under the auspices of altruism. A country with no borders will make the states fall under the rule of international law. No citizenship and no rights.

> "No society can withstand the unconditional mass migration of aliens from *every corner of the earth*. The preservation of the nation's territorial sovereignty and the culture, language, mores, tradition, and customs that make possible a harmonious community of citizens dictates that citizenship be granted only by the consent of the governed – not by the unilateral actions or 'demands' of the alien and then only to aliens who will throw off their Allegiance to their former nation and society and pledge Allegiance to America."
>
> —Mark Levin, *Immigration the Conservative Manifesto: An Excerpt from Liberty and Tyranny Conservative Manifesto*

International law and open borders, and we have CNN reporting that American citizens will be required to obtain a Real ID license to travel from State to State. Imagine that. Crossing the border **unrestricted** is more accessible than traveling to your neighboring State.

"Think your driver's license is enough to get you through US airport security and onto your domestic flight? On October 1, 2020, travelers will need a 'REAL ID-compliant' driver's license, US passport, US military I.D. or other accepted identification 'to fly within the United States.' The REAL ID Act established minimum security standards for issuing state licenses and their production. This restriction includes boarding federally regulated commercial aircraft, entering nuclear power plants, and entering federal facilities."

If we were to include the vaccine mandate and vaccine passport additionally to be required to fly on a commercial aircraft, eat at restaurants, receive medical care, and hold a job while the Federal government leaves the borders unsecured, imposing no Real ID Act requirement, no identification needed to vote, no proof of citizenship, no background checks on prior arrests, no connections to terrorism, human trafficking, drug cartel, or vaccine passport required for the illegal migrant. In contrast, the American government has armed the IRS agents to enforce compliance by the citizens to pay their taxes and to support mass immigration, which is incomprehensible.

According to the US Department of Homeland Security, to obtain a REAL-ID driver's license, the applicant must provide documentation showing their full legal name, date of birth, Social Security Number, two proofs of address of principal residence, and lawful status. In some cases, individual States may implement and enforce more requirements as needed. Leaving American borders unsecured jeopardizes the safety and security of minors and unaccompanied children. These children are crossing the border without documentation or accountability by an adult. Human traffickers are using the American borders to cross these children to be sold without defense. Is this considered a **humanity mission** to support refugees and allow undocumented people into the country on altruistic motives based on compassion without concern for the welfare and safety of the children? Are Americans now left with the responsibilities for the seven million people who have crossed the border since the Biden administration took office?

By creating a 'borderless' entry, Homeland Security will justify limiting citizens' liberties and freedoms **to add more** security measures. They first create the problem and then demand we comply. Canadians protect their borders from illegal entry of guns and insects to protect their agriculture, animals, federal convictions, drug possessions, human trafficking, and people trying to enter the country without a work permit. But the United States is allowing entry into the country, bypassing our trained Border Patrol (ICE) surveillance and Homeland Security immigration laws without recourse.

Let's define the responsibilities of ICE:

> "US Immigration and Customs Enforcement (ICE) is a federal law enforcement agency under the US Department of Homeland Security. ICE's stated mission is to protect the United States from **cross-border crime and illegal immigration** that threaten national security and public safety."
>
> —*Wikipedia*

If the states accept open borders, and the individual countries in Europe accept open borders, then the world would fall under international law. The European Union (EU) plans to implement a European militarized army to eliminate the military from individual countries. If the states submit to this Open Borders directive, the Republic and the separate state *will no longer exist.* The Republic will be broken and along with it the Constitution that was designed and written **to protect the Republic**. The former existence of the individual states that form the **United** *States* will cease to exist, and the United Nations will govern the country under the guise of the UN Charter.

Since the international law will relinquish the powers of the Republic and the individual 'States' with no borders can now be considered part of a sovereign nation, with its territory, (it) has a population, a government, and the ability to engage in diplomatic *or foreign relations* through the Secretary of State, making the United States a subject to be controlled by the oligarchs. Those who died in the Revolutionary War are rolling in their graves just about now saying, "**I died for this**?"

The UN Charter and international law cannot be enforced now because the United States still has sovereignty. The Federal government is imposing its jurisdiction on the states to comply with Federal initiatives, immigration laws, and voting interference. The FBI, CIA, Homeland Security, House of Representatives, and politicians are not following immigration laws. I wonder why? The Federal Government is pushing the narrative to allow non-citizens to vote in the presidential election under the pretense of racism. A law implemented by bureaucrats and fiefdoms. More immigration, more controlled people. Votes can make or break a country. Take this, for instance, a Chicago Commissioner Richard Boykin in 2017 calling for the UN Peacekeepers *to intervene* in the American domestic problems they first created. Do we not have our own military and National Guard to intervene should we need them?

As outlined in *The Oath of Allegiance for Enlisted Personnel*, "I_______ do solemnly swear (or affirm) that **I will support and defend** the Constitution of the United States against all enemies, foreign or domestic; that I will bear true faith and allegiance to the same."

Their obligations to protect our borders protect our financial sustainability, security, and sovereignty.

Yes, we have the Marines, the Navy Seals, the Army Special Forces, the Green Berets, and the Pararescue men, but will the UN exclude the United States Armed Forces and call in the United Nations Peacekeepers? It's interesting how we keep our men and women abroad instead of deploying them *here* to defend citizens against domestic violence, out-of-control borders, and lawbreaking politicians in office and to restore order. Chicago County Commissioner calls for UN Peacekeepers to help with Chi-Town gun violence. Boykin to ask UN for help fighting Chicago violence.

Why would he recommend the UN Peacekeepers to have any jurisdiction on American soil? Why would he initiate 'the thought' to allow foreign bodies to interfere with **domestic policing**? American taxpayers pay for homeland security, the military and police/SWAT Teams, the CIA, and the FBI, and he feels we should implement the United Nations Peacekeepers for outside intervention while we send our very best abroad.

Slowly but surely, foreign politics will be invited to interfere with state matters.

I wonder, now more than ever, if the **chief proponent** in inciting riots, burning down communities in protest, blocking traffic, and pillaging/looting establishments is all about 'stirring the embers of discontent' and whether it was planted by domestic and foreign enemies who are setting the stage for foreign infiltration. We may be at war *and not even know it.* I suppose looting, burning, and attacking Americans with violent force while inciting enough fear to silence speech and enforce stricter gun laws will make everything so much better. The globalists are watching Americans intently, planting as many **obstacles** to disorient, waiting for the right opportunity for that '*perfect*' crisis to arise so they can set their plan into action.

> "Never let a good **crisis** go to waste."
>
> —*Saul Alinsky*, a Socialist sympathizer

> "The UN Charter and the United Nations as an organization were established on October 26, 1945. The UN Charter is a multilateral treaty that serves as the organization's Constitution. The UN Charter contains a **supremacy clause that makes it the highest authority**

> of international law. The clause states that the UN Charter shall prevail in the event of a conflict between the obligations of the members of the United Nations under the present charter and their obligations under any other international agreement."
>
> —*https://legal-dictionary.thefreedictionary.com/UN+Charter+and+United+Nations*

> Subject defined, "One that is placed *under authority* or control such as one subject to a **monarch** and governed by the monarch's law (2) One who lives in the territory of enjoys the protection of, **and owes Allegiance to a sovereign power or State**."
>
> —*https://www.merriam-webster.com/dictionary/subject*

In his book *Global Financial Apocalypse Prophesied*, Wilfred J. Hahn wrote, "You cannot have two superpowers. You **cannot pledge** your Allegiance to two separate governments. You will love the one and hate the other,' as Christ poignantly instructed us." They pull our strings and watch us dance.

CHAPTER 22

UNDERMINING THE AMERICAN BY WAY OF EUGENICS

> "Every wise woman builds her house, but a foolish one tears it down with her own hands."
>
> —Proverbs 14:1, BSB

Eugenics and ethnic cleansing are more similar than one might believe. One is committed without knowledge, and the other is *purposeful.* Both have affected tens of millions of people in America and throughout the world for centuries. It's the process in which people in affluential positions decide who will live and who will die by convincing those who can be easily swayed. There are too many cultural societies that are guilty of murdering people and the unborn to discuss in one chapter. Still, we can speak of a few associated with the theory of collectivism.

Let's begin by defining infanticide (or *infant* **homicide**) as "the **intentional** killing of infants or offspring" (*Wikipedia, Infanticide*).

> "Infanticide was a **widespread practice** *throughout human history* to **dispose** of unwanted children to prevent resources from being spent on the weak or disabled (the *undesirables*). At the same time, others suffered cruel, barbaric acts in newborn sacrifice. Unwanted infants were abandoned to die by environmental exposure (heat) or thrown over cliffs, while in other societies like China,

> with the one-child act, they murdered their daughters. Infanticide was practiced in Ancient Greece, Rome, Native Indians, China, and the Aztecs, to name just a few. The purpose of infanticide (infant homicide) was to dispose of people unfit and unwanted. While infanticide is the intentional killing of infants, homicide is defined as the killing of one person by another, regardless of intention *or legality*."
>
> —The American Heritage Dictionary of the English Language, 5th Edition

Understanding the context of infanticide and homicide, what social construct deemed it just to end a life? Who dictates what is ethically right and what is morally wrong? Do we depend on our "own" understanding or blindly follow manufactured laws to tell us what is morally and ethically right? Do we cherry-pick for convenience who life is worthy and who is deserving of death?

> "Trust in the Lord with all your heart. Do not lean on *your own* understanding."
>
> —Proverbs 3:5, BSB

A film documentary called *The History of Eugenics in America* discusses a dark period when medical professionals and institutions performed unconsented sterilization and castrations on children and people with disabilities—approved by a State Eugenics Board, social workers, psychologists, medical personnel, and the *Supreme Court*. In the 1900s, people like the English Barons exploited the less fortunate through **unregulated** capitalism, keeping the people within a two-class system; these "Barons" like the Carnegie Institute of Washington, Rockefeller Foundation, Harriman Foundation, Kellogg Foundation, who had paid millions of dollars for research, basically to prove that **social problems** were essentially the results of *defective genes*, following the science of Darwinism—that the weakest links need to die off for the survival of the fittest, based on the Charles Darwin theory of natural selection.

These evil and immoral people took matters into their own hands and committed atrocities against innocent children and babies. In England, the Barons, the aristocracy, refused to aid the less fortunate, stating it would **enable** them to become dependent only to reproduce more undesirable children, allowing poverty, disease, and economic hardship to progress in aiding the natural process in the weaker population **to produce fewer children through eugenics**.

The Darwin solution, similar to the Third Reich's final solution used on the Jews, incorporates several quick solutions; I will list a few.

1. Sterilization
2. Restricting marriage laws and customs
3. Systems in mating
4. General environmental betterment
5. Polygamy (by today's standards, unwed mothers with multiple children by multiple men would be controlled by the State)
6. Euthanasia (where babies were left abandoned if it was suspected the child was born with a genetic defect)
7. Neo-Malthusianism (which means that population growth is dependent on economic growth)

Economic growth would need to be kept in check, limiting resources such as food, energy, or water. For some, this would mean starvation, while others would have the means for food.

The documentary emphasized what *America* did, with less **emphasis** on those individuals responsible for the deaths of millions of people. Propaganda quickly places the blame on "America." These aristocrats created a social construct to *displace the blame* created through the concept of a collective crime, acquitting the **source** of guilt. This proposition puts less blame on the culprits by exonerating themselves and redirecting the atrocities committed as a collective crime, which lessens the offense committed by the root cause.

People like Jack London, Alexander Graham Bell, Theodore Roosevelt, Henry Ford, and Margaret Sanger (a birth control activist). The guilt mentioned above would later need to acquiesce to the Supreme Court decision, stating that sterilization and castration were **unconstitutional**. This practice was left unchecked until 1985. No one since then has been accused of crimes against humanity, and the case was never brought to court as a criminal case, where the rich permanently caused bodily harm. Instead, the truth was swept under the rug and not spoken of. But did these tyrants disappear or **lay dormant** instead? They acted like a virulent pathogen waiting for a weakness in the social body to resurface. Busy minds never sleep.

> "Woe to those who plan **iniquity**, to those who plot **evil** on their beds! At morning's light, they carry it out because it is *in their power to do it*."
>
> —Micah 2:1, NIV

The best method to integrate a tyrant's idealisms is to plant the seeds of a social construct, presenting it as 'tolerance', altruism, and **personal rights**. It's like child's play. When you're told not to do something, you want it even more, even if you don't understand why. It's human nature—people generally do not like being told what to do. The State (*globalist*) wants women out of the house; this allows the State to raise the children and create a society "they" deem fit. So, what ploy can be introduced? Vanity. Apply neologisms and doublespeak to make the words "domestic housewife" appear demeaning and insulting. Say it often enough, and the lie becomes true. Inject feminism, oppression, and unequal pay, and **distract** them with euphemisms, and eugenics will follow. Jack London, Alexander Graham Bell, Theodore Roosevelt, Henry Ford, and Margaret Sanger will not need to interfere; you will murder your "own" undesirables and castrate your children. The globalists are brilliant! Now we have sexual dysphoria, where boys and girls have been convinced they were born in the wrong body and thus should self-mutilate with the aid of *professionals* such as those approved by a State Eugenics Board, social workers, psychologists, medical personnel, and the Supreme Court. Hormone therapy *could* solidify eugenics and *permanently* damage a child's chemistry, never to have the choice to conceive.

Hitler murdered over 60 million people; Stalin and Pol Pot did the same. Likewise, American feminists have managed to murder over 78 million unborn children through abortions. There is no need for secrecy to enforce eugenics or through the supposed "well check-ups," with the unbeknownst patient leaving the clinic sterilized. Convince the progressive woman that it's all about her body and convenience while exploiting her body and complying with the narrative the global elites have set in place.

The fetus begins with a heartbeat at five to six weeks and **can feel *pain*** as early as the first trimester (<14 weeks gestation) according to the National Institute for Health (NIH). Thill B. (2022). Fetal Pain in the First Trimester. The Linacre quarterly, 89(1), 73–100. https://doi.org/10.1177/00243639211059245. Planned Parenthood is a billion-dollar corporation. Planned Parenthood spent $45 million to get this current administration elected. According to Human Life International, in 2023: "Planned Parenthood's latest Annual Report (2018–2019) discloses its total revenue was $1,638,600,000. Of that amount, government health services reimbursements and grants accounted for over $616 million. Non-government health services revenue totaled nearly $370 million. And private contributions were nearly $600 million." Yet this organization advocated for more federal funding. Women have become a **factory-style assembly line** for money, defined as exploitation.

Also called **unregulated capitalism**: money to be made by the Barons through eugenics. Regardless of people's pocket-size worldview and what you defend, there is truth to be met. You can't help but criticize and wonder if Planned Parenthood is another ruse to implement eugenics using women like a factory-style assembly line for profit and convincing women to dispose of unwanted future people. The globalists will have no need to deceive to enforce sterilization or castration; we have sexual dysphoria imposed on our children and abortion at our fingertips. We cannot ignore that some worship the theology of Darwinians, evolution, and the survival of the fittest and the natural course to continue the human species—instead, we are deliberately performing elective surgeries with the potential for adverse side effects and health complications, through abortions, such as blood clots, perforated uterus, permanent infertility, postpartum depression, suicides, and death. No one talks about the pain and guilt that most women feel. There is no follow-up plan for what happens to the woman once she leaves the clinic. There is no statistical data to document physical complications, mental health associated with depression, or suicidal ideations.

Suppose these eugenic progressives feel that the deaths of 78 million

Americans through abortions were not enough. In that case, they will convince the rest to mutilate their children with gender-affirming surgeries and hormone therapy. There is not enough data to conclude that these practices will not somehow damage the mind, body, and spirit of future generations, crippling them mentally. We are sterilizing our children and rendering them infertile. Side effects in hormone therapy and castration cause infertility. Any parent who has condoned this procedure on their children is unfit to parent.

Gender-affirming hormone therapy uses puberty blockers to stop the normal hormonal development in young boys and girls. Medicine in a secular sense is interfering with the natural order of science and evolution through naturalism, supported by Darwinism. The question that should be asked is whether our children are being used for experimentation and for research paid out by these wealthy Barons, conspiring with the likes of Josef Mengele, the infamous Nazi surgeon who inhumanely tortured people for the sake of science. How exactly do puberty blockers work on these young adolescents' minds or children incapable of making **lifelong** impactful decisions?

Incredibly enough, these children may receive "same-day" treatment, no medical letter is needed, and no consent is required by parents even if they don't pay health insurance. Hospitals and adult-educated health professionals are performing *elective* surgeries on children too young to consent **intellectually**. The psychological evaluation would only need to say the child has been diagnosed with dysphoria for the health insurance to be approved, but what is dysphoria?

"An **emotional state** characterized by *anxiety*, *depression*, or unease. In pathology, impatience under affliction; a state of dissatisfaction, restlessness, fidgeting, or *inquietude*. A state of mind that is not a medical necessity needed to sustain life." (The American Heritage® Dictionary of the English Language, 5th Edition. https://duckduckgo.com/?va=n&t=hs&q=dysphoria&ia=definition).

"Anxiety, depression, and uneasiness; a state of mind that is not a medical necessity to sustain life" pretty much sums up the entire DSM-5 Diagnostic and Statistical in Mental Health. Mental health-defining stress alone can be associated with anxiety, depression, and uneasiness as co-occurring.

Elective surgery is not critical for life, hence the term **elective.** On the contrary, performing an elective surgery not needed to sustain life exposes children to risk factors that include permanent infertility, blood clots, *irreversible damage*, breast removal, potential diabetes, and prostate cancer, to name just a few; exploiting children to appease the sexuality in political and adult issues. Altering hormones in hormone therapy also changes the brain's chemistry in its complexities and ability to function appropriately.

So, if the client is otherwise **healthy**, the individual is opening the door to health issues that were not present. Infertility is the inability *to conceive.* The Barons are using the Art of War tactics to win their case. If the parent does not consent, then the State will. The medical profession is breaking the Hippocratic Oath "not to cause harm," which is a *social deviance*, rewiring the brain within psychological warfare to create a social construct where disinformation is leading the misinformed. Unknowingly advocating for eugenics and all done with your consent while the Barons and global elitists are reaping an infinite amount of money through non-threatening elective surgeries, while the government is distracted about a virus so deadly you need to be tested to know you have it.

The Fourteenth Amendment need not apply.

> "All persons born or naturalized in the United States, and subject to the jurisdiction thereof, are citizens under the United States and of the State wherein they reside. No State shall make or *enforce any law* which shall abridge the privileges or immunities of citizens of the United States; nor shall any State **deprive any person of life**, liberty, or property, without due process of law; nor deny to 'any person' within its jurisdiction the equal protection of the laws." Would this apply to children and the unborn?
>
> —Constitution Annotated Analysis and Interpretation of the US Constitution. https://constitution.congress.gov/constitution/amendment-14/

For those who advocate for pro-choice and feel that an unborn child has no rights to life, liberty, and *equal protection* under the US Constitution, those who enslaved human beings throughout history thought the same thing—both were unconstitutional and inhuman.

California Law AB2223 states, "This legislation removes **all penalties** from anyone violating any abortion health and safety standards when performing an abortion on a woman through all nine months of pregnancy. The bill also *hampers* law enforcement's ability to investigate and **prosecute infanticide**. Leaving a newborn baby neglected or unattended with their needs like food, water, warmth, safety, and security can cause the vulnerable to suffer and die, *will not* be implicated by law enforcement to investigate and prosecute." Could this law also be applied to a fetus that survives an abortion? Interestingly enough, note that either way, no prosecution by law enforcement will be implemented or investigated. The barons have perfected eugenics, and the women have become the progressive postmodern Canaanites, sacrificing their children to the evil barons.

What does God think about healthy feminism:

> "Blessed is the man who finds wisdom, the man who acquires understanding, for she is more profitable than silver, and her gain is better than fine gold. She is more precious than rubies; nothing you desire *compares* with her. Long life is in her right hand; in her left hand are riches and honor. All her ways are pleasant, and all her paths are peaceful."
>
> —Proverbs 3:13–17, BSB

Wisdom in scripture is referred to as feminine with the pronouns *she* and *her*. Pronouns describe the noun, the woman. But what would happen to society if *she* were to become incapable of processing wisdom, compassion, and respect for life? What will become of the species if the woman **abandons** and kills her offspring? Through Pavlov's conditioning, social construct distorts the woman's healthy ability to reason, socially constructing her to be less than what she was designed to be. No patriarchal tone is exhibited here. I am not here to condemn or make people feel horrid. I want to bring *situational awareness* that more is happening than meets the eye.

While puppeteers convince you to move to one side, *they lay traps* on the other to keep you in line. "Give them no rest and harp at social issues lest they change their minds." It's like a football playbook with preempted tactical plays. Remember, as I said before, society has been *studied extensively* by applying Pavlov's social conditioning experiment. The wealthy Barons spent millions of dollars on eugenic research. The research has been done, and we have been studied.

Is it morally wrong to stop a heartbeat or to make another feel pain? Are we to use relative speech to condone acts that spill blood and lead to death? If a tree falls in the forest, does it make a sound? If we dissect a fetus after 20 weeks with a neurological system intact, **will it cry**?

> "It is inevitable that stumbling blocks will come (*we live in a fallen world*), but **woe** to the one through whom they come! It would be better for him to have a *millstone hung around his neck* and to be thrown into the sea than to cause one of these little ones to stumble. Woe to them that cause the young to stumble, for that will not go unpunished."
>
> —Luke 17:2, CJB

Woe to those who cause the young women to stumble.

> "It is impossible that snares *will not* be set. But woe to the person *who sets them*."
>
> —Luke 17:1, CJB

> "Watch yourselves. If your brother sins, *rebuke him*, and if he repents, **forgive him**. Even if he sins against you seven times in a day, and seven times returns to say, 'I repent,' you *must* forgive him."
>
> —Luke 17:3–4, BSB

Let's contemplate the variables. If you were to conquer a country, what variables would you consider? How can you submit an entire civilization and make yourself the new oligarch? Tying in the previous chapters regarding social conditioning, we could ask the question:

Will women be targeted and purposely steered into a predictable pattern of behavior?

Can social conditioning and marketing tools help create predictive emotional and behavioral responses? The same social conditioning constructs are used within group dynamics by disrupting the cultural norms by inciting predicted emotional responses studied by globalists. The prerogative of the dominant Barons is slowly but steadily ingraining collectivism and divisiveness into the minds of women, changing their roles to become a new breed of militants and later ego alpha males. Hate their counterpart and murder their children for their self-interests. Oppose the role of the patriarch, the **father figure**, and despise the nuclear family by presenting the male as the toxic masculine patriarch, aka *a chauvinist.* But what do you call a woman who is competing with men to become the modern progressive postmodern alpha male? In films, the leading female actor degrades the male actor *intellectually* and in physical strength action-packed scenes. Wouldn't that be considered a form of chauvinism *or misandry*, **microaggressions** against the men? What would be the difference in becoming the *very character* they've been told to despise?

"Misandry is the hatred of, contempt for, or prejudice against men or boys." A form of discrimination defined by *Wikipedia*.

Misandry is a word never used in mainstream media or in social constructs. The social construct designed for women. Women have complete control over their reproductive rights. Men have zero rights. In court, if the woman lies about her pregnancy, claiming who the father is, and the man believes her and signs the birth certificate but later finds out he is not the father, he remains responsible for child support. Men can be imprisoned, even if they are not financially viable. The court tells the man, "You signed the papers!" If unmarried and the man has grown to love the child, she has **complete rights** to take the child *from him*, even if he financially supported the child, thinking the child was *his*. Where is the social justice? Would charges be pressed against her for perjury? Would the courts demand that she pay him back for lying? Should every child be DNA tested? The globalists have studied society and aided in the growing animosity towards families. They are paving the path on what happens to children. We are breaking the spirit of men, and where both sexes are exhibiting a lack of accountability.

If that *system doesn't work*, then the globalists can socially construct men to behave like women and women to behave like men, blurring the *lines of distinction* between sexual identities. Destructive and divisive. We are being led to believe that blurring the lines between men and women will somehow emasculate the women and empower her as the new progressive postmodern nihilist and superior being. She will force her revenge and make him pay for oppressing her. Maybe replace the emphasis on becoming the new alpha male.

I do not speak for all women; that would be impossible and unjust. My intent is not to hurt women but to bring *situational awareness* to how both sexes are being manipulated through propaganda to fulfill a global narrative.

The progressive postmodern self-loathing has become self-evident. Secure women do not feel the need to exploit *or insult* the existence of men or exchange the female roles they play within society. We have the unabashed chauvinist, but the use of language has changed, and the word *chauvinist* now means toxic masculinity *or is referred to* as patriarchal, changing truthful speech to relative speech. Thus, animosity is caused without a second thought through social trigger 'buzz words' to infer "All Men." In truthful speech, the "patriarch" symbolizes a father figure, not a word that has been altered to mean contempt. What woman doesn't want a good father? What woman doesn't want the love, safety, and security of her father? The love of both parents is crucial to the lifespan development of both men and women.

> "A patriarch is a man who is the *head of a family* or tribe; **a biblical figure**, regarded as a father of the human race and a respected older man. **Contrary to the root meaning of chauvinism**, it is defined "as the *belief* held by some men that men are superior to women."
>
> —Oxford American Desk Dictionary & Thesaurus. Oxford University Press, Inc., 2010 by Oxford University Press.

But the global research has continued. The Barons have created additional social constructs to turn men into beta males by redefining a *biological* woman. Even the atheistic Darwinian would object as the driving force for evolution unless you advocate for **eugenics.** Positive affirmation is received through social recognition and approval by a social construct. Biological men compete with women in sports and receive praise, accolades, and military awards, posing as women. Will biological women become **extinct** in the scheme of societal conditioning? No sons to raise. No daughters to groom. The Marxist barons have left no stone unturned.

The progressive postmodern Eve is once again lending her ear to the serpent, desiring the need to know both good and evil but now asking how I can become the new alpha where I gain more knowledge to injure my counterpart, where social media whispers have led society into sin. It was an act that broke the true equality given by God, for God did not take a bone from a man's foot for the woman to be trampled on, nor did He take the bone from the man's head for her to be above him. God took a rib from his side so that both shall walk together *equally.* For the two shall become one flesh, not two separate beings. Instead, she has been convinced of what she should love and defend, if not for herself.

For the wisdom of this world in the age of post-modernism, self-reasoning is foolishness in God's sight.

> "For the wisdom of this world is foolishness in God's sight. As it is written: 'He catches the wise in their craftiness.' And again, 'The Lord knows that the thoughts of the wise are futile.'"
>
> —1 Corinthians 3:19–20, BSB

Ralph Epperson predicted in 1989 in his book *The New World Order.* He wrote that the New World Order was scheduled to start on January 1, 2000, but the United Nations now hopes to implement the 17 Goals of the Sustainable Development Plan in 2030, which is six years from 2024. This New World Order *or the Great Reset* will enforce changes to the social construct within the family dynamics, changing traditional values within the nuclear family. What we fail to decide today will be decided for us later. Traditional marriages will decrease. The State will supersede parental rights and assume the parental position. The State will make new laws abolishing the custodial rights of parents, implementing the latest social construct under the Socialistic Marxist theology where "all women" will be employed by the State and *not allowed* to be 'stay at home' *homemakers.*

For a word now despised by progressive postmodern women, it will no longer be an alternative or life choice. Women will become a *forced* assembly line to work and in childbearing, or the scientists will clone the future. Call it a conspiracy theory, but like all conspiracy '*theories*' are based on truths. Scrutinize the truth to remove all doubt, thus placing yourself in a position to accurately defend your worldview.

Propaganda is communication that is primarily used to influence or persuade an audience to further an agenda, which may not be objective and may be selectively presenting facts to encourage a particular synthesis or perception or using '*loaded language*' **to produce an emotional** *rather than a* **rational response** to the information that is being presented (*Wikipedia, Propaganda*).

CHAPTER 23

BIOLOGICAL PSYCHOLOGY

"What we think of as free will is largely an illusion: much of thc time, we are simply operating on autopilot, and the way we think and act – and how we think and act on the spur of the moment – are a lot more susceptible to outside influence than we realize."

—Malcolm Gladwell, *The Power of Thinking without Thinking*

Malcolm Gladwell talks about the priming experiment in his book *Blink*, where he discusses the ventromedial prefrontal cortex, the area of the brain responsible for executive function, self-regulation, decision-making, and the ability to retain information, which *affects behavior* and is **highly influenced** by the outside world. He states that as much as we believe we act on *free will*, we are actually "operating on automatic pilot." Gladwell states more concisely that at the spur of the moment, we tend to act and behave more *susceptible* to outside influences than we think, **unconsciously reacting** to sounds and words automatically *without* formally thinking—autopilot. What comes to mind with autopilot in the social constructs creating trigger words within-group cultural dynamics, where scientists predicted a behavioral response? You could get a crowd to become violent if someone were to start a stampede by simply using *trigger language*. The brain that is operating on **autopilot** *will react* without hesitation.

Let's review Pavlov's dog experiment *repeatedly*, where the dogs salivated at the sound of the bell even if the food was not present. Again, anthropologists, sociologists, psychologists, medical doctors, scientists, and behaviorists have studied human behavior extensively, *monitoring the effects of influence* on behavior. The same results open for **interpretation** could be used for good or not so good. Social media, smartphones, advertisements, *and political ideology* have also studied human behavior and created ways to manipulate the many to serve their self-interests. They have collective data and have made conclusions of their own—some with good intentions and some with *not-so-good* intentions, hoping people from identity groups will "unconsciously react to sounds and words automatically without formally thinking."

> "Men (*people*) are **rarely aware** of the *real reasons* which motivate their actions."
>
> —Edward L. Bernays, *Propaganda*

Psychologists have studied human development, understanding the intellectual and environmental factors contributing to human behavior. Statistical data has been collected from multiple studies on every age group, race, and gender. This information about human development is nothing new. Evidence-based studies have been conducted to educate medical and mental health professionals to create appropriate treatment plans for their clients. The same would go for neuroscience, biopsychology, and the effects of nature vs. nurture, all of which can adversely affect our decision-making processes.

> What is biopsychology? "Biopsychology is a branch of psychology that analyzes how the brain, neurotransmitters, and other aspects of our biology **influence** our behaviors, thoughts, and feelings."
>
> —*Simply Psychology*, https://www.simplypsychology.org/theories/biological-approach

Given the definition that biopsychology analyzes how the brain's electrical impulses and biology influence one's behavior, thoughts, and feelings, it parallels Gladwell's analogy of the illusion of *free will*. In social constructs, trigger points come into play within the subconscious. Can the purposeful use of words interplay with societal thoughts and predictive behavior that one thinks is free will? Gladwell explained that the clues within the environment (usage with specific words) "create a reactionary response within the subconscious." I am not stating that Gladwell would agree with my *layman's* assumption. However, I can still gather that priming and specific (*trigger*) words can be used within identity politics, causing the same **reactionary response** detailed in the priming experiment. Read *Blink* and make the decision yourself. Priming is reacting to the unconscious. According to Gladwell, "Priming refers to when subtle triggers influence our behavior without awareness of such changes, such as introducing classical music on the subway and seeing vandalism and littering drastically decrease." If we were to change or "prime" elementary children from listening to violent and sexualized music, would the children behave differently and maybe excel in school? Probably, but the government controls the curriculum and school districts and instead pushes sexual identity as "prime."

Priming can be associated with a schema. Let's take Kendra Cherry, MS. Ed. Definition:

> "A schema interpreted by psychology is a cognitive framework or concept that helps organize and interpret information and describes the *patterns of thinking* and behavior that people use to **interpret** the world," citing Theorist Jean Piaget.
>
> —Kendra Cherry, MS. Ed., March 12, 2023. Medically reviewed by Steven Gans, MD. *What Is a Schema in Psychology?* https://www.verywellmind.com/what-is-a-schema-2795873

Patterns of thinking that help people and children to interpret the world. What if the world is relative and not truthful? Will that help us to organize, *interpret*, and analyze what is **untruthful**? Can colleges and universities, politicians, and mainstream media have the potential to be *the outside source* **influencing** how people interpret the world, interfering with how the brain responds to individuals' executive function by steering their cognition through priming and socially constructed schemes? Do they have the intellectual ability to disseminate the thinking patterns and predict the outcome? Priming uses words where the unconscious works on autopilot, *unknowingly reacting* to classical conditioning imposed on society.

> "The conscious and intelligent manipulation of the organized habits and opinions of the masses is an important element in a democratic society. Those who manipulate this unseen mechanism of society constitute an **invisible government** which is the **true ruling power** of our country."
>
> —Edward Bernays, *Propaganda*

> In psychopathology, "classical conditioning represents the learning of an association between two stimuli, the first of which (the conditioned stimulus, (CS)) predicts the occurrence of the second (with the unconditioned stimulus, (USC))." Let me repeat that statement: "**The first stimulus predicts the occurrence of the second**." Thus, "the behavior is *predictable* within a given circumstance."
>
> —Davy, Graham. 2021. *Psychopathology Research, Assessment, and Treatment in Clinical Psychology.* 3rd Edition. John and Sons. Textbooks.

Whatever that circumstance may be, the result is that society has been studied. Men, women, and children have been studied with enough evidence-based data **to make accurate predictions**. Identity groups within cultures have been studied extensively. Genders have been studied. Life span development has been—yes, *studied.*

You can gather evidence-based statistical data and pretty much make accurate predictions based on the results. Having said that, the question would now be, "Who is using this data, and for what purpose?" Could this data be used to advance an objective? Could social constructs, identity groups, gender dysphoria, and culture be staged like a football playbook? Using the psychopathology process of classical conditioning by learning the association between the first and second stimuli, resulting in a predicted outcome. It's like evaluating your opponent's playbook performance. Review past plays, how they won, and how they lost. You can create a playbook based on the strongest and weakest players. You can use this data to predict which player would be easily *swayed* or intimidated by those who are **more resistant**. You can *construct* advanced **counterattacks** based on predictability. In today's political spectrum, can advanced counterattacks be used on those who are *more resistant*? Those Americans Katie Couric said need to be deprogrammed by inciting the *more* vulnerable identity groups?

The brain creates thoughts and memories within our synapses, information that helps us navigate through reality and interpret the information we gather. Some realities are truthful and moral, while others are manipulative. How do we *interpret* what is reality and what has been manipulated? Is reality subjective, or is it an objective truth? For a serial killer, life has no meaning, but most moral people have a **universal understanding** that life has intrinsic value. It is a truthful reality for law and order but not for the murderer. These thoughts can become solidified within the brain's neurosynaptic through classical conditioning or schemas, thus becoming a reality for the individual. Can socially constructed speech, mainstream media images, and disinformation have the power to manipulate and **alter a potential reality** through falsehood? Hitler infiltrated the United States during WWII, spreading propaganda that Germany was undefeated, and the Americans believed it.

> "German agents *quietly* **infiltrated** the United States and laid the groundwork to sway public opinion in favor of Nazi Germany; All these **mental warfare activities** were funded by Germany's enormous foreign propaganda budget of $134 million per year; under these circumstances, it was difficult to warn the public that the United States was already under an **invisible** *attack of words*."
>
> —Manning, Molly Guptill, *The War of Words*

How would someone know if their perceived reality was true or false? Let's examine Plato and *The Allegory of the Cave*. What kind of reality was imposed onto those **bound and forced** to stare at a wall, seeing images and shadows behind them that have formed a perception and an imaginary reality, but was it a truthful reality? That would depend on the perception of the bound and by those outside the cave. Those bound and forced to stare at a wall relied on what they saw, but *not by those* whose reality was orchestrating the shadows and images from above. Those orchestrating knew the truth in this sense of the word, while those in the cave received a **relative reality**. So, is *The Allegory of the Cave* improbable by today's standards? Can *The Allegory of the Cave* be implemented in political psychological warfare? You decide…

CHAPTER 24

MORAL ABSOLUTES VS. MORAL RELATIVISM

> "Certain actions *determine* whether the (*moral*) action or conduct is right or wrong. Therefore, from this standpoint of a moral absolute, some things are always right, and some things are always wrong, no matter how one tries to rationalize them. Moral relativism is the belief that conflicting moral beliefs are true within subjective reasoning. This carries the idea that what you regard as a right conduct may be a right for you, *but not for me*. In relativism, what is true for the individual **replaces the search** for absolute truth."
>
> —Mark P. Cosgrove, *Foundations of Christian Thought*

In other words, in relativism, the individual would have no need *to pursue* the absolute truth. Truth to the relativist is **malleable**, where the word can mean one thing today and then be *redefined* tomorrow. Try that ideology in mathematics, physics, and medicine. Truth, conversely, brings about order, as falsehood can only bring about disorder. That's like asking the question, are you coming or are you going? In relative speech, stating that you are doing both is *illogical*.

> "These conflicting moral beliefs may exist in the case of two or more individuals or in different cultures called

> cultural relativism or in different historical epochs called historical relativism."
>
> —Ronald Nash, *Life's Ultimate Questions*

> If historical relativism is perceived as truth, can the archaeological findings be conclusive as objective *or subjective*? According to J. P. Moreland, "Moral relativism is an attempt to **undermine the claim** that there is an "objective moral law or moral absolute" that is the same for all human beings." Moral absolutes are based on standards, having a point of reference that goes beyond the subjective truths imposed *by those who wish to alter reality.* If people want to alter reality, are they working towards an agenda? If not, then why bother altering reality to begin with?
>
> —J. P. Moreland, *Scaling the Secular City*

Moreland challenges moral relativism by arguing that if relativism were true, **then all choices would be equally good**. If all choices are equally good, then even intolerance toward other beliefs can be morally correct. If so, then why should anyone practice tolerance? According to Moreland, moral relativism is always about an **individual's choice**, *whether right or wrong.* It implies that *the individual* **determines** what is right and wrong for all people and preludes to subjective reasoning with no universal point of reference. Moral relativism states that *ethics* are relative, but moral absolutism teaches that ethics are not relative.

Moreland states that moral law is grounded in God, outside human laws created by imperfect beings, unlike the Bible, written by man, *inspired by God.* Are progressive bureaucrats creating social laws based on truth or relativism to serve the citizen or the politician? Moral relativism is based on an individual's decision, but moral absolutes follow *ethical universal standards* like "You shall not murder" (Exodus 20:13, BSB). Moral relativism will only justify the actions committed by the individual or identity group of people regardless of the consequences. Could the Machiavellian form of government be imposed as a subjective when making laws that will affect only the politicians or corporate leaders but not for the benefit of the majority of citizens? Will "the end justifies the means" be assumed as a relative good government? And if so, for whom?

In other words, an objective truth from an *absolute moral perspective* **must** stem from a theistic worldview—fear of God to avoid the consequences of sin. You can say an atheist can do the right thing, but for what motives? Why do the right thing? To be a good person would be defined by what? How do you define a good person, justified by what standards?

Nihilism and relativism believe in creating new laws and standards that will benefit the one or the few—Nietzsche's version of nihilism superhuman superior race. The question now would be, who will be the ones making those relative and subjective societal laws? Will these new nihilistic laws contradict God's laws based on their relative moral standards? Will this not conflict with the social justice ideology? Shouldn't the **standards of morality** *be fair for all people* and not just for the one or the few? In a political position, will these new laws affect people disproportionately, and will the citizens have the option to vote for or against such laws without consequence?

In a relative scenario, a thief can be construed as morally subjective. Can stealing be morally subjective, and if so, *by what standards* can it apply? The same can be seen for an arsonist who can be exonerated for his moral relativism, even if it costs you your property and life. However, according to American history, some people stood up against moral relativism with regard to slavery. Should civil liberty and individual freedom be a subjective truth or a moral absolute, where freedom or enslavement is right for some and wrong for others? Could the evils of slavery have been abolished on moral relativism, or should the evils of slavery be *wrong all the time*, by all people, everywhere, making it **a universal moral absolute**? That would bring into question why some groups of people are persecuted and shamed while others are defended through postmodern social justice.

Slavery and persecution should be seen as **a morally wrong absolute** for all people and not a morally relative political-driven narrative. Dictators think along these lines that human beings are born with no intrinsic value, nor should they have the right to freedom.

Let's use an abolitionist in American history as an example. Would the thoughts of an *abolitionist* be considered 'subjective reasoning', or is it considered an **objective truth**? Using the premise of what America stands for, where all people *are created equal* and have the right to liberty, freedom, and the pursuit of happiness, or should we accept what the government has done to her while corrupting the system from within and exploiting the emotional and the vulnerable? What may be true for one may not be true for another, which is the same as saying that what is right for one *is wrong for another*? Defining the slave owner vs. the enslaved.

What would make the abolitionist's objective reasoning be right and those who enslave with "subjective reasoning" be wrong? What differentiates subjective reasoning (relative thought) from a moral objective absolute? Shouldn't moral absolutes be universally true? One could ask, "What makes the difference between someone who is educated and one who is not? Is there a difference? Is there a difference between someone skilled in surgery and someone unskilled without medical training, basing their subjective reasoning with no point of reference or education? Analytical thinking leads people to seek truthful facts, superseding subjective reasoning amplified by unreserved emotions. In science, the hypothesis or experiment, you are given a number of variables within an environmental condition, stating that the result or outcome should always be the same under the same conditions if repeated; otherwise, the hypothesis is not valid or true. If the experiment changes within the same given variables and the environmental conditions differ, will the results or outcome be the same? That would defy the laws of science. Science cannot be subjective. The result or outcome must be absolute for the experiment to be valid.

> "Scientific laws (*natural laws*) imply a cause and effect between the observed elements and must always apply under the same conditions."
>
> —*What is a scientific or natural law? ThoughtCo.* https://www.thoughtco.com/definition-of-scientific-law-605643

> "Scientific laws or laws of science are statements, based on repeated experiments or observations, that describe or predict a range of natural phenomena."
>
> —*Wikipedia*

What is a statement? Logic's building block: "A sentence that is either true or false. It cannot be both true and false, nor can it be neither true nor false. A question cannot be a statement." A statement implies that we cannot have both truth and relative truth at the same time. Either one is true, and the other is false, or neither is true or false. The counterargument is the implication that morals are either right or wrong; they can't be both.

Can language through objective and subjective reasoning both be valid? Science and language are both intellectual forms of communication. If relativism is allowed to blur the lines of distinction, society will not be able to converse. Getting from point A to point B would be virtually impossible. The same logic is referenced within the 10 Laws of Science: the Big Bang Theory, Hubble's Law of Cosmic Expansion, Kepler's Laws of Planetary Motion, Universal Law of Gravitation, Newton's Laws of Motion, Laws of Thermodynamics, Archimedes' Buoyancy Principle, Evolution and Natural Selection, Theory of General Relativity, and Heisenberg's Uncertainty Principle, each having distinct objective reasoning for being concluded as true (*10 Scientific Laws and Theories You Really Should Know* https://science.howstuffworks.com/innovation/scientific-experiments/10-scientific-laws-theories.htm).

Having said that, what do science, relative, and moral absolutes have anything to do with American history? Understanding that "America" started as a hypothesis, an experiment where people could become citizens with the freedom and liberty to govern themselves, was unheard of. The American Revolution broke away from the oligarchs, the aristocracy, and the Barons. Where manufactured subjective reasoning, believing that a form of royal blood and higher status existed, placed them above the rest of humanity.

The royal bloodline in kingship was a genealogy in Judaism, a covenant made to them by God to predict a future—a bloodline to prove the coming of their Jewish Messiah. Manmade royalty was **grossly misinterpreted** by men who became *self-appointed*. The aristocracy took a position of power to elevate themselves, claiming inheritance, a bloodline. Kings, queens, bishops, cardinals, and people in power ordained their children into kingship, giving themselves and their next generation unlimited power to rule the lesser beings. Kingship was taken from the theistic belief system (a biblical truth) and turned it into a nihilistic worldview where kingship was taken out of context. The aristocracy claimed God ordained their kingship, and God chose them exclusively, but where was this objectively written to confirm its *authenticity*? Or was their kingship subjective, to where now the people obeyed and followed as a historical and Biblical truth?

America was designed as an experiment, taking thousands of years of human experience with social injustices and severe oppression that placated the most vulnerable throughout European, the Middle East and Asian history. It was designed to create a government that would serve the people instead of exploiting them for self-interest.

Amazingly enough, the barons have crossed the sea and abandoned the aristocracy to come to America to **reestablish** *their oligarchy positions.*

Americans have had 247-plus years (depending on when this book is published) to work out the kinks and social injustices instilled by the aristocracy and the barons, who superimpose their idealism on the less educated. Suppose America were to compare itself to European countries with thousands of years of history, claiming to be refined in culture and discipline. In that case, they have acquitted themselves from their history of bloodshed, genocide, wars, and stripping countries of wealth, power, and position, and never equating the toll it took on human life, exonerating the atrocities committed by every country in Europe and the Middle East, tyranny without one accusatory word or blemish. But America is evil, and you must never forget that, and if you do, the globalists will remind you relentlessly until you understand the agenda. Hitler understood that repetition was vital in controlling the masses when he said,

> "The receptivity of the masses is very limited; their *intelligence* is small, but their power of forgetting is enormous. In consequence of these facts, all effective propaganda must be limited to a very few points and must harp on these in slogans until the last member of the public understands what you want him to understand by your slogan."
>
> —Adolf Hitler

Today, we have the anti-Americans and global supporters casting stones at a country that fought a war *against* slavery and civil injustices brought here by foreign ideologies. Remember, America is a land of immigrants. Some have migrated to contribute, and some came to destroy for self-interest. America cannot control those who migrate to cause harm except by abiding by immigration laws designed as security measures to prevent terrorism, human trafficking, illegal drugs, arms dealing, and foreign ideologies. Not everything is charitable or safe. Abraham Lincoln was given no credit for the Emancipation Proclamation, written in 1863 by a white abolitionist who fought against the system of the day. An American President who faced scrutiny, ridicule, isolation, personal and financial injury, and even death. No mention of England's bloody history, where death was a daily ritual for the monarchs and the aristocratic bloodline—no mention of the Middle East slave trade, past and present. The slave trade that operated long before America was even a thought.

Today, we quickly dismiss the slavery of the Israelites and Hebrews by the Egyptians and the Roman Empire, causing the deaths of millions of Jews and Christians by either nailing them to the city walls to instill paralyzing fear or parading them at the Roman Colosseum, where death came from being eaten alive by trained animals, was considered a form of public entertainment, like a Friday night family baseball game or paying to see a movie; let's consider that when protesting for social justice. It's interesting how the sports arenas are shaped the same as the Roman Colosseum. Cruelty was a form of entertainment designed to **distract** the populace from the State's corruption. The Roman Empire kept the people distracted while the oligarchs overtaxed and imprisoned people without due process. Not much different from today, where laws are enacted without consent, dissecting the Constitution to serve the Marxist, a Socialist acting American government inundating the people with collusions and court cases brought against anyone defying the State, all paid for by the American taxpayer.

America has a court system that fluctuates with diverse sentencing that is not equivalent to the crime committed. In one State, the guilty would get life for murder, and in another state, get five years for the same crime. In some cases, innocent people are accused without evidence and kept in prolonged court proceedings until they give up, costing the taxpayer, the modern-day serf, millions of dollars with no accountability or a receipt presented to the American taxpayer. Attorneys receive no accountability on who gets paid what and how much? Yet globalists, both foreign and domestic elitists, and mainstream media distract the public from the true narratives, exploiting the biases and the disinformation used for identity politics to those unwilling to decipher the root cause and effect, like a science experiment. Provide the variables within a given condition; the results would be the same, resulting in a predictive outcome. Globalists manipulate the emotional cause and effect orchestrated by those whose self-interests lie above their oath to the American people serving in public office. Persecuting the majority, religion, or political beliefs by indoctrinating the public consensus as a collective crime.

We are demonizing America because we are being socially conditioned to do so. This gives the politicians and self-interest groups the power to distract from their hidden motives, undermining the American mind with deception. They say, "It's just a matter of time." These self-interested identity groups are becoming the very *intolerant* group they claim to despise.

Here's an objective absolute:

> "Klaus Schwab, the founder and executive director of the Forum, said, 'Every country, from the United States to China, **must participate**, and every industry, from oil and gas to tech, must be transformed. In short, we need a 'Great Reset' *of capitalism*.'"
>
> —Imprimis-Hillsdale College's *Digest of Liberty* author Michael Rectenwald described the economic goal of the Great Reset as "capitalism with Chinese characteristics," a two-tiered economy with profitable monopolies and the State on top and Socialism for the majority below. The Great Reset is not new but a premise on old and dangerous ideologies.

> "These utopian ideologies, with their misplaced faith in the rule of so-called experts and a *corresponding* **disregard** for the people's right to rule themselves, end only in tyranny."
>
> — Michael Rectenwald, *Imprimis-Hillsdale College's Digest of Liberty*

The first migrants who entered the New World fled to escape government and religious persecution, injustice, war, disease, and starvation. Amazingly enough, the unknown educators tampered with our history books, detailing the specifics of what contributed to the mass immigration of the European settlers. These early migrants were blamed for the tragedy that ended the lives of Native Indians with disease, war, and theft, but *let us do it all over again* in today's climate with **open borders** since it worked so well the first time.

Mass immigration with no accountability. Unsupervised children entering the country with potential human traffickers. Undocumented people with no health records. No documented felonies or concerns with smuggling in drugs and fentanyl. No documented damage to our agriculture. And most of all, no documented terrorist entering the country freely. Anyone objecting to open borders is considered intolerant, deplorable, and an enemy of the State. These people need to be deprogrammed according to the anti-American groomed fascists. American priorities should be its citizens.

Open discussions on what's best for the Native Americans should be discussed. Open discussions on what's best for African Americans should be addressed, and a resolution should be made. We have political parties promising the same thing every election, failing to fulfill their campaign promises. The American taxpayer pays an endless amount of money with no checks and balances in supporting welfare and social programs. Yet, the people never seem to escape their circumstances, electing the same party repeatedly and expecting a different result, defined as insanity. We listen to politicians repeat systemic injustice as if it were fuel and the protesters the fire. Progressive politicians choose to create divisiveness, making hypnotic speeches. They create propaganda, spread disinformation, and accuse the majority of a collective crime. That will definitely bring peace, and if not, we can always resort to war. The racketeers and contractors are always open to make *more money.*

Open borders lay a financial burden on the American taxpayers who are already paying for wars, not our own, and court proceedings dictated by politicians who spend nothing to incite. Lawyers and political civil servants get paid to make accusations, and the taxpayer pays the court—just another day at work. There are no precautions with COVID-19, bringing in millions of immigrants while Americans are **mandated** and excluded from medical care, food, and jobs. Well, having Americans lose their jobs and property only opens the opportunity for the civil servant, the anti-American, to prosper in buying foreclosed homes and property at a lesser price. It also fulfills the conspiracy theory, where the United States government will enforce the theory of Marxism, a Socialist government, to where the serf will own no property. Interesting.

Marxism:

> "A totalitarian regime in which American values like freedom of speech, free-market capitalism, and private property rights *are non-existent.*"
>
> —Mark R. Levin, *American Marxism*

Back to scrutinizing immigration, where undocumented entries with MS-13 gang relations, drug cartels, human trafficking, and possibly terrorist groups infiltrate our borders *pretending* to be a refugee, but that is **highly improbable**, an impossibility until something bad happens to you. Then it becomes something important to address.

There is no thought *or probability* of people bringing in diseases with no cure or vaccination because that didn't happen to the Native Indians who died from diseases like smallpox brought in by the Europeans, *historically documented* as **possibly the first biological warfare**. Now, that's an interesting thought. Biological warfare is just a hop, skip, or jump across the border. Parents are not the only ones bringing undocumented children across the United States border. Children are entering the country without birth certificates. How can Americans protect children if they are unaccounted for? If the drug cartels are crossing the borders to make a buck by selling fentanyl to Americans, do you rationally believe they care about the welfare of children and teens? These people are at risk for human trafficking, pornography, and pedophilia in what's become a billion-dollar industry, the selling of people (as manufactured goods) for money, a modern-day progressive enslavement. This is beyond horrific in humanity when applying basic moral logic, and no *college-groomed militant* is protesting for their protection. Shouldn't social justice warriors demand their safety? The safety and security of unaccompanied children? How about the safety of American children exposed to human traffickers and drug cartels distributing fentanyl, entering the country indiscriminately? China is selling human organs on the black market. Could that be happening here in the United States? It boggles the mind to hear and read about how the anti-Americans and global sympathizers *clamor about how bad America is* without taking accountability that they are consenting to bypass laws set in place to protect Americans and those who enter the country legally.

Our government has abandoned the responsibility of all undocumented people. No one would know if these people will go missing or murdered. But the politicians preach humanitarianism and altruism while maintaining their power, exploiting the migrants for future votes by bypassing voting laws without citizenship or proof of ID. Asking for proper identification is not a form of racism. Voting is the right of American citizens who abide by the laws and contribute to the American infrastructure. It's like paying a mortgage and taxes, *and you*, the property owner, having the right to live there.

Americans are legally required to immunize themselves and their children. Students are only permitted to attend school with current immunizations. Many healthcare professionals have been State and Federally mandated to immunize or expect to lose their jobs. This applied to all physicians and nurses who were critically needed during the COVID-19 pandemic. The military is inundated with required shots, especially with deployments. Anthrax, for some members, is one of the such joys. No matter how much education or experience you may have, you don't get the flu shot; you don't get hired. The Americans must obey the mandate except for those crossing the border *illegally*.

Sounds like a gestapo's style of thinking. No shot? No papers? No, work! A preamble to the Fourth Reich, making WWII just a trial run.

Other forms of control on a trial run are the CDC, FDA, ATF, the politicians, pharmaceutical companies, and stockholders that have pushed the vaccine mandate, promoting it as being in the best interest of the people, *except* if you were the elderly and confined to a nursing home under NY State Governor Andrew Cuomo and Senator Chuck Schumer, blocked away from their families and advocates. Still, all illegal undocumented people entering the country have a clean bill of health, except for the Americans.

Mass immigration and the American Homeland Security, while we have the Real ID Act required to board airplanes, to enter governmental buildings, and Bill Gates trying to create the vaccine passport. But illegal immigrants, unvaccinated, with no state ID and no proof of vaccination, can enter the country freely and be given the right to vote. Many prefer to scoff at what should be an absolute truth, accepting relative subjective reasoning to satisfy the status quo.

The academia is also driven by politics and by financial contributors who are lobbying to indoctrinate the minds of our youth with open borders, altruism, social injustice, the 1619 project, and Critical Race Theory (CRT) designed to reeducate our youth with American history and its forced oppression. The same with the relentless rhetoric of systemic racism.

> "Fuel the ambers of discontent."
>
> —Saul Alinsky, a Socialist advocate.

Exploit the Achilles's heel and steer the people to fulfill the current progressive Marxist ideology. Society has already been studied for its predictive behavior. Marketers, sociologists, anthropologists, public health professionals, and psychologists have made a living calculating human behavior. Professionals rely on disseminating relative speech, serving subjective reasoning to civil servants who will then exploit the very people they claim to serve.

In 1619, the continent was called the New World. It was not called America, so today's laws do not apply. The New World was not called the **United States** since you need *states to begin* with and states that are thus united, hence the words the United States. The New World did not have laws, nor did it have the Declaration of Independence, the Constitution, the Bill of Rights, or the separation of States. It was called the *New World* because it was a New World.

The states did not exist, hence the word *united*, meaning more than one. Having said that several times, the New World was like a refugee camp (what we call today **colonization**) but not like our current mass immigration (**or colonization**). The new colonists did not receive entitlements, healthcare, food subsidies, housing allowance, welfare, social programs, and DACA. The new colonists did not receive representation from civil servants posed as politicians who advocated legislating for non-citizens to receive Medicaid, Medicare, Social Security, and voting rights without an ID and citizenship. However, Americans must have a State ID, the Real ID Act on their driver's license, proof of vaccination, and proof of healthcare or be prepared to face restrictions and IRS penalties.

It is *far worse* to be a citizen than it is to be an undocumented immigrant.

The American taxpayer pays for billions of dollars of entitlements. The "majority" of working-class American citizens are demonized as capitalists and convicted of guilt for a collective crime they didn't commit while identity politics demand retribution. I suppose the decades of welfare and all social programs have become irrelevant. They want your checking account, your property, your homes, and somehow your outcome as a working citizen to be evenly distributed, thus making everything fair with equal outcomes for all those who didn't sow. Retribution will have no end. Maybe we should start from the beginning, collect all the money, return it to all the taxpayers who paid for all social programs, and then give it back as a form of retribution. Then retribution and reparations would depend on what? Proof of family origins? Who are the people who will receive reparations? And when will reparation demand end? I suppose we could begin with the Native Americans, the Africans, the Asians, India, and the Jews. The Israelites were enslaved by Egypt for over 400 years. The Christians were persecuted for over two thousand years. In the end, it would conclude that every being on the planet, according to social justice, would be deserving of reparations. Unfortunately, almost everyone, everywhere has suffered in some way and somehow some injustice.

America did not come to fruition until 1776. When the New World broke away from England with the Revolutionary War. How many people died for freedom through a war that broke the British oligarchical hold on its subjects? Countries that enslaved and murdered more people than history can count. These European countries brought with them their idealisms of enslavement, persecution, and oppression because *it was done to them*. If Europeans brutally murdered their indigenous people for centuries, would they care about anyone else? Natives or the enslaved. African chiefs sold their own people for armament. The Europeans exchanged guns to enslave workers. African chiefs concerned themselves with their own form of hierarchical power, overpowering the weaker tribes. Strength and brute force were used by every country and nation. Europeans didn't just enter Africa and start taking people against their will; that would have created wars between the tribes, and the whites knew about the diseases they weren't immune to, so they didn't enter; the chiefs brought the enslaved to them. The chief made money by selling other, more vulnerable tribespeople in exchange for armaments. The white man was not eager to enter the jungle because of disease; they knew it all too well (Sowell, Thomas. *Encounter Books*, April 24, 2006).

Asians were also sold as property, following the same format of buy and sell. The people from India were sold as enslaved people as servants for the English. Slavery was already in the making, and I'm sorry to mention *an absolute truth* by saying that even the Native Indians were at war with themselves before the English stepped foot onto the shores of the New World. War brings out only the worst in people. Every nation and its people are guilty of it; it's the ugly side of human nature. Some fight to preserve and survive, and others "unfortunately" create wars for self-interest.

The more vulnerable tribes fell victim to those more ruthless.

The 247-plus years of American history, from 1619 (discovered in 1492) to 1776, were 157 years. "Britain, France, Spain, and the Netherlands were the first to colonize the New World (called Mundus Novus). Each country had different motivations for Colonization and expectations about the potential benefits," bringing with them ideologies like enslaving people to work, a common practice during the sixteenth and seventeenth centuries by all countries (*Motivations for Colonization*, National Geographic).

Facts are not contending with morality.

The English settlers (the Pilgrims) in 1620 did not fight in the Revolutionary War to free themselves from England. They did not fight in the Civil War to free the enslaved. Teaching a twisted version of American history in a classroom filled with vulnerable minds with a rudimentary level of education using textbooks tampered with disinformation. Could this be a global design to deprogram the young minds to serve the global agenda by erasing the accuracy of American history—a passive form of war against the citizens infiltrated *from within*?

> "Barrack knows that we are going to have to make sacrifices; we are going to have to change our conversation; we're going to have to change our *traditions*, **our history**; we're going to have to move into a different place as a nation."
>
> —Michelle Obama

An interesting choice of words. What is the intent, and is it a form of subjective reasoning that serves self-interest? Will this benefit her, the global elites, or the majority of Americans? Hitler used the same tactics. He took away God and, on the very same day, erected himself. A nihilist who claimed to be a Christian was far from it. He was blasphemous and deceitful. Anybody can call themselves a *Christian*, **but few rarely are.** Just because you claim to be something doesn't necessarily make it true. That is, once again, subjective relativism, only serving the one. Hitler was a progressive version of a moral relativist. His moral relativism and subjective reasoning led to the murder millions of people, including 12 million in concentration camps and six million Jews. This is where moral relativism had dire consequences—a travesty of human suffering initiated by one man and his subjective, relative reasoning.

> "Therefore, an individual, people, group, or nation that espouses and promotes moral relativism is heading for a dangerous end. The economic tsunami that we are experiencing in the United States today can be linked to the danger of moral relativism. When a scholar is groomed in one of the Ivy-League and prestigious universities of our land, and his heart has not been transformed by the supernatural power of the Gospel of Christ, we have in our hands an intellectual whose mind is full of knowledge, *but whose heart* **is left untouched and unregenerate.**"
>
> —Adarkwa, 2011

College universities are the perfect breeding ground for a college militant, socially conditioned to have contempt for people they have associated with a **collective crime** *based on the color of their skin*. Is this moral relativism that is right for one and wrong for the other? Trading one oppression for another, with us being both judge and jury without objective reasoning in due process. Guilty by association. They bite their face off despite themselves, for it's the majority that pays into the federal government, social infrastructure, student aid, and federal funding for education. The US government spends billions on foreign aid, and yet the capitalist is demonized by mainstream media, with the underlying tone in the self-righteousness narrative by the global elitist.

Strength comes in numbers. Create division, and you weaken the people. Convince the people to despise their country, and you can easily win a war while standing on foreign ground.

"If there are no moral absolutes, why have some CEOs of companies and corporations in the United States been incarcerated for misappropriating corporate funds? Why, then, do we spend millions of dollars tracking drug cartels and drug traffickers? If moral absolutes have no place in post-modernism, why do we spend billions of dollars fighting global terrorists who want to make this world an unsafe place to live? The United States should learn from history to avoid repeating it."

> "We repeat unsavory history at our peril."
> —Kennedy Ahenkora Adarkwa, PhD, *Modern Ghana*,
> September 6, 2011

CHAPTER 25

MACHIAVELLIAN GOVERNMENT DISGUISED AS SOCIALISM

> "It is not the consciousness of men that determines their being, but on the contrary, *their social being that* **determines their consciousness.**"
>
> —Karl Marx

Priming and autopilot. Let's see what history has to say about *being*.

Kitty Werthmann is an Austrian woman with a story to tell. She recounts her experiences and gives a stern warning to all Americans that history has a propensity to repeat itself if the government is left unchecked. Kitty experienced the struggles she and her family endured during WWII under the German occupation and the Nazi regime.

According to Kitty, "most people thought that Hitler rolled in and took Austria by force, but in reality, he was voted into the Austrian government in 1938. Austria was annexed by Nazi Germany. Austrian Chancellor Kurt von Schuschnigg was pressured by Hitler and forced to resign, annexing Austria to Hitler on March 11, 1938." Immediately after, Hitler appointed Nazis into political positions, and according to Kitty, they suddenly had law and order. "Three or four weeks later, everyone was employed. The government ensured that a lot of work was created through the Public Work Service." Thus, unemployment was eradicated, which brought hope to the people in 1938. Austria suffered a great depression, so most people were unemployed. Depression and inflation were high, and most people had to beg for food. The Austrians heard that Germany had jobs, and they didn't have crimes. Hitler also decided that women should have equal rights and could return to work instead of traditionally staying home and caring for their children. He devised a plan to have both parents working and out of the home, leaving the children to be raised by the public schools or German caregivers. The State took control of the young and openly indoctrinated the future without resistance (college-groomed militants). The progressive globalist mindset is to either abort your children out of convenience or have the State institutions raise your children.

Food for thought. If we don't produce children, the globalists have no potential future adversaries groomed by the undesirables. Convincing women to produce fewer children adds to the reduction of the population. Remind you that if Americans are lowering their birth rates, does that mean the rest of the world is lowering theirs? Could this be a tactic in promoting eugenics? Could this be a strategic plan by those who follow Margaret Sanger to rid the country of the undesirables? Her doctrines have convinced parents to allow their children to make detrimental decisions in self-mutilating their body parts with surgery and castration of boys. We have medical institutions experimenting with hormone therapy that could render the child infertile. Forced castration and sterilization did not work under the Constitution, but if they can manipulate the minds and convince the *undesirables* to destroy their children, the globalists shall inherit the earth.

Exemplifying the perfect scenario, according to Margaret Sanger, the founder of Planned Parenthood. Some people today could blame Margaret Sanger for the Holocaust. Hitler followed the eugenic plans written by Sanger, where he incorporated her ideas in devising the concentration camps, genocides, and eugenics. We have become a country that advocates for **death** *instead* of for life.

We end the heartbeat and call it a clump of cells.

Abortions are funded by the federal government and paid by the reluctant American taxpayer without *their consent.* The Pro-Choice subjective truth should not be imposed on the reluctant taxpayer *or forced* on the Pro-Life moral absolute.

What about equality between men and women? Women will enter the workforce, according to Hitler, and the children will be *left to the*

State (daycare centers, schools), thus becoming Hitler's youth. Should we have equality when it comes to the military? Should women be **drafted** and forced into the infantry? Should only men be drafted? Then what's to become of gender equality? If feminism wants to compete with men, then the feminist should be expected to perform at the *same level*, **without exceptions**. Any soldier performing less becomes a liability and more work for the group, squad, or battalion. During WWII, women were expected to serve in the military because of a 'new law' *entailing equality* for women. According to Kitty, the army recruited women into service, and their children were given "around-the-clock" care every day, **seven days a week**, by "*trained* psychologists."

Interesting to note, she said, "The children were being indoctrinated by trained psychologists seven days a week." I suppose that only good can come from that. To give up your children while you serve in 'battle' with the Austrian mothers. "Women without marketable skills were placed in positions more suited for men. These women eventually were placed on the front lines. They came back from the War with the same '*mental disabilities*' and Post Traumatic Stress that crippled men." This patriarchal toxic masculinity where millions of men suffering from Shell Shock, too broken to function, came home to no jobs, then went straight into the 1920s Depression. Only to wait a few more years to enter into WWII carrying the same traumas and night terrors without relief.

To put this into a reasonable perspective, Americans were forced into the Great War in 1914-1918 and then faced the Great Depression in 1929-1933. Then came WWII 1939-1945. The Americans entered the War in 1941 after the attack on Pearl Harbor, killing 2,400 Americans, including civilians, and another thousand people were wounded. We had the Korean War in 1950-1953, Vietnam from 1964-1975, Desert Storm 1990-2001, and 9/11 from 2001 to the present. What am I saying with this? That men were predominately called to service, coming back with mental and physical disabilities and crippling trauma. Hitler sent women into War to experience the same fate. The question now is, "Who was raising the children?"

These men came back mentally and physically damaged from War to find their jobs taken and to grapple with Post-Traumatic Stress Disorder (PTSD) called Shell Shock or Battle Fatigue to raise children and be husbands. Today's feminists call men patriarchs, misogynists, and toxic masculinity without recounting the effect on lifespan development in the past 110 years. It will not be good for women to be drafted, but women should support the men.

Pacifists would object to our involvement in War, *and to some extent*, I agree, especially involving Americans in War started by politicians. Most people don't want War, but you need to *prepare for War* because there will always be those who salivate for it. We cannot all hold hands and sing kumbaya with dictators and totalitarianism roaming the earth and finding their way into political positions where their decisions can cause detriment. However, the feminist will get what she asks for and make no qualms about it; she will regret her decision. I have served but was fortunate enough to choose my job; with a draft implemented, you may not have that luxury. The feminist may get a desk job, or work in medicine, *but then again* adhering to equality, she may not. Maybe the man will get the desk job or the hospital job, and the woman will be recruited into the infantry, whether pregnant or not. Perhaps she'll experience the movie theatrics, in which the female hero *plows* through men without a scratch. Reality is frightening for both genders. Progressive films, the music industry, and mainstream media are promoting women as alpha females, believing that they are as equally strong as men. Good luck with that. Should we ever have to engage in a domestic war fought on American soil, with beta males, hormone therapy, castration, identity politics, pronouns, drugs, and our racial divide? How will people face Post-Traumatic Stress, Shell Shock, or Battle Fatigue? Would we fight to protect the country as a unified people, or will we find war *offensive*?

What we see in films does not give the sufferings of war the justice it deserves. The realities of war are devastating but, at times, unavoidable. Some may say that men are the reason for wars, but truth be known, evil people initiate wars, and many men and women have lost their lives because of it. No one truly understands war and death until you experience it. Then reality becomes a whole different language. Men have suffered shell shock, battle fatigue, and Post-Traumatic Stress disorder (PTSD) for centuries. Imagine living with trauma with no relief in sight.

Hitler continued with his tactics. He ended religion in the school system. According to Kitty, "Our education system was nationalized."

Instead of saying the pledge of allegiance for justice for all or a prayer, they were ordered to sing, "Deutschland, Deutschland, Uber Alles."

Amazingly, Stalin said the same thing: "By May 31, 1937, there **should not** be one single church left within the borders of Soviet Russia, and the idea of God will have been banished from the Soviet Union as a remnant of the Middle Ages. Which has been used for the purpose of oppressing the working class."

Did Joseph Stalin imply that God oppresses the working class? The Middle Ages opened the doors to oppression, and now we will install a new form of oppression through Socialism/Communism. Could this be perceived as the working *middle class*? Did God oppress the working class, or did the aristocracy oppress man? The dictators, the monarchy, King Henry VIII, and let us not forget Queen "Bloody" Mary, the Roman Empire, the Communist, the fascist, the Socialist, and the Catholic Church all having played a monumental role in the human travesty with their deep-seated oppression and human cruelty. Blame God, they say, not the Machiavellian nihilist, the *god complex* **narcissist**. It's so much easier to condemn and accuse God for the manmade miseries implored while exonerating themselves from any wrongdoings. The audacity of the *godless* boggles the mind. Their hands are drenched in blood as they wipe it clean against their pants and then go about their day.

Hitler initiated Sunday as National Youth Day. The children attended school all week, and now Hitler demanded the children attend school on Sunday. Parents had no choice but to comply. If they did not send their children to school, they would receive a **stiff warning** on the first offense. "The second time, they would be fined the equivalent of $300, and the third time they would be **subject to jail**." And then things got worse; the students were politically indoctrinated for the first two hours before National Youth Day even started. This sounds all too familiar with today's academia with its mandatory global studies, 'white privilege' rhetoric associations with collective crimes based on color, and sexualizing our children. Inundate the students' minds with contempt for America, forcing on them a sense of progressive postmodern conformity so as not to dare venture outside their religious or political ideology. It keeps them part of an ideological identity group pressed down with peer pressure and shame with school district punishment for not conforming. How does this pattern of indoctrination apply to the majority of adults? State motor vehicles implementing the Real ID Act. This Act means you cannot enter a government building or travel without an updated driver's license. You can enter the country illegally, get social services paid for by the American taxpayer, and stay at hotels for $700 a night in New York City, but you, as a citizen, will not be allowed to enter a public building without the ID. What's next for the citizen?

Hitler initiated social health care, where the government controls the doctors, what they will be paid, and how many patients they will be **mandated** to see. I suppose American doctors won't mind bartering for payments with milk and bread like Romania did under Nicolae Ceaușescu just thirty-plus years ago. Kitty said their "tax rate soared to 80% of their income to **support** their *universal healthcare system*." Ask Sweden how they support their universal healthcare system. Their tax rate per income is 60 percent. Ironically, the system is paid through *capitalism* to support a Socialist program. That's like buying a battery-operated car and charging it with a gasoline-operated generator. Process the absolute truth around that (The Common Funds. 2020. International Healthcare System Profile. https://www.commonwealthfund.org/international-health-policy-center/countries/sweden).

Is that "equal wealth distribution" for doctors where the Socialist government will determine their pay? I sometimes wonder if the insurance companies are deliberately making reimbursement increasingly difficult for physicians and frustrating for the patient to finally give up on their endeavors, allowing the government to intervene and control healthcare. Thus, introducing the international healthcare Socialist system. It's just a thought, *a conspiracy theory* ... I'm sure it has no merit.

"All daycare and education were free. High schools were taken over by the government, and college tuition was subsidized. Everyone was **entitled to free handouts**, such as food stamps, clothing, and housing."

It sounds like Bernie Sanders's campaign promises to promote Socialism while having a net worth of $3 million in 2023 gained through capitalism.

Globalists believe a crisis should never go to waste, whereas a pandemic can be quite useful. With federal mandates for the unvaccinated, you were not permitted to work, and you were shamed and kept **isolated**. Businesses went bankrupt, foreclosed, and short sales left open for the wealthy to purchase at a much *cheaper* price. It would behoove them to keep the buildings boarded to give the appearance of a crippling economy with no job opportunities. Would this be an opportune time for domestic and foreign globalists to invest, thus contributing to eliminating free enterprise? For decades, the government has imposed impossible demands on business owners, including renovating small businesses to accommodate disabilities. These renovations can cost the owner thousands of dollars to provide disability access, brails, more oversized entrance doors, bathroom stalls, ramps, etc. Instead of these public provisions being paid for by the federal government, to which taxpayers contribute trillions of dollars each year to help maintain the social infrastructure, the small business entrepreneurs are left with paying overhead costs and healthcare insurance for their employees and are forced to hire people to satisfy diversity (DEI) who are not qualified.

Another *Art of War* tactic used during the German occupation of Austria was robbing the citizens of their right to defend themselves. Kitty remembers that "the Nazis mandated the people to **register** *their guns.* They said the best way to catch criminals was to match the serial numbers to their guns. Complying with the law, all the law-abiding Austrians had guns registered. Registering the guns allowed the Germans to know who had guns. When the gestapo told the people to turn in their guns, they knew who had them."

In the United States, we have the Bureau of Alcohol, Tobacco, Firearms and Explosives (ATF), which has the serial numbers of every gun registered, not the serial numbers crossing the border unsupervised by Homeland Security.

I wonder how different the war would have ended if the Austrians had maintained their right to bear arms during WWII, equivalent to the American Constitution and the citizen's right to bear arms. But guns cause crimes. There is no emphasis on the criminal act of the perpetrator or on the global philosophy that "the end justifies the means." The pacifist listens only to the "Gun-Free Zone" theory and truly believes that a "sign" will somehow deter the terrorists from harming our children, who are left open and vulnerable to violence committed by evil people or the mentally incapacitated.

Kitty said that Hitler had enforced censorship on speech: "Anyone speaking against the government was arrested and taken away."

This sounds very much like the social construct of 'hate speech' and disinformation. Where hate speech *begets* a hate crime, which leads to punishment, giving power to the unelected official bureaucrats, fiefdoms, and social and mainstream media gatekeepers who are equipped to bypass the Constitution and Law, deciding and declaring what is disinformation. We are being discouraged from questioning the status quo for fear of the wrath of the gatekeeper demonization or shaming us into collective conformity.

Don Lemon, from CNN, says, "Unvaccinated people should be '**shunned**' or '*left behind*'" (*Washington Examiner*. Asher Notheis. September 16, 2021).

I suppose Don Lemon ordained himself the *gatekeeper* of my household. The Hitlerian concept has reached global proportion on college campuses, discouraging free thinking and open discussion to the point that students have become the *gestapos*, threatening speakers into silence with threats of violence and ridicule. It all sounds like fascism, where the student has been given the authority to threaten anyone disagreeing with them while advocating for tolerance. With that mindset, society can threaten anyone with harm for not complying with their subjective relativism. Let's discuss who will have the authority to vote. Who will decide the outcome?

"This election *reform package*, if passed by the Senate, would **transfer authority** over on how elections are administered from the states to the 'federal government' and make permanent many voting rules that opponents say lead to voter fraud." Epoch Times wrote: "On March 3, the Democrat-led House passed H.R. 1, the **For the People Act of 2021**, a law introduced by Rep. John Sarbanes (D-Md.)."

This law changes the Republic and how each state governs its state. If the federal government becomes corrupt, then the **elections will be corrupt**, thus making the American government an oligarchy—not working on the premise of democracy they speak so diligently on working toward.

An unconstitutional law is where the states lose their power to regulate their election laws according to the will of the people. Does the United States have amendments to defend the citizens' voting rights? Which within American history has taken decades to constitutionally implement. Laws to serve the American citizens. The African American men were given the right to vote in 1870. The women's suffrage movement fought for the right to vote in 1920. We have the potential *opportunists*, dictators, barons, and oligarchs who are navigating their way into government to circumvent the citizen's rights to vote by changing laws and exploiting immigration.

If the *supposed* political party pays for someone to cross the border by promising them money, they can manipulate them to vote to support **their party**. The immigrant wouldn't know any different, undermining the American taxpayer who is unknowingly providing the financial means and opportunity for the politicians **to exploit both** the citizen and the immigrant. Complying with George Soros's Open Society Foundation, the politicians undermine the American mind by using charity and altruism: no borders, no voting rights, no speech, no sovereign nation will equate to no country. The United States will fall into the hands of the United Nations and international law. "What Republicans and Democrats Want to Change About Elections?" by THE EPOCH TIMES March 19, 2021. https://www.theepochtimes.com/what-republicans-and-democrats-want-to-change-about-elections_3739348.html?).

If an overabundance of illegal immigrants is given the right to vote, then the taxpaying citizen will no longer have the power to speak. This changes the course of the elections and how the states act as a **Republic**. These same politicians want to eradicate the *electoral vote*, the same electoral vote that protects the State. Each State governs its own laws without coercion from the Federal government. If the Federal government had full authority over the outcome of the elections and if voter fraud were to occur in the federal government, then how would the Americans know? Can we trust in the Department of Justice, Congress, or the CIA? This would undermine the constitutional rights of the Americans and give the power to the undocumented immigrants, who, in turn, give the American government unlimited power, returning America back to the *aristocracy*. With that logic, we have lost the American Revolutionary, a failed experiment because its citizens failed to protect her.

> "America will never be destroyed from the outside. If we falter and lose our freedoms, it will be because **we destroyed ourselves.**"
>
> —Abraham Lincoln

Some might say we are all immigrants, and you would be right. Still, most immigrants came here *legally*, and documented giving the current population **the time to financially support** without the heavy burden of taxation. The Native Americans suffered *under the influx of immigration* and never recovered to their former self. This influx and uncontrolled immigration will once again take from the Native Americans whatever they have left. Let's take the abstract reality of the former speaker of the House, Nancy Pelosi, a politician who was never voted into office by the people, managed to accrue excessive wealth and position in power through stocks and inside trading, privy to inside information concealed from the public where she received no stock trading penalties or lawsuits. If we surrender our free speech, how can the average American citizen be expected to contend or fight against any new laws created by politicians and fiefdoms who have an invested interest in our demise?

Using the politically correct double-edged sword to justify their relatively subjective speech using words like "deplorable, extremist, fascist, right-wingers, nationalists, patriots, patriarchs, toxic masculinity, MAGA supporters are a danger to democracy," and those associated with the 'white collective crime.' They work on the premise of 'moral relativity,' subjected by the '*coiner*,' **with no set rules or point of reference**, as they diligently work to eradicate and dissect the 'outdated' Constitution and attack the electoral vote, protecting the rights of the state. It's a global attempt to eradicate binding documents that defend the citizens' rights against an oligarchical form of government.

Advocating for speech censorship allows the government to consciously and unscrupulously bully you into submission. Remember 'priming and autopilot' in free will. You do, as they say, the American progressive postmodern subject will comply. Identity groups are advocating speech censorship while unknowingly constructing the stage for all to be censored, for what you do to me, *within the laws*, will be done to you. Progressive postmodern censorship will apply to all identity groups. It's all a matter of time before you hang yourself with your unconscious consent. Starting with college campuses, being the *easiest and most compliant* in grooming as the professors' pets, using undisciplined emotions instead of logic. Jordan Peterson stated that freedom of speech "is the forthright to defend **all your other rights**." If you cannot speak, you cannot defend. Without the ability to speak out your thoughts, you cannot think or communicate effectively unencumbered. Without speech, we would become animals trapped and imprisoned in silence. Words become speech, **and speech becomes actions**. Speech becomes the right to defend your values, your convictions, and your right to life.

> "Speech is the **representation of the mind**, and writing is the representation of speech."
>
> —Aristotle

Our forefathers painstakingly wrote the Constitution, highlighting the importance of the right to speech and bear arms to protect the citizens from those who would wish them harm. Consider this scenario: if you surrender your right to speak, you surrender your right to defend. If you were to surrender your right to bear arms, would the rest of the world give up their guns as well? Will the politicians give up their armament and bodyguards? Will they put up a fence to keep the citizens at arm's length while they corrupt the country *without resistance*? Consider this: in 1990, there was a Russian revolt against the government to regain their independence from the Soviet Union. An **unarmed nation** resorted to fighting back against the government by throwing stones. Imagine that? Nineteen ninety was only thirty-four-plus years ago. Are we ready to repeat history and return to serfdom?

> "To conquer a nation, **first disarm** *its citizens.*"
>
> —Adolf Hitler

This quote cannot be verified, but in any event, there is truth behind it unless you prefer pitchforks and stones.

> "**They have the guns**, and therefore, we are for peace and for reformation through the 'ballot.' When **we have the guns**, then it will be through the *bullet*."
>
> —Saul Alinsky, a domestic terrorist

Kitty said, "Many people who were arrested were not only Jews but priests and ministers who spoke up against the regime." She noted that "Totalitarianism" didn't come to her country overnight. It took five years to integrate the Hitlerian social construct, from 1938 to 1943, before her country realized that dictatorship had occurred. She said that if her countrymen had realized what was happening to their country, they would have fought against the Nazis with their dying breath. A citizen will only defend what they love. If you are led to despise your country and hate her, then the enemy has won the hidden Art of War without them lifting a finger against the citizen.

> "Show me where it says that protests are supposed to be polite **and peaceful**?"
>
> —Chris Cuomo

Apparently, Chris Cuomo, an American journalist, has never read the Constitution. So here, Chris Cuomo, I would be more than happy to reeducate you:

> "The First Amendment to the US Constitution protects the freedom of speech, religion, and the press. It also protects the right to **peaceful protest** and to petition the government."
>
> —First Amendment by History.com Editors. July 27, 2023. *First Amendment - Rights, US Constitution & Freedoms* (history.com)

Is Cuomo advocating for "not so peaceful" protesting, which advocates for what? Kitty stated that totalitarianism crept into her country **gradually**. Such as social constructs under the premise of good intentions and social justice (and "not so peaceful" protesting) under false political pretenses or subjective relativism. Conditioning the masses that the theory of Socialism is much more desirable and socially just than being free. Social justice is a prelude to Socialism, shared equity with equal outcomes, free healthcare, free social programs, and free welfare controlled by the government. The cost of immigration is staggering, with N.Y. and California introducing reparations on top of that. Who is going to pay for this? The Socialist, the politician, or the capitalist taxpayer? I think the latter.

Collapsing the country's financial system and national debt is nothing more than treason. Nothing is free that someone else did not pay for. Social constructs associating collective crimes and arresting people without due process related to January 6. Guilty by association. Tactics used to divide people will somehow bring order and peace, or is this a political ruse to infiltrate our social construct? According to Kitty, it took only five years for a dictator to implement totalitarianism in Austria during an open war. How long will it take if the war is happening underneath our feet? The world knows they cannot defeat America, so the Art of Psychological warfare is infiltrated by planting seeds of discontent—no need to declare open war. Allow the citizens to murder themselves without cost and loss of resources. The enemy can walk across the border, disguise itself, and enter without resistance. The enemy can cut his hair, put on a tie and suit, and infiltrate the system from within. We can even have Democrats posing as Republicans or vice versa. Anyone can be deceitful. No one is immune to evil. Amazingly enough, each American presidential administration is approximately four years long, and it took five years to transform the country's government. A lot of political damage can be done in five years and set up for the next political administration to finish the agenda.

The battles we face with tolerance versus intolerance are planting seeds of systemic racism, traditional non-conformity, the patriarchal father figure, Christianity (the Godhead), and speech censorship, punishable by unknown lawmakers and gatekeepers in charge of deciding what is considered disinformation. Implementing gun control undermines the Constitution, conforming our children to global citizenry, glamorizing Socialism, grooming college students into Marxists, dismantling the nuclear family, removing the importance of the father, and taking the matriarch out of the home. Obamacare Socialist healthcare system allows for bigger government to create dependency, not independence, exploiting the underrepresented and the vulnerable and assisting substance abuse users with free syringes keeping the addiction active. The State is advocating sexualizing, castrating, and mutilating our children's bodies, grooming mental dysphoria, rendering our children infertile. Margaret Sanger would be beaming with pride when a progressive postmodern society implements eugenics *without force or resistance.* Drug the rest. Inciting civil unrest and anarchy, looting with no repercussions, and criminalizing anyone who 'speaks up' to defend *or oppose* the rule of the gestapo. Barrack Obama quoted his deliberate attempt to "fundamentally change America" but didn't specify how.

> "We are five days away from fundamentally transforming the United States of America."
>
> —Barrack Obama, October 30, 2008, Missouri

> "We are going to have to change our conversation; **we're going to have to change our traditions, our history**; we're going to have to *move into a different* place as a nation."
>
> —Michelle Obama, May 14, 2008

> "Keep people **from their history**, and they are *easily controlled.*"
>
> —Karl Marx

Kitty continues that "her countrymen had only broomsticks for weapons to fight" against oppression. The whole idea sounds almost unbelievable, to think that someone we elected into office whose full intent was to "transform the United States" with the intention to erode our national sovereignty piece by piece by inciting systemic racism. Doesn't any of this sound familiar?

> "The New World Order will have to be built from the bottom up rather than from the top down … but **an end run on the national sovereignty**, '*eroding it piece by piece*' will accomplish much more than the 'old-fashion *frontal assault.*'"
>
> —Richard Garner-Council

Direct war or "frontal assault" will not be needed "to fundamentally transform a country"; you would only need to convince the population of a racial divide. Socially reconstruct the country's idealisms. Dissect the Constitution. Have the citizens despise their nationalism, inundating their minds with systemic racism, oppression, and relentless, repetitive rhetoric of the white man's collective crime. At the same time, multiple foreign and domestic billionaires are using their platform of expertise to solidify the invasion. We have Bill Gates, the leading financial contributor to the World Health Organization (WHO), with his connections with pharmaceutical companies, farming, and in the production of synthetic meat. We have George Soros (and his newly appointed son Alexander Soros), with his Open Society Foundation (formally known as the Open Borders Foundation) and political affiliation in politics, who have never run for office or been voted into office. Kaepernick and Mark Cuban also have used sports as a political arena to promote their paid public propaganda. We have Mark Cuban acting on the words of Richard Garner on foreign relations "to erode" our national sovereignty 'piece by piece' by using one variable in degrading the National Anthem and making it the norm.

Demonizing our American history by inciting the fans to burn their flag, kneel against the National Anthem, and make bold claims that American sovereignty is based on oppression and systemic racism. Speaking to a crowd of fans consisting of every race, color, and gender, all present together to support their beloved team? What does Mark Cuban, a billionaire, have to gain in disturbing traditional peace? More money, more power, or an unknown accolade by some domestic anti-American or foreign globalist sympathizer, or better yet, has he joined the global elitists and sold out his country for thirty pieces of silver? Maybe Mark Cuban should take a trip to Potter's field and bring along Kaepernick for company. Satan will be waiting for them right there where Judas Iscariot was found standing with open arms.

> "America is truly the greatest country in the world. Don't let freedom slip away. After America, there is no place to go."
>
> —Kitty Werthmann

> "For a time is coming when people **will no longer listen to sound** *and wholesome teaching.* They will follow their own desires and will look for teachers who will tell them whatever their itching ears want to hear. They will reject the truth and chase after myths. But you should keep a clear mind in every situation."
>
> —2 Timothy 4:3–5, BSB

> "Most importantly, I want to remind you that 'in the last days' *scoffers will come,'* **mocking the truth** and following their own desires."
>
> —2 Peter 3:3, BSB

"Paul Joseph Goebbels was a German politician and Reich Minister of Propaganda of Nazi Germany from 1933 to 1945. He was known for his 'skills' in public speaking. He advocated progressively harsher and more discrimination against the '*undesirable*,' like the Jews in the Holocaust and those who opposed and resisted the German Reich. Goebbels took great interest in the use of propaganda and relative speech to promote and elevate the Nazi party's idealisms. After the Nazis Seized Power in 1933, Goebbels **exerted his control** and position to manipulate the '*news media*,' the arts, and all information generated and circulating throughout Germany." In today's society, we call this '*disinformation*' **guarded by the gatekeepers** who will decide what people will hear and see. "Goebbels was particularly enamored in using the relatively new media of radio and film for propaganda purposes. The progressive movement is present in every nuance and storyline of American cinema. Projecting progressive idealisms penetrating the social construct, projecting a perception of reality posed by a script."

> "A lie told once remains a lie, but a lie told a thousand times *becomes the truth.*"
>
> —Joseph Goebbels

Since history is bound to repeat itself, and we have ignored discernment, we find similarities in the usage of propaganda orchestrated in WWII's progressions, assimilating the identity politics movement. Does any of this sound familiar, with platforms and mainstream media censoring speech, pushing social constructs relentlessly instead of processing the news? Assigned gatekeepers whose sole job is to disseminate what is considered disinformation and to block truthful speech that may injure global politics. One might argue that speech should be controlled to prevent those who may or may not offend. But to what extent are we willing to sacrifice our American right to avoid offending? Jordan Peterson said that speech allows us to think out loud, communicate with one another, and **engage in decision-making, problem-solving**, and political communication. It's like having someone defend you in a court of law. You need speech to **defend your innocence**. Even the guilty get their time in court. Speech is supposed to *bring light to the truth* through evidence and witnesses. Without speech, the court will make its own decision, and determination not on your behalf but on theirs. How can it be on your behalf if no one is allowed to speak in your defense? Oligarchs, barons, and the wealthy who think along these lines **will misrepresent anyone** who is not conducive to their political ruling.

It also serves to allow us to defend all our other rights. If a political party can create laws to prevent people from speaking, then we have lost the country. Without the right to speech, the government can superimpose its authority over the citizen to an extent that is unlimited. Repressing speech opens the door for society to return to an era once controlled by the barons and the oligarchs. People have become so fixated on presumed misinformation and hate speech that their minds have become clouded with deceptions of subjective reasoning and relative speech. You couldn't see the truth if it stood before you. You have been **conditioned to see what the gatekeepers demand you to see**, similar to Winston in the novel *1984*. A frightening potential version of reality if left unchecked.

But this leaves another question: Does a media platform gatekeeper have the authority to dictate what 'disinformation' is without holding the proper credentials in education held by professionals? Medical doctors and nurses are not even allowed to speak. Even the former President of the United States was censored and deplatformed from social media. Regardless of your political preference, the most powerful position on earth was silenced, *making the gatekeepers* **the most potent fiefdoms**. If they can stop a president, what will prevent them *from silencing you*? Given the present authority and power to these **faceless gatekeepers** positioned to represent themselves as the "Ministry of truth," we have entered an Orwellian state of mind.

> "The further society *drifts from the truth*, the more it will **hate those who speak it**."
>
> —George Orwell

> "Wisdom will save you from evil people, from those whose words are twisted."
>
> —Proverbs 2:12, BSB

CHAPTER 26

FACELESS OLIGARCHS

"Who are the most powerful people in America?" Philip Hamburger wrote for Prager University to explain how fiefdoms rule the law. Fiefdoms are unelected bureaucrats empowered to make decisions affecting American citizens without reproach. These "administrative states" include the FDA, FCC, IRS, ATF, and CDC, to name only a few. In medieval times, there was a king—an unelected official who held supreme authority, subjugating the many without societal laws to protect the subjects. You could checkmate the king and attempt to regain your freedom, but what can you do when thousands of little bureaucrats act like kings with no checks or balances?

What is a fiefdom? It's "an organization or department over which **one dominant person or group exercises control**; an area over which a person or organization *exerts authority or influence*; the domain controlled by a **feudal lord**; territory over which rule or control is exercised" (The Free Dictionary).

Hamburger explains that these "three-letter bureaucrats" have become so powerful they have convinced us of their unlimited authority. While fiefdoms exist within the country, what happens if they elevate themselves to a higher global position, such as in the UN? The UN has instituted a plan to implement the 17 Sustainable Development Goals by 2030, intending to control every aspect of global resources. "Global" means they will control every continent. "All resources" includes food, water, healthcare, farming, and education. This approach would transform them into "thousands of little kings" elected without consent *or vote.*

> "The Constitution is not a document for the government **to restrain the people**: it is an instrument for the people *to restrain the government.*"
>
> —Patrick Henry

It is disturbing when people say we should do away with the Constitution because it is an outdated document written by 'dead white men' from another era. What does that mean? The Constitution protects us from tyranny. With the existence of fiefdoms, how do you restrain what you did not elect? How do you stop what you didn't consent to? These three-letter bureaucrats wield their convoluted bureaucracy, called **red tape**, to wear us down into accepting their authority under progressive postmodern social constructs without opposition or resistance.

Most people work to maintain societal infrastructure while financially supporting the world. Unless you are a professional protester or a college-groomed militant, you have endless time with zero accountability. Protesters who cause billions of dollars in damage somehow believe destruction will restore order. Oddly, no insurance companies complain about losses or raise an outcry over property damage and looting. No monetary losses are reported or recouped. That is an **interesting** thought.

> "This is not an argument against government regulation per se, but against regulation imposed by bureaucrats rather than by the elected lawmakers whom we can hold accountable at the next election."
>
> —Philip Hamburger, December 10, 2018, Prager U

Consider farming: how does genetically engineered food (GMO) affect it? GMOs have tampered with our food supply, claiming to provide more food for the planet. The truth is American farmers already produce enough food to feed the world, but they are regulated to dump excess food to maintain prices. It's called "**supply and demand**." Too much of a product lowers costs; too little increases prices. This isn't rocket science. If the government controls food, water, and meat, it wields monumental authority over the food supply.

Imagine if the United Nations, European Union, Socialist/Communist, or the proposed "One World Government" of the Great Reset decided who to feed and who to deprive. History offers a grim precedent: during Stalin's Socialist regime, food supply control led to the starvation of over 3.9 million people, **primarily middle-class farmers** (Imagine *farmers* starving to death). By today's standards, such social injustice could escalate into billions—a disaster beyond comprehension. Can college-groomed militants recognize the hidden agenda of globalism, or are they too steeped in indoctrination?

Bill Gates, a billionaire, has invested in synthetic meat, arguing it offsets climate change. While the idea of avoiding harm to animals is appealing, eating synthetic meat grown in a petri dish or consuming genetically modified organisms (GMOs) is a dangerous alternative. They're already encouraging people to eat bugs. Playing God by creating artificial food mimics the hubris of opening Pandora's box or recreating the forbidden fruit from Eden.

No good comes from tampering with food and genetics forbidden knowledge. Irresponsible pseudo-scientists toy with genetics beyond their comprehension. Recreating the first bite of the apple—seeking the knowledge of good and evil—reflects humanity's obsession with power. Those tampering with genetics also tamper with nuclear weapons, like tyrants who lack responsibility for humanity, exemplifies this recklessness.

The globalists preach systemic justice, genetic foods, and climate change advocacy while disregarding the existential threat of chemical weapons. These weapons indiscriminately poison the air, land, and water. They fulfill their purpose without conscience. If such weapons are used, debates about climate change, food, and diversity will become irrelevant.

There are scientists who created GMO seeds designed to grow only once or twice; after that, they stop producing. Farmers must buy more seeds from a *monopolized bureaucratic entity*, becoming dependent on them for future crops. This practice has negatively impacted poverty-stricken countries worldwide. Meanwhile, the UN, through its "17 Goals" initiative, claims to aim for the eradication of poverty and hunger, all while being fully aware of the corruption in the GMO food industry. Motivated by money, greed, and a desire to manipulate the masses, these industries view people as the greatest commodity and the essential source of their thirst for power. This mirrors the mindset of Socialists and Communists. It's astonishing how one ideology bleeds into another, given decades to control every aspect of human needs and resources with the goal of monopolizing them. Remember, "he that holds the conch ... wins" (a reference to *Lord of the Flies* by William Golding).

> "Here's the larger danger: *As bureaucracy grows*, individual freedom **diminishes**."
>
> —Philip Hamburger

This is why it's imperative to convince people that freedom is an *unnecessary evil* and that Socialism is the way of the future—altruism controlled by the unelected. How did we get into this mess, and, more importantly, how do we get out of it? America's Founding Fathers recognized the dangers of governmental control from the start. They despised being dictated to by unelected individuals and built numerous protections into the US Constitution, beginning with the very first line after the Preamble:

"All legislative Powers herein granted shall be vested in a Congress of the United States, which shall consist of a Senate and House of Representatives."

All legislative powers—not some.

Critics who claim the Constitution is outdated must answer a critical question: How can freedom and liberties ever be outdated? Suggesting **freedom no longer applies** is similar to putting slavery back on the table. Eroding the Constitution piece by piece, limiting freedom of speech and the right to bear arms, is like dismantling a puzzle—removing one piece at a time until the image is unrecognizable. We have political movements doing precisely that, arguing the Constitution needs to be "overhauled" to meet today's *postmodern* standards.

But what are these supposed "standards"? How should this new, progressive Constitution be written to fit modern reality? Should it rely on relative and subjective interpretations where laws shift meaning depending on the moment? Should we create a "truth" that benefits only the wealthy and powerful while exploiting the unknowing? Such pretensions of social justice mask an agenda that benefits social elites, creating a nihilistic "new standard of laws" that serves no one but themselves.

Social media perpetuates this chaos by constantly redefining **its undefined set of rules.** Undefined rules mean there's no clear understanding of truth, similar to the *1984* concept of the "Ministry of Truth." This is nihilism applied to political philosophy, where chaos begets disorder. Social justice warriors mistakenly believe they fight for a noble cause but end up destroying their own existence and way of life.

> "You need to flood a country's public square with *enough sewage* ... you need to raise enough questions ... spread enough dirt ... plant enough conspiracy theorizing. **Let citizens no longer know what to believe.** Once they lose trust in their leaders, in political institutions, mainstream media, and in each other, **possibly in truth**, the game's won."
>
> —Barack Obama, speaking at Stanford University about challenges to democracy

This statement alone is a public betrayal. Moreover, we are not a democracy. America is a *Constitutional Republic* by design, created to maintain checks and balances. Our Founding Fathers warned against tampering with the Constitution, but many ignore their warnings. People have become too complacent, distracted by trivialities, and herded like cattle to the slaughter. Even a cow senses danger at the slaughterhouse, yet many humans fail to recognize the signs.

Tribal groups and social justice warriors have convinced themselves of a *false sense of power*, **unaware of the damage they inflict** on their communities and country. Politicians, mainstream media, and corporate CEOs employ *The Art of War* tactics on the public, consciously aiding globalists. Defunding the police and removing authority from society only sows more disorder.

Education has strayed far from its original purpose, moving away from mathematics, economics, English, and history to serve global social constructs and foreign conglomerates. School boards promote the sexualization of children through curricula and library books while advocating for the separation of church and state—a misunderstanding of its original intent, which was to *protect religious freedoms* **from government**

interference. Meanwhile, terms like Christian nationalism, ethnocentrism, and extremism are used as trigger words, repeated until society internalizes the message, a tactic reminiscent of Hitlerian propaganda.

Religion and patriotism are now forbidden topics in schools, yet the sexualization of children is deemed morally acceptable. This erosion of mental and moral health is not about protecting children but about bending their psyches to align with intolerant adult agendas. The modern school system has become a breeding ground for Marxism, led by figures resembling Bill Ayers of the past.

If a state eliminates its community-based police force, it opens the door for selective policing by the State. Without parental intervention and advocacy for their children's welfare, the State will step in and program the youth as future serfs. A society cannot function without a police force to maintain order, and globalists understand this all too well. This gives them the opportunity to replace local police with a handpicked modern-day gestapo—foreign or domestic anti-American sympathizers trained to enforce conformity under their guidelines. The Nazis perfected such policing, and globalists are assembling similar mechanisms to exploit. Opportunists strike at just the right moment, using neologisms and doublespeak to manipulate the masses. They position themselves as Orwellian gatekeepers, the self-appointed "Ministry of Truth," labeling dissent as disinformation.

MSNBC often uses the term *confederates* in relative speech. Historically, however, Republicans were the Union, and Confederates were Southern Democrats who fought to maintain slavery. Bureaucracy manipulates public perception while unelected, unaccountable fiefdoms craft laws in their favor, convoluting them with relative language and distorting truth.

> "How long, you simpletons, will you insist on being **simpleminded**?
> How long will you mockers relish your mocking?
> How long will you fools hate knowledge?
> Come and listen to my counsel.
> I'll share my heart with you **and make you wise**."
> —Proverbs 1:22–23, NLT

Philip Hamburger asserts that only Congress can make the nation's laws. Congress cannot divest itself of this responsibility or delegate it to bureaucracy. For the first hundred years of America's history, this principle was upheld. However, this changed when figures like Woodrow Wilson championed centralized bureaucratic power. Wilson, a **former university professor** and self-described "*progressive reformer*," grew impatient with the democratic process. Instead of **persuading the American people**, he **shifted lawmaking authority from Congress** to unelected bureaucrats. Franklin D. Roosevelt followed Wilson's example, undermining the Constitution he had sworn to uphold.

Politicians are elected to serve the country and represent the interests of its citizens, not their own. However, they have increasingly allied themselves with wealthy conglomerates, CEOs, and foreign globalists, intent on buying their way into control "with or without your consent." This undermines the trust of the American people. FDR's presidency, for example, introduced an "alphabet soup" of bureaucratic agencies during WWII. It's noteworthy, as some historians suggest, that Pearl Harbor—strategically vital to US defense—was left vulnerable before the Japanese attack. Could the loss of life have been used to rally public support for entering the war? For a deeper exploration, *The Shadows of Power: The Council on Foreign Relations and the American Decline* by James Perloff offers valuable insights.

"FDR's presidency produced an alphabet soup of new government programs. Congress passed laws, but gaps were filled by unelected bureaucrats," Hamburger explains. Consider the Affordable Care Act of 2009, or "Obamacare." The original bill was over 2,500 pages long, yet by 2013, an additional 10,000 pages of regulations had been appended."

"How do we rein in these faceless monarchs?" Hamburger asks. Congress must hold these bureaucrats accountable for creating burdensome rules. American citizens should have the legal ability to challenge laws that deviate from their intended purpose. Yet, most people lack the time or resources to fight these faceless monarchs. Bureaucrats understand this **imbalance and exploit it with endless red tape**, *wearing down* even the most determined individuals.

As the founders declared, "No regulation without representation." These "dead white men" wrote the Constitution to secure the government and protect the people. Today's politicians argue the Constitution is outdated and must be rewritten. **But to whose advantage**? Theirs *or ours*? This same logic is used to argue against the electoral vote. Without it, populous states like California and New York would dominate every election, rendering smaller states **voiceless and powerless**. Our Republic ensures that every state counts, regardless of population, preserving the balance of power. Abandoning the Electoral College would create a de facto tyranny of the majority.

The Constitution was not "written to restrain the people; it was written to restrain the government." How can such a carefully constructed document—designed to protect inalienable rights—be considered outdated? To dissect it and abandon its protections is to invite slavery. Freedom or enslavement—it is a choice. Rights to property, sustenance, and self-governance would vanish under a subjective system ruled by tyrants. **Piece by piece**, the country would crumble, leaving only the will of domestic and foreign oligarchs.

How can ordinary citizens contend with "thousands of little kings?" These unelected officials work alongside globalists and anti-American Socialist sympathizers, exhausting the nation with inflation, taxation, and political correctness. They **distract the public** with one issue while executing more destructive agendas in the shadows. Laws are intentionally convoluted with legal jargon, financially straining citizens while robbing them of understanding. New social constructs glamorize Marxism, falsely presenting Socialism as a path to freedom for all.

> "Engage people with what they expect; it is what they are able to discern and confirms their projections. **It settles them into predictable patterns of response**, **occupying their minds** while you wait for the extraordinary moment—that which they cannot anticipate."
>
> —Sun Tzu, *The Art of War*

They have convinced the young that being cared for 'collectively' is more desirable than freedom and work ethics. The elitists cling to a hidden narrative designed to benefit only the few. Diversity was not created to protect the underrepresented and oppressed; **it was a tactic to create**

division and discord. A country at war with itself is far easier to control. Globalists work tirelessly behind the scenes to unravel the American fabric, making its citizens believe the nation should burn. They overwhelm us with an **endless flood of meaningless words**, too burdensome for hardworking Americans to *untangle*. Meanwhile, we're occupied with working and paying taxes for elites to squander—and then demand more. Ultimately, we are all in the same pot, destined to suffer the same fate.

The end will justify the means, regardless of your emotional or political stance.

> "For the wisdom of this world is foolishness in God's sight. As it is written: 'He catches the wise in their craftiness.' And again, 'The Lord knows that the thoughts of the wise are futile.'"
>
> —1 Corinthians 3:19–20, BSB

> "What 'good fortune' for governments that the **people do not think**."
>
> —Adolf Hitler

> "However [political parties] may now and then answer popular ends, they are likely, in the course of time and things, to become potent engines (bureaucrats, Socialist/Communist global sympathizers) by which cunning, ambitious, **and unprincipled men will be enabled to subvert the power of the people and to 'usurp' for themselves the reins of Government**, destroying afterward the very engines which have lifted them to (an) unjust dominion."
>
> —George Washington

George Washington's words remain true today. Truth is based on objectivity and moral absolutes, not relative interpretations. Order versus chaos. Wisdom versus foolishness. A party advocating for a larger government diminishes the individual's will. Democratic Socialism is merely a euphemism for Communism.

> "There is no difference between Communism and Socialism, except in the means of achieving the same ultimate end: Communism proposes to enslave men by force, Socialism—by vote. It is merely the difference between murder and suicide."
>
> —Ayn Rand

> "Socialism is the doctrine that man has no right to exist for his own sake, that his life and his work **do not belong to him**, but belong to society; that the only justification of his existence is his service to society, and that society **may dispose of him** in any way it pleases for the sake of whatever it deems to be its own tribal, *collective good*."
>
> —Ayn Rand, *The Ayn Rand Lexicon: Objectivism from A to Z*

A "collective good" according to whom? Who will sustain this "good"? Will it be the American taxpayer, who has already paid billions in foreign aid while those nations continue to suffer poverty and hunger? Will it be the UN, an entity of immense wealth and power, rendering the American taxpayer increasingly insignificant? Citizens unwittingly fund politicians who misrepresent them, indirectly paying their enemies for their own demise.

College militants have been 'convinced' that the utopian ideals of Socialism will cure systemic racism and oppression. But this illusion demands submission: your freedom, property, voice, and ability to defend yourself must be relinquished for the "general good." Your intrinsic value and soul will also be demanded because, **in this postmodern worldview**, there is no God. The nihilistic Superman will own you. These unelected world leaders promise a utopia—a government that will rule over you. Trusting such leaders is like the blind *leading the blind*. Will they not both fall into a pit? Yes, they will.

Faceless oligarchs and bureaucrats claim they have your best interests at heart while asserting they have nothing to gain. Meanwhile, American politicians and bureaucrats act like Hollywood actors, deceiving the public year after year. They discuss government corruption in Congress as if they are fighting for us, yet no one is fired or held accountable. These politicians no longer care about being caught. To them, the average citizen is **powerless.**

Mainstream media drowns us with opinions, crafting deceptive narratives that convince us we are oppressed. This reminds me of *The Lord of the Flies*, a 1954 novel by William Golding. Once required reading, it has fallen out of favor. No foreign entity has your best interest in mind; globalists view you only as a means to an end.

> "If a house is **divided**, it cannot stand."
>
> —Mark 3:25, BSB

If you believe Socialism is the answer to your problems, I have swampland in Florida for sale. It's good "stable ground" on which to build your house.

CHAPTER 27

THE REPUBLIC IDEOLOGY & CAPITALISM

Socialism deprives individuals of incentives, creating dependency, social demands, and expected entitlements—to reap where they did not sow.

"You cannot legislate the poor into freedom by legislating the wealthy out of freedom. What one person receives without working, another must work for without receiving. The government cannot give to 'anybody' anything that the government does not first 'take' from somebody else. When half the people get the idea that they do not have to work because it does no good to work because somebody else is going to get what they worked for, that, my friend, is about the end of any nation."

> "You cannot 'multiply' wealth by 'dividing' it."
>
> —Dr. Adrian Rogers, 1931

Even scripture upholds the expectation to work *and not be a burden*:

> "We were not idle when we were with you. We never accepted food from anyone without paying for it. We worked hard day and night so we would not be a burden to any of you."
>
> —2 Thessalonians 3:7–11, NLT

The disciples did not reap what they had not sown.

We often confuse charity with dependency. Able-bodied men and women should work to provide for themselves and their families. This is not similar to enslavement or indentured servitude. Yet, as people migrate to new countries and burden the existing populace, the lines blur. In *Political Questions,* Larry Arnhart summarizes Karl Marx's political idealism in the *Communist Manifesto*:

"Another weakness in a Socialist economy is the **lack of material incentives to work**. The *motto for a Marxist economy must be*: 'From each according to his ability, to each according to his needs!' (p. 531, Marx). But if the people know that what they receive will not be proportionate to what they contribute, won't they be tempted to become free riders with no motivation to work? Why would people work hard if it didn't increase their wealth? In fact, Socialist governments have been forced to allow some capitalist economics to avoid economic catastrophes." (*Political Questions,* p. 278)

Interestingly, even Sweden's international healthcare system relies on capitalism to avoid economic collapse. Now consider that under Socialism, individuals lose the freedom to choose whether to work *or not.* The freedom to quit, to retire, or to travel is replaced with the obligation to serve the State. Citizens become modern-day proletariats under the command of a Socialist government and its fiefdoms.

Subjects under such regimes, like in China, are required to comply. If deemed enemies of the State, individuals lose access to even the most basic liberties. Jobs, loans, public transportation, and social associations are stripped away. State mandates forbid them from leaving the country, leaving them to face imprisonment or die. Some may even be reduced to "assets" through involuntary organ donation.

Under such conditions, what incentive remains to work or pursue education when one cannot keep what they earn? Communism posits that people work for the betterment of society, yet even now, taxpayers fund social programs and foreign aid without transparency or restraint. In Communism, **gatekeepers determine** who receives resources and who is deprived. Are you a good subject or a criminal in the eyes of the State? Public shaming, as seen with Don Lemon and Andrew Cuomo's rhetoric during the vaccine mandates, exemplifies the "pebble" ripple effect—a precursor to introducing larger stones of control.

Socialism advocates for **communal ownership** of production, distribution, and exchange. But who regulates the community? Who *oversees the distribution* of goods? Let's dissect this: someone must lead. Property will no longer belong to individuals but to the State. And who grants authority to redistribute it? The "community" will not govern itself; it will be ruled by the few.

The UN's "17 Goals of Sustainability" provides insight into this framework. By 2030, the UN aims to control borders, armies, self-defense, speech, and elections while punishing "hate speech" and dissent under international law. College militants, ironically advocating fascism, further this agenda.

Social and mainstream media gatekeepers determine what constitutes hate speech or disinformation, punishing platforms with fines for non-compliance. There are no clear guidelines, only rules rewritten daily to align with Socialist goals. Words are weaponized; accusations are punishable by law. This diminishes the value of the Bill of Rights and Constitution, inundating Americans with convoluted bureaucratic laws.

Under Socialism, societal exhaustion is the first step toward revolution. Traditional values and societal norms are abandoned for undefined constructs with no reference point.

> "Any revolutionary change must be preceded by a passive, affirmative, non-challenging attitude toward change among the mass of our people. **They must feel so frustrated, so defeated**, so lost, *so futureless in the prevailing system* that they are willing *to let go of the past* and chance the future."
>
> —Saul Alinsky, *Rules for Radicals*

"Socialism is synonymous with leftism, welfarism, radicalism, progressivism, social democracy, Communism, and Marxism. Within Marxism, the theory defines Socialism as a transitional social state between the **overthrow of capitalism and the realization of Communism**." The labor movement plays a key role in this transition. https://www.merriam-webster.com/thesaurus/socialism

Ayn Rand, a Russian-American novelist, philosopher, and creator of Objectivism, describes Socialism as a progressive movement toward Communism:

> "There is no difference between Communism and Socialism, except in the same ultimate end: Communism proposes to enslave men by force, and Socialism—by the vote. It is merely the difference between murder and suicide."
>
> —Ayn Rand

In America, college militants glamorize Socialism and Communism as virtuous while demonizing capitalism. But will Socialism solve societal problems once the government gains total control over its subjects? History offers no example where granting absolute power to a government was ever good for the people.

> "Utopianism substitutes *glorious predictions and unachievable promises* **for knowledge, science, and reason** while laying claim to them all. Yet there is nothing new in *deception disguised as hope* and nothing original in abstraction framed as progress. A heavenly society is said to be within reach. If only the individual surrenders more of his liberty and being for the general good, meaning the good as prescribed by the State. If he refuses, he will be tormented and **ultimately coerced into compliance**, *for conformity is essential.*"
>
> —Mark R. Levin, *Ameritopia: The Unmaking of America*

George Orwell echoes this sentiment in *Wigan Pier, Marxism, and the Working Class.* He critiques Marxism's "Theory of Suffering," noting that many self-proclaimed Socialists have motives far removed from genuine love for the working class:

"It might be said, however, that even if the 'theoretical-oriented, book-trained Socialist is not a working man himself, at least ... he is actuated by the love of the working class. He is endeavoring to shed his bourgeois status and fight on the side of the proletariat—obviously, that must be his motive. But is it? Sometimes, I look at the Socialist … the intellectual tract-writing type of Socialist with his pullover, his fuzzy hair, and his Marxist quotations, and wonder what the devil his motive really is … it's really difficult to believe it's the love of anybody. Especially if the working class, from whom he is, of all people, *the furthest removed*."

> "The truth is that to many people, calling a Socialist revolution does not mean a movement of the masses with which they hope to '**associate themselves**'—*it means a set of reforms* **which *we***, the clever ones, are going to *impose on them*, the lower order."
>
> —George Orwell

Orwell observed that many intellectual Socialists despise the bourgeoisie, even as they often *belong to this class themselves*. Their hatred of "**exploiters**" manifests as **a self-righteous crusade** to *impose reforms* on others.

Larry Arnhart summarizes Aristotle's observations in *Political Science: The Study of Regimes*:

"**Only human beings** have the capacity for logos—**the capacity for speech and reason**. The Greek word logos denotes either speech or reason and can, therefore, be translated as reasonable speech. The most profound association comes from the *mutual understanding* of the meaning of life. For human beings, living together means not just sharing in things of the body but the sharing of thoughts. A human community is a '**state of mind**.' While animals possess *perceptual thought*, only human beings possess '**conceptual thought**.'" (p. 45, Arnhart)

Conceptual thinking involves identifying patterns and connections, **addressing key underlying issues**, and using reason to derive solutions or alternatives. *Conceptual thinking* defined: Graham Davy. 2021. Psychopathology, 3rd Edition. Wiley Blackwell. **Without** freedom of speech, individuals *cannot* fully conceptualize ideas or reason effectively, limiting their ability to resolve problems within their communities or themselves.

Aristotle noted that humans, despite their capacity for reason, often prioritize **self-interest** over the common good.

> "Human beings are born with different capacities; if they are free, *they are not equal*. And if they are equal, **they are not free**."
>
> —Aleksandr Solzhenitsyn

Andrew Lobaczewski further explored human diversity in *Political Ponerology*: "The psychopath … can do anything at all and still have that **strange advantage** over the majority of people who are kept in line by their consciences. … *Some people*—whether they have a conscience or not—favor the ease of inertia, while others are filled with dreams and wild ambitions. Some human beings are brilliant and talented, some are dull-witted, and most, conscience or not, are somewhere in between" (p. 11, Lobaczewski).

This underscores the inherent *inequality* in human nature, which defies the Socialist promise of equality in outcomes.

Abraham Lincoln echoed this sentiment when he defined equality as "equality of opportunity, **not equality of results**." He described it as affording all an "unfettered start and a fair chance in the race of life." (p. 184, Arnhart)

David C. Pack's observation encapsulates the current state of the world: "The world has changed, and humanity has entered a dark period that few recognize for what it is. Troubles are sweeping the globe and noticeably with greater force; deceit, division, disorder, instability, lawlessness, corruption, and conflict of every kind are intensifying."

CHAPTER 28

THE WILL OF THE TYRANT

> "Power is in *tearing human minds to pieces* and putting them together again in '**new shapes**' of your own choosing."
>
> —George Orwell, *1984*

> "A party seeks power entirely for its own sake. We are not **interested** in the good of others; we are interested *solely* in power, pure power … and we know that no one ever seizes power with the intention of relinquishing it. Power is not a means; it is an end. One does not establish a dictatorship in order to safeguard a revolution; one makes the *revolution* in order to establish the dictatorship. The object of persecution is persecution. The object of torture is torture. The object of power is power. Now you begin to understand me."
>
> —George Orwell, *1984*

If that statement doesn't give you chills, Machiavelli's observation may:

> "Everyone sees what you appear to be; **few experience** what you really are."
>
> —Niccolò Machiavelli, *The Prince*

> "People should either be caressed or crushed. If you do them minor damage, they will get their revenge, **but if**

> **you cripple them**, *there is nothing they can do.* If you need to injure someone, do it in such a way that you do not have to fear their vengeance."
>
> —Niccolò Machiavelli

The power struggle within political parties incites societal chaos by encouraging identity politics and tribalism. Groups act as though they are operating independently, *yet in reality*, they have been '**groomed**,' like Pavlov's dogs, primed for **reactionary** *autopilot.* Globalists have studied human behavior, sociologists and psychologists analyzing group dynamics and emotional responses. Armed with this knowledge, globalists **manipulate outcomes** by provoking specific reactions, much like an older sibling antagonizing the younger to elicit a predictable response.

Politicians and globalists have constructed a framework of trigger words—**carefully crafted** to 'provoke emotional responses' within **targeted groups**. These politically incorrect or offensive words spark outrage and fuel divisiveness, creating social chaos. It's like throwing wood onto an already roaring fire. The "grand puppet masters" keep the people emotionally fueled and distracted while pulling the strings behind the scenes.

> "Politically correct methods are the lifegiving broth of evil and perfect poisons for men such as Lenin, Mao, or Bill Clinton. Those men clothed their evil under the false fabric of doing good for their society. The concepts that make political correctness work, especially when embraced and supported by the government and a bankrupt media, are ideal for their **nefarious purposes**. Political correctness is a sharp stake wielded by the left to destroy free speech, eliminate diverse opinions, kill open discussions, and destroy America. Political correctness is not a method to enhance moderation, politeness, and logic in disputes **but a technique** to stop debate and kill the possibility of further thought."
>
> —William Kaliher

Kaliher's interpretation reflects the aggressive tactics used against conservative speakers on college campuses, where students attack opponents with labels like *-phobias*, racism, oppression, and 'white privilege.' Civil discourse is shut down before logic or reason can take hold. Colleges are **replacing one conformity** *with another*, steering students into 'new' social constructs disguised as altruistic motives.

Globalists claim to oppose traditional American values, yet they quietly embed Marxist ideologies into education and culture. The Constitution was designed to protect the people, not the government. The question becomes: how do you convince a **'free-thinking society'** to accept a Socialist or Communist regime without resistance? The *Art of War* offers insight: plant seeds of discontent and divisiveness through psychological warfare.

> "Bravery without forethought causes a man to fight blindly and desperately like a mad bull. Such an opponent must not be encountered with brute force **but may be lured into an ambush** and slain."
>
> —Sun Tzu, *The Art of War*

> "I use emotion for the many **and logic for the few**."
>
> —Adolf Hitler

Deprogramming begins by altering textbooks and subtly rewriting history. Control healthcare, making insurance unaffordable and inaccessible. **Fatigue** medical providers with excessive administrative tasks until they consent to socialized healthcare. Introduce inflation and mass immigration to disrupt societal norms and financial bankrupcy. Devalue the nuclear family, replacing terms like mother, father, son, and daughter with gender-neutral pronouns. Label dissenters intolerant or guilty of various *-isms* to suppress rebellion.

These tactics mirror McCarthyism, weaponizing Marxist strategies within the White House. Nancy Pelosi's promotion of pronoun-neutral language exemplifies the undermining of traditional communication, sowing confusion and disorientation.

> "The supreme *Art of War* is to **subdue the enemy** without fighting. Be extremely subtle, even to the point of formlessness. Be extremely mysterious, even to the point of soundlessness. Thereby, you can be the director of the opponent's fate."
>
> —Sun Tzu, *The Art of War*

The conglomerate elitists continue to disrupt social cohesiveness within communities by exploiting emotional instability and suppressing rational thought. They manipulate the progressive postmodern feminist, encouraging her to **battle for the alpha male position**, creating beta males in the process. She abandons her role as an alpha matriarch, leaving her children or aborting them. Drugs further debilitate society, with biowarfare enacted through the state's allowance of substance abusers to live on the streets, supplying them with clean needles instead of reform keeping them contained. The state claims altruistic motives, insisting these measures are preventative, all while watching these individuals suffer and die.

Others are sedated with 'legal substances' like energy drinks, caffeine, and nicotine. Society is demoralized through explicit sexual content in films and music, while truthful speech is replaced by relativism to avoid offense, fostering a society built on deceit. Divisiveness is injected into the populace, making it easier to control a 'fractured and self-conflicted' mass. Without the need to exhaust resources or manpower by forming an army, identity politics is **weaponized** to 'pit groups' against each other.

The oppressed are elevated to become 'new oppressors,' with perceived former oppressors forced into submission through guilt and labeled with collective crimes. Feminists assume the alpha male role while underrepresented identity *groups* dominate, using shame and accusations to **suppress the majority**. God is systematically removed from public spaces, including courts, eroding the moral foundation where 'truth' was once sworn before *Him*. Bureaucratic laws, tangled in red tape, leave citizens **lowering their heads** to avoid the wrath of progressive nihilists.

Science and biology are distorted, with evil redefined as good and vice versa. Speech is censored, with even the right to defend oneself criminalized. Only a select few—politicians, conglomerates, UN peacekeepers, and future European armies—will be allowed to bear arms.

Innocent, law-abiding citizens are branded guilty of collective crimes, their personal property confiscated in the name of equal wealth distribution and the "common good."

Creativity, success, and work ethic are extinguished as words are redefined through neologisms, their meanings warped to appease those in power. **Individual thought** diminishes under the weight of a collective mind engineered through fear, fallacies, and the rejection of traditions painstakingly developed over centuries. Open borders overwhelm social infrastructure, adding to taxation, financially bankrupting the nation. The value of the dollar decreases, driving society into a digital currency or credit system controlled by the state, where wealth can be turned off with the flick of a switch.

Customs and border protections are disregarded, enabling the unchecked potential flow of drugs, weapons, disease, human trafficking, and criminal activity. Agricultural safeguards become irrelevant. Citizens are forced to comply and accept the influx of unvetted immigrants adding to the financial burden placed on the state.

Social and mainstream media propagate opinionated journalism disguised as news, inundating society with a **relentless barrage of propaganda** that drowns independent thought. Repeated slogans and narratives saturate every network, drilling into the public mind until compliance is achieved.

> "The receptivity of the masses is very limited; their intelligence is small, but their power of forgetting is enormous. In consequence of these facts, **all effective propaganda** must be limited to a very few points and must harp on these in slogans until the last member of the public understands what you want him to understand."
>
> —Adolf Hitler

The film and music industries perpetuate the Marxist agenda, subtly embedding social constructs into unsuspecting minds. The music industry manipulates the **musical frequencies** to affect moods, while films serve as modern-day equivalents of the Roman Colosseum, distracting the masses while advancing political agendas. In Orwell's *1984*, Winston is forced to sit obediently before a screen, absorbing Big Brother's messaging. Hollywood conditions its audiences in a similar manner, dictating to the audience what is entertaining and acceptable, regardless of moral implications.

Actors, part of the elite, use their craft to hypnotize and deceive, earning millions while living in opulence. At awards shows, they pontificate from the stage, injecting their political idealisms, corralling fans into their moral relativism **and ridiculing** dissenters. This is *The Art of War* applied—subduing society without direct conflict, infiltrating from within to weaken resistance.

> "What is the alternative to working 'inside' the system? A mess of rhetorical garbage about 'Burn the system down!' Yippie yells, 'Do it!' or 'Do your thing.' What else? Bombs? Sniping? **Silence when police are killed, and screams of 'murdering fascist pigs' when others are killed?** Attacking and baiting the police? Public suicide? 'Power comes out of the barrel of a gun!' is an absurd rallying cry when the other side has all the guns."
>
> —Saul Alinsky

> "They have the guns, and therefore, we are for peace and reformation **through the ballot**. *When we have the guns*, then it will be through **the bullet**."
>
> —Saul Alinsky

> "**Ridicule** is man's most potent weapon." A skill perfected by journalist.
>
> —Saul Alinsky, *Rules for Radicals*

Taking over a country requires careful planning, wealth, power, and patience. Seeds are planted across all aspects of society, like a pathogen invading a 'body' undetected until symptoms appear. Hitler, Stalin, and Pol Pot used these tactics, and today, figures like Kim Jong-un and the Chinese Communist Party (CCP) employ similar strategies. Foreign entities claim to offer solutions for peace, but their true motives lie in advancing their own agendas. They cherry-pick issues, *siding with groups* that cause 'the most harm' **to further their cause.**

Why would billionaires with access to political power care about the opinions or outcomes of ordinary citizens? To a tyrant, the people are only a means to an end.

George Orwell's dystopian novel *1984* explores the dangers of totalitarianism, warning of a world governed by **propaganda**, *surveillance*, and censorship. Orwellian phrases such as "Big Brother" and "doublespeak" have since become widely recognized.

What is meant by "doublespeak?"

Doublespeak is a language that deliberately obscures, disguises, distorts, or reverses the meaning of words. It often takes the form of euphemisms, making the 'language' sound more **palatable**. It may also involve intentional ambiguity or actual inversions of meaning. Doublespeak is most closely associated with political language, where it serves to disguise the nature of truth. https://en.wikipedia.org/wiki/Doublespeak

An example of this is transforming political speech, 'hate speech into a hate crime', or the use of pronouns with no clear or definitive rules. This epitomizes the modern-day progressive Marxist agenda, which changes the meanings of words to serve nihilist purposes. Doublespeak creates ambiguity, disrupting language and the ability to communicate effectively—an intentional strategy outlined in many political playbooks.

In comparison, neologisms also play a role in relative speech.

"Neologism is a new word, usage, or expression. In psychology, a neologism is a newly coined word, typically by a person affected with schizophrenia, that is **meaningless** except to the coiner. It is often a combination of two existing words or *a distortion* of an existing word." (Merriam-Webster Dictionary)

The "coiner" represents an individual or identity group expressing a term primarily for their own benefit.

"For this reason I was born and have come into the world, to testify to the truth. Everyone who belongs to the truth listens to my voice." "What is truth?" Pilate asked (John 18:37, BSB).

If there is no truth, there can be no consensus or point of reference. Without a foundation for truth, people will believe whatever they are told, submitting to dominant or socially constructed entities because they lack a point of reference to discern otherwise.

> "Wisdom will save you from evil people, *from those* whose words are **twisted**."
>
> —2 Peter 2:12, NLT

> "A word **without meaning** is merely a sound."
>
> —Tolkien, *Tolkien* (Film, 2019, Fox Searchlight Pictures)

> "It's a beautiful thing, the destruction of words."
>
> —George Orwell, *1984*

CHAPTER 29

CITIZENSHIP VS. SERVITUDE

> "Never attempt to win by force what can be won by deception."
>
> —Niccolò Machiavelli, *The Prince*

Does diversity truly unite us? Edward J. Erler provides insight into the topic of citizenship and immigration:

"President Trump's zero-tolerance policy for illegal border crossers has provoked a hysterical reaction from Democrats, establishment Republicans, the progressive-liberal media, Hollywood radicals, and 'the deep state.' What particularly motivated the ire of these Trump-haters was the fact that the zero-tolerance policy would require the separation of parents and children at the border. The hysteria was, of course, completely insincere and fabricated, given that the policy of separating children and parents was nothing new—it had been a policy of the Obama and Bush administrations as well."

This presents a quandary: thousands of American children are separated from their parents each year due to arrests or convictions for violent and non-violent crimes. Many of those arrested are single mothers whose infants become wards of the State until sentences are served. Should there be a difference between illegals breaking the law by crossing the border and Americans held accountable for their crimes? Are we cherry-picking issues to rouse the public while ignoring other truths?

Additional concerns arise about children crossing borders with people

who may not be their parents. Should these children be detained until legal guardianship is verified to protect them from human traffickers? This is the purpose of immigration laws—to regulate the influx of people and protect the vulnerable. Not everyone crossing the border is in need; some come with nefarious motivations. Border patrol agents **are trained to identify** these threats.

Another question arises: why are migrants primarily traveling north to the US when Mexico spans 761,610 square miles and offers 5,800 miles of pristine coastline? Mexico, the world's 13th largest country, is three times the size of Texas. Why bypass opportunities within Mexico to reach the US? Does this relate to government corruption and political intent to open US borders to implement international law? Could it be a ploy to introduce human trafficking, drug cartels, gang-related crimes, and poverty into **unsuspecting** American communities? This influx disorients citizens, forcing them into hypervigilance out of fear, lest they appear intolerant or selfish.

Notably, wealthier neighborhoods like Martha's Vineyard and Malibu, or properties owned by celebrities like Oprah Winfrey, are not affected by the influx of migrants. Does the US government's leniency toward illegal immigration relate to potential future voters, given the advocacy for "no ID" voting? Identification requirements are criticized as discriminatory, yet undermining **voting integrity** violates constitutional rights granted **only to citizens.** This doublespeak implies that requesting ID is oppressive, part of a broader agenda that aligns with George Soros's **Open Borders** Foundation (now called Open **Society** Foundation).

Is this altruistic façade simply a ruse to dismantle the Republic through federal interference? The Open Society Foundation seeks to **abolish borders** and **end US sovereignty** under the guise of humanitarianism. Perhaps "Open Borders" was too transparent, prompting the name change to something more **palatable** (Doublespeak).

Skeptics may dismiss such claims as conspiracy theories, yet possibilities arise: Are migrants being incentivized to cross the border with promises of financial entitlements funded by taxpayers? Are cartels exploiting people for profit, locking them in unsafe transport? More probable is that global elites and business conglomerates seek a borderless country, filling it with illegal immigrants who can vote without ID, **effectively overriding the rights** of American citizens.

Without borders, the US ceases to be a nation. The UN could claim jurisdiction under the UN Charter, subjecting Americans to international law and the "One World Government" (OWG) envisioned in the "Great Reset." A **stateless America** would render citizenship, voting, and property ownership meaningless. Freedoms and liberties would vanish, leaving individuals as subjects of the New World Order. The education system already introduces concepts of "global citizenship" to prepare future generations for servitude under this regime.

If migrants are **escaping tyranny** and cartels in their countries, would their arrival not expose Americans to similar dangers? Would the cartels not follow them? And if not, how would we know? The US already faces an opioid crisis, fentanyl deaths, and human trafficking. Why is the US expected to police the world and provide humanitarian aid at the expense of its citizens? Isn't this the responsibility of the UN? Or are they waiting until 2030 to implement their 17 Goals and Sustainment Act, **contingent** on the collapse of American sovereignty?

Southern Mexico and Belize offer beautiful countrysides, yet the migration persists northward. Are we appeasing the Open Society Foundation's agenda to make America indistinguishable from other nations? This aligns with the UN's Developmental Initiative, encouraging illegal immigration **despite** the trillion-dollar national deficit and bypassing laws meant to protect citizens.

While Homeland Security exists to safeguard borders, enforcement falters, leaving citizens vulnerable. The CIA, tasked with national security, is scarcely effective at protecting one individual, let alone millions.

Similar patterns are evident in Europe and England, where overpopulation and financial strain overwhelm its infrastructure. The taxpayer bears the burden, whether in England or the US Foundations like the Open Society Foundation remain untaxed, advocating for humanitarianism while burdening citizens with exorbitant infrastructure costs, unsustainable overpopulation, and potential cultural deviance.

Meanwhile, the US military is deployed to foreign wars, creating enemies and casualties among young soldiers. Diplomacy is absent, and the UN remains silent, preserving its self-interest. By 2030, the UN claims to have solutions, **but only after overseeing the destruction it facilitated**. Their promise to rebuild positions them as saviors—a 'chilling parallel' to the actions of an anti-Christ.

We send our brave men and women to secure freedom *in other countries*, **yet we fail to secure** and defend our homeland. The US military remains dispersed or killed, while anti-American protestors 'nitpick' the splinter in the soldier's eye, ignoring the **log in their own**. They hold picket signs, glue themselves to the ground, destroy college campuses, and deface art in protests against social injustice. Yet, they are nowhere to be found at American borders to protect children or protest drug cartels and human trafficking. These protests **appear** staged and strategically orchestrated.

> "We are asked to believe something incredible: that the American character **is defined only** by its '**unlimited acceptance** of diversity.'"
>
> —Edward J. Erler

Americans are judged not only by their character but also by how deeply others can 'pick their pockets' while crying out *oppression*.

Erler continues, "In the 2016 presidential campaign, Donald Trump appealed to the importance of citizens and borders. In other words, Trump took his stand on behalf of nation-state and citizenship against the idea of a homogenous world-state populated by '**universal persons**.'"

The social construct of referring to immigrants as "**universal persons**" is telling. American civil servants swear an oath to protect the interests of **American citizens first**, not foreign entities. The term "universal person" or "global citizen" signifies subjugation under international law rather than allegiance to one's nation.

"The homogenous world-state—the European Union on a global scale—will not be a constitutional democracy; it will be the administration of '**universal personhood**' without the **inconvenience** of having to *rely on the consent* of the governed."

Schools now teach children to identify as "global citizens," subtly deflecting their allegiance away from American citizenship. Meanwhile, the education system inundates children with topics on sexual identities and body dysphoria, neglecting civics education that would instill an **understanding of their responsibilities** *as citizens.*

> "Freedom is never more than **one generation away** from extinction. We didn't pass it to our children in the bloodstream. It must be fought for, protected, and handed on for them to do the same."
>
> —Ronald Reagan

> "I will make mere lads their leaders, and children will rule over them. **The people will oppress one another**, man against man, neighbor against neighbor; the young will rise up against the old, and the base against the honorable. A man will seize his brother within his father's house: 'You have a cloak—you be our leader! Take charge of this heap of rubble.'"
>
> —Isaiah 3:4–6, BSB

> "Who is like the wise person, and who knows the '**interpretation**' of a matter?"
>
> —Ecclesiastes 8:1, HCSB

The idea of "universal personhood" envisions governance by unelected and unaccountable bureaucrats. These administrative fiefdoms magnify their power, expanding reach in ways that erode individual freedoms. Edward J. Erler, in his 2018 article *Does Diversity Really Unite Us?*, warns that universal persons would not hold citizenship or the right to vote. Instead, they would become clients or subjects of serfdom, with individual rights **supplanted** by the "collective welfare" **determined** by bureaucrats.

> "If a man in the state of nature so free, as has been said; if he be 'absolute lord of his own person and processions', equal to the greatest, **and subject to nobody**, *why will he part with his freedom*? Why would he give up his empire and subject himself to the dominion and control of any other power? To which it is obvious to answer, that though in the State of nature, he hath such a right, yet enjoyment

> of it is very uncertain, and constantly exposed to the invasion of others."
>
> —John Locke, *Two Treatises of Government*

Locke interpreted that 'equality of outcomes' is **inherently unattainable**. Hierarchies exist by nature: professors are not equal to students, commanding officers are not equal to privates, and experienced individuals differ from the inexperienced. Andrew Lobaczewski, in *Political Ponerology*, explains, "The answer (to a conscience) will depend largely on what your desires happen to be because people **are not all the same**. Even the profoundly unscrupulous are not all the same. Some people—whether they have a conscience or not—favor the ease of inertia, while others are filled with dreams and wild ambitions. Some human beings are brilliant and talented, some are dull-witted, and most, conscience or not, are somewhere in between."

This differentiation underscores that people persevere or cling to inertia based on their **intrinsic motivations**. Studies such as the *Marshmallow Test* illustrate this contrast. **The ability to delay gratification correlates** with better outcomes in later life, **distinguishing** those with discipline from those who *succumb* to impulse.

For the psychopath, peace is never an option. Tyrants will always exist—those who thirst to subjugate their fellow man. History shows they came to the New World with both good and ill intentions: some sought refuge and peace, while others aimed for *domination*.

Tucker Carlson, in *Ship of Fools*, asserts, "Progressive liberalism no longer views self-preservation as a rational goal of the nation-state. Rather, it insists that **self-preservation and national security must be subordinate** *to openness and diversity*. America's immigration policies, we are told, should demonstrate our commitment to diversity because an important part of the American character is openness, and our commitment to diversity is an affirmation of 'who we are as Americans.' If this carries a risk to our security, it is a small price to pay. Indeed, the willing assumption of risk adds authenticity to our commitment. This should not be surprising."

> "Greater diversity **means inevitably** that we have ***less in common***, and the more we encourage diversity, the

less we honor the common good. Any honest and clear-sighted observer should be able to see that diversity is a solvent that dissolves the unity and cohesiveness of a nation—and we should not be deceived into believing that its proponents do not understand the full impact of their advocacy!"

—Tucker Carlson, *Ship of Fools: How a Selfish Ruling Class Is Bringing America to the Brink of Revolution*

"President George W. Bush, no less than President Obama, was an advocate of a 'borderless world.' A supporter of amnesty and a path to citizenship for illegal aliens, he frequently stated that 'family values don't stop at the border' and **embraced the idea** that 'universal values **transcend** a nation's sovereignty.'"

—Tucker Carlson

What did Bush and Obama mean by "embracing the idea of universal values to transcend a nation's sovereignty?" These former Presidents, who swore an oath to protect the Constitution and safeguard the security of American citizens, appeared to advocate for a borderless world. Did they deceive the country when they pledged to act in its best interest, undermining their oath and deceiving the American people? To compound matters, "thousands of little unelected bureaucrats (fiefdoms: feudal lords)" push foreign interests and create unconstitutional laws that do not serve the governed.

Consider George Soros and his 'newly appointed' son, Alex Soros. What does a billionaire gain from promoting open borders (through the Open Society Foundation) in countries where he holds no personal stake? George Soros is a man who has shown no remorse for his participation in the persecution of Jews during WWII. At the age of fourteen, he informed on Jews to the Nazis, acting as a stool pigeon for the gestapo. Why would someone **indifferent** to the suffering of his own people care for others unconnected to him? A boy who aided the Nazis in targeting the most vulnerable—women, children, and the elderly—will he not raise his sons with the same indifference?

"The one who sows injustice will reap disaster."

—Proverbs 22:8

Soros also has a controversial history in global economics. He influenced the Philippine financial banking system into bankruptcy and manipulated the British currency, similar to insider trading but on a national scale. The Rothschild family, similarly, financed Napoleonic wars and the French Revolution, setting global objectives as early as the 1800s, shortly after the signing of the Declaration of Independence.

Klaus Schwab, founder of the World Economic Forum (WEF), also has historical ties to the Nazi regime. His father, Eugen Wilhelm Schwab, was the director of Escher Wyss AG, a contractor for the Third Reich. Klaus Schwab himself was mentored by Henry Kissinger, former US Secretary of State.

> "What distinguishes Sun Tzu's *The Art of War* from Western writers in terms of strategy is the **emphasis on the psychological and political elements** over the purely military."
>
> —Henry Kissinger

Kissinger's influence is evident in the plan for global control. "Today's Americans would be outraged if the UN troops entered Los Angeles to restore order; **tomorrow, they would be grateful**. This would be especially true if they were told there was an outside threat from beyond, whether real or promulgated, that threatened our very existence. It is then that all people of the world pledge with world leaders to deliver them from this evil. **The one thing that every man fears is the unknown**. When presented with this scenario, 'individual rights' will be **willingly relinquished** for the guarantee of their well-being granted to them by their world government" (Henry Kissinger, addressing the Bilderberg meeting in Evian, France, May 21, 1992).

If Governor Gavin Newsom were removed from office, California's problems might be mitigated, but that's **not the objective**. He is fulfilling *his role* in a larger plan to '**dismantle**' the state. The puppet masters manipulate Americans like pawns on a chessboard, and Europe is no exception.

> "Their tongues are deadly arrows; they speak deception. With his mouth, *a man speaks peace* to his neighbor, but in his heart, **he sets a trap for him**."
>
> —Jeremiah 9:8, BSB

CHAPTER 30

THE ORGANIZER'S FIRST JOB IS TO INFILTRATE FROM WITHIN

> "Infiltration into **the key positions** of trade unions, cooperatives, *and citizens' groups* must be **skillfully planned**, especially in sensitive areas (identity politics, gender, and elections). Sympathizers and fellow travelers are to be groomed to show a false face to the enemy. Popular issues are to be exploited to fan the discontent with the *status quo* **into raging hostility**."
>
> —Kent Clizbe, *Willing Accomplices: Political Correctness and Hate-America-First Political Platform and Destroy America*

Saul Alinsky, in his 1971 book *Rules for Radicals*, laid out a strategy for social disruption. "You must help the people in the community to feel so frustrated, so defeated, so lost, so futureless in the prevailing system that they are willing to let go of the past and chance the future. Plant seeds by **creating an organization** (*that*) **must shake up the prevailing patterns** of their lives, agitate, create disenchantment and discontent."

This strategy involves creating a future unknown and chancing the future, governed by unelected powers. Social constructs of 'discontent' are cultivated by grooming the vulnerable through repetitive conditioning, where 'lies' become accepted truths. Charismatic public servants deliver hypnotic speeches, convincing identity groups of their good intentions while exploiting them to further hidden agendas. Speeches not aligned with the Constitution.

> "With the current values, to produce, if not a passion, affirmative, non-challenging climate fan the embers of **hopelessness** into a flame of fight."
>
> —Saul Alinsky

Notably, Alinsky dedicated his book to Lucifer, "the first rebel to go against the establishment and win his kingdom." Is this an example of moral relativism or a moral absolute? It would seem to align with subjective reasoning by the "coiner," **not intended** for the majority.

"Anomaly" refers to something *deviating* from what is standard, normal, or expected.

"Norm" refers to an **accepted standard or behavior agreed** on by most people.

> "The organizer's first job is to create the issues or problems, and organizations must be based on *many issues* (**simultaneously**, keeping the masses distracted from finishing a thought). The organizer **must first rub raw the resentments** of the people of the community and fan the latent hostilities of many of the people to the point of overt expression. **He must search out controversy** and issues rather than avoid them, for unless there is controversy, people are not concerned enough to act."
>
> —Saul Alinsky, *Rules for Radicals*

Disruption becomes the primary strategy—agitate, divide, and **exhaust** until people **accept new constructs** as the new norm.

Constant rhetoric on systemic racism, rape culture, 'white privilege,' and collective crimes against marginalized groups disrupts society without offering a resolution. Dialogue is silenced, and open discussions are replaced with ridicule, intolerance, and violent objections. Academic institutions foster this by condemning conservative speakers and *training students* into '**reactionary autopilot**.' A careful listener will notice classroom discussions often veer into pro-Marxist ideology, priming students against traditional American values.

> "If his forces are united, **separate them**."
>
> —Sun Tzu, *The Art of War*

The *12 Rules for Radicals* were written by an anti-American who exploited 1960s and 1970s college students protesting the Vietnam War to further his agenda of transforming America into a Socialist/Communist state.

Consider Senator Joseph McCarthy, who sought to expose Communist infiltration within the US government during the 1950s. His efforts, branded as "McCarthyism," resulted in public ridicule and dismissal as "unsubstantiated allegations."

> "One thing to remember in discussing the Communists in our government is that we are not dealing with spies who get 'thirty pieces of silver' to steal the blueprints of a new weapon. We are dealing with a far more sinister type of activity because it **permits the enemy** to guide and shape our policy."
>
> —Senator Joseph McCarthy

Alinsky himself remarked, "True revolutionaries do not flaunt their radicalism. They cut their hair, put on suits, and '**infiltrate the system**' *from within*."

How do you minimize or eradicate the damage caused by such infiltration? Alinsky provides a chilling answer:

"**Pick the target**, freeze it, personalize it, and polarize it. Cut off the support network and isolate the target from sympathy (the majority, political party, the unvaccinated, Christians, partiots). Go after people and not institutions; people hurt faster than institutions. This is cruel but very effective."

Mainstream media applies these tactics daily. Conservatives are interrupted, **ridiculed**, discredited, and silenced before their message can be understood. Rhetorical questions are posed to steer the audience,

filling in answers meant to suppress critical thinking. This strategy isn't limited to one political party; manipulation is wielded across the spectrum.

> "For the time will come when men (*and women*) will not **tolerate sound doctrines**, but with itching ears, they will gather around themselves teachers *to suit their own desires.* So, they will turn their ears **away from the truth** and turn aside to myths."
>
> —2 Timothy 4:3–4, BSB

Truth? "We shall have none of that," they say.

CHAPTER 31

The Rule of Reasoning: "What Is Good Government?"

Socialist sympathizers often speak as if people are 'innately good' and suggest that socioeconomic equality, equal wealth distribution, and equal outcomes will elevate social awareness and morality. Yet, one must ask: do people truly appreciate favorable circumstances, or do they develop **self-awareness** through work ethics and personal effort?

Socialist ideology presumes that individuals will willingly work for the betterment of society while **setting aside** self-interest, incentives, and personal growth. This ideology kills ambition and discourages the drive to challenge oneself. Such policies echo the idea of giving every child a 'trophy' or replacing letter grades with vague assessments like "exceeding," "meeting," or "not meeting" expectations.

> "If I were the Devil, I'd take from those who have and give to those who wanted until I have **killed the incentive of the ambitious**."
>
> —Paul Harvey, *If I Were the Devil*

Within the rule of reason, can the betterment of society rest solely on socioeconomic equality? Can it prevent war, violence, tribalism, and moral decay? Will Socialism alone erase the plagues of human history to create a utopia? Divine laws were given to guide people toward moral and ethical behavior, yet society often ignores them. If we fail to respect the laws of God, why would we respect the laws of man?

Nihilists use bureaucracy and fiefdoms to enact laws serving their interests under the guise of social justice. How long will people endure unconstitutional laws that contradict natural laws, the US Constitution, and divine principles? Could one simply **rewrite** the Ten Commandments? Which laws would be changed, and why?

> "You must not murder. You must not commit adultery. You must not steal. You must not **testify falsely against** your neighbor. You must not covet your neighbor's house, wife, husband, or anything else that belongs to your neighbor."
>
> —Exodus 20:13–17, NLT

These moral laws are universal. No one rejoices when a loved one is murdered, their home is burglarized, or their spouse is unfaithful. Whether theist *or atheist*, these standards hold true.

Yet, we now find ourselves governed by political and foreign entities making decisions without consent, prioritizing their interests. The premise of God's laws has been overshadowed by nihilistic bureaucracies. Man's intrinsic value—**a divine gift of existence** without fear of enslavement—faces erasure by governments seeking ultimate control.

Nietzsche envisioned this in his concept of the "Superman," where, "**creating new values by superior human beings** was the highest expression of the will to power that is the fundamental reality of life. In creating new values, human beings **take the place of God**" (Larry Arnhart, *Political Questions*).

> "The 'truth' is a terrible thing, **but not compared** to falsehood."
>
> —Jordan Peterson

Historically, governments often ruled subjects as property, not as citizens. Under the proposed One World Government or International Law, people would once again become "subjects"—stripped of the Constitution, voting rights, due process, and self-defense. Speech and religion would be censored, and the government would **replace God**.

Arnhart recounts Cesare Borgia's Machiavellian tactics:

"When Borgia took Romagna, he appointed an unusually cruel man to restore peace where the **previous rulers 'had created disorder**.' Once the agent had done *his job*, Borgia publicly punished him by having him cut in two and his body displayed in the public square. The ferocity of that spectacle left the people at the same time satisfied and stupefied."

Borgia's actions exemplified "**good government**" under a philosophy where the end justifies the means. Future governments might adopt similar tactics—manipulating identity politics, inflating national deficits, controlling resources, and **fabricating crises** under the guise *of restoring order.*

> "Human beings are the most political animals because they are the only animals endowed with the ability for '**reasoned speech**.' However, politics often *manifests* **not as the rule of reason** but as the *human desire* **to dominate others for selfish ends**."
>
> —Larry Arnhart

Thrasymachus argued that reasoned speech could be **weaponized for deception and power**. Similarly, *The Art of War* teaches that warfare relies on deception:

1. "If his forces *are united*, **separate them**." Disdain for nationalism and patriotism is encouraged, with accusations of ethnocentrism repeated until lies become truth.
2. "If the country is 'sovereign' and its subjects in accord, **divide them and occupy their minds** while waiting for an extraordinary moment *they cannot anticipate*."

Global elites leverage 'psychological and anthropological' studies *to manipulate society*, exploiting racial tensions, identity politics, and sexual dysphoria. Predictive algorithms and psychological conditioning, similar to Pavlov's experiments, prime people for reactionary behavior.

> "His primary target is '**the mind**' of the opposing commander. Sun Tzu realized that an indispensable preliminary to battle was to attack **the mind of the enemy**."
>
> —Sun Tzu

The enemy becomes the nationalist, the patriot, and the law-abiding citizen holding onto traditional rights. Once stripped of free speech, self-defense, and faith, society will conform to a global narrative.

> "Power is in **tearing human minds to pieces** and putting them together again in new shapes of your own choosing."
>
> —George Orwell, *1984*

In 1982, the documentary *No Place to Hide* aired an interview with Larry Grathwohl, who asked Bill Ayers about counter-revolution strategies. Ayers claimed people would need **re-education to adopt new ways of thinking**. When asked about *dissenters* (Defined as people who refuse to accept), such as "die-hard capitalists," Ayers estimated that **25 million Americans would need to be eliminated**. Despite these statements, Ayers faced no consequences and later became a *professor of education*.

> "Ayers became a professor at the University of Illinois, and his wife, Bernadine Dohrn, spent 23 years as director of Northwestern University's **Children and Family** *Justice Center*."
>
> —Jesse Kelly, *The Anti-Communist Manifesto*

I highly recommend reading *The Anti-Communist Manifesto* by Jesse Kelly. It is both frightening and deeply insightful. Research Bill Ayers and the people *he and his wife* **were connected to**. This will illuminate much about the deliberate efforts to dismantle the nuclear family, the patriarch, political parties, and the majority group. You will be astonished by what you uncover and who the key players are.

Pray for discernment, for what you see and hear may not be what it seems.

CHAPTER 32

THE MANIPULATION FOR POWER

> "We studied ourselves since we felt **something strange** *had taken over our minds*, and something valuable was leaking away irretrievably. The world of **psychological reality and moral values** seemed **suspended** as if in a chilly fog. Human feelings and sudden solidarity lost their meaning, 'as did patriotism *and our old established criteria*.'"
>
> —Andrew Lobaczewski, *Political Ponerology: A Science on the Nature of Evil Adjusted for Political Purposes*

Robert Greene wrote the New York Times bestseller *The 48 Laws of Power* and *The Art of Seduction*, praised by Henry Kissinger, former Secretary of Foreign Affairs to the United States. I won't outline every law for copyright constraints, but I will appeal to the laws that support my thoughts on the tactic used by *The Art of War*. The first law in question is Law #3.

LAW 3: Conceal Your Intentions

"Keep people **off-balance** and in the dark by never *revealing the purpose* behind your actions. If they have no clue what you are up to, *they cannot* **prepare a defense**. Guide them '**far enough down the wrong**

path, envelop them in enough smoke,' and by the time they realize your intentions, it will be too late."

"*The game is won* ..."

An interesting thought, yet a familiar statement made by Barack Obama during his speech at Stanford University. This has nothing to do with parties but everything to do **with political intent**.

> "You need to **flood a country's public square with enough sewage** ... you need to raise enough questions ... spread enough dirt ... plant enough conspiracy theorizing. **Let citizens no longer know what to believe**. Once they lose trust in their leaders, in political institutions, mainstream media, and in each other, in possibly in truth, *the game's won*."
>
> —Barack Obama, speaking at Stanford University about challenges to democracy

To correct the former President's speech, this country was not built *on democracy*. We are a **Constitutional Republic**. As Joseph Goebbels, Hitler's number one propagandist, quoted: "If something is said *often enough, people will believe it as being true*." Goebbels's speech was not intended to clarify the dissemination of disinformation but to condone censorship, under the premise that **the government will decide what truthful speech is** *and what is false*, following the statement "flooding the country's public square with enough sewage." Did he conceal his intentions to fuel racial tensions with his new movie on Netflix? I must be one of those people caught up in conspiracy theorizing.

LAW 11: Learn to Keep People Dependent on You

"Make people depend on you for their happiness and prosperity, and you have nothing to fear. **Never teach them enough** so that they can do *without you*."

Does this sound like conspiracy theorizing? Am I making this up? Could this be social deprogramming? Create **dependency** without any future hope or incentives? People tend to believe that "others" **somehow** "owe" them something without working for it. No logic in the sense of accountability and outcome of one's circumstance. Pity me instead and allow me to accuse others of a collective crime without due process. This allows the indignant to inflict pain and insult without recourse. This allows the wealthy to exploit the vulnerable while claiming social justice and feeding the flames of discontent.

Socialism was brought under the guise of social programs and dependency. People are forced to pay for Social Security when working, and now the elderly depend on the government to support them, even after all the money has been recklessly spent, keeping the people in a state of **uncertainty**. Money that is *rightfully* theirs.

LAW 31: Control the Options: Get Others to Play with the Cards You Deal

"The **best deceptions** are the ones *that seem* to give the other person **a choice**: Your victims feel that they are in control but are actually your puppets. Give people options that come out in your favor, *whichever one they choose*. Force them to make choices between the 'lesser of two evils,' both of which **serve your purpose**."

A college-groomed militant is taught to be **intolerant** of anyone who does not agree with them—yet calling a *conservative* a fascist. Let's define what a fascist is according to Merriam-Webster:

"A political philosophy, movement, or regime that exalts nation and often race *above the individual* and **advocates** a centralized 'autocratic government' headed by a **dictatorial leader**, severe economic and social regimentation, and forcible suppression of opposition; a tendency toward or actual exercise of strong autocratic or dictatorial control."

The United States has a sitting President, the Constitution, the Declaration of Independence, the Bill of Rights, the US Senate, Congress, the House of Representatives, checks and balances, the Federal Bureau of Investigation (FBI), the Central Intelligence Agency (CIA), the Supreme Court, governors, and mayors who represent their states. Another reason why the Electoral College is so '*important*': **it allows each state to have a voice**. Otherwise, politicians would only need to **concentrate their**

campaigns *in a few states that support* their party. This would allow a political party to win every election.

This negates the perceived centralized autocratic authority under a dictator. We, the people, vote civil servants into political positions. **Politicians do not vote themselves into office**—except that is exactly what's happening now, breaking American laws.

Capitalism is only available in a free country. A Socialist/Communist country does not have capitalism except for an economy subjected to stringent governmental control. In a Socialist or fascist government, the people are not free to own property or keep what they sow, which would define oppression. *If the government owns everything you have,* **it will also own you**. Everything you sow or own belongs to the master (*the government*).

If the corporation abuses its position of power, it has committed an evil against society. If the government abuses the laws, it has committed an evil against its citizens. The means of capitalism **is not the sin**. Sin is committed by the perpetrator **who abuses their power**.

To understand how our forefathers designed American government and politics, see the breakdown in Hillsdale College *1776 Curriculum: High School, American Government & Politics: Pursuing Truth, Defending Liberty*. Some college-militarized students may need to be **re-educated** because, *without citizenship*, we become subjects to unelected bureaucrats with no country.

LAW 33: DISCOVER EACH MAN'S THUMBSCREW

"Everyone has a **weakness**, *a gap* in the castle wall. That weakness is usually an insecurity, an 'uncontrollable emotion' *or need*; it can also be a small pleasure (or the need for revenge and thirst for power, no matter the cost). Either way, *once found*, it is a 'thumbscrew', you can turn to **your advantage**."

Identity groups may fall under this premise. Find their Achilles's heel, expose their weakness and the need to belong, and use the **emotional trigger points** to your advantage. It's all very simple. The orchestrators would only need to stand behind enemy lines, instigate, allow the people to fight within themselves, plant the seed of discontent, and then absolve themselves of any wrongdoing.

Remember that society has been extensively studied, and people will follow their 'itching ears' and **innermost desires** while caring very little for the truth. Whoever appeals to their pocket-sized worldview will gain the **unchallenged intellect**.

LAW 43: WORK ON THE HEARTS AND MINDS OF OTHERS

"Coercion creates a reaction that will eventually work against you. You must seduce others into wanting to move in your direction. A person you have seduced becomes your loyal pawn. And a way to *seduce others* is to operate on their '**individual psychologies and weaknesses**.' Soften up the **resistant** by working on their emotions, playing on what they hold dear and what they fear."

> "Know how to be all things to all men. Proteus, a Greek god with the ability to change shape at will, to be whatever the moment required, transformed himself into a lion, then a serpent, a panther, a boar, running water, and finally a leafy tree, when his brother tried to seize him. A discreet Proteus, a scholar among scholars, a saint among saints. That is the art of winning over everyone, for like attracts like. Take note of temperaments and adapt yourself to that of each person you meet, follow the lead of the serious and jovial in turn, changing your mood discreetly."
>
> —Baltasar Gracián (1601–1658) as quoted in Robert Greene, *The 48 Laws of Power*

The social construct of reality for society is that nothing is real. Suppose you do not have just laws, **given to us by God**, and written foundational laws established by careful thinkers, given to us by our forefathers. In that case, you will inadvertently position a progressive nihilist to control society by the unelected unknowns with an agenda they intend to fulfill—and fulfill they will, with **or without your consent**.

CHAPTER 33

CRITICAL THINKING FOR THE AMERICAN

> "Never attempt to win **by force** what can be won *by deception.*"
>
> —Niccolò Machiavelli, *The Prince*

> "It is difficult to free fools from the chains they revere."
>
> —Voltaire

Within the laws of logic, corporate astronaut, rocket scientist, and space telescope engineer Leslie Wickman, PhD, explains the concept of critical thinking and its importance in group dynamics. She writes, "The distinction between something being 'true' or 'false' can only have **meaning if sound reason applies**. Without logic, there could be no such thing as true and false. The notion of logic includes right reason and valid inferences. **Reason requires** systematicity where **basic logic** can be grasped by understanding the fundamental laws of identity, non-contradiction, excluded middle, and rational inferences. This states that the Law of the Excluded Middle says that one of two mutually contradictory statements has to be true; *there is no third* or 'undecided' option; and the Law of Rational Inference says that if A=B, and B=C, then A must = C."

> "It would be nearly impossible to get along in the real world *without logic*."
>
> —Leslie Wickman, *God of the Big Bang*

As mentioned in Chapter 9 *Relativism vs. Absolute Truth*, Dr. Wickman explains the concept of critical thinking and its importance in group dynamics. Dr. Wickman further explains the Law of Non-Contradiction states that a contradictory statement cannot be true. It would be nearly impossible to get along in the real world without logic. If a statement is true, its contradictory statement *cannot also be true*. And if any universal accepted morality and historical fact claims to offer a **universal context for truth**, anything *contrary* to that "universal truth" will have to be false.

> "In this era of postmodernity, the notion of 'true' and 'false' has to be questioned."
>
> —Leslie Wickman, *God of the Big Bang*

Many college students and young adults claim, "That may be true for you, but not for me." This imposes a relative reality that is not constituted in truth or logic, imposing someone's subjective relativity and expecting others to accept it without empirical logic or reason.

The statement, "If the laws of logic are true, then relevant truth contradicts the laws of logic," implies there can be no third or undecided option. Truth is truth, *whether* we like it or not, or whether it interferes with our personal interests. To say, "I don't like that 2+2=4," *is irrelevant*. Truth, based on logic, does not cater to worldview, relativity, *or feelings*. Mathematics does not change to suit preferences; it is objective truth founded on empirical evidence.

Truth becomes a point of reference, not a hypothetical hypothesis or delusional reality coined by an 'individual' based solely on specific intellect, feeling, or mood. Truth and logic prevent us from reinventing the wheel or indulging in schizophrenia.

According to anthropology, there are *multiple* cultures within a society, each with its own norms or traditions. However, universal norms exist that the majority can agree on. For instance, if a group believes in killing children for sport, this is not a universal truth since most moral individuals understand it to be wrong. Universal truth helps society maintain cohesion and open communication. Without it, society would spiral into constant conflict.

> "*Y'hoshua* (Christ) showed his **frustration** with stubborn human hearts and heads in the face of *reason and evidence*."
>
> —Luke 16:31, NKJV

> "For the time will come when people will not put up with sound doctrine. Instead, to suit their own desires, **they will gather around them** a great number of **teachers to say what their itching ears want to hear**."
>
> —2 Timothy 4:3, NKJV

The concept of "itching ears" reveals how emotional preference can override logic. Emotion is subjective, not rooted in objective fact. Safe spaces, for example, create a false sense of security, conditioning individuals into conformity and isolating them from societal realities. These conditions weaken critical thinking, distorting facts and logic not to say also weakens resiliency in the face of adversities.

Sun Tzu's *The Art of War* advises creating war within undetected—placing individuals in **key positions** to manipulate systems. Politicians, lawyers, and professors can subtly condition others, pouring poison into their minds while pretending to serve the public good.

Objective reasoning stands apart from subjective experience. Objectivity involves **observable** facts, while *subjectivity* **relies on personal perception**, which can *vary widely*. Subjective reasoning, unmoored from logic, creates unpredictability.

> "A self-defeating statement is one that fails to meet its own standard."
>
> —Norman Geisler and Frank Turek

> "In fact, we humans have **a fatal tendency to try to adjust the truth** to fit our desires rather than adjusting our desires to fit the truth."
>
> —Norman Geisler and Frank Turek, *I Don't Have Enough Faith to Be an Atheist*

"We **demand truth in virtually** every area of our lives," they argue. Whether in medicine, law, or finance, truth is paramount. No one wants a doctor who disregards lab results or a court that ignores evidence. Yet, when it comes to political correctness, many accept the notion that truth is relative. The notion of relative truth can mean a number of things to a number of people with no universal consensus. Any thing outside truth defines an opinion, a self perception.

> "Perhaps Augustine was right when he said, 'We love the truth when it enlightens us, but we hate it when it **convicts us**.'"
>
> —Norman Geisler and Frank Turek, *I Don't Have Enough Faith to Be an Atheist*

> "Indeed, when Gentiles, who do not have the Law, do by nature what the Law requires, they are a Law to themselves, even though they do not have the Law … and **their conscience also bearing witness,** *and their thoughts* either accusing or defending them."
>
> —Romans 12:14–16, NKJV

In other words, we are innately capable of deciphering what is morally truthful, what is right or wrong, what is subjective and what is objective. We can distinguish truth from lies unless we turn a "blind eye" to satisfy our pocket-sized worldview, but that would be intentional *and subjective.*

Kennedy Ahenkora Adarkwa, PhD, explains, "Moral absolutism is concerned with right and wrong conduct. The absolute is what determines whether the action or conduct is right or wrong. Therefore, from the standpoint of moral absolute, some things are always right, and some things are always wrong, no matter how one tries to rationalize them. **Moral absolutism emerges from a theistic worldview.**"

To say that something is true means you must **compare it to a standard *or reference*** to define it as truth. For example, in solving a quadratic problem, you need the quadratic formula ($ax^2 + bx + c = 0; x = -b \pm \sqrt{(b^2 - 4ac)} / 2a$) and the order of operations (PEMDAS: Parentheses, Exponents, Multiplication, Division, Addition, and Subtraction). Following *this objective path* **ensures you arrive at a correct and consistent answer**. A subjective approach to solving such problems would yield multiple incorrect answers.

This principle applies beyond mathematics. Imagine a pharmacist preparing medications based on subjective reasoning, leading to inconsistencies in frequency, and potency. Such errors could be dangerous, even lethal. Similarly, consider asking for change: would you accept it if someone handed you a one-dollar bill instead of a hundred, claiming it was their "subjective" view of equivalence?

> "Moral relativism contradicts moral absolutes because it insists that what is true for the individual **replaces the search for absolute truth**."
>
> —Mark P. Cosgrove, *Foundations of Christian Thought*

> "Moral relativism is an attempt to undermine the claim that there is no objective moral law or moral absolute that is **the same for all human beings**."
>
> —J. P. Moreland, *Scaling the Secular City*

J. P. Moreland argues, "If relativism is true, **then all choices are equally good**. If all choices are equally good, then even *intolerance* toward other beliefs can be morally correct. Why, then, should anyone practice tolerance? Moral relativism is always about an individual's choice, whether right or wrong. In relativism, **the individual determines what is right and what is wrong**, no matter how it affects others."

If relativism were true, could a thief in a court of law justify robbery by claiming that stealing is "morally good" from their perspective? Whose reasoning would prevail—the victim's or the thief's?

Had people not stood against moral relativism during the era of slavery, would slavery ever have been abolished? Slavery falls under moral absolutes—it is *always morally wrong*, **for all people**, in all circumstances.

> "If there are no moral absolutes, why then have some CEOs of companies and corporations in the United States been incarcerated for misappropriation of corporate funds? Why do we spend millions tracking drug cartels and traffickers? Why do we spend billions fighting global terrorists who seek to make the world unsafe if all subjective reasoning is equally valid?"
>
> —Kennedy Ahenkora Adarkwa, PhD, adjunct professor of evangelism

Moral absolutes maintain standards of right and wrong, universally applied and understood. **They eliminate guesswork about what is just**, *ensuring fairness and equality for all.*

CHAPTER 34

THE SUPREMACY OF ACTING ABOVE THE LAW.

18 US Code § 2385: Advocating Overthrow of Government

"Whoever knowingly or willfully advocates, abets, advises, or teaches the duty, necessity, desirability, or propriety of 'overthrowing or destroying the government of the United States or the government of any State, Territory, District or Possession thereof, or the government of any political subdivision therein, by force or violence, or by the assassination of any officer of any such government; or whoever, with intent to cause the overthrow or destruction of any such government, prints, publishes, edits, issues, circulates, sells, distributes, or publicly displays any written or printed matter advocating, advising, or teaching the duty, necessity, desirability, or propriety of overthrowing or destroying any government in the United States by force or violence, or attempts to do so; **or whoever organizes or helps or attempts to organize any society, group, or assembly of persons who teach, advocate, or encourage** the overthrow or destruction of any such government by force or violence or becomes or is a member of, or affiliated with, any such society, group, or assembly of persons, knowing the purposes thereof—shall be fined under this title or imprisoned not more than twenty years, or both, and shall be ineligible for employment by the United States or any department or agency thereof, for the five years next following his conviction."

Would this law apply to violent protesters who have burned or defaced public property and assaulted people? Would organizations such as the Bail Project be subject to legal scrutiny under this statute? The orchestration of large-scale **protests and riots does not occur by chance**; someone with an agenda organizes and funds these movements. Perhaps it is worth questioning why those sworn to protect American citizens and uphold the law have failed to do so. Instead, unelected bureaucrats, foreign and domestic elites, corporate conglomerates, and political insiders appear to operate with impunity, undermining American principles.

The Bail Project

Tucker Carlson remarked, "Bail Projects are funding the riots, **but who is funding the project**?" Carlson pointed to billionaire Michael Novogratz as a key figure, providing financial support for efforts that resulted in billions of dollars of property damage. Why have insurance companies, which absorb the financial losses from this destruction, not pursued legal action against these bail initiatives?

The apparent purpose of these riots is to create discord, exploiting crises to push hidden agendas. What narrative is the mainstream media, along with politicians, Hollywood, and the music industry, reinforcing through their selective focus? What does a billionaire gain by funding unrest and inciting a civil war? These acts undermine public order, yet those responsible are often released without conviction or significant legal consequences.

> "They take bribes to let the wicked go free, and they punish the innocent."
>
> —Isaiah 5:23

The Justice Department's failure to prosecute such actions raises questions about the rule of law. Section 18 US Code § 2385 clearly states the penalties for advocating violence or organizing groups aimed at government overthrow.

"If two or more persons conspire to commit any offense named in this section, each shall be fined under this title or imprisoned not more than twenty years, or both, and shall be ineligible for employment by the

United States or any department or agency thereof, for the five years next following his conviction."

Does this reality resonate with college militants? Those convicted would be barred from employment for five years after serving their sentence, while the professors and orchestrators remain untouched in their tenured positions.

Public violence, destruction of property, and instilling fear are not peaceful protests but criminal acts. The Constitution guarantees the right to peaceful assembly—not lawlessness reminiscent of third-world insurgencies. Marxism, by its very nature, threatens the Republic by advocating for the abolition of traditional family structures, obsolve freedoms and liberties and private property.

Patrisse Cullors, a founder of Black Lives Matter, openly described herself as a *trained* Marxist. This admission raises questions about the movement's intentions and whether it serves broader ideological goals. The adoption of the Communist fist as a symbol further blurs the lines between civil rights advocacy and Marxist political agendas. Again expoiting the vulnerable.

> "If one can design propaganda or psychological operations **that bypass the consciousness and rational faculties of the individual**, *targeting instead* suppressed emotions and hidden desires, it is 'possible' *to move people* to adopt beliefs and behaviors **without them being aware** of the 'underlying motivations leading them on.' [If] we understand the mechanism and motives of the group mind, is it not impossible to control and regiment the masses according to our will without their knowing it?"
>
> —Edward Bernays, *Propaganda*

> "If those in charge of our society—politicians, corporate executives, and owners of press and television—**can dominate our ideas**, [they] will be secure in power. They will not need **soldiers** patrolling the streets."
>
> —Howard Zinn

> "When people attempt to rebel against the iron logic of Nature, they come into conflict with the very same principles to which they owe their existence as human beings (freedom and liberty). Their actions *against Nature* must lead to their own downfall."
>
> —Adolf Hitler

> "Knowing their thoughts, Jesus (*Yehoshua*) said to them, 'Every kingdom divided against itself will be laid waste, and every city or household 'divided' **against itself** will not stand.'"
>
> —Luke 12:25, BSB

> "There will always be those who desire to control others and those who will listen. George Orwell '*The Lord of the Flies* **explores the dark side of humanity**, the savagery that *underlies* even the most civilized human beings. A novel intended as a tragic parody of children's adventure tales, illustrating humankind's intrinsic evil Nature.'"
>
> —William Golding, *The Lord of the Flies*

> "'Stir up the waters to catch fish: **Anger and emotions are strategically 'counterproductive**.' You must always stay 'calm and objective.' But if you can make your enemies angry while staying calm yourself, you gain a decided advantage. Put your enemies **off-balance**: Find the 'chink' ***in their vanity*** through which you can 'rattle them,' and you hold the strings.'"
>
> —Robert Greene, *The 48 Laws of Power*

Chink defined: "A narrow opening, such as a crack or fissure." A small opening into the minds of people. Find their Achilles's heel and then manipulate from there by pulling their strings.

Strings, pitchforks, broomsticks, and rocks? I am not the only one who has read these books. What are the underlying advantages of pulling our strings? Emotions, coercions, testing those who resist. Politicians are advocating for gun control, calling American citizens extremists for wanting to exercise their right to defend themselves. Are we allowing politicians to convince us to give up our right to bear arms? Making the law-abiding citizens pay for a crime they didn't commit. Criminals break the law and use arsenals to harm our children and communities, and law enforcement goes after the law-abiding citizens who lawfully registered their guns. Shall we fight with pitchforks, broomsticks, and rocks? Shall we become the progressive Russian gulag? Can the "dark side of humanity" **usher in the perfect crisis**, exhausting the nation and leaving the Americans defenseless?

> "'Brute force must first 'stifle' **the resistance of an exhausted nation**: People possessing *military or leadership skills* **must be disposed of**, and anyone appealing to moral values and legal principles must be silenced. The new principles are never explicitly enunciated. People must learn the new unwritten law via painful experience (gatekeepers, disinformation). The stultifying influence of this deviant world of concepts finishes the job, and common sense demands caution and endurance.'"
>
> —Andrew M. Lobaczewski, *Political Ponerology: A Science on the Nature of Evil Adjusted for Political Purposes*

Interesting set of 'words.' No God, no sovereign country, no ownership, and no family. We will possess nothing that will give the individual strength to oppose the oligarchs.

Planting the seeds to incite civil war without a declaration by an **unidentified** enemy. Arresting people for not wearing a mask, unconstitutional mandates, and blocking them from employment for noncompliance brings to mind the Nazi regime all over again. Even the court system is turning "a blind eye," working behind closed doors. If judges and politicians continue to abuse their position of power without punishment for ethical misconduct and or criminal recourse, what will become of the citizens? What will become of the country?

Let me use a simple analogy to prove a point. Children are not equal to their parents, students are not equal to their teachers, employees are not equal to their employers, and a coach is not equal to their players. The judge is above the plaintiffs, the defendants, the jury and the attorneys, but **they are not** above the law. The same principle can be applied to any organization positioned in power. Whatever organization "it" may be cannot be equal to the rest, but with power come responsibilities and sworn into office to conduct themselves according to ethical standards. There is no such thing as a utopian society. Someone must lead, and some must follow, but the question is, **who will lead, and who will follow**?

Let's just say, for argument's sake, that Socialism is implemented in the New World Order and wealth distribution is controlled by the UN organization; what will become of the [UN Peacekeepers]? Will they be paid more money than the socioeconomics of the rest of the population when global Socialism institutes equal wealth distribution? The laws of equal distribution will be distributed by whom? And by what standards of income will be applied. Will money incentivize the Peacekeepers to protect the UN **against their subjects**? Once they realize that the subjects have consented to forfeit their freedoms and liberties. Will the Peacekeepers pledge their allegiance to the United States to serve and protect the Americans, or will they defend the global elites? They will serve the higher hierarchical order. Look at it this way: Socialism will not have a middle class. It will only have the upper class and the lower class; one will be in power and the other a subject. Reinstating the Russian Marxist/Leninist ideology on the once-powerful capitalist Westerner. The proletariat and bourgeoisie will exist under Communism. The middle class will have been eliminated, and a free society will have been destroyed with systemic destruction from within, orchestrated by stirring emotional hatred into a predictable response like Pavlov's experiment.

Now think about this: "The United Nations is considered an Internationalist stationed on **American soil**, occupying office space in New York City. 'The United Nations Headquarters is located in the heart of New York City on 1st Avenue between 42nd and 48th Street. This 18-acre site has been declared **international territory** (on American soil) and belongs to the 193+/- Member States of the United Nations.'"

"The plot ... UN Secretariat: 'In 1946, the United Nations (UN) was looking for a location for their new headquarters in New York. The original plan was to use the grounds of the 1939 World Fair in Flushing Meadow Park in Queens. But when a project known as X-City on Manhattan's eastern border failed to materialize, **John D. Rockefeller Jr**. bought the 18-acre plot and donated it to the United Nations. This site was then used to build the UN's headquarters. The whole area was converted into international territory and **officially *did not belong*** to the United States.'"—http://www.aviewoncities.com/nyc/unitednations.htm

The Peacekeepers *are already here* on American soil. With the United States' recruitment 'failing,' what will become of the United States *without a military defense*, dispersed all over the world and a nation **exhausted** with fighting among themselves with racial divide? Would our relations be so unrepairable that we would succumb to tyranny?

> "Supreme excellence consists of breaking the enemy's resistance without fighting."
>
> —Sun Tzu, *The Art of War*

One World Order infiltration here on American soil; we won't have to travel far to fight a war.

> "'Let every nation know, whether it wishes us well or ill, that we shall pay any price, bear any burden, meet any hardship, support any friend, oppose any foe to assure the survival and the success of liberty.'"
>
> —John F. Kennedy

Pray for discernment.

CHAPTER 35

DECONSTRUCTING THE INDIVIDUAL'S SENSE OF SELF

> "Whose fault was it that I was poor or uneducated and unadmired? Obviously, the fault of the rich, well-schooled, and respected. How convenient, then, that the demands of revenge and abstract justice dovetailed. It was **only right to recompense** *from those more fortunate than me.*"
>
> —Jordan Peterson, *Maps of Meaning – The Architecture of Belief*

> "You can't hold a man down without staying down with him' and 'Character, not circumstance, makes the person."
>
> —Booker T. Washington

Anthony Benvin, a former university professor who has worked for over twenty-four years in the financial services industry, wrote, "Perhaps, we see Socialism through the romanticized superficiality of its ethic." "Help your neighbor" is certainly a better ethic than "help yourself." And in fact, Socialism can work when entered into on small, interpersonal, and voluntary scales; that is when we have the opportunity to individually negotiate, choose, and control how much and with whom we will "socialize." Such coerced Socialism, like coerced "charity," is no more than organized theft. It doesn't work, **and history is littered** with the carcasses and corpses of its failed attempts.

When we are given the opportunity to help our neighbors, we invariably first choose to help ourselves. The proof? Eric Hobsbawm, avowed Socialist and defender of Communism, died with an Estate of 1.8 million dollars. Pete Seeger? His estate is estimated at $4.2 million. There is no indication that any of them are or were *particularly interested* **in redistributing their own wealth**; no redistribution checks have been forthcoming from them or their estates. The Marxian commandment is to each according to his needs, but without capitalism, there can be no progress because there is no capital to invest. Without capitalism, there can be no charity because there is no wealth to charitably distribute."

> "But the question remains: **What are your needs, and who will decide what they are**? Who will oversee the distribution? Will they not take for themselves first?"
>
> —Anthony Benvin, *Deconstructing the Socialist*, American Thinker, February 6, 2014

> "Don't interfere with anything in the Constitution. That must be maintained, for it safeguards our liberties."
>
> —Abraham Lincoln

> "[You must help] the people in the community ... feel so frustrated, so defeated, so lost, so futureless in the prevailing system that they are willing to let go of the past and chance the future. [An] organizer must shake up the prevailing patterns of their lives–**agitate, create disenchantment and discontent** with the current values, to produce, if not a passion for change, at least a passive, affirmative, non-challenging climate. [You must] fan the embers of hopelessness into a flame of fight."
>
> —Saul Alinsky, *Rules for Radicals*

> "Always remember the first rule of power from the *Rules for Radicals*—Power is not only what you have, *but what the enemy thinks you have.*"
>
> —Saul Alinsky

> "Children exposed to this insidious self-hate are (being) **programmed** to hate themselves, their ancestors and predecessors, their country's founders, and leaders, past and present. The final result is as if Zinn planted a guided missile, with a time-delayed fuse, aimed at the heart of our nation."
>
> —Kent Clizbe, *Willing Accomplices*

> "Nationalism and patriotism are the two most evil forces that I know of."
>
> —Oliver Stone

The National Anthem has nothing to do with racism. It is solely a reminder of what we stand for, to not forget those who made the ultimate sacrifices. If her people will not defend her, then who will?

> "*If a kingdom is divided against itself*, **it cannot stand**. If a home is divided against itself, it cannot stand."
>
> —Mark 3:25, BSB

In 1959, C. Wright Mills wrote *The Sociological Imagination.* He gave us his intellectual view of Socialism, according to his biased intellect. I had no choice but to read their failed attempt to coerce me. If I were physically capable of rolling my eyes to the back of my head, I would have stared directly at the student behind me, and with every ounce of discipline I could muster, I remained quiet. I dissected the main points from Chapter One, and that was enough for me.

"The Sociological Imagination: Chapter One: The Promise" by C. Wright Mills (1959) discusses the **deconstruction of human character**. Let's be reminded of the date on which this paper was written: *1959.* That was approximately 65 years ago (from 2024), depending on the year you read this book.

Our current social discourse was planned by Mills more than six decades ago. The truth is, it's been planned since the 1800s. Suppose you cannot conquer a people with Marxism if the people **hold firmly** to faith, freedom, liberties, and the strength of nuclear families. Karl Marx knew to conquer America; the Socialist must plant the seeds of discontent, dismantle the roles that men and women play within society and in the family dynamics, and most of all, remove all remnants of God. Destroy the middle class. That way, you will be left with only the rich and the poor. Introduce racial divide, and should war knock on your front doorstep, *there'll be no one to come to your defense*.

The removal of God will give the social elitist the position of nihilistic gods (*little g*). Dissect each sentence and listen to the underlying tone and message:

> "Nowadays, people often feel that their private lives are a series of traps. They sense that within their everyday worlds, they cannot overcome their troubles, and in this feeling, they are often quite correct. What **ordinary people** *are directly aware of* and what they try to do are bounded by the private orbits in which they live; **their visions and their powers are limited** to the close-up scenes of job, family, and neighborhood; in other milieux, they move vicariously and remain spectators. And the more aware they become, ***however vaguely***, of ambitions and of threats which transcend their immediate locales, the more trapped they seem to feel."
>
> —C. Wright Mills, *The Sociological Imagination*

On the other hand, in God's ethos, God created Man in his image. Until we sinned and fell from grace. We are now created in Adam's image. In other words, **we are not ordinary people**. Even the 'lowest human being' **has intrinsic value**, where God will leave the *99 for the one.*

> "Male and female He created them, and *He* blessed them. And in the day, they were created, He called them 'man.' When Adam was 130 years old, he had a son *in his own likeness*, **after his own image**; and he named him Seth."
>
> —Genesis 5:2–3, BSB

Mills begins by insulting the average American's intelligence, "these ordinary people with their limited powers," and I saw no student object. We are being 'conditioned' to what we should convict and what we should embrace. The author must be correct; who am I to object?

> "Underlying this sense of being trapped are seemingly impersonal changes in the very structure of continent-wide societies. The facts of contemporary history are also facts about the success and the failure of individual men and women. When a society is industrialized, *a peasant becomes a worker*."
>
> —C. Wright Mills

I'm confused by this rhetoric. Does this mean that anyone who works to provide for himself and his/her family is defined as a peasant? Would this perceived peasant have the choice to work, quit, or venture out to become an entrepreneur, thus taking the position of the feudal lord like the author?

Please explain to me, Sir Mills, how do you suppose that the bare necessities to live on are to be obtained? Should an entire society become imprisoned waiting on handouts from social programs and governmental dependencies? Are we to stand idle in lines waiting for handouts from some unknown entity who has been given 'the power' *to distribute what* **they think I should receive or decide what my needs are**? What if I disagree? An entity that was put into a position *without* an election **to rule over me**. An entity that will tell me how 'ordinary and limited' I am? A potential global entity that will first take out for themselves before distributing it to their fellow serf. I suppose the assigned Jews who were put in charge to oversee the holocaust victims were also treated with civility, **as long as they obeyed**.

In some cases, they behaved worse than the Nazi's treatment of them *only to save themselves first* from the same cruelty the others were given. They were convicted and hanged for war crimes. If we become the serfs, will the assigned people protect us from those who are ruling over us? If not, then who will save us from the potential crimes committed against humanity **if the criminals** are the global entity?

To define "a feudal lord" has now become relative speech, a neologism being redefined as the businessman, vilifying the capitalist. "When classes rise or fall, a person is employed or unemployed; when the rate of investment goes up or down." Who controls the investment and economic systems? **Are they not the same entities that control the banks**? The Federal Banking System and the Federal Reserves that control interest and inflations? All interwoven with other banks across the globe. All consorting against the ordinary man and woman, acting as the feudal lords. All this is under the assumption that the ordinary man and woman are limited in their mental capacity and thus need to be positioned and staged like chess pieces on a board game.

They ask themselves, "How do we exploit these **ordinary people** *with limited mental capacity*? Do the everyday businessman and the entrepreneur control the overall welfare of the public by raping its constituent that provides for him as well? Do we not all gain in business and the freedom to provide for ourselves? The freedom of business plays into the social infrastructure, which provides jobs, healthcare, 401K, and some money for education. How will these ordinary people obtain money to live? This 'ordinary person,' defined as the majority, is the one who maintains the country's infrastructure **and pays for all social programs**. This analogy, and truthful absolute, would make the ordinary man and woman the most powerful. And how do you control the most powerful? The Government instituted socialized programs disguised as welfare, all social programs, DACA, Financial aid, abortion, healthcare, and so forth. All social programs **are without incentives**. So, the 'ordinary people' **can remain where they are**, under the thumb of a Socialist, since all their perceptions of being taken care of "needs" are met.

> "Seldom aware of the intricate connection between the patterns of their own lives and the course of world history, ordinary people do not usually know what this connection means for the kinds of people they are becoming and for the kinds of history-making in which they might take part. They **do not possess the quality of mind essential to grasp** the interplay of individuals and society."
>
> —C. Wright Mills

I about fell off my chair with that last statement. This is how a Socialist thinks. How would people know about the interplays of history when they are being played, text books tampered with and lied to? When academic institutions corrupt and limit the student's ability to access the truth. "Interplay of history" tell that to any young man or woman who fought wars and suffered or died at the hands of the enemy. School districts hand out history textbooks that have been tampered with and replaced with progressive postmodern narratives inundated with hidden agendas—changing the meaning of words to satisfy relative truth, turning everyday societal norms into chaos, and keeping people *unstable and unified*. Our footing has become weak, and we are losing our **internal desire for truth** while eradicating *our healthy ability to reason*. We have lost the strength to fight against a reality based on relativism and false narratives. Corrupting the children and waiting for the traditionalists and conservative "dinosaurs to die off" is what Chris Evans, *a mediocre actor*, said during an interview. Forcing the idealism that the LGBQ+ narrative should be ingrained into the minds of children is irresponsible. A choice made by a consenting adult, and anyone objecting is then summed up as preventing others from moving forward. Identifying a large group of people as dinosaurs and waiting for them to die off is diabolical.

The globalists and the mainstream media have picked and chosen words taken out of context *to bend the truth*. The global elitists are robbing us of truthful absolutes and replacing them with new narratives embedded with hatred and contempt. It is easier to dismantle a country "piece by piece" than to "openly declare war among its own citizens." Convince the masses to see themselves as victims, and then have them attack one another while destroying their own private property in a frenzy. Have the property owners declare bankruptcy, short sale, stolen goods, and then have the banks or government take over their property. During the pandemic, how many people lost their businesses and their homes at no fault of theirs but lost to the governmental mandate placed on them? Now, what becomes of these **empty buildings, houses, and spaces**? Maybe **bought up** by wealthy conglomerates at a fraction of their cost? Like a short sale? A bankruptcy? The loss of property, global isolation. No vaccine, no job. Sounds like the perfect crisis to me.

We have identity groups destroying public property, burning down their cities, looting their neighborhood businesses, and then calling it a "semi-peaceful demonstration." This is called a Saul Alinsky tactic when he said, "fan the ambers of discontent," add wood to the fire, instigate, and watch the people behave in a predictive manner—using identity groups to do their bidding. If this continues, the people will have nothing left to bargain with and will be more than willing to give up their liberties for a bigger government, more social programs, and subsidies like retribution to give the government more control **to restore what they destroyed**. The government, domestic and foreign elites, sit back and watch with delight. They say to themselves Pavlov was right. Social conditioning works; people will react to the sound of a bell—or should I say, trigger words.

Based on a progressive or, should I say, 'regressive' thought. We are to beg like ordinary people, submitting to treasonous politicians to help restabilize the same country they worked diligently to ***destabilize***. People will then realize they've been had. The globalists stand at a distance, clenching their hands on foreign ground, aided by anti-American sympathizers who have sold out their own country to the highest bidder, whether it was unknowingly done or purposeful. Both domestic and foreign enemies wait patiently to take down America and its people, for it's the only thing that stands in their way for complete control of the entire world. **You cannot have two superpowers**. One must fall for the other to be elevated, so they distract us while they work behind the scenes, using identity politics like pawn pieces on a board game.

> "Of biography and history, of self and world. They cannot cope with their personal troubles in such ways as to control the structural transformations that usually lie behind them."
>
> —C. Wright Mills

Again, these ordinary people who cannot cope with their "personal troubles" while the borders are unsecured, our national deficit in the trillions of dollars and continuing to grow without restraint, contending with foreign wars not our own, and civil unrest orchestrated by the unknowns. Still defined as "personal troubles." It's an '**eighth wonder of the world**' how the average American is able to rise in the morning, tie their shoelaces, brush their teeth, and spit at the same time. The ordinary—"We the people"—who appear to walk about life *aimlessly*, **without purpose, rhythm, or reason**. These conservative and modest democrat dinosaurs are unable to wake up (from the unwoke) within a society programmed as a drone, not understanding the world around us, to the very least.

> "Surely it is no wonder. In what period have so many people been so totally exposed at so fast a pace to such earthquakes of change? That Americans have not known such catastrophic changes as the men and women of other societies are due to historical facts that are now quickly becoming 'merely history,' and revolutions occur; people feel the intimate grip of new kinds of authority. **Totalitarian societies** rise and are smashed to bits—or ***succeed* fabulously**."
>
> —C. Wright Mills

What totalitarian government in world history has ever "succeeded fabulously" without first murdering millions of its own citizens? The statement alone is a travesty and an abhorrent deceit.

In Socialism, there is no systemic racism, no gender issues, no identity crisis, and no immoral psychopathic criminals. People who function under this form of totalitarian regime will equally die. There, you will find equality in its truest form, along with all the innocent people who perished in the past under the Socialistic regimes—equality in death to all those who rebelled and to all those who consented. No history book or document paper will remember their names, gender, age of innocence, or skin color. Just dead, forgotten people, the world **ground their memories into *fine, thin air*.**

How convenient is it to take the stance to exonerate foreign Socialist and Communist Governments that have caused untold human suffering in search of their ultimate power? Anti-domestic and foreigner sympathizers wipe away thousands of years of human atrocities committed on foreign lands to turn around and accuse the United States of being 'far worse' in human oppression than ever existed. These people need to read books and expose their ignorance.

> "Otherwise, you will follow the blind—will you both not fall into a pit?"
>
> —Matthew 15:14, BSB

> "Even when they do not panic, people (collectively) often sense that the older ways of feeling and thinking have *collapsed* and that newer beginnings are 'ambiguous' to the point of moral stasis."
>
> —C. Wright Mills

Read that sentence a few more times until you get the 'gist' of what he just said!

> "Is it any wonder that ordinary people feel they cannot cope with the larger worlds with which they are so suddenly confronted? That they cannot understand the meaning of their epoch for their own lives. That—in defense of selfhood—**they become morally insensible**, trying to remain altogether private individuals. Is it any wonder that they come to be possessed by a sense of the trap?"
>
> —C. Wright Mills

A private individual exercising their right to liberty, freedom, self-defense, sovereignty, and the pursuit of happiness, you have defined as "morally insensible?" Does *1984* come to mind? Does 2+2=5 sound familiar when enforced by Big Brother? What does a Socialist care about another human being if not to exploit and to gain elite hood, power, assets, and property? "Ordinary people" who cling to their old values and citizen rights within the Constitution and absolute truths. Confuse their minds with relative speech by inundating them with social constructs and crises *to sheer exhaustion.*

> "It is not only information that they need—in this Age of Fact, information often **dominates their attention and overwhelms their capacities** to assimilate it. It is not only the skills of 'reason' that they need—**although their**

> **struggles** to acquire these often exhaust their limited moral energy."
>
> —C. Wright Mills

Mind-boggling. This Socialist is emotionally influencing the groomed militant, unaware and without resistance. Exhausting "their limited moral energy."

Is this why we are inundated with technology, where the young have their faces pressed against a screen, mesmerized by social mainstream media, selfies, and physical isolation? We are bombarded with narratives from both sides of the political spectrum, promulgating the public screen within earshot 24/7 without giving the mind a rest. I *despise* the fact that even public gas stations install TV screens. You can't even pump your gas without static and noise.

Can the mainstream media be silent for fifteen seconds?

Absolutely not! Lest you have a chance to think in silence.

Social conditioning takes the form of experimentation. Public and social identity groups are studied like lab rats within their habitat. Information is gathered by a group of professional progressives: the sociologist, the anthropologist, the psychiatrist, the psychologist, politicians, social media conglomerates, bankers, and trained experts with marketing tools. These professionals have researched the social dynamics and have collected enough data to market the tactics needed to manipulate society in any direction they see fit, like Pavlov dogs' experiment into social conditioning at a much larger scale.

Read this part carefully:

For the *Sociological Imagination* "is the capacity to shift from one perspective to another—**from the political to the psychological**; from examination of a *single family* to comparative assessment of the national budgets of the world; from **the theological school to the military** establishment."

In other words, they have covered all angles, and we have been studied extensively by these *social intellectuals* perfecting Pavlov's experiment.

The author continues with the social construct of the family dynamics as a failed institution:

> "Consider marriage. Inside a marriage, a man and a woman may experience personal troubles, but when the divorce rate during the first four years of marriage is 250 out of every 1,000 attempts, this is an indication of a structural issue having to do with the **institutions of marriage and the family** and other institutions that bear on them."
>
> —C. Wright Mills

Is the institution of marriage being construed as a human error? Mills failed to mention the moral indignity in keeping the sanctity of marriage—no mention of ethical and moral responsibility towards your spouse and your family. He didn't say that social programs have created a dependency on government assistance, deleting the importance of the 'father figure' in the home. Demonizing the patriarch. No accountability. There is no mention of stability for children and the parents' interpersonal dependence on one another and living a life devoid of human emotion, stability, security, and the foundation of the home. Separated from the guidance and wisdom of God.

> Mr. Mills implies that the government should be the institution of marriage and caretakers of the family, especially the children, hence the reason to eradicate the nuclear family and for the state to position themselves as head of household. Convince the woman of her independence and to ***work more*** and leave your children at a daycare 24/7 for job advancement, money, and vanity. Convince the man he is not needed and to despise his children with forced child support. Give the power to the women or abort the 'fetus' for a plethora of reasons. In any event, the death of a potential being *is still death*, regardless of the state in development. Did Mills expect people to become a factory assembly line to serve and worship the Socialist elite?
>
> —Mills, C. Wright, *The Social Imagination*

There you have it—*The Sociological Imagination.* It is a social construct, with precise, methodical plans devised by 'intellectuals' who seem to know the human spirit better than the people themselves. The only thing I can conclude with this … is to pray for discernment.

CHAPTER 36

AMERICAN INSIGHT

"The way to have good and safe government **is not to trust it all to one**, but to *divide it* among the many, distributing to everyone exactly the functions he is competent. It is by dividing and subdividing these republics from the great national one down through all its subordinations until it ends in the administration of every man's farm by himself, by placing under everyone what his own eye may superintend that all will be done for the best.

> "What has destroyed liberty and the rights of man in every government which has ever existed under the sun? **The generalizing and concentrating all cares and powers into one body.**"
>
> —Thomas Jefferson

> "There is now evidence, plenty, to convince any sentient being that proposals and references to a 'new world order' invariably **are tied to efforts to erode national sovereignty** and lead toward world government through steady political and economic merger on regional and global levels."
>
> —William F. Jasper

> "We are going to have to change our conversation; we're going to have **to change our traditions, our history**;

> we're going to have to move into a different place as a nation."
>
> —Michelle Obama, May 14, 2008

What are all these quotes trying to say? Did Thomas Jefferson and William F. Jasper try to warn Americans of something? Does Michelle Obama know something we don't? Does she have any connection with Bill Ayers? Is it paramount for the globalist elitists and political parties to undermine and discredit our forefathers? If you intend to weaken the enemy and destroy your opposition, you will need to find fault and discredit while exonerating yourself from any malicious intent. Remember the saying, "You are only as strong as the weakest link." The global elitists sit in the dark, contemplating their next course of action, like a football playbook. They wait for the precise moment for Pavlov's social conditioning—predictable responses playing into identity politics, where tribal groups are **too preoccupied to notice** the multiple fires arising 'only ten feet from where they stand.' Add wood to the fire and watch it escalate the emotional discourse, drowning their minds and exhausting them into obedience.

> "Engage people with what they expect; it is what they are able to discern and confirm their projections. **It settles them into predictable patterns of response, occupying their minds** while you wait for the extraordinary moment which they cannot anticipate."
>
> —Sun Tzu, *The Art of War*

The world watches how Americans behave within these identities under any discord of social problems and then judges them accordingly—not based on stereotyping, as many would say, but by *a reality* **for all to see and witness**. They watch how we rip and tear each other apart like a pack of wolves. The globalists do not call attention to themselves and their inequities. Instead, they exploit the most vulnerable, convincing them to display severe judgment against anyone not agreeing with them. The globalists carefully 'discriminate' against anyone exhibiting a potential threat against the elites, weaponizing designed trigger words, neologisms, or images distributed by mainstream media. They teach the ones **willing**

to listen to spread contempt toward each other by implementing the art of deception through psychological warfare. The Pied Piper plays the flute, and the people dance to its tune. Why? Because they can. We no longer strive for wisdom, knowledge, discipline, critical thought, *or moral behavior.*

Be leery of the man who listens to the crowd and foams at the mouth for the chance to cause harm. They thirst for blood and then claim to be both judge and jury. For the relative justice they demand on their neighbor will be the same rule of justice applied to them. For that man or woman who desires evil from within is seen as an opportunist, waiting for the right prey, the right crisis, and the right opportunity to make others pay for a crime they didn't commit, thus causing more harm than good.

> "For the word of God is living and active and sharper than any two-edged sword—piercing right through to a '**separation of soul and spirit, joint and marrow**,' and **able to judge the thoughts and intentions of the heart**. No creature is hidden from *Him*, but all are naked and exposed to the eyes of Him to whom we must give account."
>
> —Hebrews 4:12–13, BSB

> "For there is nothing hidden that will not be disclosed, and nothing concealed that will not be made known and brought to light."
>
> —Luke 8:17, BSB

> "The heart is more deceitful than anything else and incurable—who can understand it? I, Yahweh (*Hashem*), **examine the mind**; I test the heart to give to each according to his way, according to what ***his actions deserve***."
>
> —Jeremiah 17:9–10, HCSB

In other words, be careful with what you say and what you do, for all your hidden intent will be brought to light. To the atheist, remember this:

you are only 50 percent right or 50 percent wrong; that's a big gamble when ***Hashem*** proclaimed that **each will receive** what his or her actions deserve.

Have you ever wondered what happened to the fifty-six men who signed the Declaration of Independence? What American textbooks have forgotten to mention and failed to educate:

"Five signers were captured by the British **as traitors and tortured before they died**. Twelve had their homes ransacked and burned; two lost their sons serving in the Revolutionary Army; another had two sons captured; nine of the 56 fought and **died from wounds** during the Revolutionary War. Carter Braxton of Virginia, a wealthy planter and trader, saw his ships swept away by the British Navy. He sold his home and properties to pay his debts **and died in rags**. Thomas McKean was so hounded by the British that he was forced to move his family almost constantly. He served in Congress **without pay**, and his family was kept in hiding. His possessions were taken from him, and poverty was his reward. Vandals/soldiers looted the properties of Dillery, Hall, Clymer, Walton, Gwinnett, Heyward, Ruttledge, and Middleton.

At the battle of Yorktown, Thomas Nelson Jr. noted that British General Cornwallis had taken over the Nelson home for his headquarters. He quietly urged General George Washington to open fire. The home was destroyed, and Nelson died bankrupt. Francis Lewis had his home and properties destroyed. The enemy jailed his wife, who died within a few months. John Hart and his 13 children fled for their lives. His fields and his gristmill were laid to waste. For more than a year, he lived in forests and caves, returning to find his wife dead and his children vanished." Political Vel Craft Veil of Politics, The 56 Men who Signed The 1776 Declaration of Independence. Retrieved from https://politicalvelcraft.org/2014/07/04/the-56-men-who-signed-the-1776-declaration-of-independence/

Credit to the sacrifices made by these men who constructed the Declaration of Independence goes unnoticed. The same can be said about the great Greek philosopher Socrates, with his plethora of wisdom, who was given '**a death sentence for basically disrupting the political norm**' and uprooting the powers held by politicians. Remember that freedom is never free. Someone fought, sacrificed, and died for you to live free. Freedom needs to be fought for every day, for there will always be those willing to take from you and leave you for dead.

These men signed the Declaration of Independence, **knowing fully** that they were committing treason, punishable by death. These men were of noble birth, educated lawyers, jurists, merchants, and farmers who sacrificed everything and fought for liberty and freedom for all.

The American Revolution set the momentum for subsequent wars that led to civil rights for the enslaved, the Civil War, the Suffrage movement, and the civil rights march. It was a long and arduous battle against those who wished to control. America had a beginning and a middle, and now the progressive postmodernists want to regress American history. Change our point of reference to lead us into a future that is unknown, led by fiefdoms. Bringing forth the idealism that this generation **is more righteous, more virtuous, and more enlightened** than our forefathers were while having sacrificed nothing *except for protesting* based on emotional outbursts.

The Civil War came to free the enslaved. The feminist movement brought the freedom to vote, to become citizens, and the civil rights movement for all to have an unfettered start. No other nation or country in history has sacrificed its citizens as much as America in such a short period of time.

No one!

I suppose their lives didn't matter. The lives of the abolitionists who fought against slavery didn't matter. The Revolutionary War and the Civil War, having taken the lives of thousands, didn't matter—wars caused by those with selfish and evil intent. The innocent lives that were sacrificed have become but a blur to this generation of college militants who have been steered by professors pulling their strings and **speaking through them** like a ventriloquist. No one can even remember the fallen soldier's last name or even their first. Many of them lie in graves with no headstones and no one to grieve over them. We have become a cold nation. We steal and spill blood and then move on without remorse. We cherry-pick what we feel is unjust, and for all others, *we ignore.*

The only lives that matter are those whose Achilles's heel can stir the pot to serve the global agenda the most. As sad as it is, we entertain the collective vengeance while satisfying the Machiavellian form of good government to where the "end will justify the means." The question is, will all color, race, gender, and self-identity groups meet the same fate? Communism cares very little, if nothing at all, about your political group identity. You are only an orchestrated means to an end. If you think not, ask Winston (*1984*); I'm sure he would have a different tale to tell.

A team is only as strong as when united and held together for the greater good. If the team is split apart, the serpent is free to wander among the people to whisper his ill intent, all without opposition. Eve disobeyed God's command, and we paid for the sin. Today, the groomed militants listen to the lie that fuels the heart: Shall we all be punished for their sins? Probably.

CHAPTER 37

THE CONSTRUCT OF LAWLESSNESS TO GROUP IDENTITY

"The commander of fifty and the dignitary, the counselor, the cunning magician, and the clever enchanter. 'I will make mere lads their leaders, and children will rule over them.' The people will oppress one another, man against man, neighbor against neighbor; the young will rise up against the old, and the base against the honorable. A man will seize his brother within his father's house, "You have a cloak—you be our leader! Take charge of this heap of rubble."

—Isaiah 3:4–6, BSB

"In the modern day, there **appears to be forces operating** through the mainstream media and popular culture, which are attempting to increase **the individual's proclivity to engage in certain types of group identification**. Namely, group identifications that 'divide the population' *into conflicting groups*. This phenomenon had potentially dire consequences for both the stability and freedom of a society, as it allows those in power to institute *the age-old tactic* **of divide and conquer**. Machiavelli noted that

> those who held power over the population **have long realized** that '**a population is always stronger**' *than those who rule over it.*"
>
> —Academy of Ideas (Edward Bernays and Group Psychology: Manipulating the Masses); Machiavelli *Discourse on Livy*

> "*Divide the many and weaken the force* which was '**strong while it was united**' ... those methods which promote division."
>
> —Machiavelli (1469–1527)

> "If your enemy is secure at all points, be prepared for him. If he is in superior strength, evade him. If your opponent is 'temperamental,' **seek to irritate him** (stir trouble; agitate). Pretend to be weak, that he may grow arrogant. If he is taking his ease, **give him no rest**. *If his forces are united*, **separate them**. If sovereign and subject are in accord, put a 'division' between them. Attack him where he is unprepared, appear where you are not expected."
>
> —Sun Tzu, *The Art of War*

Michelle Obama is very good at reopening the wounds, by giving those *who listen*, **no rest**. If any pseudo-politician has the **proclivity to manipulate a controlled group**, *it would be her.* Watch all her videos and speeches, especially those directed towards young black students. She does not praise them for what they have accomplished ***but implores them*** to be incessantly reminded of their oppression even after graduating from a prestigious Ivy League College. She will exploit anyone willing to listen.

> "By dividing a population along lines as race, class, religion, gender, or political preference, *or in other words*, **into groups naturally prone to clash**, the effects of group psychology render rational discourse and **debate**

> **between individuals** ***in these*** **separate groups** extremely unlikely."
>
> —Edward Bernays, *Academy of Ideas*

> "Each Group … **considers its own standards ultimate and indisputable** *and tends to dismiss all contrary* or different standards as 'indefensible.'"
>
> —Edward Bernays, *Crystallizing Public Opinion*

> "For the time will come when men **will not tolerate sound doctrine**, but with itching ears they will gather around themselves **teachers to suit** their own desires."
>
> —2 Timothy 4:3, BSB

For those old enough to remember the saying, "I hear no evil, see no evil, and speak no evil," it describes isolating their minds, **removing themselves entirely** *from any possibility of further thought.* Leaving rational thinking to the wasteside.

> "A society dominated by such groups is thus easily divided in increasingly hostile conflicts and as a result not only does the '**population as a whole become weakened**,' as Machiavelli pointed out, but its **eyes are diverted away from the actions being operated behind the scenes** constitute in the words of Bernays, the invisible government who controls the destinies of millions."
>
> —Edward Bernays, *Propaganda*

> "While there is nothing wrong in deriving a sense of belonging based on the commonalities we share with others, it is the '**misguided identity**' primarily on **our group membership**."
>
> —Edward Bernays

Group membership is similar to gang-ship. Once you identify yourself as part of an identity group *or gang*, then you are **expected to follow** the group or gang dynamics. If you fail to agree or follow on all accounts, the group will assault and ostracize you faster than you can blink your eye. The group membership is only the means to an end.

> "The existence of a society based on individual rights and personal liberties is dependent on a population which has developed this capacity for individual consciousness or in other words, on a society of individuals who understand themselves and treat others as individuals first and foremost."
>
> —Erich Neumann, *The Origins and History of Consciousness*

> This would explain the desire to control the masses, but within groups. As 'Neumann continues,' "**the group an group-consciousness were dominate** ... [the individual] was not an autonomous, individualized entity with a knowledge, morality, volition, *and activity of its own;* **it functions solely as a part of the group,** and the group with its superordinate power was the only real subject."
>
> —Edward Bernays

One will become the mass while the other becomes the ruler. How is that different from the slave from its master?

In a Socialist/Communist form of government, there will be no such thing as a utopian society. *It is unattainable.* Racial warfare will be controlled, but at what cost? Equal wealth distribution will be collected, first taken from the taxpaying citizen, aka the masses—it is not taken from the rich and the powerful. How many times has the politician campaigned to take from the 1 percent? They can't because **they themselves** *fall under* the 1 percent. It's a ruse. The rich manipulators will remain as the rich manipulators. Do you think that Jeff Bezos, Amazon CEO, who became the first trillionaire in history, is going to share his money with the law-abiding taxpaying commoner or the lawless protestor? Do you think he will participate in the equal wealth distribution, taking from the haves to give to the have-nots? To take from the haves to give to the have-nots is not designed to take from the 1 percent *but a strategic ploy* to eliminate the middle class. Do you think his mind will change to serve the global ruse for the greater and collective good? Do you think his sole purpose will be to share his wealth with the undisciplined, misdirected, and unruly identity groups whose **behavior is predictable** and often incited? Do you think he cares about your feelings and how you identify? You are untrustworthy, destructive, and a liability. Identity groups and various cultures have been studied, I repeat, ***extensively*** and will be exploited until the objective has been met. Division serves a purpose, and it will not be in your best interest.

> "The proclivity of individuals to date to engage in group identification is not only a danger to the freedom and stability of a society, but it is also '**a repression of consciousness'** back to a primitive psychological state."
>
> —Edward Bernays

Acting without 'discipline and behaving without self-control' will only lead you into a pit where **no one will have any use for you**.

CHAPTER 38

ARTIFICIAL INTELLIGENCE

Can Artificial Intelligence (AI) be used to **shape public opinion**? Can visual repetition become an **unshaken reality**? Can the mainstream media choose what it will reveal while keeping truthful events undisclosed?

Rob Smith wrote an article for the World Economic Forum in 2018, highlighting the dangers of Artificial Intelligence (AI):

> "Fake news and **fake videos generated by AI** could have a big impact on public opinion, disrupting all layers of society, *from politics to media*."
>
> —Rob Smith

Wendell Wallach, Chair of the World Economic Forum Global Future Council on Technology, Values, and Policy and the author of *A Dangerous Master: How to Keep Technology from Slipping Beyond our Control*, says, "Social media is already 'combining insights into human psychology' **and how to manipulate opinions**, and it will become more sophisticated over the coming years."

> "Facial recognition, fingerprinting, and synthetic imaging *can put you anywhere at any time*, **regardless of truth and innocence.**"
>
> —Rob Smith

Could an isolated incident such as war images be constructed where the true enemy appears as the victim? Is that implausible? An improbability? If words can be weaponized or changed into relative speech to serve the narrative, couldn't AI be manipulated to **construct images to present a specific outcome**? Can mainstream media use their paid platform by multiple contributors to disrupt the norms of society by using AI images as a form of *psychological warfare*, with the sole intent to incite a predictable and preconditioned response from group identities and Socialist sympathizers?

As mentioned several times before, Pavlov's dog experiment used operative and classical conditioning to predetermine the dog's responses. Anthropologists, psychologists, sociologists, psychiatrists, and **commercialized marketing tools** have collected enough data on group dynamics to be useful for *the mainstream media gatekeepers*. Collective data and evidence-based information **can predict behavior superimposed onto group dynamics** *and steer identity groups* in any direction the gatekeeper wields it.

> "These tools will not only be used as propaganda by states to 'confuse and destabilize competing powers' but also as *new methods* employed by political leaders and political parties **for tracking, manipulating, and managing citizens within a country**."
>
> —Rob Smith

So, what does this entail? Is everything you see and hear truthful, *or is it just a means* to lead you in a **predetermined path**? Can these images affect how we see politics, academia, and group dynamics? Can they *shape how we see competing and opposing views*? Can the 'gatekeepers' steer our behavior into a predictable response?

> See also YouTube: "Description: The World Economic Forum is the international organization committed to improving the state of the world through public-private cooperation in the spirit of global citizenship."
>
> —Rob Smith, *3 ways AI [Artificial Intelligence] could threaten our world, and what we need to do to stay safe.* Retrieved from https://www.weforum.org/

agenda/2018/03/3-ways-ai-could-threaten-our-world-and-what-we-need-to-do-to-stay-safe

Be mindful that the World Economic Forum (WEF) is by invitation only. This group of people is making decisions that will **impact the world economic system** and will affect each and every one of us. Media, businessmen, and Hollywood elites are all part of the "invitation only." Imagine that—using the Oscars as a political platform to inject their ideologies under their crafty ruse of acting. Professional skilled actors and the music industry are doing **what they do best**: entertaining *and deceiving through images and lyrics*, **luring the audience** by using operative and classical conditioning marketing tools.

I am left to wonder why Prince Harry defected to the United States—a bipartisan to the Royal British family and part of the invitation only to the WEF. Working the system from within. https://www.weforum.org/

The bigger technology gets, the more invasive AI will become. Using facial recognition, eye scanning, and fingerprinting **can someday be used against you**. That is not an improbability or a conspiracy theory. No, this has been in the plan for decades. Biometrics was subtly introduced during the pandemic as a means to *verify immunity* before boarding a plane or going shopping at a mall.

> "In the last few years, we have experienced various uses of biometrics in our daily lives. Several mobile phone manufacturers have brought **fingerprint technology** for smartphones; Siri, Cortana, and Amazon's Echo Dot bring **voice recognition**; and Windows 10's Hello brings facial recognition for login. Moreover, biometric technology is now the latest public demand in many areas like border security."
>
> —Biometric Today

How is it being used in border security? **The border is completely left open**, and yet we need 'biometrics' *to spy on traveling American citizens*. In retrospect, it makes sense to help ensure public safety, national security, and convenience in the process at airports. Biometrics are not being used for border security; it's just needed to monitor citizens. Everything starts with good intentions until some politician *or fiefdom* finds a better use for it.

Amazon Groceries will be implementing the 'Just Walk Out' system using AI technology.

> "Amazon One allows shoppers to securely checkout with nothing more than the 'palm of their hand' by looking at both the palm and its underlying vein structure to create a **unique palm signature** for identity matching."
>
> —Dilip Kumar, vice president, AWS Applications

"For the theist, you would understand what that means.

> "...required all people small and great, rich and poor, free and slave, to receive a mark on their right hand or on their forehead (facial and iris recognition), **so that no one could buy or sell unless** he had the mark."
>
> —Revelation 13:16–17 BSB

The system will scan your items when you pull an item off the shelves. If the government adopts China's credit system and Big Brother, will you be able to shop? The same with digital currency. If the government shuts off your ability to access your money, will you be able to survive?

Next will be Amazon food shopping where you will need to be microchipped to buy food. But if you are an enemy of the state, you don't get to eat. China does this, using a credit system. If they consider you a bad citizen, they plaster your face in the public square to shame you. You are deprived of getting a bank loan, a job, riding public transportation, or leaving the country. Big Brother is watching a lot more than you think...

Giving up our liberties, privacy, and freedom for convenience. Technology will someday come back to injure us in the most horrific way...*if not already.*

CHAPTER 39

ARE AMERICANS BECOMING SOVIETIZED?

"Just as an animal predator will adopt all kinds of stealthy functions **to stalk their prey, cut them out of the herd, get close to them, and reduce their resistance**, so does the psychopath construct all kinds of elaborate camouflage composed of words and appearances—lies and manipulations—to 'assimilate' their prey."

—Andrew Lobaczewski, *Political Ponerology*

"I want to raise a generation of young people '**devoid**' *of emotion, imperious,* **relentless, and cruel**."

—Adolf Hitler, hanging on a wall at Auschwitz

We recently learned that the Department of Defense is reviewing its rosters to 'spot **extremist** sentiments.' The US Postal Service recently admitted it uses *tracking programs* **to monitor Americans**' social media postings. There is no mention of active sleeper cells or recruitment of foreign terrorists for training camps here in the US. Yet, the government feels the need to spy on its citizens instead of raiding sleeper cells in an attempt to prevent potential terrorism.

"CNN recently alleged that the Biden administration's Department of Homeland Security is considering ***partnering with private surveillance***

***firms* to circumvent government prohibitions** on scrutinizing Americans' online activity."

We have public signs announcing schools participating in the "A Gun Free Zone," putting our children in harm's way. Advertising that no safety measures have been implemented except for a 'sign,' **that can neither protect nor act**. Satisfying a status quo of '**inviting the psychopath**' for the first five minutes of fame and then the government advocating the confiscation of our guns is a Machiavelli style of good government. Allowing the murdering of our innocent children at the cost of inducting Machiavelli's style of good government, where "the end justifies the means." If that doesn't work we can always resort to fear-mongering.

If gun violence was actually a detriment to society, according to the government and civil servants, then **why not** institute 24-hour police surveillance **or post security guards** to protect our children? Instead, they advocate for "lawn signs," letting the perpetrators know that the school is a "Gun Free Zone." Is this a formal invite?

> "A time will come when **nothing makes sense**. The state must declare '**the child**' to be the 'most precious treasure' of the people. As long as the 'government is '**perceived**' as working for the 'benefit' of the children (gun control), the people will 'happily ***endure almost any curtailment*** of liberty and almost any **deprivation**.'"
>
> —Adolf Hitler

The FBI and CIA, the police, and security guards protect the White House. The politicians are protected, as American royalty, Hollywood film stars, and music icons are protected, except for the American children. Are we expendable, and these *enlightened globalists* are not? Either we inundate our children with mental illness and sexual dysphoria or keep them in harm's way. We send our children to institutions that are potentially dangerous to receive a quasi-education, inundating them with adult political issues.

We have allowed medical establishments to diagnose our children of sexual dysphoria, prescribe medication, hormone blockers and surgery, to sterilize and mutilate their young bodies before they are mature enough to understand the lifelong ramifications of their decisions. These children cannot join the service, buy a pack of cigarettes, drink alcohol, or purchase healthcare, yet they can consent to elected surgery without the knowledge of long-term evidence-based data.

Society fills them with drugs like heroin, opioids, fentanyl, energy drinks, glue, vape, cigarettes, alcohol, and coffee. And if that doesn't get them, we murder them before they can take their first breath. With eugenics in mind and billions of dollars in revenue, using fetal mutilated parts for genetic testing and food flavoring, we have postmodern women becoming emotionally disoriented, clamoring **uncontrollably** for their right to end a life without discussing preempted measures, nor exercising foresight.

> "Woe to those who call evil good and good evil, who turn darkness to light and light to darkness, who replace bitter with sweet and sweet with bitter. Woe to those who are wise in their own eyes and clever in their own sight."
>
> —Isaiah 5:20–21, BSB

What else can contribute to a nation becoming Sovietized? "What unites current woke activists such as Oprah Winfrey, LeBron James, Mark Zuckerberg, and the Obamas are their huge estates and their multimillion-dollar wealth. Just as the select few of the old Soviet nomenklatura had their Black Sea dachas, America's loudest top-down revolutionaries prefer living in Martha's Vineyard, Beverly Hills, Montecito, and Malibu." Victor Davis Hanson

All the while, Michelle Obama speaks about systemic racism, Socialism, and equal wealth distribution. She states that she has experienced racism continuously by the American people even though her husband was elected as President and served two terms in office. The former First Lady is orchestrating the art of manipulation, speaking through subtle inferences in promoting Socialism, not for her, but for us. Will she participate in equal wealth distribution and 'equal outcome' for all? That is a delusion for us to bite into. At the 2024 DNC Convention Michelle Obama said, " She (her mother) and my father didn't aspire to be wealthy—in fact, they were 'suspicious' of folks who took more than they needed." I wonder if the former First Lady's parents would be suspicious of her with her multimillion-dollar estates. Did she take more than what was needed? Will she and former President Barrack Obama participate in the equal wealth distribution of their net worth of 70 million dollars? I'm just asking…

Are anti-Americans any different than a stool pigeon rooting out all potential enemies of the people? The same tactics were used by the North Koreans, secret police, and all the Nazi sympathizers who occupied countries. Who didn't turn in a Jew or a Christian for safety or rations? We have the Schumers and the Pelosis, whose main narrative is to censor speech and dictate who will hold office before the votes are even counted. It took years for Tucker Carlson to reveal the truth behind the January 6th Insurrection through controversial videotapes deemed classified by the FBI and the courts. They knew the truth all along and yet allowed a false narrative to be disseminated into the public arena.

> "Don't do as the wicked do, and don't follow the path of evildoers. Don't even think about it; don't go that way. Turn away and keep moving. For evil people can't sleep until they've done their evil deed for the day. They can't rest until they've caused someone to stumble.
>
> They eat the food of wickedness and drink the wine of violence."
>
> —Proverbs 4:14–17, NLT

They follow each other like lost sheep, pulled by strings and lured by puppet masters who are intentionally leading them into a pit.

> "An evil man is held captive by his own sins; **they are ropes** that catch and hold him."
>
> —Proverbs 5:22, NLT

> "I know all the things that you do, that you are neither hot nor cold. I wish that you were one or the other! But since you are like lukewarm water, neither hot nor cold, I will spit you out of my mouth!"
>
> —Revelation 3:15, NLT

Did you find this offensive, that God finds lukewarm people repulsive?

If protesters defend one side but advocate hatred toward another, is that defined as social justice? If you defend the people who call themselves Palestinians and hate the Jews who are attending American universities and threaten professors who teach, is that a form of social justice? Shouldn't social justice be defined as those who defend equality for peace, a fair start in life, and seek out solutions to make society a better place to live in? They speak on one hand for good and do evil with the other. Lukewarm people.

Chaos breeds chaos, and nothing good is derived by those who harbor ill intent—those who wait for the right opportunity to exert their will on another.

Since when did Americans encourage co-workers or fellow students to turn in others in private conversation or their open idealism? That is a WWII tactic of citizen espionage. Why do thousands of people scour the internet to find any probability to discredit their neighbor while they have a log in their own eye? Thought criminalities are presumed guilty of systemic and immigration racism and discrimination against anti-vaccine. Take them down, they say. Report them to the YouTube and Facebook gatekeeping police, or have the FBI follow them and use AI to falsely accuse them of a crime. We are not progressing as a nation; we are regressing toward a nihilistic monarchy. Anyone defying the government runs the fear of being doxed or hunted down for an incorrect thought and found guilty without the court's proceedings. The CIA and FBI are becoming as ideological as the old KGB. If that doesn't work, you can always tack on the word **extremism** to any group identity to demonize any group unwilling to compromise or conform.

Tack on Homeland Security, who are allowing millions of undocumented immigrants to enter the country without vaccination status, possible felony or criminal history, human traffickers, terrorists, and drug cartels. Homeland Security is allowing an indiscriminate amount of people to enter the country, while Americans are scanned at airports, expected to carry the Real ID, and forced into political vaccinations they question. We have state government officials, the House of Representatives, Congress, and unfortunately, the Supreme Court. They interject the FBI agents to clamor within identity groups' protests to 'defund the police' with the full intent to usher in the new **handpicked** KGB. All they need to do now is exhaust the police forces and force them to quit, leaving the neighborhood without any interference. Use social media to portray the police as violent criminals, and the new KGB will be 'hand-picked' through martial law. Are some police officers corrupt? Yes, but it's a **high improbability** that 'all police officers' are bad.

What did George Soros have to say about the Trump administration?

> "Clearly, I consider the Trump Administration a danger to the world, but I regard it as a purely temporary phenomenon, that will disappear in 2020 or even sooner. I give President Trump credit for motivating his core supporters (Constitutionalists) brilliantly, but for every core supporter he has created a greater number of core opponents **who are equally strongly motivated**. That's why I 'expect' a Democratic landslide in 2018."
>
> —George Soros
>
> (https://www.youtube.com/watch?v=ux- UdJyzJo)

George Soros, who is connected with the World Economic Forum (WEF) and the United Nations (UN), is a man who exposed and aided the Nazis in rounding up fellow Jews. How many deaths did he contribute to while stealing their property? He spoke with such confidence and conviction, almost implying that he knows something we don't. House Speaker Nancy Pelosi also made a comment regarding Trump: "Oh, he will never be President." Did our constitutional right to vote become obsolete? Has our government become the modern-day Joseph Stalin who said,

"Those who cast the vote **decide nothing**. Those who count the votes **decide everything**."

When that doesn't work then we clamor repetitive 'election deniers.' It doesn't matter what party you defend if your vote doesn't count. What else can be done to coerce the citizen? "In modern America, the Pulitzer Prizes and the Emmys, Grammys, Tony's, and Oscars don't necessarily reflect the year's best work, but often the most politically correct work from the most woke. The Soviets offered no apologies for extinguishing freedom. Instead, they boasted that they were advocates for equity, champions of the underclass, enemies of privilege—and therefore, could terminate anyone or anything they pleased." Hanson, 2021.

How do you subjugate the majority?

How do you subjugate the majority who are able-bodied men? You deprogram their minds. You instill doubt and fear. You attack them with words, priming and deprogramming society's current perception into one collective thought like a well-organized Pavlov's dogs experiment. Priming words—"toxic masculinity," "patriarchy," "high pay scale," and "being useless." De-emasculate men and create a generation of beta males, weakening the potential defense to our nation if we were to be called into war. Introduce men into women's sports. Merge biological sexes into one and convince those willing to listen that both sexes are the same. You would think progressive feminists would be outraged that men are crossing over into their athletic playing field. Instead of affirmative action being instituted between men and women, a male identifying as a woman will be recognized **as more deserving**. Men will win and dominate the women's place in sports. Imagine taking the best athletes in basketball to play against the best in women players. How will women defend themselves against the group identifying as women?

We had two distinctions, and now we have none. We had the truth, and now we have relative speech. The more we water down reality, the more we distance ourselves from truth.

> "And for this cause, God shall send them a strong delusion, that they should believe a lie."
>
> —2 Thessalonians 2:11, NKJV

Does God want us to believe the lie? No. But if you desire the lie, then it will become your truth because the individual **or group wills it**. Have corrupt men found another way to subjugate women where "she" politely follows in obedience to serve political correctness? With that thought in mind, can corporate leaders and politicians bet against women in athletic competitions, knowing full well the outcome? I suppose this would be a legal form of inside trading, betting against an unequal playing field. Biological men have cornered the corporate market and now they have cornered the Olympics. We went from progressive to regressive with no objection from the feminists.

The same can be said: if you are born today with white skin, you are immediately guilty of a crime you have yet to commit. Appropriating the mind in **social conditioning 'implies'** that racism will continue without an **unforeseeable** end. Every generation to come will claim oppression and demand reparations. If it is not this, then it will be that. And if not that, then it will be this: color, gender, socioeconomics, language, religion, political stance—and the list can go on and on forever without ceasing. Each generation will only create a new formality to resist, overpower, and make demands burdening the unprotected group. The progressive nihilist only proves that without God and moral absolutes, the spirit becomes unrelenting, and a truthful reality will become a blur without definition.

> "It would not be impossible to prove with sufficient repetition and a 'psychological understanding' of the people concerned that a square is, in fact, a circle. They are mere words, and words can be molded until they clothe ideas and disguise. Think of the press as a great keyboard on which the government can play."
>
> —Joseph Goebbels

According to Victor Hanson, "The Soviet surveillance resembles the Department of Defense, which is reviewing its personnel rosters to spot extremist sentiments." **But who are these extremists**? Is it the spy, the terrorist, the Socialist sympathizer, or is it the Christian nationalist and the patriot?

"The US Postal Service recently admitted it uses tracking programs to monitor the social media postings of Americans." Hanson, 2021.

If this is true, then wouldn't it be disconcerting to know that the US Postal Service controls the distribution of mail-in ballots? Wouldn't the US Postal Service know if a person was deceased (more than ten years) or a person no longer residing at this residence? To track and monitor Americans using modern-day technology.

One can only wonder if that, in any way, can spill into our elections.

How can the US Postal Service commit a federal offense and not be raided or investigated by the Federal Bureau of Investigation (FBI)?

> "CCP Leader Lays Out Plan to Control the Global Internet; In a January 2017 speech, Xi said, 'the power to control the internet' had become the 'new focal point of [China's] national strategic contest' **and singled out the United States** as a 'rival force' standing in the way of the regime's ambition. The ultimate goal was for the Chinese Communist Party (CCP) **to control all content** so that the regime could wield what Xi describes as 'discourse to power' over communications and discussions on the world stage."
>
> —Nicole Hao and Cathy He, *Epoch Times: Truth & Tradition*, May 5–11, 2021

"Discourse to power?" Where did I hear those words before? Oh yes, Machiavelli's *The Prince* and *Discourses.*

> "Some find affirmation for the 'common belief' that Machiavelli was a teacher of evil because he taught 'political leaders how to win and hold power **through force and fraud**.'"
>
> —Political Questions, Larry Arnhart, *Power in Politics: Machiavelli's The Prince of Discourse*

Another question to ponder: would the full control of the internet cause a monumental problem for future forms of communication and a black web of opportunity for the elitist to censor speech and interfere with elections? Will this enable the globalists to usher in the Orwellian society foretold by George Orwell?

> "In sum, in a cyberwar scenario, the US government may not have control over a very strategic area of its military operations—cyber. Even if it secures military and government domains and IP addresses, the targets in cyber warfare are likely to be civilian, and the US

> government requires private sector infrastructure to operate." If that is the case, then our **military security** is dependent on the private sector instead of being controlled by United States military intelligence. Along with being too distracted by the global pandemic, economic crisis, civil uprising, systemic racism, Roe v. Wade, defunding the police, and promoting anarchy, we have lost interest and concern for our national security.
>
> —Westby, Jody, September 24, 2016, *7 Days Before Obama Gives Away Internet & National Security*

The Obama administration also gave Google server rights and domain access to United States military intelligence. We have all our American medical records online—the Medical Administrative Records (MAR)—all implemented under the command of the Obama administration. Everything on the internet is open for the dark web to potentially access.

> "Obama's actions amount to 'one small step' **for internationalism** and one giant leap for surrendering America's control over an invention we have every right and responsibility to control and manage."
>
> —Bradley Blakeman, professor of politics and public policy at Georgetown University, August 1, 2016

The internet is the most powerful social platform capable of swaying people toward a good or undesirable direction. It would be comparable to maneuvering a herd in any direction the social media gatekeepers and global elitists see fit—Winston's Big Brother. They have studied the masses enough to know what their "itching ears want to hear, and what their eyes want to see" (2 Timothy 4:3-4, NLT). They can make the public believe they can't live without social media and every other materialistic and technological nonsense they can get their hands on.

> "In America, where and for what reason you riot determines whether you face any legal consequences. The

> Soviet Union was run by a pampered elite, exempt from the ramifications of their own radical ideologies."
>
> —Hanson, 2021

> Imagine that! The pampered elites. Would that include the untouchable Hollywood elite, the music and film industry promoting demonic images and political ideologies with public shaming? How about the journalists, politicians, state government, bankers, billionaires, sports owners, athletes, and global elitists? This is what happens when the progressive man, the modern-day nihilist, as Nietzsche described, "will create new values through a new 'master morality' of nobility." Where the nihilist is free to create "new values by (supposedly) believing themselves to be these superior human beings (to which they find themselves **the enlightened ones**), which will form the highest expression of the 'will of power' that is the fundamental reality of life."
>
> —Political Questions, Larry Arnhart

This raises questions about Biden's attempt to establish a Disinformation Governance Board that appears synonymous with the Orwellian *1984* Ministry of Truth. If the government controls speech, then it can control reality thus affecting social constructs. In creating these new social constructs under the premise of social justice (which is defined by whom?), they circumvent God's laws by creating new manmade *relative moral laws.* Human beings will now take the place of God and not feel the need to answer to a higher being. The tyrant's rebellious nature has placed himself above God, creating whatever laws he sees fit to accomplish his goal of undermining his fellow man. Women are also prone to this very deceit. "My body, my choice" is a **diversion** to convince women to self-mutilate and perform consented eugenics, ridding society of any future children labeled as 'deplorable and undesirable' according to the global elitists.

Victor Davis Hanson, a syndicated columnist Published an article on May 7, 2021, "*Americans Becoming Sovietized? 10 Warning Signs about the Woke Left's Radical Agenda.*" I won't outline every warning sign for copyright constraints, but I can outline a few Soviet global terms that Americans *and non-Americans* should be aware of: "Introduce ideological indoctrination (social constructs); Soviet (*American and European*) surveillance to **ferret out ideological dissidents** in social media (arresting people for speaking out in social media)**;** The Soviet (American academia) educational system sought 'not to enlighten' but to 'indoctrinate' young minds in **proper government-approved thought** and to 'oversee' compliance with the official narrative that a 'flawed America' must **confess, apologize for** and **renounce** its *evil foundations*; The Soviets mastered Trotskyization, or the **rewriting and airbrushing away of history to fabricate a present reality**" also projected in the writing of the *Manifesto of the Communist Party and its genesis*, (Marxists Internet Archive) published in 1848, Karl Marx and Friedrich Engels declared: "In bourgeois society ... the past dominates the present. In a Communist society, the "**present**" *dominates the past*; Soviet *socialist* (American judicial system) prosecutors and courts are 'weaponized' according to **ideology**; and (global *Socialist*) advocate for equity, **champions of the underclass**, 'enemies of the privilege' — and therefore could terminate anyone or anything they pleased, thus defending their thought-control efforts, forced re-education sessions, scripted confessionals, mandatory apologies and cancel culture on the pretense that we need *long-overdue* "**fundamental transformation**."

Are Americans expected to engage with the New World Government, the One World Order, the Great Reset, and **fundamentally** declare *the Year Zero*? "Year Zero is an idea put into practice by Pol Pot in Democratic Kampuchea **that all culture and traditions within a society must be completely destroyed** or discarded and that a 'new revolutionary culture' **must replace it** starting from scratch." Year Zero (political notion) Wikipedia

The Daily Stanford Archives Nov. 3, 1976 published "*Bad Teaching*" referring to Donald J. Harris, an Economist professor at Stanford University. Bill Behn, Mark Johnson, and David Hawes wrote, "One argument raised two years ago in the Economic Department in opposition to the permanent appointing of visiting Prof. Donald Harris, a Marxist scholar, was that his excellence as a teacher attracted students to study in his area of instruction. Harris was described as **too charismatic**, a '**pied piper**' leading students **astray from neo-classical economics**.

In brief, Harris taught "bad" courses too well." Harris also authored the book *Capital Accumulation and Income Distribution*. Published by Stanford University Press January 1, 1976. Would it be a disbelief to see the connection between Professor and his daughter Kamala Harris when she appeared to paraphrase Karl Marx, "We have the ability to see what can be, '**unburdened by what has been.**'"

Karl Marx, "Move forward into a future *unburdened by what has been*; the present will dominate the past."

> "Barrack knows that we are going to have to make sacrifices; we are going to have to change our conversation; we're going to have to '***change our traditions***,' **our history**; we're going to have to *move into a different place* as a nation."
>
> —Michelle Obama

Barrack Obama, "We are five days away from '**fundamentally transforming**' the United States of America."

The Art of War states: "**Be extremely subtle** even to the point of ***formlessness***. Be extremely mysterious even to the point of *soundlessness*. Thereby, you can be the director of the opponent's fate."

A lot has been said, and many may agree or choose to disagree—and that is your right. The point is not *to just* agree or to instantly *disagree*. The point is to open a **dialogue**, to question the unquestionable without fear of retaliation. To seek what is hidden and not visible or transparent. To question what you have deemed to be your reality, a reality that *may or may not be* your own. Wisdom is not for everyone. **Truth is not for everyone**, but blessed is s/he who seeks and prays for discernment. Blessed is s/he who is not easily swayed by crafty, charismatic, and hypnotic speeches. Seek discernment regardless of whether you are a theist, agnostic, or atheist, **for truth and logic are the same for all**.

> "Men (*people*) are **rarely aware** of the real reasons which **motivate their actions**."
>
> —Edward L. Bernays, Propaganda

> "**Guard your heart above all else**, for it '**determines**' the course of your life. Avoid all perverse talk; **stay away from corrupt speech**. Look straight ahead and fix your eyes on what lies before you. Mark out a straight path for your feet; stay on the safe path. Don't get sidetracked; keep your feet from following evil."
>
> —Proverbs 4:23-27, NLT

You do not have to agree with what I wrote; *that's not the point.* The point is to **examine your convictions** and to seek discernment. Rather than accept a pocket-size worldview to fit a particular idealism, allow yourself to think **outside the public domain** of what the social constructs and identity groups have dictated. Seek out the uncomfortable truth; you'd be amazed at what you'd find. God bless your journey.

> "Ask, and it shall be given you; seek, and ye shall find; knock, and it shall be opened unto you."
>
> —Matthew 7:7 KJV

About the Author

The author served in the United States Air Force and Air National Guard, retiring as a Senior Master Sergeant (SMSgt) after serving as a Nursing Superintendent and Non-Commissioned Officer in Charge (NCOIC) of Flight Operational Medicine. She completed her bachelor's degree at Penn State University and earned her graduate degree in Clinical Mental Health from Moravian University. Her interests lie in neuropsychotherapy and integrative mental health.

Printed in the United States
by Baker & Taylor Publisher Services